MW01489864

THE
LIFE AND LETTERS OF
CHARLES DARWIN

Including an Autobiographical Chapter

EDITED BY HIS SON
FRANCIS DARWIN

IN TWO VOLUMES
VOL. I

NEW YORK
D. APPLETON AND COMPANY
1897

Ch. Darwin

PREFACE.

In choosing letters for publication I have been largely guided by the wish to illustrate my father's personal character. But his life was so essentially one of work, that a history of the man could not be written without following closely the career of the author. Thus it comes about that the chief part of the book falls into chapters whose titles correspond to the names of his books.

In arranging the letters I have adhered as far as possible to chronological sequence, but the character and variety of his researches make a strictly chronological order an impossibility. It was his habit to work more or less simultaneously at several subjects. Experimental work was often carried on as a refreshment or variety, while books entailing reasoning and the marshalling of large bodies of facts were being written. Moreover, many of his researches were allowed to drop, and only resumed after an interval of years. Thus a rigidly chronological series of letters would present a patchwork of subjects, each of which would be difficult to follow. The Table of Contents will show in what way I have attempted to avoid this result.

In printing the letters I have followed (except in a

few cases) the usual plan of indicating the existence of omissions or insertions. My father's letters give frequent evidence of having been written when he was tired or hurried, and they bear the marks of this circumstance. In writing to a friend, or to one of his family, he frequently omitted the articles: these have been inserted without the usual indications, except in a few instances (*e. g.* vol. i. p. *177*), where it is of special interest to preserve intact the hurried character of the letter. Other small words, such as *of*, *to*, &c., have been inserted usually within brackets. I have not followed the originals as regards the spelling of names, the use of capitals, or in the matter of punctuation. My father underlined many words in his letters; these have not always been given in italics,— a rendering which would unfairly exaggerate their effect.

The Diary or Pocket-book, from which quotations occur in the following pages, has been of value as supplying a frame-work of facts round which letters may be grouped. It is unfortunately written with great brevity, the history of a year being compressed into a page or less; and contains little more than the dates of the principal events of his life, together with entries as to his work, and as to the duration of his more serious illnesses. He rarely dated his letters, so that but for the Diary it would have been all but impossible to unravel the history of his books. It has also enabled me to assign dates to many letters which would otherwise have been shorn of half their value.

Of letters addressed to my father I have not made much use. It was his custom to file all letters received, and when his slender stock of files (" spits " as he called them) was exhausted, he would burn the letters of several years, in order that he might make use of the liberated "spits." This process, carried on for years, destroyed nearly all letters received before 1862. After that date he was persuaded to keep the more interesting letters, and these are preserved in an accessible form.

I have attempted to give, in Chapter III., some account of his manner of working. During the last eight years of his life I acted as his assistant, and thus had an opportunity of knowing something of his habits and methods.

I have received much help from my friends in the course of my work. To some I am indebted for reminiscences of my father, to others for information, criticisms, and advice. To all these kind coadjutors I gladly acknowledge my indebtedness. The names of some occur in connection with their contributions, but I do not name those to whom I am indebted for criticisms or corrections, because I should wish to bear alone the load of my short-comings, rather than to let any of it fall on those who have done their best to lighten it.

It will be seen how largely I am indebted to Sir Joseph Hooker for the means of illustrating my father's life. The readers of these pages will, I think, be grateful to Sir Joseph for the care with which he has preserved his valuable collection of letters, and I should wish to add my acknowledgment of the generosity with which he has placed it at my disposal, and for the kindly encouragement given throughout my work.

To Mr. Huxley I owe a debt of thanks, not only for much kind help, but for his willing compliance with my request that he should contribute a chapter on the reception of the 'Origin of Species.'

Finally, it is a pleasure to acknowledge the cour-

tesy of the publishers of the ‘Century Magazine’ who
have freely given me the use of their illustrations. To
Messrs. Maull and Fox and Messrs. Elliott and Fry I
am also indebted for their kindness in allowing me the
use of reproductions of their photographs.

FRANCIS DARWIN.

CAMBRIDGE,
October, 1887.

TABLE OF CONTENTS.

LIST OF ILLUSTRATIONS.

LIFE AND LETTERS

OF

CHARLES DARWIN.

CHAPTER I.

THE DARWIN FAMILY.

THE earliest records of the family show the Darwins to have been substantial yeomen residing on the northern borders of Lincolnshire, close to Yorkshire. The name is now very unusual in England, but I believe that it is not unknown in the neighbourhood of Sheffield and in Lancashire. Down to the year 1600 we find the name spelt in a variety of ways—Derwent, Darwen, Darwynne, &c. It is possible, therefore, that the family migrated at some unknown date from Yorkshire, Cumberland, or Derbyshire, where Derwent occurs as the name of a river.

The first ancestor of whom we know was one William Darwin, who lived, about the year 1500, at Marton, near Gainsborough. His great grandson, Richard Darwyn, inherited land at Marton and elsewhere, and in his will, dated 1584. "bequeathed the sum of 3s. 4d. towards the settynge up of the Queene's Majestie's armes over the quearie (choir) doore in the parishe churche of Marton." *

The son of this Richard, named William Darwin, and

---

* We owe a knowledge of these earlier members of the family to researches amongst the wills at Lincoln, made by the well-known genealogist, Colonel Chester.

described as " gentleman," appears to have been a successful
man. Whilst retaining his ancestral land at Marton, he acquired through his wife and by purchase an estate at Cleatham, in the parish of Manton, near Kirton Lindsey, and
fixed his residence there. This estate remained in the family
down to the year 1760. A cottage with thick walls, some
fish-ponds and old trees, now alone show where the " Old
Hall " once stood, and a field is still locally known as the
" Darwin Charity," from being subject to a charge in favour
of the poor of Marton. William Darwin must, at least in
part, have owed his rise in station to his appointment in 1613
by James I. to the post of Yeoman of the Royal Armoury of
Greenwich. The office appears to have been worth only £33
a year, and the duties were probably almost nominal ; he
held the post down to his death during the Civil Wars.

The fact that this William was a royal servant may explain
why his son, also named William, served when almost a boy
for the King, as " Captain-Lieutenant " in Sir William Pel-
ham's troop of horse. On the partial dispersion of the royal
armies, and the retreat of the remainder to Scotland, the
boy's estates were sequestrated by the Parliament, but they
were redeemed on his signing the Solemn League and Cove-
nant, and on his paying a fine which must have struck his
finances severely ; for in a petition to Charles II. he speaks
of his almost utter ruin from having adhered to the royal
cause.

During the Commonwealth, William Darwin became a
barrister of Lincoln's Inn, and this circumstance probably led
to his marriage with the daughter of Erasmus Earle, serjeant-
at-law ; hence his great-grandson, Erasmus Darwin, the Poet,
derived his Christian name. He ultimately became Recorder
of the city of Lincoln.

The eldest son of the Recorder, again called William, was
born in 1655, and married the heiress of Robert Waring, a
member of a good Staffordshire family. This lady inherited
from the family of Lassells, or Lascelles, the manor and hall
of Elston, near Newark, which has remained ever since in the

family.* A portrait of this William Darwin at Elston shows him as a good-looking young man in a full-bottomed wig.

This third William had two sons, William, and Robert who was educated as a barrister. The Cleatham property was left to William, but on the termination of his line in daughters reverted to the younger brother, who had received Elston. On his mother's death Robert gave up his profession and resided ever afterwards at Elston Hall. Of this Robert, Charles Darwin writes † :—

"He seems to have had some taste for science, for he was an early member of the well-known Spalding Club ; and the celebrated antiquary Dr. Stukeley, in 'An Account of the almost entire Sceleton of a large Animal,' &c., published in the 'Philosophical Transactions,' April and May 1719, begins the paper as follows: 'Having an account from my friend Robert Darwin, Esq., of Lincoln's Inn, a person of curiosity, of a human sceleton impressed in stone, found lately by the rector of Elston,' &c. Stukeley then speaks of it as a great rarity, 'the like whereof has not been observed before in this island to my knowledge.' Judging from a sort of litany written by Robert, and handed down in the family, he was a strong advocate of temperance, which his son ever afterwards so strongly advocated :—

From a morning that doth shine,
From a boy that drinketh wine,
From a wife that talketh Latine,
Good Lord deliver me!

---

* Captain Lassells, or Lascelles, of Elston was military secretary to Monk, Duke of Albemarle, during the Civil Wars. A large volume of account books, countersigned in many places by Monk, are now in the possession of my cousin Francis Darwin. The accounts might possibly prove of interest to the antiquarian or historian. A portrait of Captain Lassells in armour, although used at one time as an archery-target by some small boys of our name, was not irretrievably ruined.

† What follows is quoted from Charles Darwin's biography of his grandfather, forming the preliminary notice to Ernst Krause's interesting essay, 'Erasmus Darwin,' London, 1879, p. 4.

"It is suspected that the third line may be accounted for by his wife, the mother of Erasmus, having been a very learned lady. The eldest son of Robert, christened Robert Waring, succeeded to the estate of Elston, and died there at the age of ninety-two, a bachelor. He had a strong taste for poetry, like his youngest brother Erasmus. Robert also cultivated botany, and, when an oldish man, he published his 'Principia Botanica.' This book in MS. was beautifully written, and my father [Dr. R. W. Darwin] declared that he believed it was published because his old uncle could not endure that such fine caligraphy should be wasted. But this was hardly just, as the work contains many curious notes on biology—a subject wholly neglected in England in the last century. The public, moreover, appreciated the book, as the copy in my possession is the third edition."

The second son, William Alvey, inherited Elston, and transmitted it to his granddaughter, the late Mrs. Darwin, of Elston and Creskeld. A third son, John, became rector of Elston, the living being in the gift of the family. The fourth son, and youngest child, was Erasmus Darwin, the poet and philosopher.

The table on page 5 shows Charles Darwin's descent from Robert, and his relationship to some other members of the family, whose names occur in his correspondence. Among these are included William Darwin Fox, one of his earliest correspondents, and Francis Galton, with whom he maintained a warm friendship for many years. Here also occurs the name of Francis Sacheverel Darwin, who inherited a love of natural history from Erasmus, and transmitted it to his son Edward Darwin, author (under the name of "High Elms") of a 'Gamekeeper's Manual' (4th Edit. 1863), which shows keen observation of the habits of various animals.

It is always interesting to see how far a man's personal characteristics can be traced in his forefathers. Charles Darwin inherited the tall stature, but not the bulky figure of Erasmus; but in his features there is no traceable resemblance to those of his grandfather. Nor, it appears, had

TABLE OF RELATIONSHIP.

ROBERT DARWIN of Elston.
b. 1682, d. 1754.

William Alvey.
b. 1726, d. 1783.

ERASMUS, m. (1) Mary Howard; m. (2) Eliz. Chandos-Pole.
b. 1731, d. 1802.   b. 1740, d. 1770.   b. 1747, d. 1832.

Robert Waring.
b. 1724, d. 1816.

ROBERT WARING.
b. 1767, d. 1848.
m. Susannah Wedgwood.

Charles.
b. 1758,
d. 1778.

Violetta, m. Samuel Tertius Galton.

Francis Sacheverel.
b. 1786, d. 1859.

Anne m. Samuel Fox.

William Brown.
b. 1774, d. 1841.

William Darwin Fox.

Francis Galton.

Reginald Darwin.

Edward Darwin, "High Elms."

Charlotte, m. Francis Rhodes, now Francis Darwin of Creskeld and Elston.

Sarah, m. Edward Noel.

CHARLES ROBERT DARWIN.
b. Feb. 12, 1809, d. Apr. 19, 1882.

Erasmus the love of exercise and of field-sports, so character-istic of Charles Darwin as a young man, though he had, like his grandson, an indomitable love of hard mental work. Be-nevolence and sympathy with others, and a great personal charm of manner, were common to the two. Charles Darwin possessed, in the highest degree, that "vividness of imagina-tion" of which he speaks as strongly characteristic of Eras-mus, and as leading "to his overpowering tendency to theo-rise and generalise." This tendency, in the case of Charles Darwin, was fully kept in check by the determination to test his theories to the utmost. Erasmus had a strong love of all kinds of mechanism, for which Charles Darwin had no taste. Neither had Charles Darwin the literary temperament which made Erasmus a poet as well as a philosopher. He writes of Erasmus : * "Throughout his letters I have been struck with his indifference to fame, and the complete absence of all signs of any over-estimation of his own abilities, or of the success of his works." These, indeed, seem indications of traits most strikingly prominent in his own character. Yet we get no evidence in Erasmus of the intense modesty and simplicity that marked Charles Darwin's whole nature. But by the quick bursts of anger provoked in Erasmus, at the sight of any inhumanity or injustice, we are again reminded of him.

On the whole, however, it seems to me that we do not know enough of the essential personal tone of Erasmus Dar-win's character to attempt more than a superficial compari-son ; and I am left with an impression that, in spite of many resemblances, the two men were of a different type. It has been shown that Miss Seward and Mrs. Schimmelpenninck have misrepresented Erasmus Darwin's character.† It is, however, extremely probable that the faults which they exag-gerate were to some extent characteristic of the man ; and this leads me to think that Erasmus had a certain acerbity or severity of temper which did not exist in his grandson.

---

* 'Life of Erasmus Darwin,' p. 68.   † Ibid., pp. 77, 79, &c.

The sons of Erasmus Darwin inherited in some degree his intellectual tastes, for Charles Darwin writes of them as follows :

"His eldest son, Charles (born September 3, 1758), was a young man of extraordinary promise, but died (May 15, 1778) before he was twenty-one years old, from the effects of a wound received whilst dissecting the brain of a child. He inherited from his father a strong taste for various branches of science, for writing verses, and for mechanics. . . . He also inherited stammering. With the hope of curing him, his father sent him to France, when about eight years old (1766–'67), with a private tutor, thinking that if he was not allowed to speak English for a time, the habit of stammering might be lost ; and it is a curious fact, that in after years, when speaking French, he never stammered. At a very early age he collected specimens of all kinds. When sixteen years old he was sent for a year to [Christ Church] Oxford, but he did not like the place, and thought (in the words of his father) that the 'vigour of his mind languished in the pursuit of classical elegance like Hercules at the distaff, and sighed to be removed to the robuster exercise of the medical school of Edinburgh.' He stayed three years at Edinburgh, working hard at his medical studies, and attending 'with diligence all the sick poor of the parish of Waterleith, and supplying them with the necessary medicines.' The Æsculapian Society awarded him its first gold medal for an experimental inquiry on pus and mucus. Notices of him appeared in various journals ; and all the writers agree about his uncommon energy and abilities. He seems like his father to have excited the warm affection of his friends. Professor Andrew Duncan . . . . spoke . . . . about him with the warmest affection forty-seven years after his death when I was a young medical student at Edinburgh . . . .

"About the character of his second son, Erasmus (born 1759), I have little to say, for though he wrote poetry, he seems to have had none of the other tastes of his father. He had, however, his own peculiar tastes, viz., genealogy, the col-

iecting of coins, and statistics. When a boy he counted all
the houses in the city of Lichfield, and found out the number of inhabitants in as many as he could; he thus made a
census, and when a real one was first made, his estimate was
found to be nearly accurate. His disposition was quiet and
retiring. My father had a very high opinion of his abilities,
and this was probably just, for he would not otherwise have
been invited to travel with, and pay long visits to, men so distinguished in different ways as Boulton the engineer, and Day
the moralist and novelist." His death by suicide, in 1799,
seems to have taken place in a state of incipient insanity.

Robert Waring, the father of Charles Darwin, was born
May 30, 1766, and entered the medical profession like his
father. He studied for a few months at Leyden, and took
his M. D.* at that University on Feb. 26, 1785. "His father"
(Erasmus) "brought † him to Shrewsbury before he was
twenty-one years old (1787), and left him £20, saying, 'Let
me know when you want more, and I will send it you.' His
uncle, the rector of Elston, afterwards also sent him £20, and
this was the sole pecuniary aid which he ever received . . .
Erasmus tells Mr. Edgeworth that his son Robert, after
being settled in Shrewsbury for only six months, 'already
had between forty and fifty patients.' By the second year
he was in considerable, and ever afterwards in very large,
practice."

---

* I owe this information to the kindness of Professor Rauwenhoff, Director of the Archives at Leyden. He quotes from the catalogue of doctors that "Robertus Waring Darwin, Anglo-britannus," defended (Feb.
26, 1785) in the Senate a Dissertation on the coloured images seen after
looking at a bright object, and "Medicinæ Doctor creatus est a clar. Para-
dijs." The archives of Leyden University are so complete that Professor
Rauwenhoff is able to tell me that my grandfather lived together with a
certain "Petrus Crompton, Anglus," in lodgings in the Apothekersdijk.
Dr. Darwin's Leyden dissertation was published in the 'Philosophical
Transactions,' and my father used to say that the work was in fact due to
Erasmus Darwin.—F. D.

† 'Life of Erasmus Darwin,' p. 85.

Robert Waring Darwin married (April 18, 1796) Susannah, the daughter of his father's friend, Josiah Wedgwood, of Etruria, then in her thirty-second year. We have a miniature of her, with a remarkably sweet and happy face, bearing some resemblance to the portrait by Sir Joshua Reynolds of her father; a countenance expressive of the gentle and sympathetic nature which Miss Meteyard ascribes to her.* She died July 15, 1817, thirty-two years before her husband, whose death occurred on November 13, 1848. Dr. Darwin lived before his marriage for two or three years on St. John's Hill; afterwards at the Crescent, where his eldest daughter Marianne was born; lastly at the "Mount," in the part of Shrewsbury known as Frankwell, where the other children were born. This house was built by Dr. Darwin about 1800, it is now in the possession of Mr. Spencer Phillips, and has undergone but little alteration. It is a large, plain, square, red-brick house, of which the most attractive feature is the pretty green-house, opening out of the morning-room.

The house is charmingly placed, on the top of a steep bank leading down to the Severn. The terraced bank is traversed by a long walk, leading from end to end, still called "the Doctor's Walk." At one point in this walk grows a Spanish chestnut, the branches of which bend back parallel to themselves in a curious manner, and this was Charles Darwin's favourite tree as a boy, where he and his sister Catherine had each their special seat.

The Doctor took a great pleasure in his garden, planting it with ornamental trees and shrubs, and being especially successful in fruit-trees; and this love of plants was, I think, the only taste kindred to natural history which he possessed. Of the "Mount pigeons," which Miss Meteyard describes as illustrating Dr. Darwin's natural-history taste, I have not been able to hear from those most capable of knowing. Miss Meteyard's account of him is not quite accurate in a few points. For instance, it is incorrect to describe Dr. Darwin

---

* 'A Group of Englishmen,' by Miss Meteyard, 1871.

2

as having a philosophical mind; his was a mind especially
given to detail, and not to generalising. Again, those who
knew him intimately describe him as eating remarkably little,
so that he was not "a great feeder, eating a goose for his dinner, as easily as other men do a partridge."* In the matter
of dress he was conservative, and wore to the end of his life
knee-breeches and drab gaiters, which, however, certainly did
not, as Miss Meteyard says, button above the knee—a form
of costume chiefly known to us in grenadiers of Queen Anne's
day, and in modern wood-cutters and ploughboys.

Charles Darwin had the strongest feeling of love and respect for his father's memory. His recollection of everything
that was connected with him was peculiarly distinct, and he
spoke of him frequently; generally prefacing an anecdote
with some such phrase as, "My father, who was the wisest
man I ever knew, &c. . . ." It was astonishing how clearly
he remembered his father's opinions, so that he was able to
quote some maxims or hint of his in most cases of illness.
As a rule, he put small faith in doctors, and thus his unlimited belief in Dr. Darwin's medical instinct and methods of
treatment was all the more striking.

His reverence for him was boundless and most touching.
He would have wished to judge everything else in the world
dispassionately, but anything his father had said was received
with almost implicit faith. His daughter Mrs. Litchfield remembers him saying that he hoped none of his sons would
ever believe anything because he said it, unless they were
themselves convinced of its truth,—a feeling in striking contrast with his own manner of faith.

A visit which Charles Darwin made to Shrewsbury in 1869
left on the mind of his daughter who accompanied him a
strong impression of his love for his old home. The then
tenant of the Mount showed them over the house, &c., and
with mistaken hospitality remained with the party during the
whole visit. As they were leaving, Charles Darwin said, with

---

*'A Group of Englishmen,' p. 263.

a pathetic look of regret, "If I could have been left alone in
that green-house for five minutes, I know I should have been
able to see my father in his wheel-chair as vividly as if he
had been there before me."

Perhaps this incident shows what I think is the truth, that
the memory of his father he loved the best, was that of him
as an old man. Mrs. Litchfield has noted down a few words
which illustrate well his feeling towards his father. She describes him as saying with the most tender respect, "I think
my father was a little unjust to me when I was young, but
afterwards I am thankful to think I became a prime favourite
with him." She has a vivid recollection of the expression of
happy reverie that accompanied these words, as if he were
reviewing the whole relation, and the remembrance left a deep
sense of peace and gratitude.

What follows was added by Charles Darwin to his autobiographical 'Recollections,' and was written about 1877
or 1878.

"I may here add a few pages about my father, who was
in many ways a remarkable man.

"He was about 6 feet 2 inches in height, with broad
shoulders, and very corpulent, so that he was the largest
man whom I ever saw. When he last weighed himself, he
was 24 stone, but afterwards increased much in weight. His
chief mental characteristics were his powers of observation
and his sympathy, neither of which have I ever seen exceeded
or even equalled. His sympathy was not only with the dis-
tresses of others, but in a greater degree with the pleasures
of all around him. This led him to be always scheming to
give pleasure to others, and, though hating extravagance, to
perform many generous actions. For instance, Mr. B——, a
small manufacturer in Shrewsbury, came to him one day, and
said he should be bankrupt unless he could at once borrow
£10,000, but that he was unable to give any legal security.
My father heard his reasons for believing that he could ultimately repay the money, and from [his] intuitive perception

of character felt sure that he was to be trusted. So he advanced this sum, which was a very large one for him while young, and was after a time repaid.

"I suppose that it was his sympathy which gave him unbounded power of winning confidence, and as a consequence made him highly successful as a physician. He began to practise before he was twenty-one years old, and his fees during the first year paid for the keep of two horses and a servant. On the following year his practice was large, and so continued for about sixty years, when he ceased to attend on any one. His great success as a doctor was the more remarkable, as he told me that he at first hated his profession so much that if he had been sure of the smallest pittance, or if his father had given him any choice, nothing should have induced him to follow it. To the end of his life, the thought of an operation almost sickened him, and he could scarcely endure to see a person bled—a horror which he has transmitted to me—and I remember the horror which I felt as a schoolboy in reading about Pliny (I think) bleeding to death in a warm bath. . . .

"Owing to my father's power of winning confidence, many patients, especially ladies, consulted him when suffering from any misery, as a sort of Father-Confessor. He told me that they always began by complaining in a vague manner about their health, and by practice he soon guessed what was really the matter. He then suggested that they had been suffering in their minds, and now they would pour out their troubles. and he heard nothing more about the body. . . . Owing to my father's skill in winning confidence he received many strange confessions of misery and guilt. He often remarked how many miserable wives he had known. In several instances husbands and wives had gone on pretty well together for between twenty and thirty years, and then hated each other bitterly; this he attributed to their having lost a common bond in their young children having grown up.

"But the most remarkable power which my father possessed was that of reading the characters, and even the thoughts of those whom he saw even for a short time. We had many instances of the power, some of which seemed almost supernatural. It saved my father from ever making (with one exception, and the character of this man was soon discovered) an unworthy friend. A strange clergyman came to Shrewsbury, and seemed to be a rich man ; everybody called on him, and he was invited to many houses. My father called, and on his return home told my sisters on no account to invite him or his family to our house ; for he felt sure that the man was not to be trusted. After a few months he suddenly bolted, being heavily in debt, and was found out to be little better than an habitual swindler. Here is a case of trustfulness which not many men would have ventured on. An Irish gentleman, a complete stranger, called on my father one day, and said that he had lost his purse, and that it would be a serious inconvenience to him to wait in Shrewsbury until he could receive a remittance from Ireland. He then asked my father to lend him £20, which was immediately done, as my father felt certain that the story was a true one. As soon as a letter could arrive from Ireland, one came with the most profuse thanks, and enclosing, as he said, a £20 Bank of England note, but no note was enclosed. I asked my father whether this did not stagger him, but he answered 'not in the least.' On the next day another letter came with many apologies for having forgotten (like a true Irishman) to put the note into his letter of the day before. . . . [A gentleman] brought his nephew, who was insane but quite gentle, to my father ; and the young man's insanity led him to accuse himself of all the crimes under heaven. When my father afterwards talked over the matter with the uncle, he said, 'I am sure that your nephew is really guilty of . . . a heinous crime.' Whereupon [the gentleman] said, 'Good God,' Dr. Darwin, who told you ; we thought that no human being knew the fact except ourselves!' My father told me the story many years after the event, and I asked him how he distinguished the true from the false self-accusations ; and it was very characteristic of my father that he said he could not explain how it was.

"The following story shows what good guesses my father could make. Lord Shelburne, afterwards the first Marquis of Lansdowne, was famous (as Macaulay somewhere remarks) for his knowledge of the affairs of Europe, on which he greatly prided himself. He consulted my father medically, and afterwards harangued him on the state of Holland. My father had studied medicine at Leyden, and one day [while there] went a long walk into the country with a friend who took him to the house of a clergyman (we will say the Rev. Mr. A——, for I have forgotten his name), who had married an Englishwoman. My father was very hungry, and there was little for luncheon except cheese, which he could never eat. The old lady was surprised and grieved at this, and assured my father that it was an excellent cheese, and had been sent her from Bowood, the seat of Lord Shelburne. My father wondered why a cheese should be sent her from Bowood, but thought nothing more about it until it flashed across his mind many years afterwards, whilst Lord Shelburne was talking about Holland. So he answered, 'I should think from what I saw of the Rev. Mr. A——, that he was a very able man, and well acquainted with the state of Holland.' My father saw that the Earl, who immediately changed the conversation, was much startled. On the next morning my father received a note from the Earl, saying that he had delayed starting on his journey, and wished particularly to see my father. When he called, the Earl said, 'Dr. Darwin, it is of the utmost importance to me and to the Rev. Mr. A—— to learn how you have discovered that he is the source of my information about Holland.' So my father had to explain the state of the case, and he supposed that Lord Shelburne was much struck with his diplomatic skill in guessing, for during many years afterwards he received many kind messages from him through various friends. I think that he must have told the story to his children; for Sir C. Lyell asked me many years ago why the Marquis of Lansdowne (the son or grandson of the first marquis) felt so much interest about me, whom he had never seen, and my family. When forty new members (the forty thieves as they were then called) were added to the Athenæum Club, there was much canvassing to be one of them; and without my having asked any one, Lord Lansdowne proposed me and got me elected. If I am right in my supposition, it was a queer concatenation of events that my father not eating cheese half-a-century before in Holland led to my election as a member of the Athenæum.

"The sharpness of his observation led him to predict with remarkable skill the course of any illness, and he suggested endless small details of relief. I was told that a young doctor in Shrewsbury, who disliked my father, used to say that he was wholly unscientific, but owned that his power of predicting the end of an illness was unparalleled. Formerly when he thought that I should be a doctor, he talked much to me about his patients. In the old days the practice of bleeding largely was universal, but my father maintained that far more evil was thus caused than good done; and he advised me if ever I was myself ill not to allow any doctor to take more than an extremely small quantity of blood. Long before typhoid fever was recognised as distinct, my father told me that two utterly distinct kinds of illness were confounded under the name of typhus fever. He was vehement against drinking, and was convinced of both the direct and inherited evil effects of alcohol when habitually taken even in moderate quantity in a very large majority of cases. But he admitted and advanced instances of certain persons who could drink largely during their whole lives without apparently suffering any evil effects, and he believed that he could often beforehand tell who would thus not suffer. He himself never drank a drop of any alcoholic fluid. This remark reminds me of a case showing how a witness under the most favourable circumstances may be utterly mistaken. A gentleman-farmer was strongly urged by my father not to drink, and was encouraged by being told that he himself never touched any spirituous liquor. Whereupon the gentleman said, 'Come,

come, Doctor, this won't do—though it is very kind of you to say so for my sake—for I know that you take a very large glass of hot gin and water every evening after your dinner.' * So my father asked him how he knew this. The man answered, 'My cook was your kitchen-maid for two or three years, and she saw the butler every day prepare and take to you the gin and water.' The explanation was that my father had the odd habit of drinking hot water in a very tall and large glass after his dinner; and the butler used first to put some cold water in the glass, which the girl mistook for gin, and then filled it up with boiling water from the kitchen boiler.

"My father used to tell me many little things which he had found useful in his medical practice. Thus ladies often cried much while telling him their troubles, and thus caused much loss of his precious time. He soon found that begging them to command and restrain themselves, always made them weep the more, so that afterwards he always encouraged them to go on crying, saying that this would relieve them more than anything else, and with the invariable result that they soon ceased to cry, and he could hear what they had to say and give his advice. When patients who were very ill craved for some strange and unnatural food, my father asked them what had put such an idea into their heads; if they answered that they did not know, he would allow them to try the food, and often with success, as he trusted to their having a kind of instinctive desire; but if they answered that they had heard that the food in question had done good to some one else, he firmly refused his assent.

"He gave one day an odd little specimen of human nature. When a very young man he was called in to consult with the family physician in the case of a gentleman of much distinction in Shropshire. The old doctor told the wife that the illness was of such a nature that it must end fatally.

---

* This belief still survives, and was mentioned to my brother in 1884 by an old inhabitant of Shrewsbury.—F. D.

My father took a different view and maintained that the gentleman would recover: he was proved quite wrong in all respects (I think by autopsy) and he owned his error. He was then convinced that he should never again be consulted by this family; but after a few months the widow sent for him, having dismissed the old family doctor. My father was so much surprised at this, that he asked a friend of the widow to find out why he was again consulted. The widow answered her friend, that 'she would never again see the odious old doctor who said from the first that her husband would die, while Dr. Darwin always maintained that he would recover!' In another case my father told a lady that her husband would certainly die. Some months afterwards he saw the widow, who was a very sensible woman, and she said, 'You are a very young man, and allow me to advise you always to give, as long as you possibly can, hope to any near relative nursing a patient. You made me despair, and from that moment I lost strength.' My father said that he had often since seen the paramount importance, for the sake of the patient, of keeping up the hope and with it the strength of the nurse in charge. This he sometimes found difficult to do compatibly with truth. One old gentleman, however, caused him no such perplexity. He was sent for by Mr. P——, who said, 'From all that I have seen and heard of you I believe that you are the sort of man who will speak the truth, and if I ask, you will tell me when I am dying. Now I much desire that you should attend me, if you will promise, whatever I may say, always to declare that I am not going to die.' My father acquiesced on the understanding that his words should in fact have no meaning.

" My father possessed an extraordinary memory, especially for dates, so that he knew, when he was very old, the day of the birth, marriage, and death of a multitude of persons in Shropshire; and he once told me that this power annoyed him; for if he once heard a date, he could not forget it; and thus the deaths of many friends were often recalled to his mind. Owing to his strong memory he knew an extraordinary number of curious stories, which he liked to tell, as he was a great talker. He was generally in high spirits, and laughed and joked with every one—often with his servants—with the utmost freedom; yet he had the art of making every one obey him to the letter. Many persons were much afraid of him. I remember my father telling us one day, with a laugh, that several persons had asked him whether Miss ——, a grand old lady in Shropshire, had called on him, so that at last he enquired why they asked him; and he was told that Miss ——, whom my father had somehow mortally offended, was telling everybody that she would call and tell 'that fat old doctor very plainly what she thought of him.' She had already called, but her courage had failed, and no one could have been more courteous and friendly. As a boy, I went to stay at the house of ——, whose wife was insane; and the poor creature, as soon as she saw me, was in the most abject state of terror that I ever saw, weeping bitterly and asking me over and over again, ' Is your father coming?' but was soon pacified. On my return home, I asked my father why she was so frightened, and he answered he was very glad to hear it, as he had frightened her on purpose, feeling sure that she would be kept in safety and much happier without any restraint, if her husband could influence her, whenever she became at all violent, by proposing to send for Dr. Darwin; and these words succeeded perfectly during the rest of her long life.

"My father was very sensitive, so that many small events annoyed him or pained him much. I once asked him, when he was old and could not walk, why he did not drive out for exercise; and he answered, ' Every road out of Shrewsbury is associated in my mind with some painful event.' Yet he was generally in high spirits. He was easily made very angry, but his kindness was unbounded. He was widely and deeply loved.

"He was a cautious and good man of business, so that he hardly ever lost money by an investment, and left to his children a very large property. I remember a story showing how easily utterly false beliefs originate and spread. Mr. E——, a squire of one of the oldest families in Shropshire, and head partner in a bank, committed suicide. My father was sent for as a matter of form, and found him dead. I may mention, by the way, to show how matters were managed in those old days, that because Mr. E—— was a rather great man, and universally respected, no inquest was held over his body. My father, in returning home, thought it proper to call at the bank (where he had an account) to tell the managing partners of the event, as it was not improbable that it would cause a run on the bank. Well, the story was spread far and wide, that my father went into the bank, drew out all his money, left the bank, came back again, and said, ' I may just tell you that Mr. E—— has killed himself,' and then departed. It seems that it was then a common belief that money withdrawn from a bank was not safe until the person had passed out through the door of the bank. My father did not hear this story till some little time afterwards, when the managing partner said that he had departed from his invariable rule of never allowing any one to see the account of another man, by having shown the ledger with my father's account to several persons, as this proved that my father had not drawn out a penny on that day. It would have been dishonorable in my father to have used his professional knowledge for his private advantage. Nevertheless, the supposed act was greatly admired by some persons; and many years afterwards, a gentleman remarked, ' Ah, Doctor, what a splendid man of business you were in so cleverly getting all your money safe out of that bank ! '

"My father's mind was not scientific, and he did not try to generalize his knowledge under general laws; yet he formed a theory for almost everything which occurred. I do not think I gained much from him intellectually ; but his example ought to have been of much moral service to all his children. One of his golden rules (a hard one to follow) was, ' Never become the friend of any one whom you cannot respect.' "

Dr. Darwin had six children : * Marianne, married Dr.
Henry Parker ; Caroline, married Josiah Wedgwood ; Erasmus Alvey ; Susan, died unmarried ; Charles Robert ; Catherine, married Rev. Charles Langton.

The elder son, Erasmus, was born in 1804, and died unmarried at the age of seventy-seven.

He, like his brother, was educated at Shrewsbury School
and at Christ's College, Cambridge.   He studied medicine at
Edinburgh and in London, and took the degree of Bachelor
of Medicine at Cambridge.   He never made any pretence of
practising as a doctor, and, after leaving Cambridge, lived a
quiet life in London.

There was something pathetic in Charles Darwin's affection for his brother Erasmus, as if he always recollected his
solitary life, and the touching patience and sweetness of his
nature.   He often spoke of him as " Poor old Ras," or " Poor
dear old Philos "—I imagine Philos (Philosopher) was a relic
of the days when they worked at chemistry in the tool-house
at Shrewsbury—a time of which he always preserved a pleasant memory.   Erasmus being rather more than four years
older than Charles Darwin, they were not long together at
Cambridge, but previously at Edinburgh they lived in the
same lodgings, and after the Voyage they lived for a time together in Erasmus' house in Great Marlborough Street.   At
this time also he often speaks with much affection of Erasmus in his letters to Fox, using words such as "my dear good
old brother."   In later years Erasmus Darwin came to Down
occasionally, or joined his brother's family in a summer holiday.   But gradually it came about that he could not, through
ill health, make up his mind to leave London, and then they
only saw each other when Charles Darwin went for a week at
a time to his brother's house in Queen Anne Street.

The following note on his brother's character was written
by Charles Darwin at about the same time that the sketch of
his father was added to the ' Recollections ':—

* Of these Mrs. Wedgwood is now the sole survivor.

"My brother Erasmus possessed a remarkably clear mind with extensive and diversified tastes and knowledge in literature, art, and even in science. For a short time he collected and dried plants, and during a somewhat longer time experimented in chemistry. He was extremely agreeable, and his wit often reminded me of that in the letters and works of Charles Lamb. He was very kind-hearted. . . . His health from his boyhood had been weak, and as a consequence he failed in energy. His spirits were not high, sometimes low, more especially during early and middle manhood. He read much, even whilst a boy, and at school encouraged me to read, lending me books. Our minds and tastes were, however, so different, that I do not think I owe much to him intellectually. I am inclined to agree with Francis Galton in believing that education and environment produce only a small effect on the mind of any one, and that most of our qualities are innate."

Erasmus Darwin's name, though not known to the general public, may be remembered from the sketch of his character in Carlyle's 'Reminiscences,' which I here reproduce in part :—

"Erasmus Darwin, a most diverse kind of mortal, came to seek us out very soon ('had heard of Carlyle in Germany, &c.') and continues ever since to be a quiet house-friend, honestly attached ; though his visits latterly have been rarer and rarer, health so poor, I so occupied, &c., &c. He had something of original and sarcastically ingenious in him, one of the sincerest, naturally truest, and most modest of men ; elder brother of Charles Darwin (the famed Darwin on Species of these days) to whom I rather prefer him for intellect, had not his health quite doomed him to silence and patient idleness. . . . My dear one had a great favour for this honest Darwin always ; many a road, to shops and the like, he drove her in his cab (Darwingium Cabbum comparable to Georgium Sidus) in those early days when even the charge of omnibuses

was a consideration, and his sparse utterances, sardonic often,
were a great amusement to her. 'A perfect gentleman,' she
at once discerned him to be, and of sound worth and kindliness in the most unaffected form." *

Charles Darwin did not appreciate this sketch of his
brother; he thought Carlyle had missed the essence of his
most lovable nature.

I am tempted by the wish of illustrating further the
character of one so sincerely beloved by all Charles Darwin's
children, to reproduce a letter to the *Spectator* (Sept. 3, 1881)
by his cousin Miss Julia Wedgwood.

"A portrait from Mr. Carlyle's portfolio not regretted by
any who loved the original, surely confers sufficient distinction to warrant a few words of notice, when the character
it depicts is withdrawn from mortal gaze. Erasmus, the only
brother of Charles Darwin, and the faithful and affectionate
old friend of both the Carlyles, has left a circle of mourners
who need no tribute from illustrious pen to embalm the
memory so dear to their hearts; but a wider circle must
have felt some interest excited by that tribute, and may
receive with a certain attention the record of a unique and
indelible impression, even though it be made only on the
hearts of those who cannot bequeath it, and with whom, therefore, it must speedily pass away. They remember it with the
same distinctness as they remember a creation of genius; it
has in like manner enriched and sweetened life, formed a
common meeting-point for those who had no other; and, in
its strong fragrance of individuality, enforced that respect for
the idiosyncracies of human character without which moral
judgment is always hard and shallow, and often unjust.
Carlyle was one to find a peculiar enjoyment in the combination of liveliness and repose which gave his friend's society an
influence at once stimulating and soothing, and the warmth

* Carlyle's 'Reminiscences,' vol. ii. p. 208.

of his appreciation was not made known first in its posthumous expression; his letters of anxiety nearly thirty years ago, when the frail life which has been prolonged to old age was threatened by serious illness, are still fresh in my memory. The friendship was equally warm with both husband and wife. I remember well a pathetic little remonstrance from her elicited by an avowal from Erasmus Darwin, that he preferred cats to dogs, which she felt a slur on her little ' Nero; ' and the tones in which she said, ' Oh, but you are fond of dogs! you are too kind not to be,' spoke of a long vista of small, gracious kindnesses, remembered with a tender gratitude. He was intimate also with a person whose friends, like those of Mr. Carlyle, have not always had cause to congratulate themselves on their place in her gallery,—Harriet Martineau. I have heard him more than once call her a faithful friend, and it always seemed to me a curious tribute to something in the friendship that he alone supplied; but if she had written of him at all, I believe the mention, in its heartiness of appreciation, would have afforded a rare and curious meeting-point with the other ' Reminiscences,' so like and yet so unlike. It is not possible to transfer the impression of a character; we can only suggest it by means of some resemblance; and it is a singular illustration of that irony which checks or directs our sympathies, that in trying to give some notion of the man whom, among those who were not his kindred, Carlyle appears to have most loved, I can say nothing more descriptive than that he seems to me to have had something in common with the man whom Carlyle least appreciated. The society of Erasmus Darwin had, to my mind, much the same charm as the writings of Charles Lamb. There was the same kind of playfulness, the same lightness of touch, the same tenderness, perhaps the same limitations. On another side of his nature, I have often been reminded of him by the quaint, delicate humour, the superficial intolerance, the deep springs of pity, the peculiar mixture of something pathetic with a sort of gay scorn, entirely remote from contempt, which distinguish the Ellesmere of Sir Arthur Helps' earlier dialogues. Perhaps

we recall such natures most distinctly, when such a resemblance is all that is left of them. The character is not merged
in the creation; and what we lose in the power to communicate our impression, we seem to gain in its vividness. Erasmus Darwin has passed away in old age, yet his memory
retains something of a youthful fragrance; his influence gave
much happiness, of a kind usually associated with youth, to
many lives besides the illustrious one whose records justify,
though certainly they do not inspire, the wish to place this
fading chaplet on his grave."

The foregoing pages give, in a fragmentary manner, as
much perhaps as need be told of the family from which
Charles Darwin came, and may serve as an introduction to
the autobiographical chapter which follows.

CHAPTER II.

AUTOBIOGRAPHY.

[MY father's autobiographical recollections, given in the present chapter, were written for his children,—and written without any thought that they would ever be published. To many this may seem an impossibility; but those who knew my father will understand how it was not only possible, but natural. The autobiography bears the heading, 'Recollections of the Development of my Mind and Character,' and end with the following note :—" Aug. 3. 1876. This sketch of my life was begun about May 28th at Hopedene,* and since then I have written for nearly an hour on most afternoons." It will easily be understood that, in a narrative of a personal and intimate kind written for his wife and children, passages should occur which must here be omitted; and I have not thought it necessary to indicate where such omissions are made. It has been found necessary to make a few corrections of obvious verbal slips, but the number of such alterations has been kept down to the minimum.—F. D.]

A GERMAN Editor having written to me for an account of the development of my mind and character with some sketch of my autobiography, I have thought that the attempt would amuse me, and might possibly interest my children or their children. I know that it would have interested me greatly to have read even so short and dull a sketch of the mind of my grandfather, written by himself, and what he thought and did, and how he worked. I have attempted to write the following account of myself, as if I were a dead man in another world looking back at my own life. Nor have I found this

---

* Mr. Hensleigh Wedgwood's house in Surrey.

3

difficult, for life is nearly over with me. I have taken no pains about my style of writing.

I was born at Shrewsbury on February 12th, 1809, and my earliest recollection goes back only to when I was a few months over four years old, when we went to near Abergele for sea-bathing, and I recollect some events and places there with some little distinctness.

My mother died in July 1817, when I was a little over eight years old, and it is odd that I can remember hardly anything about her except her death-bed, her black velvet gown, and her curiously constructed work-table. In the spring of this same year I was sent to a day-school in Shrewsbury, where I stayed a year. I have been told that I was much slower in learning than my younger sister Catherine, and I believe that I was in many ways a naughty boy.

By the time I went to this day-school * my taste for natural history, and more especially for collecting, was well developed. I tried to make out the names of plants,† and collected all sorts of things, shells, seals, franks, coins, and minerals. The passion for collecting which leads a man to be a systematic naturalist, a virtuoso, or a miser, was very strong in me, and was clearly innate, as none of my sisters or brother ever had this taste.

---

* Kept by Rev. G. Case, minister of the Unitarian Chapel in the High Street. Mrs. Darwin was a Unitarian and attended Mr. Case's chapel, and my father as a little boy went there with his elder sisters. But both he and his brother were christened and intended to belong to the Church of England; and after his early boyhood he seems usually to have gone to church and not to Mr. Case's. It appears (*St. James' Gazette*, Dec. 15, 1883) that a mural tablet has been erected to his memory in the chapel, which is now known as the ' Free Christian Church.'

† Rev. W. A. Leighton, who was a schoolfellow of my father's at Mr. Case's school, remembers his bringing a flower to school and saying that his mother had taught him how by looking at the inside of the blossom the name of the plant could be discovered. Mr. Leighton goes on, " This greatly roused my attention and curiosity, and I inquired of him repeatedly how this could be done?"—but his lesson was naturally enough not transmissible.—F. D.

One little event during this year has fixed itself very firmly in my mind, and I hope that it has done so from my conscience having been afterwards sorely troubled by it; it is curious as showing that apparently I was interested at this early age in the variability of plants! I told another little boy (I believe it was Leighton, who afterwards became a well-known lichenologist and botanist), that I could produce variously coloured polyanthuses and primroses by watering them with certain coloured fluids, which was of course a monstrous fable, and had never been tried by me. I may here also confess that as a little boy I was much given to inventing deliberate falsehoods, and this was always done for the sake of causing excitement. For instance, I once gathered much valuable fruit from my father's trees and hid it in the shrubbery, and then ran in breathless haste to spread the news that I had discovered a hoard of stolen fruit.

I must have been a very simple little fellow when I first went to the school. A boy of the name of Garnett took me into a cake shop one day, and bought some cakes for which he did not pay, as the shopman trusted him. When we came out I asked him why he did not pay for them, and he instantly answered, "Why, do you not know that my uncle left a great sum of money to the town on condition that every tradesman should give whatever was wanted without payment to any one who wore his old hat and moved [it] in a particular manner?" and he then showed me how it was moved. He then went into another shop where he was trusted, and asked for some small article, moving his hat in the proper manner, and of course obtained it without payment. When we came out he said, "Now if you like to go by yourself into that cake-shop (how well I remember its exact position) I will lend you my hat, and you can get whatever you like if you move the hat on your head properly." I gladly accepted the generous offer, and went in and asked for some cakes, moved the old hat and was walking out of the shop, when the shopman made a rush at me, so I dropped the cakes and ran for dear life, and was astonished by being greeted with shouts of laughter by my false friend Garnett.

I can say in my own favour that I was as a boy humane, but I owed this entirely to the instruction and example of my sisters. I doubt indeed whether humanity is a natural or innate quality. I was very fond of collecting eggs, but I never took more than a single egg out of a bird's nest, except on one single occasion, when I took all, not for their value, but from a sort of bravado.

I had a strong taste for angling, and would sit for any number of hours on the bank of a river or pond watching the float; when at Maer* I was told that I could kill the worms with salt and water, and from that day I never spitted a living-worm, though at the expense probably of some loss of success.

Once as a very little boy whilst at the day school, or before that time, I acted cruelly, for I beat a puppy, I believe, simply from enjoying the sense of power; but the beating could not have been severe, for the puppy did not howl, of which I feel sure, as the spot was near the house This act lay heavily on my conscience, as is shown by my remembering the exact spot where the crime was committed. It probably lay all the heavier from my love of dogs being then, and for a long time afterwards, a passion. Dogs seemed to know this, for I was an adept in robbing their love from their masters.

I remember clearly only one other incident during this year whilst at Mr. Case's daily school,—namely, the burial of a dragoon soldier; and it is surprising how clearly I can still see the horse with the man's empty boots and carbine suspended to the saddle, and the firing over the grave. This scene deeply stirred whatever poetic fancy there was in me.

In the summer of 1818 I went to Dr. Butler's great school in Shrewsbury, and remained there for seven years till Midsummer 1825, when I was sixteen years old. I boarded at

---

* The house of his uncle, Josiah Wedgwood.

this school, so that I had the great advantage of living the life of a true schoolboy; but as the distance was hardly more than a mile to my home, I very often ran there in the longer intervals between the callings over and before locking up at night. This, I think, was in many ways advantageous to me by keeping up home affections and interests. I remember in the early part of my school life that I often had to run very quickly to be in time, and from being a fleet runner was generally successful; but when in doubt I prayed earnestly to God to help me, and I well remember that I attributed my success to the prayers and not to my quick running, and marvelled how generally I was aided.

I have heard my father and elder sister say that I had, as a very young boy, a strong taste for long solitary walks; but what I thought about I know not. I often became quite absorbed, and once, whilst returning to school on the summit of the old fortifications round Shrewsbury, which had been converted into a public foot-path with no parapet on one side, I walked off and fell to the ground, but the height was only seven or eight feet. Nevertheless the number of thoughts which passed through my mind during this very short, but sudden and wholly unexpected fall, was astonishing, and seem hardly compatible with what physiologists have, I believe, proved about each thought requiring quite an appreciable amount of time.

Nothing could have been worse for the development of my mind than Dr. Butler's school, as it was strictly classical, nothing else being taught, except a little ancient geography and history. The school as a means of education to me was simply a blank. During my whole life I have been singularly incapable of mastering any language. Especial attention was paid to verse-making, and this I could never do well. I had many friends, and got together a good collection of old verses, which by patching together, sometimes aided by other boys, I could work into any subject. Much attention was paid to learning by heart the lessons of the previous day; this I could effect with great facility, learning forty or fifty

lines of Virgil or Homer, whilst I was in morning chapel ; but
this exercise was utterly useless, for every verse was forgotten
in forty-eight hours.   I was not idle, and with the exception of
versification, generally worked conscientiously at my classics,
not using cribs.   The sole pleasure I ever received from such
studies, was from some of the odes of Horace, which I admired greatly.

When I left the school I was for my age neither high nor
low in it ; and I believe that I was considered by all my masters and by my father as a very ordinary boy, rather below
the common standard in intellect.   To my deep mortification
my father once said to me, "You care for nothing but shooting, dogs, and rat-catching, and you will be a disgrace to
yourself and all your family."   But my father, who was the
kindest man I ever knew and whose memory I love with all
my heart, must have been angry and somewhat unjust when
he used such words.

Looking back as well as I can at my character during
my school life, the only qualities which at this period promised
well for the future, were, that I had strong and diversified
tastes, much zeal for whatever interested me, and a keen
pleasure in understanding any complex subject or thing.   I
was taught Euclid by a private tutor, and I distinctly remember the intense satisfaction which the clear geometrical proofs
gave me.   I remember, with equal distinctness, the delight
which my uncle gave me (the father of Francis Galton) by
explaining the principle of the vernier of a barometer.   With
respect to diversified tastes, independently of science, I was
fond of reading various books, and I used to sit for hours
reading the historical plays of Shakespeare, generally in an
old window in the thick walls of the school.   I read also other
poetry, such as Thomson's 'Seasons,' and the recently published poems of Byron and Scott.   I mention this because
later in life I wholly lost, to my great regret, all pleasure from
poetry of any kind, including Shakespeare.   In connection
with pleasure from poetry, I may add that in 1822 a vivid
delight in scenery was first awakened in my mind, during a

riding tour on the borders of Wales, and this has lasted longer than any other æsthetic pleasure.

Early in my school days a boy had a copy of the ' Wonders of the World,' which I often read, and disputed with other boys about the veracity of some of the statements ; and I believe that this book first gave me a wish to travel in remote countries, which was ultimately fulfilled by the voyage of the *Beagle*. In the latter part of my school life I became passionately fond of shooting ; I do not believe that any one could have shown more zeal for the most holy cause than I did for shooting birds. How well I remember killing my first snipe, and my excitement was so great that I had much difficulty in reloading my gun from the trembling of my hands. This taste long continued, and I became a very good shot. When at Cambridge I used to practise throwing up my gun to my shoulder before a looking-glass to see that I threw it up straight. Another and better plan was to get a friend to wave about a lighted candle, and then to fire at it with a cap on the nipple, and if the aim was accurate the little puff of air would blow out the candle. The explosion of the cap caused a sharp crack, and I was told that the tutor of the college remarked, "What an extraordinary thing it is, Mr. Darwin seems to spend hours in cracking a horse-whip in his room, for I often hear the crack when I pass under his windows."

I had many friends amongst the schoolboys, whom I loved dearly, and I think that my disposition was then very affectionate.

With respect to science, I continued collecting minerals with much zeal, but quite unscientifically—all that I cared about was a new-*named* mineral, and I hardly attempted to classify them. I must have observed insects with some little care, for when ten years old (1819) I went for three weeks to Plas Edwards on the sea-coast in Wales, I was very much interested and surprised at seeing a large black and scarlet Hemipterous insect, many moths (Zygæna), and a Cicindela which are not found in Shropshire. I almost made up my mind to begin collecting all the insects which I could find

dead, for on consulting my sister I concluded that it was not
right to kill insects for the sake of making a collection.
From reading White's 'Selborne,' I took much pleasure in
watching the habits of birds, and even made notes on the
subject.   In my simplicity I remember wondering why every
gentleman did not become an ornithologist.

Towards the close of my school life, my brother worked
hard at chemistry, and made a fair laboratory with proper
apparatus in the tool-house in the garden, and I was allowed
to aid him as a servant in most of his experiments. He made
all the gases and many compounds, and I read with great
care several books on chemistry, such as Henry and Parkes'
'Chemical Catechism.' The subject interested me greatly,
and we often used to go on working till rather late at night.
This was the best part of my education at school, for it showed
me practically the meaning of experimental science.   The
fact that we worked at chemistry somehow got known at school,
and as it was an unprecedented fact, I was nicknamed
"Gas." I was also once publicly rebuked by the head-master,
Dr. Butler, for thus wasting my time on such useless subjects;
and he called me very unjustly a "poco curante," and as I
did not understand what he meant, it seemed to me a fearful
reproach.

As I was doing no good at school, my father wisely took
me away at a rather earlier age than usual, and sent me (Oct.
1825) to Edinburgh University with my brother, where I
stayed for two years or sessions.   My brother was completing
his medical studies, though I do not believe he ever really intended to practise, and I was sent there to commence them.
But soon after this period I became convinced from various
small circumstances that my father would leave me property
enough to subsist on with some comfort, though I never
imagined that I should be so rich a man as I am; but my
belief was sufficient to check any strenuous efforts to learn
medicine.

The instruction at Edinburgh was altogether by lectures,
and these were intolerably dull, with the exception of those

on chemistry by Hope ; but to my mind there are no advantages and many disadvantages in lectures compared with reading. Dr. Duncan's lectures on Materia Medica at 8 o'clock on a winter's morning are something fearful to remember. Dr. —— made his lectures on human anatomy as dull as he was himself, and the subject disgusted me. It has proved one of the greatest evils in my life that I was not urged to practise dissection, for I should soon have got over my disgust ; and the practice would have been invaluable for all my future work. This has been an irremediable evil, as well as my incapacity to draw. I also attended regularly the clinical wards in the hospital. Some of the cases distressed me a good deal, and I still have vivid pictures before me of some of them ; but I was not so foolish as to allow this to lessen my attendance. I cannot understand why this part of my medical course did not interest me in a greater degree ; for during the summer before coming to Edinburgh I began attending some of the poor people, chiefly children and women in Shrewsbury : I wrote down as full an account as I could of the case with all the symptoms, and read them aloud to my father, who suggested further inquiries and advised me what medicines to give, which I made up myself. At one time I had at least a dozen patients, and I felt a keen interest in the work. My father, who was by far the best judge of character whom I ever knew, declared that I should make a successful physician,—meaning by this one who would get many patients. He maintained that the chief element of success was exciting confidence ; but what he saw in me which convinced him that I should create confidence I know not. I also attended on two occasions the operating theatre in the hospital at Edinburgh, and saw two very bad operations, one on a child, but I rushed away before they were completed. Nor did I ever attend again, for hardly any inducement would have been strong enough to make me do so; this being long before the blessed days of chloroform. The two cases fairly haunted me for many a long year.

My brother stayed only one year at the University, so that

during the second year I was left to my own resources ; and
this was an advantage, for I became well acquainted with
several young men fond of natural science. One of these
was Ainsworth, who afterwards published his travels in As-
syria ; he was a Wernerian geologist, and knew a little about
many subjects. Dr. Coldstream was a very different young
man, prim, formal, highly religious, and most kind-hearted ;
he afterwards published some good zoological articles. A
third young man was Hardie, who would, I think, have made
a good botanist, but died early in India. Lastly, Dr. Grant,
my senior by several years, but how I became acquainted
with him I cannot remember; he published some first-rate
zoological papers, but after coming to London as Professor
in University College, he did nothing more in science, a fact
which has always been inexplicable to me. I knew him well ;
he was dry and formal in manner, with much enthusiasm
beneath this outer crust. He one day, when we were walking together, burst forth in high admiration of Lamarck and
his views on evolution. I listened in silent astonishment, and
as far as I can judge without any effect on my mind. I had
previously read the ' Zoonomia ' of my grandfather, in which
similar views are maintained, but without producing any effect
on me. Nevertheless it is probable that the hearing rather
early in life such views maintained and praised may have
favoured my upholding them under a different form in my
' Origin of Species.' At this time I admired greatly the
' Zoonomia ; ' but on reading it a second time after an interval of ten or fifteen years, I was much disappointed ; the
proportion of speculation being so large to the facts given.

Drs. Grant and Coldstream attended much to marine
Zoology, and I often accompanied the former to collect animals in the tidal pools, which I dissected as well as I could.
I also became friends with some of the Newhaven fishermen,
and sometimes accompanied them when they trawled for
oysters, and thus got many specimens. But from not having
had any regular practice in dissection, and from possessing
only a wretched microscope, my attempts were very poor,

Nevertheless I made one interesting little discovery, and read, about the beginning of the year 1826, a short paper on the subject before the Plinian Society. This was that the so-called ova of Flustra had the power of independent movement by means of cilia, and were in fact larvæ. In another short paper I showed that the little globular bodies which had been supposed to be the young state of *Fucus loreus* were the egg-cases of the wormlike *Pontobdella muricata*.

The Plinian Society was encouraged and, I believe, founded by Professor Jameson : it consisted of students and met in an underground room in the University for the sake of reading papers on natural science and discussing them. I used regularly to attend, and the meetings had a good effect on me in stimulating my zeal and giving me new congenial acquaintances. One evening a poor young man got up, and after stammering for a prodigious length of time, blushing crimson, he at last slowly got out the words, " Mr. President, I have forgotten what I was going to say." The poor fellow looked quite overwhelmed, and all the members were so surprised that no one could think of a word to say to cover his confusion. The papers which were read to our little society were not printed, so that I had not the satisfaction of seeing my paper in print ; but I believe Dr. Grant noticed my small discovery in his excellent memoir on Flustra.

I was also a member of the Royal Medical Society, and attended pretty regularly; but as the subjects were exclusively medical, I did not much care about them. Much rubbish was talked there, but there were some good speakers, of whom the best was the present Sir J. Kay-Shuttleworth. Dr. Grant took me occasionally to the meetings of the Wernerian Society, where various papers on natural history were read, discussed, and afterwards published in the 'Transactions.' I heard Audubon deliver there some interesting discourses on the habits of N. American birds, sneering somewhat unjustly at Waterton. By the way, a negro lived in Edinburgh, who had travelled with Waterton, and gained his livelihood by stuffing birds, which he did excellently : he gave me lessons

for payment, and I used often to sit with him, for he was a
very pleasant and intelligent man.

Mr. Leonard Horner also took me once to a meeting of
the Royal Society of Edinburgh, where I saw Sir Walter
Scott in the chair as President, and he apologised to the
meeting as not feeling fitted for such a position. I looked at
him and at the whole scene with some awe and reverence,
and I think it was owing to this visit during my youth, and
to my having attended the Royal Medical Society, that I felt
the honour of being elected a few years ago an honorary
member of both these Societies, more than any other similar
honour. If I had been told at that time that I should one
day have been thus honoured, I declare that I should have
thought it as ridiculous and improbable, as if I had been told
that I should be elected King of England.

During my second year at Edinburgh I attended ———'s
lectures on Geology and Zoology, but they were incredibly
dull. The sole effect they produced on me was the determination never as long as I lived to read a book on Geology,
or in any way to study the science. Yet I feel sure that I
was prepared for a philosophical treatment of the subject ;
for an old Mr. Cotton in Shropshire, who knew a good deal
about rocks, had pointed out to me two or three years previously a well-known large erratic boulder in the town of
Shrewsbury, called the "bell-stone"; he told me that there
was no rock of the same kind nearer than Cumberland or
Scotland, and he solemnly assured me that the world would
come to an end before any one would be able to explain how
this stone came where it now lay. This produced a deep
impression on me, and I meditated over this wonderful stone.
So that I felt the keenest delight when I first read of the
action of icebergs in transporting boulders, and I gloried in
the progress of Geology. Equally striking is the fact that I,
though now only sixty-seven years old, heard the Professor,
in a field lecture at Salisbury Craigs, discoursing on a trap-
dyke, with amygdaloidal margins and the strata indurated on
each side, with volcanic rocks all around us, say that it was a

fissure filled with sediment from above, adding with a sneer that there were men who maintained that it had been injected from beneath in a molten condition. When I think of this lecture, I do not wonder that I determined never to attend to Geology.

From attending ——'s lectures, I became acquainted with the curator of the museum, Mr. Macgillivray, who afterwards published a large and excellent book on the birds of Scotland. I had much interesting natural-history talk with him, and he was very kind to me. He gave me some rare shells, for I at that time collected marine mollusca, but with no great zeal.

My summer vacations during these two years were wholly given up to amusements, though I always had some book in hand, which I read with interest. During the summer of 1826 I took a long walking tour with two friends with knapsacks on our backs through North Wales. We walked thirty miles most days, including one day the ascent of Snowdon. I also went with my sister a riding tour in North Wales, a servant with saddle-bags carrying our clothes. The autumns were devoted to shooting chiefly at Mr. Owen's, at Woodhouse, and at my Uncle Jos's,* at Maer. My zeal was so great that I used to place my shooting-boots open by my bed-side when I went to bed, so as not to lose half a minute in putting them on in the morning ; and on one occasion I reached a distant part of the Maer estate, on the 20th of August for black-game shooting, before I could see : I then toiled on with the gamekeeper the whole day through thick heath and young Scotch firs.

I kept an exact record of every bird which I shot throughout the whole season. One day when shooting at Woodhouse with Captain Owen, the eldest son, and Major Hill, his cousin, afterwards Lord Berwick, both of whom I liked very much, I thought myself shamefully used, for every time after I had fired and thought that I had killed a bird, one of the two acted as if loading his gun, and cried out, "You must not

* Josiah Wedgwood, the son of the founder of the Etruria Works.

count that bird, for I fired at the same time," and the gamekeeper, perceiving the joke, backed them up. After some
hours they told me the joke, but it was no joke to me, for I
had shot a large number of birds, but did not know how
many, and could not add them to my list, which I used to do
by making a knot in a piece of string tied to a button-hole.
This my wicked friends had perceived.

How I did enjoy shooting! but I think that I must have
been half-consciously ashamed of my zeal, for I tried to persuade myself that shooting was almost an intellectual employment; it required so much skill to judge where to find most
game and to hunt the dogs well.

One of my autumnal visits to Maer in 1827 was memorable from meeting there Sir J. Mackintosh, who was the best
converser I ever listened to. I heard afterwards with a
glow of pride that he had said, "There is something in that
young man that interests me." This must have been chiefly
due to his perceiving that I listened with much interest to
everything which he said, for I was as ignorant as a pig about
his subjects of history, politics, and moral philosophy. To
hear of praise from an eminent person, though no doubt apt
or certain to excite vanity, is, I think, good for a young man,
as it helps to keep him in the right course.

My visits to Maer during these two or three succeeding
years were quite delightful, independently of the autumnal
shooting. Life there was perfectly free; the country was
very pleasant for walking or riding; and in the evening there
was much very agreeable conversation, not so personal as it
generally is in large family parties, together with music. In
the summer the whole family used often to sit on the steps of
the old portico, with the flower-garden in front, and with the
steep wooded bank opposite the house reflected in the lake,
with here and there a fish rising or a water-bird paddling
about. Nothing has left a more vivid picture on my mind
than these evenings at Maer. I was also attached to and
greatly revered my Uncle Jos; he was silent and reserved, so
as to be a rather awful man; but he sometimes talked openly

with me. He was the very type of an upright man, with the clearest judgment. I do not believe that any power on earth could have made him swerve an inch from what he considered the right course. I used to apply to him in my mind the well-known ode of Horace, now forgotten by me, in which the words "nec vultus tyranni, &c.," * come in.

Cambridge 1828–1831.—After having spent two sessions in Edinburgh, my father perceived, or he heard from my sisters, that I did not like the thought of being a physician, so he proposed that I should become a clergyman. He was very properly vehement against my turning into an idle sporting man, which then seemed my probable destination. I asked for some time to consider, as from what little I had heard or thought on the subject I had scruples about declaring my belief in all the dogmas of the Church of England; though otherwise I liked the thought of being a country clergyman. Accordingly I read with care ' Pearson on the Creed,' and a few other books on divinity; and as I did not then in the least doubt the strict and literal truth of every word in the Bible, I soon persuaded myself that our Creed must be fully accepted.

Considering how fiercely I have been attacked by the orthodox, it seems ludicrous that I once intended to be a clergyman. Nor was this intention and my father's wish ever formally given up, but died a natural death when, on leaving Cambridge, I joined the *Beagle* as naturalist. If the phrenologists are to be trusted, I was well fitted in one respect to be a clergyman. A few years ago the secretaries of a German psychological society asked me earnestly by letter for a photograph of myself; and some time afterwards I received the proceedings of one of the meetings, in which it seemed that the shape of my head had been the subject of a public discus-

---

* Justum et tenacem propositi virum
Non civium ardor prava jubentium,
Non vultus instantis tyranni
Mente quatit solidâ.

sion, and one of the speakers declared that I had the bump of reverence developed enough for ten priests.

As it was decided that I should be a clergyman, it was necessary that I should go to one of the English universities and take a degree; but as I had never opened a classical book since leaving school, I found to my dismay, that in the two intervening years I had actually forgotten, incredible as it may appear, almost everything which I had learnt, even to some few of the Greek letters. I did not therefore proceed to Cambridge at the usual time in October, but worked with a private tutor in Shrewsbury, and went to Cambridge after the Christmas vacation, early in 1828. I soon recovered my school standard of knowledge, and could translate easy Greek books, such as Homer and the Greek Testament, with moderate facility.

During the three years which I spent at Cambridge my time was wasted, as far as the academical studies were concerned, as completely as at Edinburgh and at school. I attempted mathematics, and even went during the summer of 1828 with a private tutor (a very dull man) to Barmouth, but I got on very slowly. The work was repugnant to me, chiefly from my not being able to see any meaning in the early steps in algebra. This impatience was very foolish, and in after years I have deeply regretted that I did not proceed far enough at least to understand something of the great leading principles of mathematics, for men thus endowed seem to have an extra sense. But I do not believe that I should ever have succeeded beyond a very low grade. With respect to Classics I did nothing except attend a few compulsory college lectures, and the attendance was almost nominal. In my second year I had to work for a month or two to pass the Little-Go, which I did easily. Again, in my last year I worked with some earnestness for my final degree of B. A., and brushed up my Classics, together with a little Algebra and Euclid, which latter gave me much pleasure, as it did at school. In order to pass the B. A. examination, it was also necessary to get up Paley's 'Evidences of Christianity,' and his 'Moral Philosophy.' This was done in a thorough manner, and I am convinced that I could have written out the whole of the 'Evidences' with perfect correctness, but not of course in the clear language of Paley. The logic of this book and, as I may add, of his 'Natural Theology,' gave me as much delight as did Euclid. The careful study of these works, without attempting to learn any part by rote, was the only part of the academical course which, as I then felt and as I still believe, was of the least use to me in the education of my mind. I did not at that time trouble myself about Paley's premises; and taking these on trust, I was charmed and convinced by the long line of argumentation. By answering well the examination questions in Paley, by doing Euclid well, and by not failing miserably in Classics, I gained a good place among the οἱ πολλοὶ or crowd of men who do not go in for honours. Oddly enough, I cannot remember how high I stood, and my memory fluctuates between the fifth, tenth, or twelfth, name on the list.*

Public lectures on several branches were given in the University, attendance being quite voluntary; but I was so sickened with lectures at Edinburgh that I did not even attend Sedgwick's eloquent and interesting lectures. Had I done so I should probably have become a geologist earlier than I did. I attended, however, Henslow's lectures on Botany, and liked them much for their extreme clearness, and the admirable illustrations; but I did not study botany. Henslow used to take his pupils, including several of the older members of the University, field excursions, on foot or in coaches, to distant places, or in a barge down the river, and lectured on the rarer plants and animals which were observed. These excursions were delightful.

Although, as we shall presently see, there were some redeeming features in my life at Cambridge, my time was sadly wasted there, and worse than wasted. From my passion for shooting and for hunting, and, when this failed, for riding

* Tenth in the list of January 1831.

across country, I got into a sporting set, including some dissipated low-minded young men. We used often to dine together in the evening, though these dinners often included men of a higher stamp, and we sometimes drank too much, with jolly singing and playing at cards afterwards. I know that I ought to feel ashamed of days and evenings thus spent, but as some of my friends were very pleasant, and we were all in the highest spirits, I cannot help looking back to these times with much pleasure.

But I am glad to think that I had many other friends of a widely different nature. I was very intimate with Whitley,* who was afterwards Senior Wrangler, and we used continually to take long walks together. He inoculated me with a taste for pictures and good engravings, of which I bought some. I frequently went to the Fitzwilliam Gallery, and my taste must have been fairly good, for I certainly admired the best pictures, which I discussed with the old curator. I read also with much interest Sir Joshua Reynolds' book. This taste, though not natural to me, lasted for several years, and many of the pictures in the National Gallery in London gave me much pleasure : that of Sebastian del Piombo exciting in me a sense of sublimity.

I also got into a musical set, I believe by means of my warm-hearted friend, Herbert,† who took a high wrangler's degree. From associating with these men, and hearing them play, I acquired a strong taste for music, and used very often to time my walks so as to hear on week days the anthem in King's College Chapel. This gave me intense pleasure, so that my backbone would sometimes shiver. I am sure that there was no affectation or mere imitation in this taste, for I used generally to go by myself to King's College, and I sometimes hired the chorister boys to sing in my rooms. Never-

---

* Rev. C. Whitley, Hon. Canon of Durham, formerly Reader in Natural Philosophy in Durham University.

† The late John Maurice Herbert, County Court Judge of Cardiff and the Monmouth Circuit.

theless I am so utterly destitute of an ear, that I cannot perceive a discord, or keep time and hum a tune correctly; and it is a mystery how I could possibly have derived pleasure from music.

My musical friends soon perceived my state, and sometimes amused themselves by making me pass an examination, which consisted in ascertaining how many tunes I could recognise when they were played rather more quickly or slowly than usual. 'God save the King,' when thus played, was a sore puzzle. There was another man with almost as bad an ear as I had, and strange to say he played a little on the flute. Once I had the triumph of beating him in one of our musical examinations.

But no pursuit at Cambridge was followed with nearly so much eagerness or gave me so much pleasure as collecting beetles. It was the mere passion for collecting, for I did not dissect them, and rarely compared their external characters with published descriptions, but got them named anyhow. I will give a proof of my zeal: one day, on tearing off some old bark, I saw two rare beetles, and seized one in each hand; then I saw a third and new kind, which I could not bear to lose, so that I popped the one which I held in my right hand into my mouth. Alas! it ejected some intensely acrid fluid, which burnt my tongue so that I was forced to spit the beetle out, which was lost, as was the third one.

I was very successful in collecting, and invented two new methods; I employed a labourer to scrape during the winter, moss off old trees and place it in a large bag, and likewise to collect the rubbish at the bottom of the barges in which reeds are brought from the fens, and thus I got some very rare species. No poet ever felt more delighted at seeing his first poem published than I did at seeing, in Stephens' 'Illustrations of British Insects,' the magic words, "captured by C. Darwin, Esq." I was introduced to entomology by my second cousin, W. Darwin Fox, a clever and most pleasant man, who was then at Christ's College, and with whom I became extremely intimate. Afterwards I became well acquainted,

and went out collecting, with Albert Way of Trinity, who in
after years became a well-known archæologist; also with H.
Thompson of the same College, afterwards a leading agricult-
urist, chairman of a great railway, and Member of Parliament. It seems therefore that a taste for collecting beetles is
some indication of future success in life!

I am surprised what an indelible impression many of the
beetles which I caught at Cambridge have left on my mind.
I can remember the exact appearance of certain posts, old
trees and banks where I made a good capture. The pretty
Panagæus crux-major was a treasure in those days, and here
at Down I saw a beetle running across a walk, and on picking
it up instantly perceived that it differed slightly from *P. crux-
major*, and it turned out to be *P. quadripunctatus*, which is
only a variety or closely allied species, differing from it very
slightly in outline. I had never seen in those old days Licinus alive, which to an uneducated eye hardly differs from
many of the black Carabidous beetles; but my sons found
here a specimen, and I instantly recognized that it was new
to me; yet I had not looked at a British beetle for the last
twenty years.

I have not as yet mentioned a circumstance which influenced my whole career more than any other. This was my
friendship with Professor Henslow. Before coming up to
Cambridge, I had heard of him from my brother as a man
who knew every branch of science, and I was accordingly prepared to reverence him. He kept open house once every
week when all undergraduates, and some older members of
the University, who were attached to science, used to meet
in the evening. I soon got, through Fox, an invitation, and
went there regularly. Before long I became well acquainted
with Henslow, and during the latter half of my time at Cambridge took long walks with him on most days; so that I was
called by some of the dons "the man who walks with Henslow;" and in the evening I was very often asked to join his
family dinner. His knowledge was great in botany, entomology, chemistry, mineralogy, and geology. His strongest

taste was to draw conclusions from long-continued minute observations. His judgment was excellent, and his whole mind well balanced; but I do not suppose that any one would say that he possessed much original genius. He was deeply religious, and so orthodox that he told me one day he should be grieved if a single word of the Thirty-nine Articles were altered. His moral qualities were in every way admirable. He was free from every tinge of vanity or other petty feeling ; and I never saw a man who thought so little about himself or his own concerns. His temper was imperturbably good, with the most winning and courteous manners ; yet, as I have seen, he could be roused by any bad action to the warmest indignation and prompt action.

I once saw in his company in the streets of Cambridge almost as horrid a scene as could have been witnessed during the French Revolution. Two body-snatchers had been arrested, and whilst being taken to prison had been torn from the constable by a crowd of the roughest men, who dragged them by their legs along the muddy and stony road. They were covered from head to foot with mud, and their faces were bleeding either from having been kicked or from the stones ; they looked like corpses, but the crowd was so dense that I got only a few momentary glimpses of the wretched creatures. Never in my life have I seen such wrath painted on a man's face as was shown by Henslow at this horrid scene. He tried repeatedly to penetrate the mob; but it was simply impossible. He then rushed away to the mayor, telling me not to follow him, but to get more policemen. I forget the issue, except that the two men were got into the prison without being killed.

Henslow's benevolence was unbounded, as he proved by his many excellent schemes for his poor parishioners, when in after years he held the living of Hitcham. My intimacy with such a man ought to have been, and I hope was, an inestimable benefit. I cannot resist mentioning a trifling incident, which showed his kind consideration. Whilst examining some pollen-grains on a damp surface, I saw the tubes exserted, and instantly rushed off to communicate my surprising discovery to him. Now I do not suppose any other professor of botany could have helped laughing at my coming in such a hurry to make such a communication. But he agreed how interesting the phenomenon was, and explained its meaning, but made me clearly understand how well it was known; so I left him not in the least mortified, but well pleased at having discovered for myself so remarkable a fact, but determined not to be in such a hurry again to communicate my discoveries.

Dr. Whewell was one of the older and distinguished men who sometimes visited Henslow, and on several occasions I walked home with him at night. Next to Sir J. Mackintosh he was the best converser on grave subjects to whom I ever listened. Leonard Jenyns,* who afterwards published some good essays in Natural History,† often stayed with Henslow, who was his brother-in-law. I visited him at his parsonage on the borders of the Fens [Swaffham Bulbeck], and had many a good walk and talk with him about Natural History. I became also acquainted with several other men older than me, who did not care much about science, but were friends of Henslow. One was a Scotchman, brother of Sir Alexander Ramsay, and tutor of Jesus College: he was a delightful man, but did not live for many years. Another was Mr. Dawes, afterwards Dean of Hereford, and famous for his success in the education of the poor. These men and others of the same standing, together with Henslow, used sometimes to take distant excursions into the country, which I was allowed to join, and they were most agreeable.

Looking back, I infer that there must have been something in me a little superior to the common run of youths, otherwise the above-mentioned men, so much older than me and higher in academical position, would never have allowed

---

* The well-known Soame Jenyns was cousin to Mr. Jenyns' father.

† Mr. Jenyns (now Blomefield) described the fish for the Zoology of the *Beagle;* and is author of a long series of papers, chiefly Zoological.

me to associate with them. Certainly I was not aware of any such superiority, and I remember one of my sporting friends, Turner, who saw me at work with my beetles, saying that I should some day be a Fellow of the Royal Society, and the notion seemed to me preposterous.

During my last year at Cambridge, I read with care and profound interest Humboldt's 'Personal Narrative.' This work, and Sir J. Herschel's 'Introduction to the Study of Natural Philosophy,' stirred up in me a burning zeal to add even the most humble contribution to the noble structure of Natural Science. No one or a dozen other books influenced me nearly so much as these two. I copied out from Humboldt long passages about Teneriffe, and read them aloud on one of the above-mentioned excursions, to (I think) Henslow, Ramsay, and Dawes, for on a previous occasion I had talked about the glories of Teneriffe, and some of the party declared they would endeavour to go there; but I think that they were only half in earnest. I was, however, quite in earnest, and got an introduction to a merchant in London to enquire about ships; but the scheme was, of course, knocked on the head by the voyage of the *Beagle*.

My summer vacations were given up to collecting beetles, to some reading, and short tours. In the autumn my whole time was devoted to shooting, chiefly at Woodhouse and Maer, and sometimes with young Eyton of Eyton. Upon the whole the three years which I spent at Cambridge were the most joyful in my happy life; for I was then in excellent health, and almost always in high spirits.

As I had at first come up to Cambridge at Christmas, I was forced to keep two terms after passing my final examination, at the commencement of 1831; and Henslow then persuaded me to begin the study of geology. Therefore on my return to Shropshire I examined sections, and coloured a map of parts round Shrewsbury. Professor Sedgwick intended to visit North Wales in the beginning of August to pursue his famous geological investigations amongst the older rocks, and Henslow asked him to allow me to accompany him.* Accordingly he came and slept at my father's house.

A short conversation with him during this evening produced a strong impression on my mind. Whilst examining an old gravel-pit near Shrewsbury, a labourer told me that he had found in it a large worn tropical Volute shell, such as may be seen on the chimney-pieces of cottages ; and as he would not sell the shell, I was convinced that he had really found it in the pit. I told Sedgwick of the fact, and he at once said (no doubt truly) that it must have been thrown away by some one into the pit; but then added, if really embedded there it would be the greatest misfortune to geology, as it would overthrow all that we know about the superficial deposits of the Midland Counties. These gravel-beds belong in fact to the glacial period, and in after years I found in them broken arctic shells. But I was then utterly astonished at Sedgwick not being delighted at so wonderful a fact as a tropical shell being found near the surface in the middle of England. Nothing before had ever made me thoroughly realise, though I had read various scientific books, that science consists in grouping facts so that general laws or conclusions may be drawn from them.

Next morning we started for Llangollen, Conway, Bangor, and Capel Curig. This tour was of decided use in teaching me a little how to make out the geology of a country. Sedgwick often sent me on a line parallel to his, telling me to bring back specimens of the rocks and to mark the stratification on a map. I have little doubt that he did this for my good, as I was too ignorant to have aided him. On this tour

* In connection with this tour my father used to tell a story about Sedgwick : they had started from their inn one morning, and had walked a mile or two, when Sedgwick suddenly stopped, and vowed that he would return, being certain "that damned scoundrel " (the waiter) had not given the chambermaid the sixpence intrusted to him for the purpose. He was ultimately persuaded to give up the project, seeing that there was no reason for suspecting the waiter of especial perfidy.—F. D.

I had a striking instance of how easy it is to overlook phenomena, however conspicuous, before they have been observed by any one. We spent many hours in Cwm Idwal, examining all the rocks with extreme care, as Sedgwick was anxious to find fossils in them ; but neither of us saw a trace of the wonderful glacial phenomena all around us ; we did not notice the plainly scored rocks, the perched boulders, the lateral and terminal moraines. Yet these phenomena are so conspicuous that, as I declared in a paper published many years afterwards in the 'Philosophical Magazine,'* a house burnt down by fire did not tell its story more plainly than did this valley. If it had still been filled by a glacier, the phenomena would have been less distinct than they now are.

At Capel Curig I left Sedgwick and went in a straight line by compass and map across the mountains to Barmouth, never following any track unless it coincided with my course. I thus came on some strange wild places, and enjoyed much this manner of travelling. I visited Barmouth to see some Cambridge friends who were reading there, and thence returned to Shrewsbury and to Maer for shooting; for at that time I should have thought myself mad to give up the first days of partridge-shooting for geology or any other science.

Voyage of the 'Beagle' from December 27, 1831, to October 2, 1836.

On returning home from my short geological tour in North Wales, I found a letter from Henslow, informing me that Captain Fitz-Roy was willing to give up part of his own cabin to any young man who would volunteer to go with him without pay as naturalist to the Voyage of the *Beagle*. I have given, as I believe, in my MS. Journal an account of all the circumstances which then occurred; I will here only say that I was instantly eager to accept the offer, but my father strongly objected, adding the words, fortunate for me,

---

* 'Philosophical Magazine,' 1842.

"If you can find any man of common sense who advises you to go I will give my consent." So I wrote that evening and refused the offer. On the next morning I went to Maer to be ready for September 1st, and, whilst out shooting, my uncle * sent for me, offering to drive me over to Shrewsbury and talk with my father, as my uncle thought it would be wise in me to accept the offer. My father always maintained that he was one of the most sensible men in the world, and he at once consented in the kindest manner. I had been rather extravagant at Cambridge, and to console my father, said, "that I should be deuced clever to spend more than my allowance whilst on board the *Beagle;*" but he answered with a smile, "But they tell me you are very clever."

Next day I started for Cambridge to see Henslow, and thence to London to see Fitz-Roy, and all was soon arranged. Afterwards, on becoming very intimate with Fitz-Roy, I heard that I had run a very narrow risk of being rejected, on account of the shape of my nose! He was an ardent disciple of Lavater, and was convinced that he could judge of a man's character by the outline of his features; and he doubted whether any one with my nose could possess sufficient energy and determination for the voyage. But I think he was afterwards well satisfied that my nose had spoken falsely.

Fitz-Roy's character was a singular one, with very many noble features: he was devoted to his duty, generous to a fault, bold, determined, and indomitably energetic, and an ardent friend to all under his sway. He would undertake any sort of trouble to assist those whom he thought deserved assistance. He was a handsome man, strikingly like a gentleman, with highly courteous manners, which resembled those of his maternal uncle, the famous Lord Castlereagh, as I was told by the Minister at Rio. Nevertheless he must have inherited much in his appearance from Charles II., for Dr. Wallich gave me a collection of photographs which he had made, and I was struck with the resemblance of one to Fitz-

---

* Josiah Wedgwood.

Roy; and on looking at the name, I found it Ch. E. Sobieski Stuart, Count d'Albanie, a descendant of the same monarch.

Fitz-Roy's temper was a most unfortunate one. It was usually worst in the early morning, and with his eagle eye he could generally detect something amiss about the ship, and was then unsparing in his blame. He was very kind to me, but was a man very difficult to live with on the intimate terms which necessarily followed from our messing by ourselves in the same cabin. We had several quarrels; for instance, early in the voyage at Bahia, in Brazil, he defended and praised slavery, which I abominated, and told me that he had just visited a great slave-owner, who had called up many of his slaves and asked them whether they were happy, and whether they wished to be free, and all answered "No." I then asked him, perhaps with a sneer, whether he thought that the answer of slaves in the presence of their master was worth anything? This made him excessively angry, and he said that as I doubted his word we could not live any longer together. I thought that I should have been compelled to leave the ship; but as soon as the news spread, which it did quickly, as the captain sent for the first lieutenant to assuage his anger by abusing me, I was deeply gratified by receiving an invitation from all the gun-room officers to mess with them. But after a few hours Fitz-Roy showed his usual magnanimity by sending an officer to me with an apology and a request that I would continue to live with him.

His character was in several respects one of the most noble which I have ever known.

The voyage of the *Beagle* has been by far the most important event in my life, and has determined my whole career; yet it depended on so small a circumstance as my uncle offering to drive me thirty miles to Shrewsbury, which few uncles would have done, and on such a trifle as the shape of my nose. I have always felt that I owe to the voyage the first real training or education of my mind; I was led to attend closely to several branches of natural history, and thus my powers of observation were improved, though they were always fairly developed.

The investigation of the geology of all the places visited was far more important, as reasoning here comes into play. On first examining a new district nothing can appear more hopeless than the chaos of rocks ; but by recording the stratification and nature of the rocks and fossils at many points, always reasoning and predicting what will be found elsewhere, light soon begins to dawn on the district, and the structure of the whole becomes more or less intelligible. I had brought with me the first volume of Lyell's 'Principles of Geology,' which I studied attentively; and the book was of the highest service to me in many ways. The very first place which I examined, namely St. Jago in the Cape de Verde islands, showed me clearly the wonderful superiority of Lyell's manner of treating geology, compared with that of any other author, whose works I had with me or ever afterwards read.

Another of my occupations was collecting animals of all classes, briefly describing and roughly dissecting many of the marine ones; but from not being able to draw, and from not having sufficient anatomical knowledge, a great pile of MS. which I made during the voyage has proved almost useless. I thus lost much time, with the exception of that spent in acquiring some knowledge of the Crustaceans, as this was of service when in after years I undertook a monograph of the Cirripedia.

During some part of the day I wrote my Journal, and took much pains in describing carefully and vividly all that I had seen ; and this was good practice. My Journal served also, in part, as letters to my home, and portions were sent to England whenever there was an opportunity.

The above various special studies were, however, of no importance compared with the habit of energetic industry and of concentrated attention to whatever I was engaged in, which I then acquired. Everything about which I thought or read was made to bear directly on what I had seen or was likely to see ; and this habit of mind was continued during the five years of the voyage. I feel sure that it was this training which has enabled me to do whatever I have done in science.

Looking backwards, I can now perceive how my love for science gradually preponderated over every other taste. During the first two years my old passion for shooting survived in nearly full force, and I shot myself all the birds and animals for my collection ; but gradually I gave up my gun more and more, and finally altogether, to my servant, as shooting interfered with my work, more especially with making out the geological structure of a country. I discovered, though unconsciously and insensibly, that the pleasure of observing and reasoning was a much higher one than that of skill and sport. That my mind became developed through my pursuits during the voyage is rendered probable by a remark made by my father, who was the most acute observer whom I ever saw, of a sceptical disposition, and far from being a believer in phrenology ; for on first seeing me after the voyage, he turned round to my sisters, and exclaimed, " Why, the shape of his head is quite altered."

To return to the voyage. On September 11th (1831), I paid a flying visit with Fitz-Roy to the *Beagle* at Plymouth. Thence to Shrewsbury to wish my father and sisters a long farewell. On October 24th I took up my residence at Plymouth, and remained there until December 27th, when the *Beagle* finally left the shores of England for her circumnavigation of the world. We made two earlier attempts to sail, but were driven back each time by heavy gales. These two months at Plymouth were the most miserable which I ever spent, though I exerted myself in various ways. I was out of spirits at the thought of leaving all my family and friends for so long a time, and the weather seemed to me inexpressibly gloomy. I was also troubled with palpitation and pain about the heart, and like many a young ignorant man, especially one with a smattering of medical knowledge, was convinced that I had heart disease. I did not consult any doctor, as I fully expected to hear the verdict that I was not fit for the voyage, and I was resolved to go at all hazards.

I need not here refer to the events of the voyage—where we went and what we did—as I have given a sufficiently full account in my published Journal. The glories of the vegetation of the Tropics rise before my mind at the present time more vividly than anything else; though the sense of sublimity, which the great deserts of Patagonia and the forest-clad mountains of Tierra del Fuego excited in me, has left an indelible impression on my mind. The sight of a naked savage in his native land is an event which can never be forgotten. Many of my excursions on horseback through wild countries, or in the boats, some of which lasted several weeks, were deeply interesting: their discomfort and some degree of danger were at that time hardly a drawback, and none at all afterwards. I also reflect with high satisfaction on some of my scientific work, such as solving the problem of coral islands, and making out the geological structure of certain islands, for instance, St. Helena. Nor must I pass over the discovery of the singular relations of the animals and plants inhabiting the several islands of the Galapagos archipelago, and of all of them to the inhabitants of South America.

As far as I can judge of myself, I worked to the utmost during the voyage from the mere pleasure of investigation, and from my strong desire to add a few facts to the great mass of facts in Natural Science. But I was also ambitious to take a fair place among scientific men,—whether more ambitious or less so than most of my fellow-workers, I can form no opinion.

The geology of St. Jago is very striking, yet simple: a stream of lava formerly flowed over the bed of the sea, formed of triturated recent shells and corals, which it has baked into a hard white rock. Since then the whole island has been upheaved. But the line of white rock revealed to me a new and important fact, namely, that there had been afterwards subsi-

dence round the craters, which had since been in action, and
had poured forth lava. It then first dawned on me that I
might perhaps write a book on the geology of the various
countries visited, and this made me thrill with delight. That
was a memorable hour to me, and how distinctly I can call to
mind the low cliff of lava beneath which I rested, with the
sun glaring hot, a few strange desert plants growing near, and
with living corals in the tidal pools at my feet. Later in the
voyage, Fitz-Roy asked me to read some of my Journal, and
declared it would be worth publishing; so here was a second
book in prospect !

Towards the close of our voyage I received a letter whilst
at Ascension, in which my sisters told me that Sedgwick had
called on my father, and said that I should take a place among
the leading scientific men. I could not at the time understand how he could have learnt anything of my proceedings,
but I heard (I believe afterwards) that Henslow had read
some of the letters which I wrote to him before the Philosophical Society of Cambridge,* and had printed them for
private distribution. My collection of fossil bones, which
had been sent to Henslow, also excited considerable attention amongst palæontologists. After reading this letter, I
clambered over the mountains of Ascension with a bounding
step, and made the volcanic rocks resound under my geological hammer. All this shows how ambitious I was ; but I think
that I can say with truth that in after years, though I cared
in the highest degree for the approbation of such men as
Lyell and Hooker, who were my friends, I did not care much
about the general public. I do not mean to say that a favourable review or a large sale of my books did not please me
greatly, but the pleasure was a fleeting one, and I am sure
that I have never turned one inch out of my course to gain
fame.

---

* Read at the meeting held November 16, 1835, and printed in a pamphlet of 31 pp. for distribution among the members of the Society.

From my return to England (October 2, 1836) to my marriage (January 29, 1839).

These two years and three months were the most active ones which I ever spent, though I was occasionally unwell, and so lost some time. After going backwards and forwards several times between Shrewsbury, Maer, Cambridge, and London, I settled in lodgings at Cambridge * on December 13th, where all my collections were under the care of Henslow. I stayed here three months, and got my minerals and rocks examined by the aid of Professor Miller.

I began preparing my ' Journal of Travels,' which was not hard work, as my MS. Journal had been written with care, and my chief labour was making an abstract of my more interesting scientific results. I sent also, at the request of Lyell, a short account of my observations on the elevation of the coast of Chile to the Geological Society.†

On March 7th, 1837, I took lodgings in Great Marlborough Street in London, and remained there for nearly two years, until I was married. During these two years I finished my Journal, read several papers before the Geological Society, began preparing the MS. for my ' Geological Observations,' and arranged for the publication of the ' Zoology of the Voyage of the *Beagle.*' In July I opened my first note-book for facts in relation to the Origin of Species, about which I had long reflected, and never ceased working for the next twenty years.

During these two years I also went a little into society, and acted as one of the honorary secretaries of the Geological Society. I saw a great deal of Lyell. One of his chief characteristics was his sympathy with the work of others, and I was as much astonished as delighted at the interest which he showed when, on my return to England, I explained to him my views on coral reefs. This encouraged me greatly, and his advice and example had much influence on me. During

---

* In Fitzwilliam Street.
† ' Geolog. Soc. Proc.' ii. 1838, pp. 446–449.

LONDON.

this time I saw also a good deal of Robert Brown; I used often to call and sit with him during his breakfast on Sunday mornings, and he poured forth a rich treasure of curious observations and acute remarks, but they almost always related to minute points, and he never with me discussed large or general questions in science.

During these two years I took several short excursions as a relaxation, and one longer one to the Parallel Roads of Glen Roy, an account of which was published in the ' Philosophical Transactions.'* This paper was a great failure, and I am ashamed of it. Having been deeply impressed with what I had seen of the elevation of the land of South America, I attributed the parallel lines to the action of the sea; but I had to give up this view when Agassiz propounded his glacier-lake theory. Because no other explanation was possible under our then state of knowledge, I argued in favor of sea-action; and my error has been a good lesson to me never to trust in science to the principle of exclusion.

As I was not able to work all day at science, I read a good deal during these two years on various subjects, including some metaphysical books; but I was not well fitted for such studies. About this time I took much delight in Wordsworth's and Coleridge's poetry; and can boast that I read the ' Excursion ' twice through. Formerly Milton's ' Paradise Lost ' had been my chief favourite, and in my excursions during the voyage of the *Beagle*, when I could take only a single volume, I always chose Milton.

From my marriage, January 29, 1839, and residence in Upper Gower Street, to our leaving London and settling at Down, September 14, 1842.

After speaking of his happy married life, and of his children, he continues : —

During the three years and eight months whilst we resided in London, I did less scientific work, though I worked as

---

* 1839, pp. 39–82.

hard as I possibly could, than during any other equal length
of time in my life. This was owing to frequently recurring
unwellness, and to one long and serious illness. The greater
part of my time, when I could do anything, was devoted to
my work on 'Coral Reefs,' which I had begun before my
marriage, and of which the last proof-sheet was corrected on
May 6th, 1842. This book, though a small one, cost me
twenty months of hard work, as I had to read every work on
the islands of the Pacific and to consult many charts. It was
thought highly of by scientific men, and the theory therein
given is, I think, now well established.

No other work of mine was begun in so deductive a spirit
as this, for the whole theory was thought out on the west
coast of South America, before I had seen a true coral reef.
I had therefore only to verify and extend my views by a careful examination of living reefs. But it should be observed
that I had during the two previous years been incessantly attending to the effects on the shores of South America of the
intermittent elevation of the land, together with denudation
and the deposition of sediment. This necessarily led me to
reflect much on the effects of subsidence, and it was easy to
replace in imagination the continued deposition of sediment
by the upward growth of corals. To do this was to form
my theory of the formation of barrier-reefs and atolls.

Besides my work on coral-reefs, during my residence in
London, I read before the Geological Society papers on the
Erratic Boulders of South America,* on Earthquakes,† and
on the Formation by the Agency of Earth-worms of Mould.‡
I also continued to superintend the publication of the 'Zoology
of the Voyage of the *Beagle*.' Nor did I ever intermit collecting facts bearing on the origin of species ; and I could
sometimes do this when I could do nothing else from illness.

In the summer of 1842 I was stronger than I had been for
some time, and took a little tour by myself in North Wales,

---

* ' Geolog. Soc. Proc.' iii. 1842.   † ' Geolog. Trans.' v. 1840.
‡ ' Geolog. Soc. Proc.' ii. 1838.

for the sake of observing the effects of the old glaciers which formerly filled all the larger valleys. I published a short account of what I saw in the 'Philosophical Magazine.'* This excursion interested me greatly, and it was the last time I was ever strong enough to climb mountains or to take long walks such as are necessary for geological work.

During the early part of our life in London, I was strong enough to go into general society, and saw a good deal of several scientific men, and other more or less distinguished men. I will give my impressions with respect to some of them, though I have little to say worth saying.

I saw more of Lyell than of any other man, both before and after my marriage. His mind was characterised, as it appeared to me, by clearness, caution, sound judgment, and a good deal of originality. When I made any remark to him on Geology, he never rested until he saw the whole case clearly, and often made me see it more clearly than I had done before. He would advance all possible objections to my suggestion, and even after these were exhausted would long remain dubious. A second characteristic was his hearty sympathy with the work of other scientific men.†

On my return from the voyage of the *Beagle*, I explained to him my views on coral-reefs, which differed from his, and I was greatly surprised and encouraged by the vivid interest which he showed. His delight in science was ardent, and he felt the keenest interest in the future progress of mankind. He was very kind-hearted, and thoroughly liberal in his religious beliefs, or rather disbeliefs; but he was a strong theist. His candour was highly remarkable. He exhibited this by becoming a convert to the Descent theory, though he had gained much fame by opposing Lamarck's views, and this after he had grown old. He reminded me that I had

---

* 'Philosophical Magazine,' 1842.

† The slight repetition here observable is accounted for by the notes on Lyell, &c., having been added in April, 1881, a few years after the rest of the ' Recollections ' were written.

many years before said to him, when discussing the opposition
of the old school of geologists to his new views, "What a
good thing it would be if every scientific man was to die when
sixty years old, as afterwards he would be sure to oppose all
new doctrines." But he hoped that now he might be allowed
to live.

The science of Geology is enormously indebted to Lyell—
more so, as I believe, than to any other man who ever lived.
When [I was] starting on the voyage of the *Beagle*, the sagacious Henslow, who, like all other geologists, believed at that
time in successive cataclysms, advised me to get and study
the first volume of the 'Principles,' which had then just been
published, but on no account to accept the views therein advocated. How differently would any one now speak of the
'Principles'! I am proud to remember that the first place,
namely, St. Jago, in the Cape de Verde archipelago, in which
I geologised, convinced me of the infinite superiority of
Lyell's views over those advocated in any other work known
to me.

The powerful effects of Lyell's works could formerly be
plainly seen in the different progress of the science in France
and England. The present total oblivion of Elie de Beaumont's wild hypotheses, such as his 'Craters of Elevation'
and 'Lines of Elevation' (which latter hypothesis I heard
Sedgwick at the Geological Society lauding to the skies), may
be largely attributed to Lyell.

I saw a good deal of Robert Brown, "facile Princeps Bo-
tanicorum," as he was called by Humboldt. He seemed to
me to be chiefly remarkable for the minuteness of his observations, and their perfect accuracy. His knowledge was
extraordinarily great, and much died with him, owing to his
excessive fear of ever making a mistake. He poured out his
knowledge to me in the most unreserved manner, yet was
strangely jealous on some points. I called on him two or
three times before the voyage of the *Beagle*, and on one occasion he asked me to look through a microscope and describe what I saw. This I did, and believe now that it was

the marvellous currents of protoplasm in some vegetable cell.
I then asked him what I had seen; but he answered me,
"That is my little secret."

He was capable of the most generous actions. When old,
much out of health, and quite unfit for any exertion, he daily
visited (as Hooker told me) an old man-servant, who lived at
a distance (and whom he supported), and read aloud to him.
This is enough to make up for any degree of scientific penuri-
ousness or jealousy.

I may here mention a few other eminent men, whom I
have occasionally seen, but I have little to say about them
worth saying. I felt a high reverence for Sir J. Herschel,
and was delighted to dine with him at his charming house at
the Cape of Good Hope, and afterwards at his London house.
I saw him, also, on a few other occasions. He never talked
much, but every word which he uttered was worth listening to.

I once met at breakfast at Sir R. Murchison's house the
illustrious Humboldt, who honoured me by expressing a wish
to see me. I was a little disappointed with the great man, but
my anticipations probably were too high. I can remember
nothing distinctly about our interview, except that Humboldt
was very cheerful and talked much.

—————— reminds me of Buckle whom I once met at Hensleigh Wedgwood's. I was very glad to learn from him his
system of collecting facts. He told me that he bought all the
books which he read, and made a full index, to each, of the
facts which he thought might prove serviceable to him, and
that he could always remember in what book he had read
anything, for his memory was wonderful. I asked him how
at first he could judge what facts would be serviceable, and
he answered that he did not know, but that a sort of instinct
guided him. From this habit of making indices, he was enabled to give the astonishing number of references on all sorts
of subjects, which may be found in his 'History of Civilisation.' This book I thought most interesting, and read it
twice, but I doubt whether his generalisations are worth any-

thing.   Buckle was a great talker, and I listened to him saying hardly a word, nor indeed could I have done so for he
left no gaps.   When Mrs. Farrer began to sing, I jumped up
and said that I must listen to her ; after I had moved away
he turned around to a friend and said (as was overheard by
my brother), "Well, Mr. Darwin's books are much better than
his conversation."

Of other great literary men, I once met Sydney Smith
at Dean Milman's house.   There was something inexplicably
amusing in every word which he uttered.   Perhaps this was
partly due to the expectation of being amused.   He was talking about Lady Cork, who was then extremely old.   This was
the lady who, as he said, was once so much affected by one
of his charity sermons, that she *borrowed* a guinea from a
friend to put in the plate.   He now said "It is generally believed that my dear old friend Lady Cork has been overlooked," and he said this in such a manner that no one could
for a moment doubt that he meant that his dear old friend
had been overlooked by the devil.   How he managed to express this I know not.

I likewise once met Macaulay at Lord Stanhope's (the
historian's) house, and as there was only one other man at
dinner, I had a grand opportunity of hearing him converse,
and he was very agreeable.   He did not talk at all too much ;
nor indeed could such a man talk too much, as long as he allowed others to turn the stream of his conversation, and this
he did allow.

Lord Stanhope once gave me a curious little proof of the
accuracy and fulness of Macaulay's memory : many historians used often to meet at Lord Stanhope's house, and in
discussing various subjects they would sometimes differ from
Macaulay, and formerly they often referred to some book to
see who was right ; but latterly, as Lord Stanhope noticed,
no historian ever took this trouble, and whatever Macaulay
said was final.

On another occasion I met at Lord Stanhope's house,
one of his parties of historians and other literary men, and.

amongst them were Motley and Grote. After luncheon I walked about Chevening Park for nearly an hour with Grote, and was much interested by his conversation and pleased by the simplicity and absence of all pretension in his manners.

Long ago I dined occasionally with the old Earl, the father of the historian; he was a strange man, but what little I knew of him I liked much. He was frank, genial, and pleasant. He had strongly marked features, with a brown complexion, and his clothes, when I saw him, were all brown. He seemed to believe in everything which was to others utterly incredible. He said one day to me, "Why don't you give up your fiddle-faddle of geology and zoology, and turn to the occult sciences?" The historian, then Lord Mahon, seemed shocked at such a speech to me, and his charming wife much amused.

The last man whom I will mention is Carlyle, seen by me several times at my brother's house, and two or three times at my own house. His talk was very racy and interesting, just like his writings, but he sometimes went on too long on the same subject. I remember a funny dinner at my brother's, where, amongst a few others, were Babbage and Lyell, both of whom liked to talk. Carlyle, however, silenced every one by haranguing during the whole dinner on the advantages of silence. After dinner Babbage, in his grimmest manner, thanked Carlyle for his very interesting lecture on silence.

Carlyle sneered at almost every one: one day in my house he called Grote's 'History' "a fetid quagmire, with nothing spiritual about it." I always thought, until his 'Reminiscences' appeared, that his sneers were partly jokes, but this now seems rather doubtful. His expression was that of a depressed, almost despondent yet benevolent, man; and it is notorious how heartily he laughed. I believe that his benevolence was real, though stained by not a little jealousy. No one can doubt about his extraordinary power of drawing pictures of things and men—far more vivid, as it appears to me, than any drawn by Macaulay. Whether his pictures of men were true ones is another question.

He has been all-powerful in impressing some grand moral truths on the minds of men. On the other hand, his views about slavery were revolting. In his eyes might was right. His mind seemed to me a very narrow one; even if all branches of science, which he despised, are excluded. It is astonishing to me that Kingsley should have spoken of him as a man well fitted to advance science. He laughed to scorn the idea that a mathematician, such as Whewell, could judge, as I maintained he could, of Goethe's views on light. He thought it a most ridiculous thing that any one should care whether a glacier moved a little quicker or a little slower, or moved at all. As far as I could judge, I never met a man with a mind so ill adapted for scientific research.

Whilst living in London, I attended as regularly as I could the meetings of several scientific socities, and acted as secretary to the Geological Society. But such attendance, and ordinary society, suited my health so badly that we resolved to live in the country, which we both preferred and have never repented of.

Residence at Down from September 14, 1842, *to the present time,* 1876.

After several fruitless searches in Surrey and elsewhere, we found this house and purchased it. I was pleased with the diversified appearance of vegetation proper to a chalk district, and so unlike what I had been accustomed to in the Midland counties; and still more pleased with the extreme quietness and rusticity of the place. It is not, however, quite so retired a place as a writer in a German periodical makes it, who says that my house can be approached only by a mule-track! Our fixing ourselves here has answered admirably in one way, which we did not anticipate, namely, by being very convenient for frequent visits from our children.

Few persons can have lived a more retired life than we

have done. Besides short visits to the houses of relations, and occasionally to the seaside or elsewhere, we have gone nowhere. During the first part of our residence we went a little into society, and received a few friends here; but my health almost always suffered from the excitement, violent shivering and vomiting attacks being thus brought on. I have therefore been compelled for many years to give up all dinner-parties; and this has been somewhat of a deprivation to me, as such parties always put me into high spirits. From the same cause I have been able to invite here very few scientific acquaintances.

My chief enjoyment and sole employment throughout life has been scientific work; and the excitement from such work makes me for the time forget, or drives quite away, my daily discomfort. I have therefore nothing to record during the rest of my life, except the publication of my several books. Perhaps a few details how they arose may be worth giving.

My several Publications.—In the early part of 1844, my observations on the volcanic islands visited during the voyage of the *Beagle* were published. In 1845, I took much pains in correcting a new edition of my ' Journal of Researches,' which was originally published in 1839 as part of Fitz-Roy's work. The success of this, my first literary child, always tickles my vanity more than that of any of my other books. Even to this day it sells steadily in England and the United States, and has been translated for the second time into German, and into French and other languages. This success of a book of travels, especially of a scientific one, so many years after its first publication, is surprising. Ten thousand copies have been sold in England of the second edition. In 1846 my ' Geological Observations on South America ' were published. I record in a little diary, which I have always kept, that my three geological books (' Coral Reefs' included) consumed four and a half years' steady work; "and now it is ten years since my return to England. How much time have I lost by illness?" I have nothing to say about these three books except that to my surprise new editions have lately been called for.*

In October, 1846, I began to work on 'Cirripedia.' When on the coast of Chile, I found a most curious form, which burrowed into the shells of Concholepas, and which differed so much from all other Cirripedes that I had to form a new sub-order for its sole reception. Lately an allied burrowing genus has been found on the shores of Portugal. To understand the structure of my new Cirripede I had to examine and dissect many of the common forms; and this gradually led me on to take up the whole group. I worked steadily on this subject for the next eight years, and ultimately published two thick volumes,† describing all the known living species, and two thin quartos on the extinct species. I do not doubt that Sir E. Lytton Bulwer had me in his mind when he introduced in one of his novels a Professor Long, who had written two huge volumes on limpets.

Although I was employed during eight years on this work, yet I record in my diary that about two years out of this time was lost by illness. On this account I went in 1848 for some months to Malvern for hydropathic treatment, which did me much good, so that on my return home I was able to resume work. So much was I out of health that when my dear father died on November 13th, 1848, I was unable to attend his funeral or to act as one of his executors.

My work on the Cirripedia possesses, I think, considerable value, as besides describing several new and remarkable forms, I made out the homologies of the various parts—I discovered the cementing apparatus, though I blundered dreadfully about the cement glands—and lastly I proved the existence in certain genera of minute males complemental to and parasitic on the hermaphrodites. This latter discovery has at last been fully confirmed; though at one time a German

---

* 'Geological Observations,' 2nd Edit. 1876. 'Coral Reefs,' 2nd Edit. 1874.

† Published by the Ray Society.

writer was pleased to attribute the whole account to my fertile imagination. The Cirripedes form a highly varying and difficult group of species to class ; and my work was of considerable use to me, when I had to discuss in the 'Origin of Species' the principles of a natural classification. Nevertheless, I doubt whether the work was worth the consumption of so much time.

From September 1854 I devoted my whole time to arranging my huge pile of notes, to observing, and to experimenting in relation to the transmutation of species. During the voyage of the *Beagle* I had been deeply impressed by discovering in the Pampean formation great fossil animals covered with armour like that on the existing armadillos ; secondly, by the manner in which closely allied animals replace one another in proceeding southwards over the Continent ; and thirdly, by the South American character of most of the productions of the Galapagos archipelago, and more especially by the manner in which they differ slightly on each island of the group ; none of the islands appearing to be very ancient in a geological sense.

It was evident that such facts as these, as well as many others, could only be explained on the supposition that species gradually become modified ; and the subject haunted me. But it was equally evident that neither the action of the surrounding conditions, nor the will of the organisms (especially in the case of plants) could account for the innumerable cases in which organisms of every kind are beautifully adapted to their habits of life—for instance, a woodpecker or a tree-frog to climb trees, or a seed for dispersal by hooks or plumes. I had always been much struck by such adaptations, and until these could be explained it seemed to me almost useless to endeavour to prove by indirect evidence that species have been modified.

After my return to England it appeared to me that by following the example of Lyell in Geology, and by collecting all facts which bore in any way on the variation of animals and plants under domestication and nature, some light might

perhaps be thrown on the whole subject.   My first note-book
was opened in July 1837.   I worked on true Baconian principles, and without any theory collected facts on a wholesale
scale, more especially with respect to domesticated productions, by printed enquiries, by conversation with skilful
breeders and gardeners, and by extensive reading.   When I
see the list of books of all kinds which I read and abstracted,
including whole series of Journals and Transactions, I am
surprised at my industry.   I soon perceived that selection
was the keystone of man's success in making useful races of
animals and plants.   But how selection could be applied to
organisms living in a state of nature remained for some time
a mystery to me.

In October 1838, that is, fifteen months after I had begun
my systematic enquiry, I happened to read for amusement
'Malthus on Population,' and being well prepared to appreciate the struggle for existence which everywhere goes on
from long-continued observation of the habits of animals and
plants, it at once struck me that under these circumstances
favourable variations would tend to be preserved, and unfavourable ones to be destroyed.   The result of this would be
the formation of new species.   Here then I had at last got a
theory by which to work; but I was so anxious to avoid
prejudice, that I determined not for some time to write even
the briefest sketch of it.   In June 1842 I first allowed myself
the satisfaction of writing a very brief abstract of my theory
in pencil in 35 pages; and this was enlarged during the summer of 1844 into one of 230 pages, which I had fairly copied
out and still possess.

But at that time I overlooked one problem of great importance; and it is astonishing to me, except on the principle of
Columbus and his egg, how I could have overlooked it and
its solution.   This problem is the tendency in organic beings
descended from the same stock to diverge in character as
they become modified.   That they have diverged greatly is
obvious from the manner in which species of all kinds can be
classed under genera, genera under families, families under

sub-orders and so forth ; and I can remember the very spot in the road, whilst in my carriage, when to my joy the solution occurred to me ; and this was long after I had come to Down. The solution, as I believe, is that the modified offspring of all dominant and increasing forms tend to become adapted to many and highly diversified places in the economy of nature.

Early in 1856 Lyell advised me to write out my views pretty fully, and I began at once to do so on a scale three or four times as extensive as that which was afterwards followed in my 'Origin of Species ; ' yet it was only an abstract of the materials which I had collected, and I got through about half the work on this scale. But my plans were overthrown, for early in the summer of 1858 Mr. Wallace, who was then in the Malay archipelago, sent me an essay "On the Tendency of Varieties to depart indefinitely from the Original Type;" and this essay contained exactly the same theory as mine. Mr. Wallace expressed the wish that if I thought well of his essay, I should send it to Lyell for perusal.

The circumstances under which I consented at the request of Lyell and Hooker to allow of an abstract from my MS., together with a letter to Asa Gray, dated September 5, 1857, to be published at the same time with Wallace's Essay, are given in the 'Journal of the Proceedings of the Linnean Society,' 1858, p. 45. I was at first very unwilling to consent, as I thought Mr. Wallace might consider my doing so unjustifiable, for I did not then know how generous and noble was his disposition. The extract from my MS. and the letter to Asa Gray had neither been intended for publication, and were badly written. Mr. Wallace's essay, on the other hand, was admirably expressed and quite clear. Nevertheless, our joint productions excited very little attention, and the only published notice of them which I can remember was by Professor Haughton of Dublin, whose verdict was that all that was new in them was false, and what was true was old. This shows how necessary it is that any new view should be explained at considerable length in order to arouse public attention.

In September 1858 I set to work by the strong advice of Lyell and Hooker to prepare a volume on the transmutation of species, but was often interrupted by ill-health, and short visits to Dr. Lane's delightful hydropathic establishment at Moor Park. I abstracted the MS. begun on a much larger scale in 1856, and completed the volume on the same reduced scale. It cost me thirteen months and ten days' hard labour. It was published under the title of the 'Origin of Species,' in November 1859. Though considerably added to and corrected in the later editions, it has remained substantially the same book.

It is no doubt the chief work of my life. It was from the first highly successful. The first small edition of 1250 copies was sold on the day of publication, and a second edition of 3000 copies soon afterwards. Sixteen thousand copies have now (1876) been sold in England; and considering how stiff a book it is, this is a large sale. It has been translated into almost every European tongue, even into such languages as Spanish, Bohemian, Polish, and Russian. It has also, according to Miss Bird, been translated into Japanese,* and is there much studied. Even an essay in Hebrew has appeared on it, showing that the theory is contained in the Old Testament! The reviews were very numerous; for some time I collected all that appeared on the 'Origin' and on my related books, and these amount (excluding newspaper reviews) to 265; but after a time I gave up the attempt in despair. Many separate essays and books on the subject have appeared; and in Germany a catalogue or bibliography on "Darwinismus" has appeared every year or two.

The success of the 'Origin' may, I think, be attributed in large part to my having long before written two condensed sketches, and to my having finally abstracted a much larger manuscript, which was itself an abstract. By this means I was enabled to select the more striking facts and conclusions.

---

* Miss Bird is mistaken, as I learn from Prof. Mitsukuri.—F. D.

I had, also, during many years followed a golden rule, namely, that whenever a published fact, a new observation or thought came across me, which was opposed to my general results, to make a memorandum of it without fail and at once ; for I had found by experience that such facts and thoughts were far more apt to escape from the memory than favourable ones. Owing to this habit, very few objections were raised against my views which I had not at least noticed and attempted to answer.

It has sometimes been said that the success of the 'Origin' proved "that the subject was in the air," or "that men's minds were prepared for it." I do not think that this is strictly true, for I occasionally sounded not a few naturalists, and never happened to come across a single one who seemed to doubt about the permanence of species. Even Lyell and Hooker, though they would listen with interest to me, never seemed to agree. I tried once or twice to explain to able men what I meant by Natural Selection, but signally failed. What I believe was strictly true is that innumerable well-observed facts were stored in the minds of naturalists ready to take their proper places as soon as any theory which would receive them was sufficiently explained. Another element in the success of the book was its moderate size ; and this I owe to the appearance of Mr. Wallace's essay ; had I published on the scale in which I began to write in 1856, the book would have been four or five times as large as the 'Origin,' and very few would have had the patience to read it.

I gained much by my delay in publishing from about 1839, when the theory was clearly conceived, to 1859 ; and I lost nothing by it, for I cared very little whether men attributed most originality to me or Wallace ; and his essay no doubt aided in the reception of the theory. I was forestalled in only one important point, which my vanity has always made me regret, namely, the explanation by means of the Glacial period of the presence of the same species of plants and of some few animals on distant mountain summits and in the arctic regions. This view pleased me so much that I wrote it out in extenso, and I believe that it was read by Hooker some years before E. Forbes published his celebrated memoir* on the subject. In the very few points in which we differed, I still think that I was in the right. I have never, of course, alluded in print to my having independently worked out this view.

Hardly any point gave me so much satisfaction when I was at work on the 'Origin,' as the explanation of the wide difference in many classes between the embryo and the adult animal, and of the close resemblance of the embryos within the same class. No notice of this point was taken, as far as I remember, in the early reviews of the 'Origin,' and I recollect expressing my surprise on this head in a letter to Asa Gray. Within late years several reviewers have given the whole credit to Fritz Müller and Häckel, who undoubtedly have worked it out much more fully, and in some respects more correctly than I did. I had materials for a whole chapter on the subject, and I ought to have made the discussion longer; for it is clear that I failed to impress my readers; and he who succeeds in doing so deserves, in my opinion, all the credit.

This leads me to remark that I have almost always been treated honestly by my reviewers, passing over those without scientific knowledge as not worthy of notice. My views have often been grossly misrepresented, bitterly opposed and ridiculed, but this has been generally done, as I believe, in good faith. On the whole I do not doubt that my works have been over and over again greatly overpraised. I rejoice that I have avoided controversies, and this I owe to Lyell, who many years ago, in reference to my geological works, strongly advised me never to get entangled in a controversy, as it rarely did any good and caused a miserable loss of time and temper.

Whenever I have found out that I have blundered, or that my work has been imperfect, and when I have been contemptuously criticised, and even when I have been over-

---

* 'Geolog. Survey Mem.,' 1846.

praised, so that I have felt mortified, it has been my greatest comfort to say hundreds of times to myself that "I have worked as hard and as well as I could, and no man can do more than this." I remember when in Good Success Bay, in Tierra del Fuego, thinking (and, I believe, that I wrote home to the effect) that I could not employ my life better than in adding a little to Natural Science. This I have done to the best of my abilities, and critics may say what they like, but they cannot destroy this conviction.

During the two last months of 1859 I was fully occupied in preparing a second edition of the 'Origin,' and by an enormous correspondence. On January 1st, 1860, I began arranging my notes for my work on the 'Variation of Animals and Plants under Domestication;' but it was not published until the beginning of 1868; the delay having been caused partly by frequent illnesses, one of which lasted seven months, and partly by being tempted to publish on other subjects which at the time interested me more.

On May 15th, 1862, my little book on the 'Fertilisation of Orchids,' which cost me ten months' work, was published: most of the facts had been slowly accumulated during several previous years. During the summer of 1839, and, I believe, during the previous summer, I was led to attend to the cross-fertilisation of flowers by the aid of insects, from having come to the conclusion in my speculations on the origin of species, that crossing played an important part in keeping specific forms constant. I attended to the subject more or less during every subsequent summer; and my interest in it was greatly enhanced by having procured and read in November 1841, through the advice of Robert Brown, a copy of C. K. Sprengel's wonderful book, 'Das entdeckte Geheimniss der Natur.' For some years before 1862 I had specially attended to the fertilisation of our British orchids; and it seemed to me the best plan to prepare as complete a treatise on this group of plants as well as I could, rather than to utilise the great mass of matter which I had slowly collected with respect to other plants.

5

My resolve proved a wise one; for since the appearance
of my book, a surprising number of papers and separate
works on the fertilisation of all kinds of flowers have appeared : and these are far better done than I could possibly
have effected.   The merits of poor old Sprengel, so long
overlooked, are now fully recognised many years after his
death.

During the same year I published in the 'Journal of the
Linnean Society' a paper "On the Two Forms, or Dimor·
phic Condition of Primula," and during the next five years,
five other papers on dimorphic and trimorphic plants.   I do
not think anything in my scientific life has given me so much
satisfaction as making out the meaning of the structure of
these plants.   I had noticed in 1838 or 1839 the dimorphism
of *Linum flavum*, and had at first thought that it was merely
a case of unmeaning variability.   But on examining the common species of Primula I found that the two forms were much
too regular and constant to be thus viewed.   I therefore became almost convinced that the common cowslip and prim-
rose were on the high road to become diœcious ;—that the
short pistil in the one form, and the short stamens in the
other form were tending towards abortion.   The plants were
therefore subjected under this point of view to trial ; but as
soon as the flowers with short pistils fertilised with pollen
from the short stamens, were found to yield more seeds than
any other of the four possible unions, the abortion-theory was
knocked on the head.   After some additional experiment, it
became evident that the two forms, though both were perfect
hermaphrodites, bore almost the same relation to one another
as do the two sexes of an ordinary animal.   With Lythrum
we have the still more wonderful case of three forms standing
in a similar relation to one another.   I afterwards found that
the offspring from the union of two plants belonging to the
same forms presented a close and curious analogy with hybrids from the union of two distinct species.

In the autumn of 1864 I finished a long paper on 'Climbing Plants,' and sent it to the Linnean Society.   The writing

of this paper cost me four months; but I was so unwell when I received the proof-sheets that I was forced to leave them very badly and often obscurely expressed. The paper was little noticed, but when in 1875 it was corrected and published as a separate book it sold well. I was led to take up this subject by reading a short paper by Asa Gray, published in 1858. He sent me seeds, and on raising some plants I was so much fascinated and perplexed by the revolving movements of the tendrils and stems, which movements are really very simple, though appearing at first sight very complex, that I procured various other kinds of climbing plants, and studied the whole subject. I was all the more attracted to it, from not being at all satisfied with the explanation which Henslow gave us in his lectures, about twining plants, namely, that they had a natural tendency to grow up in a spire. This explanation proved quite erroneous. Some of the adaptations displayed by Climbing Plants are as beautiful as those of Orchids for ensuring cross-fertilisation.

My 'Variation of Animals and Plants under Domestication' was begun, as already stated, in the beginning of 1860, but was not published until the beginning of 1868. It was a big book, and cost me four years and two months' hard labour. It gives all my observations and an immense number of facts collected from various sources, about our domestic productions. In the second volume the causes and laws of variation, inheritance, &c., are discussed as far as our present state of knowledge permits. Towards the end of the work I give my well-abused hypothesis of Pangenesis. An unverified hypothesis is of little or no value; but if any one should hereafter be led to make observations by which some such hypothesis could be established, I shall have done good service, as an astonishing number of isolated facts can be thus connected together and rendered intelligible. In 1875 a second and largely corrected edition, which cost me a good deal of labour, was brought out.

My 'Descent of Man' was published in February, 1871. As soon as I had become, in the year 1837 or 1838, convinced that species were mutable productions, I could not avoid the belief that man must come under the same law. Accordingly I collected notes on the subject for my own satisfaction, and not for a long time with any intention of publishing. Although in the 'Origin of Species' the derivation of any particular species is never discussed, yet I thought it best, in order that no honourable man should accuse me of concealing my views, to add that by the work "light would be thrown on the origin of man and his history." It would have been useless and injurious to the success of the book to have paraded, without giving any evidence, my conviction with respect to his origin.

But when I found that many naturalists fully accepted the doctrine of the evolution of species, it seemed to me advisable to work up such notes as I possessed, and to publish a special treatise on the origin of man. I was the more glad to do so, as it gave me an opportunity of fully discussing sexual selection—a subject which had always greatly interested me. This subject, and that of the variation of our domestic productions, together with the causes and laws of variation, inheritance, and the intercrossing of plants, are the sole subjects which I have been able to write about in full, so as to use all the materials which I have collected. The 'Descent of Man' took me three years to write, but then as usual some of this time was lost by ill health, and some was consumed by preparing new editions and other minor works. A second and largely corrected edition of the 'Descent' appeared in 1874.

My book on the 'Expression of the Emotions in Men and Animals' was published in the autumn of 1872. I had intended to give only a chapter on the subject in the 'Descent of Man,' but as soon as I began to put my notes together, I saw that it would require a separate treatise.

My first child was born on December 27th, 1839, and I at once commenced to make notes on the first dawn of the various expressions which he exhibited, for I felt convinced, even at this early period, that the most complex and fine shades of expression must all have had a gradual and natural origin. During the summer of the following year, 1840, I read Sir C.

Bell's admirable work on expression, and this greatly increased the interest which I felt in the subject, though I could not at all agree with his belief that various muscles had been specially created for the sake of expression. From this time forward I occasionally attended to the subject, both with respect to man and our domesticated animals. My book sold largely; 5267 copies having been disposed of on the day of publication.

In the summer of 1860 I was idling and resting near Hartfield, where two species of Drosera abound; and I noticed that numerous insects had been entrapped by the leaves. I carried home some plants, and on giving them insects saw the movements of the tentacles, and this made me think it probable that the insects were caught for some special purpose. Fortunately a crucial test occurred to me, that of placing a large number of leaves in various nitrogenous and non-nitrogenous fluids of equal density; and as soon as I found that the former alone excited energetic movements, it was obvious that here was a fine new field for investigation.

During subsequent years, whenever I had leisure, I pursued my experiments, and my book on 'Insectivorous Plants' was published in July 1875—that is, sixteen years after my first observations. The delay in this case, as with all my other books, has been a great advantage to me; for a man after a long interval can criticise his own work, almost as well as if it were that of another person. The fact that a plant should secrete, when properly excited, a fluid containing an acid and ferment, closely analogous to the digestive fluid of an animal, was certainly a remarkable discovery.

During this autumn of 1876 I shall publish on the 'Effects of Cross and Self-Fertilisation in the Vegetable Kingdom.' This book will form a complement to that on the 'Fertilisation of Orchids,' in which I showed how perfect were the means for cross-fertilisation, and here I shall show how important are the results. I was led to make, during eleven years, the numerous experiments recorded in this volume, by a mere accidental observation; and indeed it required the accident to be repeated before my attention was thoroughly

aroused to the remarkable fact that seedlings of self-fertilised
parentage are inferior, even in the first generation, in height
and vigour to seedlings of cross-fertilised parentage. I hope
also to republish a revised edition of my book on Orchids,
and hereafter my papers on dimorphic and trimorphic plants,
together with some additional observations on allied points
which I never have had time to arrange. My strength will
then probably be exhausted, and I shall be ready to exclaim
" Nunc dimittis."

Written May 1st, 1881.—' The Effects of Cross and Self-
Fertilisation ' was published in the autumn of 1876; and the
results there arrived at explain, as I believe, the endless and
wonderful contrivances for the transportal of pollen from one
plant to another of the same species. I now believe, however,
chiefly from the observations of Hermann Müller, that I ought
to have insisted more strongly than I did on the many adaptations for self-fertilisation; though I was well aware of many
such adaptations. A much enlarged edition of my ' Fertilisation of Orchids ' was published in 1877.

In this same year ' The Different Forms of Flowers, &c.,'
appeared, and in 1880 a second edition. This book consists
chiefly of the several papers on Heterostyled flowers originally
published by the Linnean Society, corrected, with much new
matter added, together with observations on some other cases
in which the same plant bears two kinds of flowers. As before remarked, no little discovery of mine ever gave me so
much pleasure as the making out the meaning of heterostyled
flowers. The results of crossing such flowers in an illegiti-
mate manner, I believe to be very important, as bearing on
the sterility of hybrids; although these results have been
noticed by only a few persons.

In 1879, I had a translation of Dr. Ernst Krause's ' Life of
Erasmus Darwin ' published, and I added a sketch of his
character and habits from material in my possession. Many
persons have been much interested by this little life, and I
am surprised that only 800 or 900 copies were sold.

In 1880 I published, with [my son] Frank's assistance, our

'Power of Movement in Plants.' This was a tough piece of work. The book bears somewhat the same relation to my little book on 'Climbing Plants,' which 'Cross-Fertilisation' did to the 'Fertilisation of Orchids;' for in accordance with the principle of evolution it was impossible to account for climbing plants having been developed in so many widely different groups unless all kinds of plants possess some slight power of movement of an analogous kind. This I proved to be the case; and I was further led to a rather wide general-isation, viz. that the great and important classes of move-ments, excited by light, the attraction of gravity, &c., are all modified forms of the fundamental movement of circumnuta-tion. It has always pleased me to exalt plants in the scale of organised beings; and I therefore felt an especial pleasure in showing how many and what admirably well adapted move-ments the tip of a root possesses.

I have now (May 1, 1881) sent to the printers the MS. of a little book on 'The Formation of Vegetable Mould, through the Action of Worms.' This is a subject of but small im-portance; and I know not whether it will interest any readers,[*] but it has interested me. It is the completion of a short paper read before the Geological Society more than forty years ago, and has revived old geological thoughts.

I have now mentioned all the books which I have pub-lished, and these have been the milestones in my life, so that little remains to be said. I am not conscious of any change in my mind during the last thirty years, excepting in one point presently to be mentioned; .nor, indeed, could any change have been expected unless one of general deterioration. But my father lived to his eighty-third year with his mind as lively as ever it was, and all his faculties undimmed; and I hope that I may die before my mind fails to a sensible ex-tent. I think that I have become a little more skilful in guessing right explanations and in devising experimental

[*] Between November 1881 and February 1884, 8500 copies have been sold.

tests ; but this may probably be the result of mere practice, and of a larger store of knowledge. I have as much difficulty as ever in expressing myself clearly and concisely ; and this difficulty has caused me a very great loss of time ; but it has had the compensating advantage of forcing me to think long and intently about every sentence, and thus I have been led to see errors in reasoning and in my own observations or those of others.

There seems to be a sort of fatality in my mind leading me to put at first my statement or proposition in a wrong or awkward form. Formerly I used to think about my sentences before writing them down; but for several years I have found that it saves time to scribble in a vile hand whole pages as quickly as I possibly can, contracting half the words; and then correct deliberately. Sentences thus scribbled down are often better ones than I could have written deliberately.

Having said thus much about my manner of writing, I will add that with my large books I spend a good deal of time over the general arrangement of the matter. I first make the rudest outline in two or three pages, and then a larger one in several pages, a few words or one word standing for a whole discussion or series of facts. Each one of these headings is again enlarged and often transferred before I begin to write *in extenso*. As in several of my books facts observed by others have been very extensively used, and as I have always had several quite distinct subjects in hand at the same time, I may mention that I keep from thirty to forty large portfolios, in cabinets with labelled shelves, into which I can at once put a detached reference or memorandum. I have bought many books, and at their ends I make an index of all the facts that concern my work ; or, if the book is not my own, write out a separate abstract, and of such abstracts I have a large drawer full. Before beginning on any subject I look to all the short indexes and make a general and classified index, and by taking the one or more proper portfolios I have all the information collected during my life ready for use.

I have said that in one respect my mind has changed
during the last twenty or thirty years. Up to the age of
thirty, or beyond it, poetry of many kinds, such as the works
of Milton, Gray, Byron, Wordsworth, Coleridge, and Shelley,
gave me great pleasure, and even as a schoolboy I took
intense delight in Shakespeare, especially in the historical
plays. I have also said that formerly pictures gave me considerable, and music very great delight. But now for many
years I cannot endure to read a line of poetry: I have tried
lately to read Shakespeare, and found it so intolerably dull
that it nauseated me. I have also almost lost my taste for
pictures or music. Music generally sets me thinking too en-
ergetically on what I have been at work on, instead of giving
me pleasure. I retain some taste for fine scenery, but it does
not cause me the exquisite delight which it formerly did.
On the other hand, novels which are works of the imagination, though not of a very high order, have been for years
a wonderful relief and pleasure to me, and I often bless all
novelists. A surprising number have been read aloud to me,
and I like all if moderately good, and if they do not end un-
happily—against which a law ought to be passed. A novel,
according to my taste, does not come into the first class
unless it contains some person whom one can thoroughly
love, and if a pretty woman all the better.

This curious and lamentable loss of the higher æsthetic
tastes is all the odder, as books on history, biographies, and
travels (independently of any scientific facts which they may
contain), and essays on all sorts of subjects interest me as
much as ever they did. My mind seems to have become a
kind of machine for grinding general laws out of large collections of facts, but why this should have caused the atrophy
of that part of the brain alone, on which the higher tastes
depend, I cannot conceive. A man with a mind more highly
organised or better constituted than mine, would not, I suppose, have thus suffered ; and if I had to live my life again,
I would have made a rule to read some poetry and listen to
some music at least once every week ; for perhaps the parts

of my brain now atrophied would thus have been kept active through use. The loss of these tastes is a loss of happiness, and may possibly be injurious to the intellect, and more probably to the moral character, by enfeebling the emotional part of our nature.

My books have sold largely in England, have been translated into many languages, and passed through several editions in foreign countries. I have heard it said that the success of a work abroad is the best test of its enduring value. I doubt whether this is at all trustworthy; but judged by this standard my name ought to last for a few years. Therefore it may be worth while to try to analyse the mental qualities and the conditions on which my success has depended; though I am aware that no man can do this correctly.

I have no great quickness of apprehension or wit which is so remarkable in some clever men, for instance, Huxley. I am therefore a poor critic: a paper or book, when first read, generally excites my admiration, and it is only after considerable reflection that I perceive the weak points. My power to follow a long and purely abstract train of thought is very limited; and therefore I could never have succeeded with metaphysics or mathematics. My memory is extensive, yet hazy: it suffices to make me cautious by vaguely telling me that I have observed or read something opposed to the conclusion which I am drawing, or on the other hand in favour of it; and after a time I can generally recollect where to search for my authority. So poor in one sense is my memory, that I have never been able to remember for more than a few days a single date or a line of poetry.

Some of my critics have said, "Oh, he is a good observer, but he has no power of reasoning!" I do not think that this can be true, for the 'Origin of Species' is one long argument from the beginning to the end, and it has convinced not a few able men. No one could have written it without having some power of reasoning. I have a fair share of invention, and of common sense or judgment, such as every fairly successful lawyer or doctor must have, but not, I believe, in any higher degree.

On the favourable side of the balance, I think that I am superior to the common run of men in noticing things which easily escape attention, and in observing them carefully. My industry has been nearly as great as it could have been in the observation and collection of facts. What is far more important, my love of natural science has been steady and ardent.

This pure love has, however, been much aided by the ambition to be esteemed by my fellow naturalists. From my early youth I have had the strongest desire to understand or explain whatever I observed,—that is, to group all facts under some general laws. These causes combined have given me the patience to reflect or ponder for any number of years over any unexplained problem. As far as I can judge, I am not apt to follow blindly the lead of other men. I have steadily endeavoured to keep my mind free so as to give up any hypothesis, however much beloved (and I cannot resist forming one on every subject), as soon as facts are shown to be opposed to it. Indeed, I have had no choice but to act in this manner, for with the exception of the Coral Reefs, I cannot remember a single first-formed hypothesis which had not after a time to be given up or greatly modified. This has naturally led me to distrust greatly deductive reasoning in the mixed sciences. On the other hand, I am not very sceptical,—a frame of mind which I believe to be injurious to the progress of science. A good deal of scepticism in a scientific man is advisable to avoid much loss of time, but I have met with not a few men, who, I feel sure, have often thus been deterred from experiment or observations, which would have proved directly or indirectly serviceable.

In illustration, I will give the oddest case which I have known. A gentleman (who, as I afterwards heard, is a good local botanist) wrote to me from the Eastern counties that the seed or beans of the common field-bean had this year everywhere grown on the wrong side of the pod. I wrote

back, asking for further information, as I did not understand
what was meant; but I did not receive any answer for a very
long time. I then saw in two newspapers, one published in
Kent and the other in Yorkshire, paragraphs stating that it
was a most remarkable fact that "the beans this year had all
grown on the wrong side." So I thought there must be some
foundation for so general a statement. Accordingly, I went
to my gardener, an old Kentish man, and asked him whether
he had heard anything about it, and he answered, "Oh, no,
sir, it must be a mistake, for the beans grow on the wrong
side only on leap-year, and this is not leap-year." I then
asked him how they grew in common years and how on leap-
years, but soon found that he knew absolutely nothing of how
they grew at any time, but he stuck to his belief.

After a time I heard from my first informant, who, with
many apologies, said that he should not have written to me
had he not heard the statement from several intelligent farmers; but that he had since spoken again to every one of them,
and not one knew in the least what he had himself meant.
So that here a belief—if indeed a statement with no definite
idea attached to it can be called a belief—had spread over almost the whole of England without any vestige of evidence.

I have known in the course of my life only three intentionally falsified statements, and one of these may have been
a hoax (and there have been several scientific hoaxes) which,
however, took in an American Agricultural Journal. It related to the formation in Holland of a new breed of oxen by
the crossing of distinct species of Bos (some of which I happen to know are sterile together), and the author had the im-
pudence to state that he had corresponded with me, and that
I had been deeply impressed with the importance of his result. The article was sent to me by the editor of an English
Agricultural Journal, asking for my opinion before republish-
ing it.

A second case was an account of several varieties, raised
by the author from several species of Primula, which had
spontaneously yielded a full complement of seed, although

the parent plants had been carefully protected from the access of insects. This account was published before I had discovered the meaning of heterostylism, and the whole statement must have been fraudulent, or there was neglect in excluding insects so gross as to be scarcely credible.

The third case was more curious: Mr. Huth published in his book on 'Consanguineous Marriage' some long extracts from a Belgian author, who stated that he had interbred rabbits in the closest manner for very many generations, without the least injurious effects. The account was published in a most respectable Journal, that of the Royal Society of Belgium; but I could not avoid feeling doubts—I hardly know why, except that there were no accidents of any kind, and my experience in breeding animals made me think this very improbable.

So with much hesitation I wrote to Professor Van Beneden, asking him whether the author was a trustworthy man. I soon heard in answer that the Society had been greatly shocked by discovering that the whole account was a fraud.* The writer had been publicly challenged in the Journal to say where he had resided and kept his large stock of rabbits while carrying on his experiments, which must have consumed several years, and no answer could be extracted from him.

My habits are methodical, and this has been of not a little use for my particular line of work. Lastly, I have had ample leisure from not having to earn my own bread. Even ill-health, though it has annihilated several years of my life, has saved me from the distractions of society and amusement.

Therefore my success as a man of science, whatever this may have amounted to, has been determined, as far as I can judge, by complex and diversified mental qualities and conditions. Of these, the most important have been—the love

---

* The falseness of the published statements on which Mr. Huth relied has been pointed out by himself in a slip inserted in all the copies of his book which then remained unsold.

of science—unbounded patience in long reflecting over any subject—industry in observing and collecting facts—and a fair share of invention as well as of common sense. With such moderate abilities as I possess, it is truly surprising that I should have influenced to a considerable extent the belief of scientific men on some important points.

DOWN HOUSE, FROM THE GARDEN.

[From the Century Magazine.

CHAPTER III.

REMINISCENCES OF MY FATHER'S EVERYDAY LIFE.

IT is my wish in the present chapter to give some idea of my father's everyday life. It has seemed to me that I might carry out this object in the form of a rough sketch of a day's life at Down, interspersed with such recollections as are called up by the record. Many of these recollections, which have a meaning for those who knew my father, will seem colourless or trifling to strangers. Nevertheless, I give them in the hope that they may help to preserve that impression of his personality which remains on the minds of those who knew and loved him—an impression at once so vivid and so untranslatable into words.

Of his personal appearance (in these days of multiplied photographs) it is hardly necessary to say much. He was about six feet in height, but scarcely looked so tall, as he stooped a good deal; in later days he yielded to the stoop; but I can remember seeing him long ago swinging his arms back to open out his chest, and holding himself upright with a jerk. He gave one the idea that he had been active rather than strong; his shoulders were not broad for his height, though certainly not narrow. As a young man he must have had much endurance, for on one of the shore excursions from the *Beagle*, when all were suffering from want of water, he was one of the two who were better able than the rest to struggle on in search of it. As a boy he was active, and could jump a bar placed at the height of the "Adam's apple" in his neck.

He walked with a swinging action, using a stick heavily
shod with iron, which he struck loudly against the ground,
producing as he went round the "Sand-walk" at Down, a
rhythmical click which is with all of us a very distinct remembrance. As he returned from the midday walk, often
carrying the waterproof or cloak which had proved too hot,
one could see that the swinging step was kept up by something of an effort. Indoors his step was often slow and
laboured, and as he went upstairs in the afternoon he might
be heard mounting the stairs with a heavy footfall, as if each
step were an effort. When interested in his work he moved
about quickly and easily enough, and often in the middle of
dictating he went eagerly into the hall to get a pinch of snuff,
leaving the study door open, and calling out the last words of
his sentence as he went. Indoors he sometimes used an oak
stick like a little alpenstock, and this was a sign that he felt
giddiness.

In spite of his strength and activity, I think he must
always have had a clumsiness of movement. He was naturally awkward with his hands, and was unable to draw at all
well.* This he always regretted much, and he frequently
urged the paramount necessity of a young naturalist making
himself a good draughtsman.

He could dissect well under the simple microscope, but I
think it was by dint of his great patience and carefulness. It
was characteristic of him that he thought many little bits of
skilful dissection something almost superhuman. He used to
speak with admiration of the skill with which he saw New-
port dissect a humble bee, getting out the nervous system
with a few cuts of a fine pair of scissors, held, as my father
used to show, with the elbow raised, and in an attitude which
certainly would render great steadiness necessary. He used
to consider cutting sections a great feat, and in the last year
of his life, with wonderful energy, took the pains to learn to

---

* The figure representing the aggregated cell-contents in 'Insectivorous Plants' was drawn by him.

cut sections of roots and leaves. His hand was not steady enough to hold the object to be cut, and he employed a common microtome, in which the pith for holding the object was clamped, and the razor slid on a glass surface in making the sections. He used to laugh at himself, and at his own skill in section-cutting, at which he would say he was "speech-less with admiration." On the other hand, he must have had accuracy of eye and power of co-ordinating his movements, since he was a good shot with a gun as a young man, and as a boy was skilful in throwing. He once killed a hare sitting in the flower-garden at Shrewsbury by throwing a marble at it, and, as a man, he once killed a cross-beak with a stone. He was so unhappy at having uselessly killed the cross-beak that he did not mention it for years, and then explained that he should never have thrown at it if he had not felt sure that his old skill had gone from him.

When walking he had a fidgetting movement with his fingers, which he has described in one of his books as the habit of an old man. When he sat still he often took hold of one wrist with the other hand ; he sat with his legs crossed, and from being so thin they could be crossed very far, as may be seen in one of the photographs. He had his chair in the study and in the drawing-room raised so as to be much higher than ordinary chairs; this was done because sitting on a low or even an ordinary chair caused him some discomfort. We used to laugh at him for making his tall drawing-room chair still higher by putting footstools on it, and then neu-tralising the result by resting his feet on another chair.

His beard was full and almost untrimmed, the hair being grey and white, fine rather than coarse, and wavy or frizzled. His moustache was somewhat disfigured by being cut short and square across. He became very bald, having only a fringe of dark hair behind.

His face was ruddy in colour, and this perhaps made people think him less of an invalid than he was. He wrote to Dr. Hooker (June 13, 1849), " Every one tells me that I look quite blooming and beautiful ; and most think I am

7

shamming, but you have never been one of those." And it must be remembered that at this time he was miserably ill, far worse than in later years. His eyes were bluish grey under deep overhanging brows, with thick bushy projecting eyebrows. His high forehead was much wrinkled, but otherwise his face was not much marked or lined. His expression showed no signs of the continual discomfort he suffered.

When he was excited with pleasant talk his whole manner was wonderfully bright and animated, and his face shared to the full in the general animation. His laugh was a free and sounding peal, like that of a man who gives himself sympathetically and with enjoyment to the person and the thing which have amused him. He often used some sort of gesture with his laugh, lifting up his hands or bringing one down with a slap. I think, generally speaking, he was given to gesture, and often used his hands in explaining anything (*e. g.* the fertilisation of a flower) in a way that seemed rather an aid to himself than to the listener. He did this on occasions when most people would illustrate their explanations by means of a rough pencil sketch.

He wore dark clothes, of a loose and easy fit. Of late years he gave up the tall hat even in London, and wore a soft black one in winter, and a big straw hat in summer. His usual out-of-doors dress was the short cloak in which Elliot and Fry's photograph represents him leaning against the pillar of the verandah. Two peculiarities of his indoor dress were that he almost always wore a shawl over his shoulders, and that he had great loose cloth boots lined with fur which he could slip on over his indoor shoes. Like most delicate people he suffered from heat as well as from chilliness; it was as if he could not hit the balance between too hot and too cold; often a mental cause would make him too hot, so that he would take off his coat if anything went wrong in the course of his work.

He rose early, chiefly because he could not lie in bed, and I think he would have liked to get up earlier than he did. He took a short turn before breakfast, a habit which began

when he went for the first time to a water-cure establishment.
This habit he kept up till almost the end of his life. I used,
as a little boy, to like going out with him, and I have a vague
sense of the red of the winter sunrise, and a recollection of
the pleasant companionship, and a certain honour and glory
in it. He used to delight me as a boy by telling me how, in
still earlier walks, on dark winter mornings, he had once or
twice met foxes trotting home at the dawning.

After breakfasting alone about 7·45, he went to work at
once, considering the 1½ hour between 8 and 9·30 one of his
best working times. At 9·30 he came into the drawing-room
for his letters—rejoicing if the post was a light one and being
sometimes much worried if it was not. He would then hear
any family letters read aloud as he lay on the sofa.

The reading aloud, which also included part of a novel,
lasted till about half-past ten, when he went back to work
till twelve or a quarter past. By this time he considered his
day's work over, and would often say, in a satisfied voice,
" *I've* done a good day's work." He then went out of doors
whether it was wet or fine ; Polly, his white terrier, went with
him in fair weather, but in rain she refused or might be seen
hesitating in the verandah, with a mixed expression of disgust
and shame at her own want of courage ; generally, however,
her conscience carried the day, and as soon as he was evidently gone she could not bear to stay behind.

My father was always fond of dogs, and as a young man
had the power of stealing away the affections of his sister's
pets ; at Cambridge, he won the love of his cousin W. D.
Fox's dog, and this may perhaps have been the little beast
which used to creep down inside his bed and sleep at the
foot every night. My father had a surly dog, who was devoted to him, but unfriendly to every one else, and when he
came back from the *Beagle* voyage, the dog remembered
him, but in a curious way, which my father was fond of telling. He went into the yard and shouted in his old manner ;
the dog rushed out and set off with him on his walk, showing no more emotion or excitement than if the same thing

had happened the day before, instead of five years ago.
This story is made use of in the 'Descent of Man,' 2nd Edit.,
p. 74.

In my memory there were only two dogs which had much
connection with my father. One was a large black and white
half-bred retriever, called Bob, to which we, as children, were
much devoted. He was the dog of whom the story of the
"hot-house face" is told in the 'Expression of the Emotions.'

But the dog most closely associated with my father was
the above-mentioned Polly, a rough, white fox-terrier. She
was a sharp-witted, affectionate dog; when her master was
going away on a journey, she always discovered the fact by
the signs of packing going on in the study, and became low-
spirited accordingly. She began, too, to be excited by seeing
the study prepared for his return home. She was a cunning
little creature, and used to tremble or put on an air of misery
when my father passed, while she was waiting for dinner, just
as if she knew that he would say (as he did often say) that
"she was famishing." My father used to make her catch
biscuits off her nose, and had an affectionate and mock-
solemn way of explaining to her before-hand that she must
"be a very good girl." She had a mark on her back where
she had been burnt, and where the hair had re-grown red
instead of white, and my father used to commend her for
this tuft of hair as being in accordance with his theory of
pangenesis; her father had been a red bull-terrier, thus the
red hair appearing after the burn showed the presence of
latent red gemmules. He was delightfully tender to Polly,
and never showed any impatience at the attentions she required, such as to be let in at the door, or out at the verandah window, to bark at "naughty people," a self-imposed
duty she much enjoyed. She died, or rather had to be killed,
a few days after his death.*

---

* The basket in which she usually lay curled up near the fire in his
study is faithfully represented in Mr. Parson's drawing, "The Study at
Down," facing page 101.

My father's midday walk generally began by a call at the greenhouse, where he looked at any germinating seeds or experimental plants which required a casual examination, but he hardly ever did any serious observing at this time. Then he went on for his constitutional—either round the "Sand-walk," or outside his own grounds in the immediate neighbourhood of the house. The "Sand-walk" was a narrow strip of land 1½ acres in extent, with a gravel-walk round it. On one side of it was a broad old shaw with fair-sized oaks in it, which made a sheltered shady walk ; the other side was separated from a neighbouring grass field by a low quickset hedge, over which you could look at what view there was, a quiet little valley losing itself in the upland country towards the edge of the Westerham hill, with hazel coppice and larch wood, the remnants of what was once a large wood, stretching away to the Westerham road. I have heard my father say that the charm of this simple little valley helped to make him settle at Down.

The Sand-walk was planted by my father with a variety of trees, such as hazel, alder, lime, hornbeam, birch, privet, and dogwood, and with a long line of hollies all down the exposed side. In earlier times he took a certain number of turns every day, and used to count them by means of a heap of flints, one of which he kicked out on the path each time he passed. Of late years I think he did not keep to any fixed number of turns, but took as many as he felt strength for. The Sand-walk was our play-ground as children, and here we continually saw my father as he walked round. He liked to see what we were doing, and was ever ready to sympathize in any fun that was going on. It is curious to think how, with regard to the Sand-walk in connection with my father, my earliest recollections coincide with my latest ; it shows how unvarying his habits have been.

Sometimes when alone he stood still or walked stealthily to observe birds or beasts. It was on one of these occasions that some young squirrels ran up his back and legs, while their mother barked at them in an agony from the tree. He always found birds' nests even up to the last years of his life, and we, as children, considered that he had a special genius in this direction. In his quiet prowls he came across the less common birds, but I fancy he used to conceal it from me, as a little boy, because he observed the agony of mind which I endured at not having seen the siskin or goldfinch, or whatever it might have been. He used to tell us how, when he was creeping noiselessly along in the "Big-Woods," he came upon a fox asleep in the daytime, which was so much astonished that it took a good stare at him before it ran off. A Spitz dog which accompanied him showed no sign of excitement at the fox, and he used to end the story by wondering how the dog could have been so faint-hearted.

Another favourite place was "Orchis Bank," above the quiet Cudham valley, where fly- and musk-orchis grew among the junipers, and Cephalanthera and Neottia under the beech boughs; the little wood "Hangrove," just above this, he was also fond of, and here I remember his collecting grasses, when he took a fancy to make out the names of all the common kinds. He was fond of quoting the saying of one of his little boys, who, having found a grass that his father had not seen before, had it laid by his own plate during dinner, remarking, "I are an extraordinary grass-finder!"

My father much enjoyed wandering slowly in the garden with my mother or some of his children, or making one of a party. sitting out on a bench on the lawn; he generally sat, however, on the grass, and I remember him often lying under one of the big lime-trees, with his head on the green mound at its foot. In dry summer weather, when we often sat out, the big fly-wheel of the well was commonly heard spinning round, and so the sound became associated with those pleasant days. He used to like to watch us playing at lawn-tennis, and often knocked up a stray ball for us with the curved handle of his stick.

Though he took no personal share in the management of the garden, he had great delight in the beauty of flowers—for instance, in the mass of Azaleas which generally stood in the drawing-room. I think he sometimes fused together his admiration of the structure of a flower and of its intrinsic beauty; for instance, in the case of the big pendulous pink and white flowers of Dielytra. In the same way he had an affection, half-artistic, half-botanical, for the little blue Lobelia. In admiring flowers, he would often laugh at the dingy high-art colours, and contrast them with the bright tints of nature. I used to like to hear him admire the beauty of a flower; it was a kind of gratitude to the flower itself, and a personal love for its delicate form and colour. I seem to remember him gently touching a flower he delighted in; it was the same simple admiration that a child might have.

He could not help personifying natural things. This feeling came out in abuse as well as in praise—*e.g.* of some seedlings—"The little beggars are doing just what I don't want them to." He would speak in a half-provoked, half-admiring way of the ingenuity of a Mimosa leaf in screwing itself out of a basin of water in which he had tried to fix it. One might see the same spirit in his way of speaking of Sundew, earth-worms, &c.*

Within my memory, his only outdoor recreation, besides walking, was riding, which he took to on the recommendation of Dr. Bence Jones, and we had the luck to find for him the easiest and quietest cob in the world, named "Tommy." He enjoyed these rides extremely, and devised a number of short rounds which brought him home in time for lunch. Our country is good for this purpose, owing to the number of small valleys which give a variety to what in a flat country would be a dull loop of road. He was not, I think, naturally fond of horses, nor had he a high opinion of their intelligence, and Tommy was often laughed at for the alarm he showed at passing and repassing the same heap of hedge-

---

* Cf. Leslie Stephen's 'Swift,' 1882, p. 200, where Swift's inspection of the manners and customs of servants are compared to my father's observations on worms, "The difference is," says Mr. Stephen, "that Darwin had none but kindly feelings for worms."

clippings as he went round the field. I think he used to feel surprised at himself, when he remembered how bold a rider he had been, and how utterly old age and bad health had taken away his nerve. He would say that riding prevented him thinking much more effectually than walking—that having to attend to the horse gave him occupation sufficient to prevent any really hard thinking. And the change of scene which it gave him was good for spirits and health.

Unluckily, Tommy one day fell heavily with him on Keston common. This, and an accident with another horse, upset his nerves, and he was advised to give up riding.

If I go beyond my own experience, and recall what I have heard him say of his love for sport, &c., I can think of a good deal, but much of it would be a repetition of what is contained in his 'Recollections.' At school he was fond of bat-fives, and this was the only game at which he was skilful. He was fond of his gun as quite a boy, and became a good shot ; he used to tell how in South America he killed twenty-three snipe in twenty-four shots. In telling the story he was careful to add that he thought they were not quite so wild as English snipe.

Luncheon at Down came after his midday walk ; and here I may say a word or two about his meals generally. He had a boy-like love of sweets, unluckily for himself, since he was constantly forbidden to take them. He was not particularly successful in keeping the "vows," as he called them, which he made against eating sweets, and never considered them binding unless he made them aloud.

He drank very little wine, but enjoyed, and was revived by, the little he did drink. He had a horror of drinking, and constantly warned his boys that any one might be led into drinking too much. I remember, in my innocence as a small boy, asking him if he had been ever tipsy ; and he answered very gravely that he was ashamed to say he had once drunk too much at Cambridge. I was much impressed, so that I know now the place where the question was asked.

After his lunch, he read the newspaper, lying on the sofa

in the drawing-room. I think the paper was the only non-scientific matter which he read to himself. Everything else, novels, travels, history, was read aloud to him. He took so wide an interest in life, that there was much to occupy him in newspapers, though he laughed at the wordiness of the debates; reading them, I think, only in abstract. His interest in politics was considerable, but his opinion on these matters was formed rather by the way than with any serious amount of thought.

After he had read his paper, came his time for writing letters. These, as well as the MS. of his books, were written by him as he sat in a huge horse-hair chair by the fire, his paper supported on a board resting on the arms of the chair. When he had many or long letters to write, he would dictate them from a rough copy; these rough copies were written on the backs of manuscript or of proof-sheets, and were almost illegible, sometimes even to himself. He made a rule of keeping *all* letters that he received; this was a habit which he learnt from his father, and which he said had been of great use to him.

He received many letters from foolish, unscrupulous people, and all of these received replies. He used to say that if he did not answer them, he had it on his conscience afterwards, and no doubt it was in great measure the courtesy with which he answered every one, which produced the universal and widespread sense of his kindness of nature, which was so evident on his death.

He was considerate to his correspondents in other and lesser things, for instance when dictating a letter to a foreigner he hardly ever failed to say to me, "You'd better try and write well, as it's to a foreigner." His letters were generally written on the assumption that they would be carelessly read; thus, when he was dictating, he was careful to tell me to make an important clause begin with an obvious paragraph "to catch his eye," as he often said. How much he thought of the trouble he gave others by asking questions, will be well enough shown by his letters. It is difficult to say anything about the general tone of his letters, they will speak for themselves. The unvarying courtesy of them is very striking. I had a proof of this quality in the feeling with which Mr. Hacon, his solicitor, regarded him. He had never seen my father, yet had a sincere feeling of friendship for him, and spoke especially of his letters as being such as a man seldom receives in the way of business :—"Everything I did was right, and everything was profusely thanked for."

He had a printed form to be used in replying to troublesome correspondents, but he hardly ever used it ; I suppose he never found an occasion that seemed exactly suitable. I remember an occasion on which it might have been used with advantage. He received a letter from a stranger stating that the writer had undertaken to uphold Evolution at a debating society, and that being a busy young man, without time for reading, he wished to have a sketch of my father's views. Even this wonderful young man got a civil answer, though I think he did not get much material for his speech. His rule was to thank the donors of books, but not of pamphlets. He sometimes expressed surprise that so few people thanked him for his books which he gave away liberally ; the letters that he did receive gave him much pleasure, because he habitually formed so humble an estimate of the value of all his works, that he was generally surprised at the interest which they excited.

In money and business matters he was remarkably careful and exact. He kept accounts with great care, classifying them, and balancing at the end of the year like a merchant. I remember the quick way in which he would reach out for his account-book to enter each cheque paid, as though he were in a hurry to get it entered before he had forgotten it. His father must have allowed him to believe that he would be poorer than he really was, for some of the difficulty experienced in finding a house in the country must have arisen from the modest sum he felt prepared to give. Yet he knew, of course, that he would be in easy circumstances, for in his 'Recollections' he mentions this as one of the reasons for his not having worked at medicine with so much zeal as he would have done if he had been obliged to gain his living.

He had a pet economy in paper, but it was rather a hobby than a real economy. All the blank sheets of letters received were kept in a portfolio to be used in making notes; it was his respect for paper that made him write so much on the backs of his old MS., and in this way, unfortunately, he destroyed large parts of the original MS. of his books. His feeling about paper extended to waste paper, and he objected, half in fun, to the careless custom of throwing a spill into the fire after it had been used for lighting a candle.

My father was wonderfully liberal and generous to all his children in the matter of money, and I have special cause to remember his kindness when I think of the way in which he paid some Cambridge debts of mine—making it almost seem a virtue in me to have told him of them. In his later years he had the kind and generous plan of dividing his surplus at the year's end among his children.

He had a great respect for pure business capacity, and often spoke with admiration of a relative who had doubled his fortune. And of himself would often say in fun that what he really *was* proud of was the money he had saved. He also felt satisfaction in the money he made by his books. His anxiety to save came in a great measure from his fears that his children would not have health enough to earn their own livings, a foreboding which fairly haunted him for many years. And I have a dim recollection of his saying, " Thank God, you'll have bread and cheese," when I was so young that I was rather inclined to take it literally.

When letters were finished, about three in the afternoon, he rested in his bedroom, lying on the sofa and smoking a cigarette, and listening to a novel or other book not scientific. He only smoked when resting, whereas snuff was a stimulant, and was taken during working hours. He took snuff for many years of his life, having learnt the habit at Edinburgh as a student. He had a nice silver snuff-box given him by Mrs. Wedgwood of Maer, which he valued much—but he rarely carried it, because it tempted him to take too many pinches. In one of his early letters he speaks of having given up snuff for a month, and describes himself as feeling "most lethargic, stupid, and melancholy." Our former neighbour and clergyman, Mr. Brodie Innes, tells me that at one time my father made a resolve not to take snuff except away from home, "a most satisfactory arrangement for me," he adds, "as I kept a box in my study to which there was access from the garden without summoning servants, and I had more frequently, than might have been otherwise the case, the privilege of a few minutes' conversation with my dear friend." He generally took snuff from a jar on the hall table, because having to go this distance for a pinch was a slight check; the clink of the lid of the snuff jar was a very familiar sound. Sometimes when he was in the drawing-room, it would occur to him that the study fire must be burning low, and when some of us offered to see after it, it would turn out that he also wished to get a pinch of snuff.

Smoking he only took to permanently of late years, though on his Pampas rides he learned to smoke with the Gauchos, and I have heard him speak of the great comfort of a cup of *maté* and a cigarette when he halted after a long ride and was unable to get food for some time.

The reading aloud often sent him to sleep, and he used to regret losing parts of a novel, for my mother went steadily on lest the cessation of the sound might wake him. He came down at four o'clock to dress for his walk, and he was so regular that one might be quite certain it was within a few minutes of four when his descending steps were heard.

From about half-past four to half-past five he worked; then he came to the drawing-room, and was idle till it was time (about six) to go up for another rest with novel-reading and a cigarette.

Latterly he gave up late dinner, and had a simple tea at half-past seven (while we had dinner), with an egg or a small piece of meat. After dinner he never stayed in the room, and used to apologise by saying he was an old woman, who

THE STUDY AT DOWN.

[From the Century Magazine.

must be allowed to leave with the ladies. This was one of the many signs and results of his constant weakness and ill-health. Half an hour more or less conversation would make to him the difference of a sleepless night, and of the loss perhaps of half the next day's work.

After dinner he played backgammon with my mother, two games being played every night; for many years a score of the games which each won was kept, and in this score he took the greatest interest. He became extremely animated over these games, bitterly lamenting his bad luck and exploding with exaggerated mock-anger at my mother's good fortune.

After backgammon he read some scientific book to himself, either in the drawing-room, or, if much talking was going on, in the study.

In the evening, that is, after he had read as much as his strength would allow, and before the reading aloud began, he would often lie on the sofa and listen to my mother playing the piano. He had not a good ear, yet in spite of this he had a true love of fine music. He used to lament that his enjoyment of music had become dulled with age, yet within my recollection, his love of a good tune was strong. I never heard him hum more than one tune, the Welsh song "Ar hyd y nos," which he went through correctly; he used also, I believe, to hum a little Otaheitan song. From his want of ear he was unable to recognize a tune when he heard it again, but he remained constant to what he liked, and would often say, when an old favourite was played, "That's a fine thing; what is it?" He liked especially parts of Beethoven's symphonies, and bits of Handel. He made a little list of all the pieces which he especially liked among those which my mother played—giving in a few words the impression that each one made on him—but these notes are unfortunately lost. He was sensitive to differences in style, and enjoyed the late Mrs. Vernon Lushington's playing intensely, and in June 1881, when Hans Richter paid a visit at Down, he was roused to strong enthusiasm by his magnificent performance on the piano. He much enjoyed good singing, and was moved al-

most to tears by grand or pathetic songs. His niece Lady
Farrer's singing of Sullivan's "Will he come" was a never-
failing enjoyment to him. He was humble in the extreme
about his own taste, and correspondingly pleased when he
found that others agreed with him.

He became much tired in the evenings, especially of late
years, when he left the drawing-room about ten, going to bed
at half-past ten. His nights were generally bad, and he often
lay awake or sat up in bed for hours, suffering much discomfort. He was troubled at night by the activity of his thoughts,
and would become exhausted by his mind working at some
problem which he would willingly have dismissed. At night,
too, anything which had vexed or troubled him in the day
would haunt him, and I think it was then that he suffered if
he had not answered some troublesome person's letter.

The regular readings, which I have mentioned, continued
for so many years, enabled him to get through a great deal
of the lighter kinds of literature. He was extremely fond of
novels, and I remember well the way in which he would anticipate the pleasure of having a novel read to him, as he lay
down, or lighted his cigarette. He took a vivid interest both
in plot and characters, and would on no account know before-
hand, how a story finished; he considered looking at the end
of a novel as a feminine vice. He could not enjoy any story
with a tragical end. for this reason he did not keenly appreciate George Eliot, though he often spoke warmly in praise of
'Silas Marner.' Walter Scott, Miss Austen, and Mrs. Gaskell,
were read and re-read till they could be read no more. He
had two or three books in hand at the same time—a novel
and perhaps a biography and a book of travels. He did not
often read out-of-the-way or old standard books, but generally kept to the books of the day obtained from a circulating
library.

I do not think that his literary tastes and opinions were
on a level with the rest of his mind. He himself, though he
was clear as to what he thought good, considered that in
matters of literary taste, he was quite outside the pale, and

often spoke of what those within it liked or disliked, as if they formed a class to which he had no claim to belong.

In all matters of art he was inclined to laugh at professed critics, and say that their opinions were formed by fashion. Thus in painting, he would say how in his day every one admired masters who are now neglected. His love of pictures as a young man is almost a proof that he must have had an appreciation of a portrait as a work of art, not as a likeness. Yet he often talked laughingly of the small worth of portraits, and said that a photograph was worth any number of pictures, as if he were blind to the artistic quality in a painted portrait. But this was generally said in his attempts to persuade us to give up the idea of having his portrait painted, an operation very irksome to him.

This way of looking at himself as an ignoramus in all matters of art, was strengthened by the absence of pretence, which was part of his character. With regard to questions of taste, as well as to more serious things, he always had the courage of his opinions. I remember, however, an instance that sounds like a contradiction to this : when he was looking at the Turners in Mr. Ruskin's bedroom, he did not confess, as he did afterwards, that he could make out absolutely nothing of what Mr. Ruskin saw in them. But this little pretence was not for his own sake, but for the sake of courtesy to his host. He was pleased and amused when subsequently Mr. Ruskin brought him some photographs of pictures (I think Vandyke portraits), and courteously seemed to value my father's opinion about them.

Much of his scientific reading was in German, and this was a great labour to him ; in reading a book after him, I was often struck at seeing, from the pencil-marks made each day where he left off, how little he could read at a time. He used to call German the "Verdammte," pronounced as if in English. He was especially indignant with Germans, because he was convinced that they could write simply if they chose, and often praised Dr. F. Hildebrand for writing German which was as clear as French. He sometimes gave a German

sentence to a friend, a patriotic German lady, and used to
laugh at her if she did not translate it fluently.   He himself
learnt German simply by hammering away with a dictionary;
he would say that his only way was to read a sentence a
great many times over, and at last the meaning occurred to
him.   When he began German long ago, he boasted of the
fact (as he used to tell) to Sir J. Hooker, who replied,
"Ah, my dear fellow, that's nothing; I've begun it many
times."

In spite of his want of grammar, he managed to get on
wonderfully with German, and the sentences that he failed to
make out were generally really difficult ones.   He never
attempted to speak German correctly, but pronounced the
words as though they were English; and this made it not a
little difficult to help him, when he read out a German sentence and asked for a translation.   He certainly had a bad
ear for vocal sounds, so that he found it impossible to perceive small differences in pronunciation.

His wide interest in branches of science that were not
specially his own was remarkable   In the biological sciences
his doctrines make themselves felt so widely that there was
something interesting to him in most departments of it.   He
read a good deal of many quite special works, and large parts
of text books, such as Huxley's 'Invertebrate Anatomy,' or
such a book as Balfour's 'Embryology,' where the detail, at
any rate, was not specially in his own line.   And in the case
of elaborate books of the monograph type, though he did not
make a study of them, yet he felt the strongest admiration for
them.

In the non-biological sciences he felt keen sympathy with
work of which he could not really judge.   For instance, he
used to read nearly the whole of 'Nature,' though so much
of it deals with mathematics and physics.   I have often heard
him say that he got a kind of satisfaction in reading articles
which (according to himself) he could not understand.   I
wish I could reproduce the manner in which he would laugh
at himself for it.

It was remarkable, too, how he kept up his interest in subjects at which he had formerly worked. This was strikingly the case with geology. In one of his letters to Mr. Judd he begs him to pay him a visit, saying that since Lyell's death he hardly ever gets a geological talk. His observations, made only a few years before his death, on the upright pebbles in the drift at Southampton, and discussed in a letter to Mr. Geikie, afford another instance. Again, in the letters to Dr. Dohrn, he shows how his interest in barnacles remained alive. I think it was all due to the vitality and persistence of his mind—a quality I have heard him speak of as if he felt that he was strongly gifted in that respect. Not that he used any such phrases as these about himself, but he would say that he had the power of keeping a subject or question more or less before him for a great many years. The extent to which he possessed this power appears when we consider the number of different problems which he solved, and the early period at which some of them began to occupy him.

It was a sure sign that he was not well when he was idle at any times other than his regular resting hours; for, as long as he remained moderately well, there was no break in the regularity of his life. Week-days and Sundays passed by alike, each with their stated intervals of work and rest. It is almost impossible, except for those who watched his daily life, to realise how essential to his well-being was the regular routine that I have sketched: and with what pain and difficulty anything beyond it was attempted. Any public appearance, even of the most modest kind, was an effort to him. In 1871 he went to the little village church for the wedding of his elder daughter, but he could hardly bear the fatigue of being present through the short service. The same may be said of the few other occasions on which he was present at similar ceremonies.

I remember him many years ago at a christening: a memory which has remained with me, because to us children it seemed an extraordinary and abnormal occurrence. I remember his look most distinctly at his brother Erasmus's funeral, as he stood in the scattering of snow, wrapped in a long black funeral cloak, with a grave look of sad reverie.

When, after an interval of many years, he again attended a meeting of the Linnean Society, it was felt to be, and was in fact, a serious undertaking ; one not to be determined on without much sinking of heart, and hardly to be carried into effect without paying a penalty of subsequent suffering. In the same way a breakfast-party at Sir James Paget's, with some of the distinguished visitors to the Medical Congress (1881), was to him a severe exertion.

The early morning was the only time at which he could make any effort of the kind, with comparative impunity. Thus it came about that the visits he paid to his scientific friends in London were by preference made as early as ten in the morning. For the same reason he started on his journeys by the earliest possible train, and used to arrive at the houses of relatives in London when they were beginning their day.

He kept an accurate journal of the days on which he worked and those on which his ill health prevented him from working, so that it would be possible to tell how many were idle days in any given year. In this journal—a little yellow Letts's Diary, which lay open on his mantel-piece, piled on the diaries of previous years—he also entered the day on which he started for a holiday and that of his return.

The most frequent holidays were visits of a week to London, either to his brother's house (6 Queen Anne Street), or to his daughter's (4 Bryanston Street). He was generally persuaded by my mother to take these short holidays, when it became clear from the frequency of " bad days," or from the swimming of his head, that he was being overworked. He went unwillingly, and tried to drive hard bargains, stipulating, for instance, that he should come home in five days instead of six. Even if he were leaving home for no more than a week, the packing had to be begun early on the previous day, and the chief part of it he would do himself. The discomfort of a journey to him was, at least latterly, chiefly in the anticipation, and in the miserable sinking feeling from which he suffered immediately before the start ; even a fairly long journey, such as that to Coniston, tired him wonderfully little, considering how much an invalid he was ; and he certainly enjoyed it in an almost boyish way, and to a curious extent.

Although, as he has said, some of his æsthetic tastes had suffered a gradual decay, his love of scenery remained fresh and strong. Every walk at Coniston was a fresh delight, and he was never tired of praising the beauty of the broken hilly country at the head of the lake.

One of the happy memories of this time [1879] is that of a delightful visit to Grasmere : " The perfect day," my sister writes, " and my father's vivid enjoyment and flow of spirits, form a picture in my mind that I like to think of. He could hardly sit still in the carriage for turning round and getting up to admire the view from each fresh point, and even in returning he was full of the beauty of Rydal Water, though he would not allow that Grasmere at all equalled his beloved Coniston."

Besides these longer holidays, there were shorter visits to various relatives—to his brother-in-law's house, close to Leith Hill, and to his son near Southampton. He always particularly enjoyed rambling over rough open country, such as the commons near Leith Hill and Southampton, the heath-covered wastes of Ashdown Forest, or the delightful " Rough " near the house of his friend Sir Thomas Farrer. He never was quite idle even on these holidays, and found things to observe. At Hartfield he watched Drosera catching insects, &c. ; at Torquay he observed the fertilisation of an orchid (*Spiranthes*), and also made out the relations of the sexes in Thyme.

He was always rejoiced to get home after his holidays ; he used greatly to enjoy the welcome he got from his dog Polly, who would get wild with excitement, panting, squeaking, rushing round the room, and jumping on and off the chairs ; and he used to stoop down, pressing her face to his, letting her lick him, and speaking to her with a peculiarly tender, caressing voice.

My father had the power of giving to these summer holidays a charm which was strongly felt by all his family. The pressure of his work at home kept him at the utmost stretch of his powers of endurance, and when released from it, he entered on a holiday with a youthfulness of enjoyment that made his companionship delightful; we felt that we saw more of him in a week's holiday than in a month at home.

Some of these absences from home, however, had a depressing effect on him; when he had been previously much overworked it seemed as though the absence of the customary strain allowed him to fall into a peculiar condition of miserable health.

Besides the holidays which I have mentioned, there were his visits to water-cure establishments. In 1849, when very ill, suffering from constant sickness, he was urged by a friend to try the water-cure, and at last agreed to go to Dr. Gully's establishment at Malvern. His letters to Mr. Fox show how much good the treatment did him; he seems to have thought that he had found a cure for his troubles, but, like all other remedies, it had only a transient effect on him. However, he found it, at first, so good for him that when he came home he built himself a douche-bath, and the butler learnt to be his bathman.

He paid many visits to Moor Park, Dr. Lane's water-cure establishment in Surrey, not far from Aldershot. These visits were pleasant ones, and he always looked back to them with pleasure. Dr. Lane has given his recollections of my father in Dr. Richardson's 'Lecture on Charles Darwin,' October 22, 1882, from which I quote :—

" In a public institution like mine, he was surrounded, of course, by multifarious types of character, by persons of both sexes, mostly very different from himself—commonplace people, in short, as the majority are everywhere, but like to him at least in this, that they were fellow-creatures and fellow-patients. And never was any one more genial, more considerate, more friendly, more altogether charming than he universally was." . . . . He "never aimed, as too often happens with good talkers, at monopolising the conversation. It was his pleasure rather to give and take, and he was as good a listener as a speaker. He never preached nor prosed, but his talk, whether grave or gay (and it was each by turns), was full of life and salt—racy, bright, and animated."

Some idea of his relation to his family and his friends may be gathered from what has gone before; it would be impossible to attempt a complete account of these relationships, but a slightly fuller outline may not be out of place. Of his married life I cannot speak, save in the briefest manner. In his relationship towards my mother, his tender and sympathetic nature was shown in its most beautiful aspect. In her presence he found his happiness, and through her, his life,— which might have been overshadowed by gloom,—became one of content and quiet gladness.

The 'Expression of the Emotions' shows how closely he watched his children; it was characteristic of him that (as I have heard him tell), although he was so anxious to observe accurately the expression of a crying child, his sympathy with the grief spoiled his observation. His note-book, in which are recorded sayings of his young children, shows his pleasure in them. He seemed to retain a sort of regretful memory of the childhoods which had faded away, and thus he wrote in his 'Recollections':—"When you were very young it was my delight to play with you all, and I think with a sigh that such days can never return."

I may quote, as showing the tenderness of his nature, some sentences from an account of his little daughter Annie, written a few days after her death :—

"Our poor child, Annie, was born in Gower Street, on March 2, 1841, and expired at Malvern at mid-day on the 23rd of April, 1851.

"I write these few pages, as I think in after years, if we live, the impressions now put down will recall more vividly her chief characteristics. From whatever point I look back at her, the main feature in her disposition which at once rises before me, is her buoyant joyousness, tempered by two other characteristics, namely, her sensitiveness, which might easily have been overlooked by a stranger, and her strong affection. Her joyousness and animal spirits radiated from her whole countenance, and rendered every movement elastic and full of life and vigour. It was delightful and cheerful to behold her. Her dear face now rises before me, as she used sometimes to come running downstairs with a stolen pinch of snuff for me, her whole form radiant with the pleasure of giving pleasure. Even when playing with her cousins, when her joyousness almost passed into boisterousness, a single glance of my eye, not of displeasure (for I thank God I hardly ever cast one on her), but of want of sympathy, would for some minutes alter her whole countenance.

"The other point in her character, which made her joy-ousness and spirits so delightful, was her strong affection, which was of a most clinging, fondling nature. When quite a baby, this showed itself in never being easy without touch-ing her mother, when in bed with her; and quite lately she would, when poorly, fondle for any length of time one of her mother's arms. When very unwell, her mother lying down beside her seemed to soothe her in a manner quite different from what it would have done to any of our other children. So, again, she would at almost any time spend half an hour in arranging my hair, 'making it,' as she called it, 'beautiful,' or in smoothing, the poor dear darling, my collar or cuffs—in short, in fondling me.

"Besides her joyousness thus tempered, she was in her manners remarkably cordial, frank, open, straightforward, natural, and without any shade of reserve. Her whole mind was pure and transparent. One felt one knew her thoroughly and could trust her. I always thought, that come what might, we should have had in our old age at least one loving soul

which nothing could have changed. All her movements
were vigorous, active, and usually graceful. When going
round the Sand-walk with me, although I walked fast, yet she
often used to go before, pirouetting in the most elegant
way, her dear face bright all the time with the sweetest smiles.
Occasionally she had a pretty coquettish manner towards me,
the memory of which is charming. She often used exaggerated language, and when I quizzed her by exaggerating what
she had said, how clearly can I now see the little toss of the
head, and exclamation of 'Oh, papa what a shame of you!'
In the last short illness her conduct in simple truth was angelic. She never once complained; never became fretful;
was ever considerate of others, and was thankful in the most
gentle, pathetic manner for everything done for her. When
so exhausted that she could hardly speak, she praised everything that was given her, and said some tea 'was beautifully
good.' When I gave her some water she said, 'I quite thank
you;' and these, I believe, were the last precious words ever
addressed by her dear lips to me.

"We have lost the joy of the household, and the solace
of our old age. She must have known how we loved her.
Oh, that she could now know how deeply, how tenderly,
we do still and shall ever love her dear joyous face! Blessings on her!

"April 30, 1851."

We his children all took especial pleasure in the games he
played at with us, but I do not think he romped much with
us; I suppose his health prevented any rough play. He used
sometimes to tell us stories, which were considered especially
delightful, partly on account of their rarity.

The way he brought us up is shown by a little story about
my brother Leonard, which my father was fond of telling.
He came into the drawing-room and found Leonard dancing
about on the sofa, which was forbidden, for the sake of the
springs, and said, "Oh, Lenny, Lenny, that's against all rules,"
and received for answer, "Then I think you'd better go out

of the room." I do not believe he ever spoke an angry word
to any of his children in his life ; but I am certain that it
never entered our heads to disobey him.   I well remember
one occasion when my father reproved me for a piece of carelessness ; and I can still recall the feeling of depression which
came over me, and the care which he took to disperse it by
speaking to me soon afterwards with especial kindness.   He
kept up his delightful, affectionate manner towards us all his
life.   I sometimes wonder that he could do so, with such an
undemonstrative race as we are ; but I hope he knew how
much we delighted in his loving words and manner.   How
often, when a man, I have wished when my father was behind
my chair, that he would pass his hand over my hair, as he
used to do when I was a boy.   He allowed his grown-up children to laugh with and at him, and was, generally speaking,
on terms of perfect equality with us.

He was always full of interest about each one's plans or
successes.   We used to laugh at him, and say he would not
believe in his sons, because, for instance, he would be a little
doubtful about their taking some bit of work for which he did
not feel sure that they had knowledge enough.   On the other
hand, he was only too much inclined to take a favourable view
of our work.   When I thought he had set too high a value on
anything that I had done, he used to be indignant and inclined
to explode in mock anger.   His doubts were part of his hu-
mility concerning what was in any way connected with
himself ; his too favourable view of our work was due to his
sympathetic nature, which made him lenient to every one.

He kept up towards his children his delightful manner of
expressing his thanks; and I never wrote a letter, or read a
page aloud to him, without receiving a few kind words of
recognition.   His love and goodness towards his little grandson Bernard were great ; and he often spoke of the pleasure
it was to him to see " his little face opposite to him" at luncheon.   He and Bernard used to compare their tastes ; e. g., in
liking brown sugar better than white, &c.; the result being,
" We always agree, don't we ? "

My sister writes :—

"My first remembrances of my father are of the delights of his playing with us. He was passionately attached to his own children, although he was not an indiscriminate child-lover. To all of us he was the most delightful play-fellow, and the most perfect sympathiser. Indeed it is impossible adequately to describe how delightful a relation his was to his family, whether as children or in their later life.

"It is a proof of the terms on which we were, and also of how much he was valued as a play-fellow, that one of his sons when about four years old tried to bribe him with sixpence to come and play in working hours. We all knew the sacred-ness of working-time, but that any one should resist sixpence seemed an impossibility.

"He must have been the most patient and delightful of nurses. I remember the haven of peace and comfort it seemed to me when I was unwell, to be tucked up on the study sofa, idly considering the old geological map hung on the wall. This must have been in his working hours, for I always picture him sitting in the horsehair arm-chair by the corner of the fire.

"Another mark of his unbounded patience was the way in which we were suffered to make raids into the study when we had an absolute need of sticking-plaster, string, pins, scissors, stamps, foot-rule, or hammer. These and other such neces-saries were always to be found in the study, and it was the only place where this was a certainty. We used to feel it wrong to go in during work-time; still, when the necessity was great we did so. I remember his patient look when he said once, 'Don't you think you could not come in again, I have been interrupted very often.' We used to dread going in for sticking-plaster, because he disliked to see that we had cut ourselves, both for our sakes and on account of his acute sensitiveness to the sight of blood. I well remember lurking about the passage till he was safe away, and then stealing in for the plaster.

"Life seems to me, as I look back upon it, to have been very regular in those early days, and except relations (and a few intimate friends), I do not think any one came to the house. After lessons, we were always free to go where we would, and that was chiefly in the drawing-room and about the garden, so that we were very much with both my father and mother. We used to think it most delightful when he told us any stories about the *Beagle*, or about early Shrewsbury days—little bits about school-life and his boyish tastes. Sometimes too he read aloud to his children such books as Scott's novels, and I remember a few little lectures on the steam-engine.

"I was more or less ill during the five years between my thirteenth and eighteenth years, and for a long time (years it seems to me) he used to play a couple of games of backgammon with me every afternoon. He played them with the greatest spirit, and I remember we used at one time to keep account of the games, and as this record came out in favour of him, we kept a list of the doublets thrown by each, as I was convinced that he threw better than myself.

"His patience and sympathy were boundless during this weary illness, and sometimes when most miserable I felt his sympathy to be almost too keen. When at my worst, we went to my aunt's house at Hartfield, in Sussex, and as soon as we had made the move safely he went on to Moor Park for a fortnight's water-cure. I can recall now how on his return I could hardly bear to have him in the room, the expression of tender sympathy and emotion in his face was too agitating, coming fresh upon me after his little absence.

"He cared for all our pursuits and interests, and lived our lives with us in a way that very few fathers do. But I am certain that none of us felt that this intimacy interfered the least with our respect or obedience. Whatever he said was absolute truth and law to us. He always put his whole mind into answering any of our questions. One trifling instance makes me feel how he cared for what we cared for. He had no special taste for cats, though he admired the pretty ways

of a kitten. But yet he knew and remembered the individu-
alities of my many cats, and would talk about the habits and
characters of the more remarkable ones years after they had
died.

"Another characteristic of his treatment of his children
was his respect for their liberty, and for their personality.
Even as quite a girl, I remember rejoicing in this sense of
freedom. Our father and mother would not even wish to
know what we were doing or thinking unless we wished to
tell. He always made us feel that we were each of us creatures whose opinions and thoughts were valuable to him, so
that whatever there was best in us came out in the sunshine
of his presence.

" I do not think his exaggerated sense of our good qualities, intellectual or moral, made us conceited, as might perhaps
have been expected, but rather more humble and grateful to
him. The reason being no doubt that the influence of his
character, of his sincerity and greatness of nature, had a
much deeper and more lasting effect than any small exalta-
tion which his praises or admiration may have caused to our
vanity."

As head of a household he was much loved and respected;
he always spoke to servants with politeness, using the expression, "would you be so good," in asking for anything. He
was hardly ever angry with his servants ; it shows how seldom
this occurred, that when, as a small boy, I overheard a servant
being scolded, and my father speaking angrily, it impressed
me as an appalling circumstance, and I remember running up
stairs out of a general sense of awe. He did not trouble himself about the management of the garden, cows, &c. He
considered the horses so little his concern, that he used to ask
doubtfully whether he might have a horse and cart to send to
Keston for Drosera, or to the Westerham nurseries for plants,
or the like.

As a host my father had a peculiar charm : the presence
of visitors excited him, and made him appear to his best

advantage. At Shrewsbury, he used to say, it was his father's wish that the guests should be attended to constantly, and in one of the letters to Fox he speaks of the impossibility of writing a letter while the house was full of company. I think he always felt uneasy at not doing more for the entertainment of his guests, but the result was successful ; and, to make up for any loss, there was the gain that the guests felt perfectly free to do as they liked. The most usual visitors were those who stayed from Saturday till Monday ; those who remained longer were generally relatives, and were considered to be rather more my mother's affair than his.

Besides these visitors, there were foreigners and other strangers, who came down for luncheon and went away in the afternoon. He used conscientiously to represent to them the enormous distance of Down from London, and the labour it would be to come there, unconsciously taking for granted that they would find the journey as toilsome as he did himself. If, however, they were not deterred, he used to arrange their journeys for them, telling them when to come, and practically when to go. It was pleasant to see the way in which he shook hands with a guest who was being welcomed for the first time ; his hand used to shoot out in a way that gave one the feeling that it was hastening to meet the guest's hands. With old friends his hand came down with a hearty swing into the other hand in a way I always had satisfaction in seeing. His good-bye was chiefly characterised by the pleasant way in which he thanked his guests, as he stood at the door, for having come to see him.

These luncheons were very successful entertainments, there was no drag or flagging about them, my father was bright and excited throughout the whole visit. Professor De Candolle has described a visit to Down, in his admirable and sympathetic sketch of my father.* He speaks of his manner as resembling that of a " savant " of Oxford or Cambridge.

---

* ' Darwin considéré au point de vue des causes de son succès.'— Geneva, 1882.

This does not strike me as quite a good comparison; in his ease and naturalness there was more of the manner of some soldiers; a manner arising from total absence of pretence or affectation. It was this absence of pose, and the natural and simple way in which he began talking to his guests, so as to get them on their own lines, which made him so charming a host to a stranger. His happy choice of matter for talk seemed to flow out of his sympathetic nature, and humble, vivid interest in other people's work.

To some, I think, he caused actual pain by his modesty; I have seen the late Francis Balfour quite discomposed by having knowledge ascribed to himself on a point about which my father claimed to be utterly ignorant.

It is difficult to seize on the characteristics of my father's conversation.

He had more dread than have most people of repeating his stories, and continually said, "You must have heard me tell," or "I dare say I've told you." One peculiarity he had, which gave a curious effect to his conversation. The first few words of a sentence would often remind him of some exception to, or some reason against, what he was going to say; and this again brought up some other point, so that the sentence would become a system of parenthesis within parenthesis, and it was often impossible to understand the drift of what he was saying until he came to the end of his sentence. He used to say of himself that he was not quick enough to hold an argument with any one, and I think this was true. Unless it was a subject on which he was just then at work, he could not get the train of argument into working order quickly enough. This is shown even in his letters; thus, in the case of two letters to Prof. Semper about the effect of isolation, he did not recall the series of facts he wanted until some days after the first letter had been sent off.

When puzzled in talking, he had a peculiar stammer on the first word of a sentence. I only recall this occurring with words beginning with w; possibly he had a special difficulty with this letter, for I have heard him say that as a boy he could not pronounce w, and that sixpence was offered him if he could say "white wine," which he pronounced "rite rine." Possibly he may have inherited this tendency from Erasmus Darwin, who stammered.*

He sometimes combined his metaphors in a curious way, using such a phrase as "holding on like life,"—a mixture of "holding on for his life," and "holding on like grim death." It came from his eager way of putting emphasis into what he was saying. This sometimes gave an air of exaggeration where it was not intended; but it gave, too, a noble air of strong and generous conviction; as, for instance, when he gave his evidence before the Royal Commission on vivisection and came out with his words about cruelty, " It deserves detestation and abhorrence." When he felt strongly about any similar question, he could hardly trust himself to speak, as he then easily became angry, a thing which he disliked excessively. He was conscious that his anger had a tendency to multiply itself in the utterance, and for this reason dreaded (for example) having to scold a servant.

It was a great proof of the modesty of his style of talking, that, when, for instance, a number of visitors came over from Sir John Lubbock's for a Sunday afternoon call he never seemed to be preaching or lecturing, although he had so much of the talk to himself. He was particularly charming when "chaffing" any one, and in high spirits over it. His manner at such times was light-hearted and boyish, and his refinement of nature came out most strongly. So, when he was talking to a lady who pleased and amused him, the combination of raillery and deference in his manner was delightful to see.

When my father had several guests he managed them well, getting a talk with each, or bringing two or three together

---

* My father related a Johnsonian answer of Erasmus Darwin's: " Don't you find it very inconvenient stammering, Dr. Darwin?" " No, sir, because I have time to think before I speak, and don't ask impertinent questions."

round his chair. In these conversations there was always
a good deal of fun, and, speaking generally, there was either
a humorous turn in his talk, or a sunny geniality which
served instead. Perhaps my recollection of a pervading element of humour is the more vivid, because the best talks were
with Mr. Huxley, in whom there is the aptness which is akin
to humour, even when humour itself is not there. My father
enjoyed Mr. Huxley's humour exceedingly, and would often
say, "What splendid fun Huxley is!" I think he probably
had more scientific argument (of the nature of a fight) with
Lyell and Sir Joseph Hooker.

He used to say that it grieved him to find that for the
friends of his later life he had not the warm affection of
his youth. Certainly in his early letters from Cambridge
he gives proofs of very strong friendship for Herbert and
Fox; but no one except himself would have said that his
affection for his friends was not, throughout life, of the
warmest possible kind. In serving a friend he would not
spare himself, and precious time and strength were willingly
given. He undoubtedly had, to an unusual degree, the power
of attaching his friends to him. He had many warm friendships, but to Sir Joseph Hooker he was bound by ties of
affection stronger than we often see among men. He wrote
in his 'Recollections,' "I have known hardly any man more
lovable than Hooker."

His relationship to the village people was a pleasant one;
he treated them, one and all, with courtesy, when he came in
contact with them, and took an interest in all relating to
their welfare. Some time after he came to live at Down he
helped to found a Friendly Club, and served as treasurer for
thirty years. He took much trouble about the club, keeping its accounts with minute and scrupulous exactness, and
taking pleasure in its prosperous condition. Every Whit-
Monday the club used to march round with band and banner,
and paraded on the lawn in front of the house. There he met
them, and explained to them their financial position in a little
speech seasoned with a few well-worn jokes. He was often

unwell enough to make even this little ceremony an exertion, but I think he never failed to meet them.

He was also treasurer of the Coal Club, which gave him some work, and he acted for some years as a County Magistrate.

With regard to my father's interest in the affairs of the village, Mr. Brodie Innes has been so good as to give me his recollections :—

"On my becoming Vicar of Down in 1846, we became friends, and so continued till his death. His conduct towards me and my family was one of unvarying kindness, and we repaid it by warm affection.

"In all parish matters he was an active assistant; in matters connected with the schools, charities, and other business, his liberal contribution was ever ready, and in the differences which at times occurred in that, as in other parishes, I was always sure of his support. He held that where there was really no important objection, his assistance should be given to the clergyman, who ought to know the circumstances best, and was chiefly responsible."

His intercourse with strangers was marked with scrupulous and rather formal politeness, but in fact he had few opportunities of meeting strangers.

Dr. Lane has described * how, on the rare occasion of my father attending a lecture (Dr. Sanderson's) at the Royal Institution, "the whole assembly . . . rose to their feet to welcome him," while he seemed "scarcely conscious that such an outburst of applause could possibly be intended for himself." The quiet life he led at Down made him feel confused in a large society; for instance, at the Royal Society's *soirées* he felt oppressed by the numbers. The feeling that he ought to know people, and the difficulty he had in remembering faces in his latter years, also added to his discomfort on

---

* Lecture by Dr. B. W. Richardson, in St. George's Hall, Oct. 22, 1882.

such occasions. He did not realise that he would be recognised from his photographs, and I remember his being uneasy
at being obviously recognised by a stranger at the Crystal
Palace Aquarium.

I must say something of his manner of working : one
characteristic of it was his respect for time ; he never forgot
how precious it was. This was shown, for instance, in the
way in which he tried to curtail his holidays; also, and more
clearly, with respect to shorter periods. He would often say,
that saving the minutes was the way to get work done ; he
showed this love of saving the minutes in the difference he
felt between a quarter of an hour and ten minutes' work; he
never wasted a few spare minutes from thinking that it was
not worth while to set to work. I was often struck by his
way of working up to the very limit of his strength, so that
he suddenly stopped in dictating, with the words, "I believe
I mustn't do any more." The same eager desire not to lose
time was seen in his quick movements when at work. I
particularly remember noticing this when he was making an
experiment on the roots of beans, which required some care
in manipulation; fastening the little bits of card upon the
roots was done carefully and necessarily slowly, but the intermediate movements were all quick ; taking a fresh bean,
seeing that the root was healthy, impaling it on a pin, fixing
it on a cork, and seeing that it was vertical, &c.; all these
processes were performed with a kind of restrained eagerness.
He always gave one the impression of working with pleasure,
and not with any drag. I have an image, too, of him as he
recorded the result of some experiment, looking eagerly at
each root, &c., and then writing with equal eagerness. I
remember the quick movement of his head up and down as
he looked from the object to the notes.

He saved a great deal of time through not having to do
things twice. Although he would patiently go on repeating
experiments where there was any good to be gained, he could
not endure having to repeat an experiment which ought, if
complete care had been taken, to have succeeded the first

9

time—and this gave him a continual anxiety that the experiment should not be wasted; he felt the experiment to be sacred, however slight a one it was. He wished to learn as much as possible from an experiment, so that he did not confine himself to observing the single point to which the experiment was directed, and his power of seeing a number of other things was wonderful. I do not think he cared for preliminary or rough observation intended to serve as guides and to be repeated. Any experiment done was to be of some use, and in this connection I remember how strongly he urged the necessity of keeping the notes of experiments which failed, and to this rule he always adhered.

In the literary part of his work he had the same horror of losing time, and the same zeal in what he was doing at the moment, and this made him careful not to be obliged unnecessarily to read anything a second time.

His natural tendency was to use simple methods and few instruments. The use of the compound microscope has much increased since his youth, and this at the expense of the simple one. It strikes us nowadays as extraordinary that he should have had no compound microscope when he went his *Beagle* voyage; but in this he followed the advice of Robt. Brown, who was an authority in such matters. He always had a great liking for the simple microscope, and maintained that nowadays it was too much neglected, and that one ought always to see as much as possible with the simple before taking to the compound microscope. In one of his letters he speaks on this point, and remarks that he always suspects the work of a man who never uses the simple microscope.

His dissecting table was a thick board, let into a window of the study; it was lower than an ordinary table, so that he could not have worked at it standing : but this, from wishing to save his strength, he would not have done in any case. He sat at his dissecting-table on a curious low stool which had belonged to his father, with a seat revolving on a vertical spindle, and mounted on large castors, so that he could turn easily from side to side. His ordinary tools, &c., were lying about on the table, but besides these a number of odds and ends were kept in a round table full of radiating drawers, and turning on a vertical axis, which stood close by his left side, as he sat at his microscope-table. The drawers were labelled, "best tools," "rough tools," "specimens," "preparations for specimens," &c. The most marked peculiarity of the contents of these drawers was the care with which little scraps and almost useless things were preserved; he held the well-known belief, that if you threw a thing away you were sure to want it directly—and so things accumulated.

If any one had looked at his tools, &c., lying on the table, he would have been struck by an air of simpleness, make-shift, and oddness.

At his right hand were shelves, with a number of other odds and ends, glasses, saucers, tin biscuit boxes for germinating seeds, zinc labels, saucers full of sand, &c., &c. Considering how tidy and methodical he was in essential things, it is curious that he bore with so many make-shifts: for instance, instead of having a box made of a desired shape, and stained black inside, he would hunt up something like what he wanted and get it darkened inside with shoe-blacking; he did not care to have glass covers made for tumblers in which he germinated seeds, but used broken bits of irregular shape, with perhaps a narrow angle sticking uselessly out on one side. But so much of his experimenting was of a simple kind, that he had no need for any elaboration, and I think his habit in this respect was in great measure due to his desire to husband his strength, and not waste it on inessential things.

His way of marking objects may here be mentioned. If he had a number of things to distinguish, such as leaves, flowers, &c., he tied threads of different colours round them. In particular he used this method when he had only two classes of objects to distinguish; thus in the case of crossed and self-fertilised flowers, one set would be marked with black and one with white thread, tied round the stalk of the flower. I remember well the look of two sets of capsules, gathered and waiting to be weighed, counted, &c., with pieces of black and of white thread to distinguish the trays in which they lay. When he had to compare two sets of seedlings, sowed in the same pot, he separated them by a partition of zinc-plate; and the zinc label, which gave the necessary details about the experiment, was always placed on a certain side, so that it became instinctive with him to know without reading the label which were the "crossed" and which were the "self-fertilised."

His love of each particular experiment, and his eager zeal not to lose the fruit of it, came out markedly in these crossing experiments—in the elaborate care he took not to make any confusion in putting capsules into wrong trays, &c., &c. I can recall his appearance as he counted seeds under the simple microscope with an alertness not usually characterising such mechanical work as counting. I think he personified each seed as a small demon trying to elude him by getting into the wrong heap, or jumping away altogether; and this gave to the work the excitement of a game. He had great faith in instruments, and I do not think it naturally occurred to him to doubt the accuracy of a scale or measuring glass, &c. He was astonished when we found that one of his micrometers differed from the other. He did not require any great accuracy in most of his measurements, and had not good scales; he had an old three-foot rule, which was the common property of the household, and was constantly being borrowed, because it was the only one which was certain to be in its place—unless, indeed, the last borrower had forgotten to put it back. For measuring the height of plants he had a seven-foot deal rod, graduated by the village carpenter. Latterly he took to using paper scales graduated to millimeters. For small objects he used a pair of compasses and an ivory protractor. It was characteristic of him that he took scrupulous pains in making measurements with his somewhat rough scales. A trifling example of his faith in authority is that he took his "inch in terms of millimeters" from an old book, in which it turned out to be inaccurately given. He had a chemical balance which dated from the days when he worked at chemistry with his brother Erasmus. Measurements of capacity were made with an apothecary's measuring glass : I remember well its rough look and bad graduation. With this, too, I remember the great care he took in getting the fluid-line on to the graduation. I do not mean by this account of his instruments that any of his experiments suffered from want of accuracy in measurement, I give them as examples of his simple methods and faith in others—faith at least in instrument-makers, whose whole trade was a mystery to him.

A few of his mental characteristics, bearing especially on his mode of working, occur to me. There was one quality of mind which seemed to be of special and extreme advantage in leading him to make discoveries. It was the power of never letting exceptions pass unnoticed. Everybody notices a fact as an exception when it is striking or frequent, but he had a special instinct for arresting an exception. A point apparently slight and unconnected with his present work is passed over by many a man almost unconsciously with some half-considered explanation, which is in fact no explanation. It was just these things that he seized on to make a start from. In a certain sense there is nothing special in this procedure, many discoveries being made by means of it. I only mention it because, as I watched him at work, the value of this power to an experimenter was so strongly impressed upon me.

Another quality which was shown in his experimental works was his power of sticking to a subject ; he used almost to apologise for his patience, saying that he could not bear to be beaten, as if this were rather a sign of weakness on his part. He often quoted the saying, "It's dogged as does it ;" and I think doggedness expresses his frame of mind almost better than perseverance. Perseverance seems hardly to express his almost fierce desire to force the truth to reveal itself. He often said that it was important that a man should know the right point at which to give up an inquiry. And I think it was his tendency to pass this point that inclined him to apologise for his perseverance, and gave the air of doggedness to his work.

He often said that no one could be a good observer unless he was an active theoriser. This brings me back to what I said about his instinct for arresting exceptions : it was as though he were charged with theorising power ready to flow into any channel on the slightest disturbance, so that no fact, however small, could avoid releasing a stream of theory, and thus the fact became magnified into importance. In this way it naturally happened that many untenable theories occurred to him; but fortunately his richness of imagination was equalled by his power of judging and condemning the thoughts that occurred to him. He was just to his theories, and did not condemn them unheard ; and so it happened that he was willing to test what would seem to most people not at all worth testing. These rather wild trials he called "fool's experiments," and enjoyed extremely. As an example I may mention that finding the cotyledons of Biophytum to be highly sensitive to vibrations of the table, he fancied that they might perceive the vibrations of sound, and therefore made me play my bassoon close to a plant. *

The love of experiment was very strong in him, and I can remember the way he would say, "I shan't be easy till I have tried it," as if an outside force were driving him. He enjoyed experimenting much more than work which only entailed reasoning, and when he was engaged on one of his books which required argument and the marshalling of facts, he felt experimental work to be a rest or holiday. Thus, while working upon the 'Variations of Animals and Plants,' in 1860–61, he made out the fertilisation of Orchids, and thought himself idle for giving so much time to them. It is interesting to think that so important a piece of research should have been

---

* This is not so much an example of superabundant theorising from a small cause, but only of his wish to test the most improbable ideas.

undertaken and largely worked out as a pastime in place of more serious work. The letters to Hooker of this period contain expressions such as, "God forgive me for being so idle: I am quite sillily interested in this work." The intense pleasure he took in understanding the adaptations for fertilisation is strongly shown in these letters. He speaks in one of his letters of his intention of working at Drosera as a rest from the 'Descent of Man.' He has described in his 'Recollections' the strong satisfaction he felt in solving the problem of heterostylism. And I have heard him mention that the Geology of South America gave him almost more pleasure than anything else. It was perhaps this delight in work requiring keen observation that made him value praise given to his observing powers almost more than appreciation of his other qualities.

For books he had no respect, but merely considered them as tools to be worked with. Thus he did not bind them, and even when a paper book fell to pieces from use, as happened to Müller's 'Befruchtung,' he preserved it from complete dissolution by putting a metal clip over its back. In the same way he would cut a heavy book in half, to make it more convenient to hold. He used to boast that he made Lyell publish the second edition of one of his books in two volumes instead of in one, by telling him how he had been obliged to cut it in half. Pamphlets were often treated even more severely than books, for he would tear out, for the sake of saving room, all the pages except the one that interested him. The consequence of all this was, that his library was not ornamental, but was striking from being so evidently a working collection of books.

He was methodical in his manner of reading books and pamphlets bearing on his own work. He had one shelf on which were piled up the books he had not yet read, and another to which they were transferred after having been read, and before being catalogued. He would often groan over his unread books, because there were so many which he knew he should never read. Many a book was at once transferred to the other heap, either marked with a cypher at the end, to show that it contained no marked passages, or inscribed, perhaps, "not read," or "only skimmed." The books accumulated in the "read" heap until the shelves overflowed, and then, with much lamenting, a day was given up to the cataloguing. He disliked this work, and as the necessity of undertaking the work became imperative, would often say, in a voice of despair, "We really must do these books soon."

In each book, as he read it, he marked passages bearing on his work. In reading a book or pamphlet, &c., he made pencil-lines at the side of the page, often adding short remarks, and at the end made a list of the pages marked. When it was to be catalogued and put away, the marked pages were looked at, and so a rough abstract of the book was made. This abstract would perhaps be written under three or four headings on different sheets, the facts being sorted out and added to the previously collected facts in different subjects. He had other sets of abstracts arranged, not according to subject, but according to periodical. When collecting facts on a large scale, in earlier years, he used to read through, and make abstracts, in this way, of whole series of periodicals.

In some of his early letters he speaks of filling several note-books with facts for his book on species; but it was certainly early that he adopted his plan of using portfolios as described in the 'Recollections.'* My father and M. de Candolle were mutually pleased to discover that they had adopted the same plan of classifying facts. De Candolle describes the method in his 'Phytologie,' and in his sketch of my father mentions the satisfaction he felt in seeing it in action at Down.

Besides these portfolios, of which there are some dozens full of notes, there are large bundles of MS. marked "used"

---

* The racks on which the portfolios were placed are shown in the illustration, "The Study of Down," facing p. 101, in the recess at the right-hand side of the fire-place.

and put away. He felt the value of his notes, and had a horror of their destruction by fire. I remember, when some alarm of fire had happened, his begging me to be especially careful, adding very earnestly, that the rest of his life would be miserable if his notes and books were to be destroyed.

He shows the same feeling in writing about the loss of a manuscript, the purport of his words being, "I have a copy, or the loss would have killed me." In writing a book he would spend much time and labour in making a skeleton or plan of the whole, and in enlarging and sub-classing each heading, as described in his 'Recollections.' I think this careful arrangement of the plan was not at all essential to the building up of his argument, but for its presentment, and for the arrangement of his facts. In his 'Life of Erasmus Darwin,' as it was first printed in slips, the growth of the book from a skeleton was plainly visible. The arrangement was altered afterwards, because it was too formal and categorical, and seemed to give the character of his grandfather rather by means of a list of qualities than as a complete picture.

It was only within the last few years that he adopted a plan of writing which he was convinced suited him best, and which is described in the 'Recollections;' namely, writing a rough copy straight off without the slightest attention to style. It was characteristic of him that he felt unable to write with sufficient want of care if he used his best paper, and thus it was that he wrote on the backs of old proofs or manuscript. The rough copy was then reconsidered, and a fair copy was made. For this purpose he had foolscap paper ruled at wide intervals, the lines being needed to prevent him writing so closely that correction became difficult. The fair copy was then corrected, and was recopied before being sent to the printers. The copying was done by Mr. E. Norman, who began this work many years ago when village schoolmaster at Down. My father became so used to Mr. Norman's hand-writing, that he could not correct manuscript, even when clearly written out by one of his children, until it had been recopied by Mr. Norman. The MS., on returning from Mr.

Norman, was once more corrected, and then sent off to the
printers.   Then came the work of revising and correcting the
proofs, which my father found especially wearisome.

It was at this stage that he first seriously considered the
style of what he had written.   When this was going on he
usually started some other piece of work as a relief.   The
correction of slips consisted in fact of two processes, for the
correction were first written in pencil, and then re-considered
and written in ink.

When the book was passing through the "slip" stage he
was glad to have corrections and suggestions from others.
Thus my mother looked over the proofs of the 'Origin.'   In
some of the later works my sister, Mrs. Litchfied, did much
of the correction.   After my sister's marriage perhaps most
of the work fell to my share.

My sister, Mrs. Litchfield, writes :—

" This work was very interesting in itself, and it was inexpressibly exhilarating to work for him.   He was always so
ready to be convinced that any suggested alteration was an
improvement, and so full of gratitude for the trouble taken.
I do not think that he ever used to forget to tell me what improvement he thought that I had made, and he used almost
to excuse himself if he did not agree with any correction.   I
think I felt the singular modesty and graciousness of his
nature through thus working for him in a way I never should
otherwise have done.

" He did not write with ease, and was apt to invert his
sentences both in writing and speaking, putting the qualifying
clause before it was clear what it was to qualify.   He corrected
a great deal, and was eager to express himself as well as he
possibly could."

Perhaps the commonest corrections needed were of obscurities due to the omission of a necessary link in the reasoning,
something which he had evidently omitted through familiarity
with the subject.   Not that there was any fault in the sequence

of the thoughts, but that from familiarity with his argument he did not notice when the words failed to reproduce his thought. He also frequently put too much matter into one sentence, so that it had to be cut up into two.

On the whole, I think the pains which my father took over the literary part of the work was very remarkable. He often laughed or grumbled at himself for the difficulty which he found in writing English, saying, for instance, that if a bad arrangement of a sentence was possible, he should be sure to adopt it. He once got much amusement and satisfaction out of the difficulty which one of the family found in writing a short circular. He had the pleasure of correcting and laughing at obscurities, involved sentences, and other defects, and thus took his revenge for all the criticism he had himself to bear with. He used to quote with astonishment Miss Martineau's advice to young authors, to write straight off and send the MS. to the printer without correction. But in some cases he acted in a somewhat similar manner. When a sentence got hopelessly involved, he would ask himself, "now what *do* you want to say?" and his answer written down, would often disentangle the confusion.

His style has been much praised; on the other hand, at least one good judge has remarked to me that it is not a good style. It is, above all things, direct and clear; and it is characteristic of himself in its simplicity, bordering on naïveté, and in its absence of pretence. He had the strongest disbelief in the common idea that a classical scholar must write good English ; indeed, he thought that the contrary was the case. In writing, he sometimes showed the same tendency to strong expressions as he did in conversation. Thus in the ' Origin,' p. 440, there is a description of a larval cirripede, "with six pairs of beautifully constructed natatory legs, a pair of magnificent compound eyes, and extremely complex antennæ." We used to laugh at him for this sentence, which we compared to an advertisement. This tendency to give himself up to the enthusiastic turn of his thought, without fear of being ludicrous, appears elsewhere in his writings.

His courteous and conciliatory tone towards his reader is remarkable, and it must be partly this quality which revealed his personal sweetness of character to so many who had never seen him. I have always felt it to be a curious fact, that he who had altered the face of Biological Science, and is in this respect the chief of the moderns, should have written and worked in so essentially a non-modern spirit and manner. In reading his books one is reminded of the older naturalists rather than of the modern school of writers. He was a Naturalist in the old sense of the word, that is, a man who works at many branches of the science, not merely a specialist in one. Thus it is, that, though he founded whole new divisions of special subjects—such as the fertilisation of flowers, insectivorous plants, dimorphism, &c.—yet even in treating these very subjects he does not strike the reader as a specialist. The reader feels like a friend who is being talked to by a courteous gentleman, not like a pupil being lectured by a professor. The tone of such a book as the 'Origin' is charming, and almost pathetic; it is the tone of a man who, convinced of the truth of his own views, hardly expects to convince others; it is just the reverse of the style of a fanatic, who wants to force people to believe. The reader is never scorned for any amount of doubt which he may be imagined to feel, and his scepticism is treated with patient respect. A sceptical reader, or perhaps even an unreasonable reader, seems to have been generally present to his thoughts. It was in consequence of this feeling. perhaps, that he took much trouble over points which he imagined would strike the reader, or save him trouble, and so tempt him to read.

For the same reason he took much interest in the illustrations of his books, and I think rated rather too highly their value. The illustrations for his earlier books were drawn by professional artists. This was the case in 'Animals and Plants,' the 'Descent of Man,' and the 'Expression of the Emotions.' On the other hand, 'Climbing Plants,' 'Insectivorous Plants,' the 'Movements of Plants,' and 'Forms of Flowers,' were, to a large extent, illustrated by some of his children—my brother George having drawn by far the most. It was delightful to draw for him, as he was enthusiastic in his praise of very moderate performances. I remember well his charming manner of receiving the drawings of one of his daughters-in-law, and how he would finish his words of praise by saying, "Tell A——, Michael Angelo is nothing to it." Though he praised so generously, he always looked closely at the drawing, and easily detected mistakes or carelessness.

He had a horror of being lengthy, and seems to have been really much annoyed and distressed when he found how the 'Variations of Animals and Plants' was growing under his hands. I remember his cordially agreeing with 'Tristram Shandy's' words, "Let no man say, 'Come, I'll write a duodecimo.'"

His consideration for other authors was as marked a characteristic as his tone towards his reader. He speaks of all other authors as persons deserving of respect. In cases where, as in the case of ——'s experiments on Drosera, he thought lightly of the author, he speaks of him in such a way that no one would suspect it. In other cases he treats the confused writings of ignorant persons as though the fault lay with himself for not appreciating or understanding them. Besides this general tone of respect, he had a pleasant way of expressing his opinion on the value of a quoted work, or his obligation for a piece of private information.

His respectful feeling was not only morally beautiful, but was I think of practical use in making him ready to consider the ideas and observations of all manner of people. He used almost to apologise for this, and would say that he was at first inclined to rate everything too highly.

It was a great merit in his mind that, in spite of having so strong a respectful feeling towards what he read, he had the keenest of instincts as to whether a man was trustworthy or not. He seemed to form a very definite opinion as to the accuracy of the men whose books he read; and made use of this judgment in his choice of facts for use in argument or as illustrations. I gained the impression that he felt this power of judging of a man's trustworthiness to be of much value.

He had a keen feeling of the sense of honour that ought to reign among authors, and had a horror of any kind of laxness in quoting. He had a contempt for the love of honour and glory, and in his letters often blames himself for the pleasure he took in the success of his books, as though he were departing from his ideal—a love of truth and carelessness about fame. Often, when writing to Sir J. Hooker what he calls a boasting letter, he laughs at himself for his conceit and want of modesty. There is a wonderfully interesting letter which he wrote to my mother bequeathing to her, in case of his death, the care of publishing the manuscript of his first essay on evolution. This letter seems to me full of the intense desire that his theory should succeed as a contribution to knowledge, and apart from any desire for personal fame. He certainly had the healthy desire for success which a man of strong feelings ought to have. But at the time of the publication of the 'Origin' it is evident that he was overwhelmingly satisfied with the adherence of such men as Lyell, Hooker, Huxley, and Asa Gray, and did not dream of or desire any such wide and general fame as he attained to.

Connected with his contempt for the undue love of fame, was an equally strong dislike of all questions of priority. The letters to Lyell, at the time of the 'Origin,' show the anger he felt with himself for not being able to repress a feeling of disappointment at what he thought was Mr. Wallace's forestalling of all his years of work. His sense of literary honour comes out strongly in these letters; and his feeling about priority is again shown in the admiration expressed in his 'Recollections' of Mr. Wallace's self-annihilation.

His feeling about reclamations, including answers to attacks and all kinds of discussions, was strong. It is simply expressed in a letter to Falconer (1863?), "If I ever felt angry towards you, for whom I have a sincere friendship, I should begin to suspect that I was a little mad. I was very sorry about your reclamation, as I think it is in every case a

mistake and should be left to others. Whether I should so
act myself under provocation is a different question." It was
a feeling partly dictated by instinctive delicacy, and partly
by a strong sense of the waste of time, energy, and temper
thus caused. He said that he owed his determination not to
get into discussions * to the advice of Lyell,—advice which
he transmitted to those among his friends who were given to
paper warfare.

If the character of my father's working life is to be understood, the conditions of ill-health, under which he worked,
must be constantly borne in mind. He bore his illness with
such uncomplaining patience, that even his children can
hardly, I believe, realise the extent of his habitual suffering.
In their case the difficulty is heightened by the fact that,
from the days of their earliest recollections, they saw him in
constant ill-health,—and saw him, in spite of it, full of pleasure in what pleased them. Thus, in later life, their perception of what he endured had to be disentangled from the
impression produced in childhood by constant genial kindness under conditions of unrecognised difficulty. No one
indeed, except my mother, knows the full amount of suffering
he endured, or the full amount of his wonderful patience.
For all the latter years of his life she never left him for a
night ; and her days were so planned that all his resting
hours might be shared with her. She shielded him from
every avoidable annoyance, and omitted nothing that might
save him trouble, or prevent him becoming overtired, or that
might alleviate the many discomforts of his ill-health. I hesitate to speak thus freely of a thing so sacred as the life-long

---

* He departed from his rule in his "Note on the Habits of the Pampas
Woodpecker, *Colaptes campestris*," 'Proc. Zool. Soc.,' 1870, p. 705 : also in
a letter published in the 'Athenæum' (1863, p. 554), in which case he
afterwards regretted that he had not remained silent. His replies to criticisms, in the later editions of the 'Origin,' can hardly be classed as infrac-
tions of his rule.

devotion which prompted all this constant and tender care.
But it is, I repeat, a principal feature of his life, that for
nearly forty years he never knew one day of the health of
ordinary men, and that thus his life was one long struggle
against the weariness and strain of sickness. And this cannot
be told without speaking of the one condition which enabled
him to bear the strain and fight out the struggle to the end.

LETTERS.

THE earliest letters to which I have access are those written by my father when an undergraduate at Cambridge.

The history of his life, as told in his correspondence, must therefore begin with this period.

CHAPTER IV.

CAMBRIDGE LIFE.

[My father's Cambridge life comprises the time between the Lent Term, 1828, when he came up as a Freshman, and the end of the May Term, 1831, when he took his degree and left the University.

It appears from the College books, that my father "admissus est pensionarius minor sub Magistro Shaw" on Oct. 15, 1827. He did not come into residence till the Lent Term, 1828, so that, although he passed his examination in due season, he was unable to take his degree at the usual time,—the beginning of the Lent Term, 1831. In such a case a man usually took his degree before Ash-Wednesday, when he was called "Baccalaureus ad Diem Cinerum," and ranked with the B. A.'s of the year. My father's name, however, occurs in the list of Bachelors "ad Baptistam," or those admitted between Ash-Wednesday and St. John Baptist's Day (June 24th) ;* he therefore took rank among the Bachelors of 1832.

He "kept" for a term or two in lodgings, over Bacon the tobacconist's : not, however, over the shop in the Market Place, now so well known to Cambridge men, but in Sidney Street. For the rest of his time he had pleasant rooms on the south side of the first court of Christ's. †

---

* "On Tuesday last Charles Darwin, of Christ's College, was admitted B. A."—*Cambridge Chronicle,* Friday, April 29, 1831.

† The rooms are on the first floor, on the west side of the middle staircase. A medallion (given by my brother) has recently been let into the wall of the sitting-room.

What determined the choice of this college for his brother Erasmus and himself I have no means of knowing. Erasmus the elder, their grandfather, had been at St. John's, and this college might have been reasonably selected for them, being connected with Shrewsbury School. But the life of an undergraduate at St. John's seems, in those days, to have been a troubled one, if I may judge from the fact that a relative of mine migrated thence to Christ's to escape the harassing discipline of the place. A story told by Mr. Herbert * illustrates the same state of things :—

" In the beginning of the October Term of 1830, an incident occurred which was attended with somewhat disagreeable, though ludicrous consequences to myself. Darwin asked me to take a long walk with him in the Fens, to search for some natural objects he was desirous of having. After a very long, fatiguing day's work, we dined together, late in the evening, at his rooms in Christ's College ; and as soon as our dinner was over we threw ourselves into easy chairs and fell sound asleep. I was the first to awake, about three in the morning, when, having looked at my watch, and knowing the strict rule of St. John's, which required men *in statu pupillari* to come into college before midnight, I rushed homeward at the utmost speed, in fear of the consequences, but hoping that the Dean would accept the excuse as sufficient when I told him the real facts. He, however, was inexorable, and refused to receive my explanations, or any evidence I could bring; and although during my undergraduateship I had never been reported for coming late into College, now, when I was a hard-working B. A., and had five or six pupils, he sentenced me to confinement to the College walls for the rest of the term. Darwin's indignation knew no bounds, and the stupid injustice and tyranny of the Dean raised not only a perfect ferment among my friends, but was the subject of expostulation from some of the leading members of the University."

My father seems to have found no difficulty in living at

---

* See p. 42.

peace with all men in and out of office at Lady Margaret's
other foundation. The impression of a contemporary of
my father's is that Christ's in their day was a pleasant, fairly
quiet college, with some tendency towards "horsiness"; many
of the men made a custom of going to Newmarket during the
races, though betting was not a regular practice. In this they
were by no means discouraged by the Senior Tutor, Mr.
Shaw, who was himself generally to be seen on the Heath on
these occasions. There was a somewhat high proportion of
Fellow-Commoners,—eight or nine, to sixty or seventy Pen-
sioners, and this would indicate that it was not an unpleasant
college for men with money to spend and with no great love
of strict discipline.

The way in which the service was conducted in chapel
shows that the Dean, at least, was not over zealous. I have
heard my father tell how at evening chapel the Dean used to
read alternate verses of the Psalms, without making even a
pretence of waiting for the congregation to take their share.
And when the Lesson was a lengthy one, he would rise and
go on with the Canticles after the scholar had read fifteen or
twenty verses.

It is curious that my father often spoke of his Cambridge
life as if it had been so much time wasted, forgetting that,
although the set studies of the place were barren enough for
him, he yet gained in the highest degree the best advantages
of a University life—the contact with men and an opportunity
for his mind to grow vigorously. It is true that he valued
at its highest the advantages which he gained from associating
with Professor Henslow and some others, but he seemed to
consider this as a chance outcome of his life at Cambridge,
not an advantage for which *Alma Mater* could claim any
credit. One of my father's Cambridge friends was the late
Mr. J. M. Herbert, County Court Judge for South Wales,
from whom I was fortunate enough to obtain some notes
which help us to gain an idea of how my father impressed
his contemporaries. Mr. Herbert writes: "I think it was in
the spring of 1828 that I first met Darwin, either at my

cousin Whitley's rooms in St. John's, or at the rooms of some
other of his old Shrewsbury schoolfellows, with many of
whom I was on terms of great intimacy. But it certainly was
in the summer of that year that our acquaintance ripened
into intimacy, when we happened to be together at Barmouth,
for the Long Vacation, reading with private tutors,—he with
Batterton of St. John's, his Classical and Mathematical Tutor,
and I with Yate of St. John's."

The intercourse between them practically ceased in 1831,
when my father said good-bye to Herbert at Cambridge, on
starting on his *Beagle* voyage. I once met Mr. Herbert, then
almost an old man, and I was much struck by the evident
warmth and freshness of the affection with which he remembered my father. The notes from which I quote end with
this warm-hearted eulogium : " It would be idle for me to
speak of his vast intellectual powers . . . but I cannot end
this cursory and rambling sketch without testifying, and I
doubt not all his surviving college friends would concur with
me, that he was the most genial, warm-hearted, generous, and
affectionate of friends ; that his sympathies were with all that
was good and true; and that he had a cordial hatred for
everything false, or vile, or cruel, or mean, or dishonourable.
He was not only great, but pre-eminently good, and just, and
loveable."

Two anecdotes told by Mr. Herbert show that my father's
feeling for suffering, whether of man or beast, was as strong
in him as a young man as it was in later years : " Before he
left Cambridge he told me that he had made up his mind not
to shoot any more ; that he had had two days' shooting at his
friend's, Mr. Owen of Woodhouse ; and that on the second
day, when going over some of the ground they had beaten
on the day before, he picked up a bird not quite dead, but
lingering from a shot it had received on the previous day;
and that it had made and left such a painful impression on
his mind, that he could not reconcile it to his conscience to
continue to derive pleasure from a sport which inflicted such
cruel suffering."

To realise the strength of the feeling that led to this resolve, we must remember how passionate was his love of sport. We must recall the boy shooting his first snipe,* and trembling with excitement so that he could hardly reload his gun. Or think of such a sentence as, " Upon my soul, it is only about a fortnight to the ' First,' then if there is a bliss on earth that is it."†

Another anecdote told by Mr. Herbert illustrates again his tenderness of heart:—

" When at Barmouth he and I went to an exhibition of 'learned dogs.' In the middle of the entertainment one of the dogs failed in performing the trick his master told him to do. On the man reproving him, the dog put on a most piteous expression, as if in fear of the whip. Darwin seeing it, asked me to leave with him, saying, 'Come along, I can't stand this any longer; how those poor dogs must have been licked.' "

It is curious that the same feeling recurred to my father more than fifty years afterwards, on seeing some performing dogs at the Westminster Aquarium; on this occasion he was reassured by the manager telling him that the dogs were taught more by reward than by punishment. Mr. Herbert goes on :—" It stirred one's inmost depth of feeling to hear him descant upon, and groan over, the horrors of the slave-trade, or the cruelties to which the suffering Poles were subjected to at Warsaw. . . . These, and other like proofs have left on my mind the conviction that a more humane or tender-hearted man never lived."

His old college friends agree in speaking with affectionate warmth of his pleasant, genial temper as a young man. From what they have been able to tell me, I gain the impression of a young man overflowing with animal spirits—leading a varied healthy life—not over-industrious in the set studies of the place, but full of other pursuits, which were followed with a

---

* ' Recollections,' p. 34.
† Letter from C. Darwin to W. D. Fox.

rejoicing enthusiasm.   Entomology, riding, shooting in the
fens, suppers and card-playing, music at King's Chapel, engravings at the Fitzwilliam Museum, walks with Professor
Henslow—all combined to fill up a happy life.   He seems to
have infected others with his enthusiasm.   Mr. Herbert relates how, during the same Barmouth summer, he was pressed
into the service of "the science"—as my father called collecting beetles.   They took their daily walks together among
the hills behind Barmouth, or boated in the Mawddach estu-
ary, or sailed to Sarn Badrig to land there at low water, or
went fly-fishing in the Cors-y-gedol lakes.   "On these occasions Darwin entomologized most industriously, picking up
creatures as he walked along, and bagging everything which
seemed worthy of being pursued, or of further examination.
And very soon he armed me with a bottle of alcohol, in which
I had to drop any beetle which struck me as not of a common
kind.   I performed this duty with some diligence in my constitutional walks; but alas! my powers of discrimination seldom enabled me to secure a prize—the usual result, on his
examining the contents of my bottle, being an exclamation,
'Well, old Cherbury'* (the nickname he gave me, and by
which he usually addressed me), 'none of these will do.'"
Again, the Rev. T. Butler, who was one of the Barmouth
reading-party in 1828, says: "He inoculated me with a taste
for Botany which has stuck by me all my life."

Archdeacon Watkins, another old college friend of my
father's, remembers him unearthing beetles in the willows
between Cambridge and Grantchester, and speaks of a certain
beetle the remembrance of whose name is "Crux major."†
How enthusiastically must my father have exulted over this
beetle to have impressed its name on a companion so that he
remembers it after half a century!   Archdeacon Watkins goes
on: "I do not forget the long and very interesting conversations that we had about Brazilian scenery and tropical vege-

---

* No doubt in allusion to the title of Lord Herbert of Cherbury.
† *Panagæus crux-major.*

tation of all sorts. Nor do I forget the way and the vehemence with which he rubbed his chin when he got excited on such subjects, and discoursed eloquently of lianas, orchids, &c."

He became intimate with Henslow, the Professor of Botany, and through him with some other older members of the University. "But," Mr. Herbert writes, "he always kept up the closest connection with the friends of his own standing; and at our frequent social gatherings—at breakfast, wine or supper parties—he was ever one of the most cheerful, the most popular, and the most welcome."

My father formed one of a club for dining once a week, called the Gourmet * Club, the members, besides himself and Mr. Herbert (from whom I quote), being Whitley of St. John's, now Honorary Canon of Durham; † Heaviside of Sidney, now Canon of Norwich; Lovett Cameron of Trinity, now vicar of Shoreham; Blane of Trinity, who held a high post during the Crimean war; H. Lowe ‡ (now Sherbrooke) of Trinity Hall; and Watkins of Emmanuel, now Archdeacon of York The origin of the club's name seems already to have become involved in obscurity. Mr. Herbert says that it was chosen in derision of another "set of men who called themselves by a long Greek name signifying 'fond of dainties,' but who falsified their claim to such a designation by their weekly practice of dining at some roadside inn, six miles from Cambridge, on mutton chops or beans and bacon." Another old member of the club tells me that the name arose because the members were given to making experiments on "birds and beasts, which were before unknown to human palate." He says that hawk and bittern were tried, and that their zeal broke down over an old brown owl, "which was indescribable." At any rate, the meetings seemed to have been successful, and to have ended with "a game of mild vingt-et-un."

---

* Mr. Herbert mentions the name as ' The Glutton Club.'
† Formerly Reader in Natural Philosophy at Durham University.
‡ Brother of Lord Sherbrooke.

Mr. Herbert gives an amusing account of the musical examinations described by my father in his 'Recollections.' Mr. Herbert speaks strongly of his love of music, and adds, "What gave him the greatest delight was some grand symphony or overture of Mozart's or Beethoven's, with their full harmonies.' On one occasion Herbert remembers "accompanying him to the afternoon service at King's, when we heard a very beautiful anthem. At the end of one of the parts, which was exceedingly impressive, he turned round to me and said, with a deep sigh, 'How's your backbone?'" He often spoke of a feeling of coldness or shivering in his back on hearing beautiful music.

Besides a love of music, he had certainly at this time a love of fine literature ; and Mr. Cameron tells me that he used to read Shakespeare to my father in his rooms at Christ's, who took much pleasure in it.   He also speaks of his "great liking for first-class line engravings, especially those of Raphael Morghen and Müller ; and he spent hours in the Fitzwilliam Museum in looking over the prints in that collection."

My father's letters to Fox show how sorely oppressed he felt by the reading of an examination : "I am reading very hard, and have spirits for nothing. I actually have not stuck a beetle this term." His despair over mathematics must have been profound, when he expressed a hope that Fox's silence is due to "your being ten fathoms deep in the Mathematics ; and if you are, God help you, for so am I, only with this difference, I stick fast in the mud at the bottom, and there I shall remain." Mr. Herbert says : "He had. I imagine, no natural turn for mathematics, and he gave up his mathematical reading before he had mastered the first part of Algebra, having had a special quarrel with Surds and the Binomial Theorem."

We get some evidence from his letters to Fox of my father's intention of going into the Church. "I am glad," he writes,* "to hear that you are reading divinity. I should

* March 18, 1829.

like to know what books you are reading, and your opinions
about them; you need not be afraid of preaching to me pre-
maturely." Mr. Herbert's sketch shows how doubts arose in
my father's mind as to the possibility of his taking Orders.
He writes, "We had an earnest conversation about going into
Holy Orders; and I remember his asking me, with reference
to the question put by the Bishop in the ordination service,
'Do you trust that you are inwardly moved by the Holy
Spirit, &c.,' whether I could answer in the affirmative, and on
my saying I could not, he said, 'Neither can I, and therefore
I cannot take orders.'" This conversation appears to have
taken place in 1829, and if so, the doubts here expressed
must have been quieted, for in May 1830, he speaks of having
some thoughts of reading divinity with Henslow.

The greater number of the following letters are addressed
by my father to his cousin, William Darwin Fox. Mr. Fox's
relationship to my father is shown in the pedigree given in
Chapter I. The degree of kinship appears to have remained
a problem to my father, as he signs himself in one letter
" $\frac{\text{cousin}}{n^2}$." Their friendship was, in fact, due to their being
undergraduates together. My father's letters show clearly
enough how genuine the friendship was. In after years, distance, large families, and ill-health on both sides, checked the
intercourse; but a warm feeling of friendship remained. The
correspondence was never quite dropped and continued till
Mr. Fox's death in 1880. Mr. Fox took orders, and worked
as a country clergyman until forced by ill-health to leave
his living in Delamere Forest. His love of natural history
remained strong, and he became a skilled fancier of many
kinds of birds, &c. The index to 'Animals and Plants,' and
my father's later correspondence, show how much help he
received from his old College friend.]

C. Darwin to J. M. Herbert.

Saturday Evening
[September 14, 1828].*

MY DEAR OLD CHERBURY,

I am about to fulfil my promise of writing to you, but I am sorry to add there is a very selfish motive at the bottom. I am going to ask you a great favour, and you cannot imagine how much you will oblige me by procuring some more specimens of some insects which I dare say I can describe. In the first place, I must inform you that I have taken some of the rarest of the British Insects, and their being found near Barmouth, is quite unknown to the Entomological world : I think I shall write and inform some of the crack entomologists.

But now for business. *Several* more specimens, if you can procure them without much trouble, of the following insects:— The violet-black coloured beetle, found on Craig Storm,† under stones. also a large smooth black one very like it ; a bluish metallic-coloured dung-beetle, which is *very* common on the hill-sides; also, if you *would* be so very kind as to cross the ferry, and you will find a great number under the stones on the waste land of a long, smooth, jet-black beetle (a great many of these); also, in the same situation, a very small pinkish insect, with black spots, with a curved thorax projecting beyond the head; also, upon the marshy land over the ferry, near the sea, under old sea-weed, stones, &c., you will find a small yellowish transparent beetle, with two or four blackish marks on the back. Under these stones there are two sorts, one much darker than the other ; the lighter-coloured is that which I want. These last two insects are *excessively rare*, and you will really *extremely* oblige me by taking all this trouble pretty soon. Remember me most kindly to

---

* The postmark being Derby seems to show that the letter was written from his cousin, W. D. Fox's house, Osmaston, near Derby.

† The top of the hill immediately behind Barmouth was called Craig-Storm, a hybrid Cambro-English word.

Butler, tell him of my success, and I dare say both of you will easily recognise these insects. I hope his caterpillars go on well. I think many of the Chrysalises are well worth keeping. I really am quite ashamed [of] so long a letter all about my own concerns; but do return good for evil, and send me a long account of all your proceedings.

In the first week I killed seventy-five head of game—a very contemptible number—but there are very few birds. I killed, however, a brace of black game. Since then I have been staying at the Fox's, near Derby; it is a very pleasant house, and the music meeting went off very well. I want to hear how Yates likes his gun, and what use he has made of it.

If the bottle is not large you can buy another for me, and when you pass through Shrewsbury you can leave these treasures, and I hope, if you possibly can, you will stay a day or two with me, as I hope I need not say how glad I shall be to see you again. Fox remarked what deuced good-natured fellows your friends at Barmouth must be; and if I did not know that you and Butler were so, I would not think of giving you so much trouble.

Believe me, my dear Herbert,

Yours, most sincerely,

CHARLES DARWIN.

Remember me to all friends.

[In the following January we find him looking forward with pleasure to the beginning of another year of his Cambridge life: he writes to Fox—

" I waited till to-day for the chance of a letter, but I will wait no longer. I must most sincerely and cordially congratulate you on having finished all your labours. I think your place a *very good* one considering by how much you have beaten many men who had the start of you in reading. I do so wish I were now in Cambridge (a very selfish wish, however, as I was not with you in all your troubles and misery), to join in all the glory and happiness, which dangers

gone by can give.   How we would talk, walk, and entomologise !   Sappho should be the best of bitches, and Dash, of
dogs : then should be ' peace on earth, good will to men,'—
which, by the way, I always think the most perfect description of happiness that words can give."]

C. Darwin to W. D. Fox.

Cambridge, Thursday [February 26, 1829].

MY DEAR FOX,

When I arrived here on Tuesday I found to my great
grief and surprise, a letter on my table which I had written to
you about a fortnight ago, the stupid porter never took the
trouble of getting the letter forwarded.   I suppose you have
been abusing me for a most ungrateful wretch ; but I am sure
you will pity me now, as nothing is so vexatious as having
written a letter in vain.

Last Thursday I left Shrewsbury for London, and stayed
there till Tuesday, on which I came down here by the ' Times.'
The first two days I spent entirely with Mr. Hope,* and did
little else but talk about and look at insects ; his collection is
most magnificent, and he himself is the most generous of
entomologists ; he has given me about 160 new species, and
actually often wanted to give me the rarest insects of which
he had only two specimens.   He made many civil speeches,
and hoped you will call on him some time with me, whenever
we should happen to be in London.   He greatly compliments
our exertions in Entomology, and says we have taken a wonderfully great number of good insects.   On Sunday I spent
the day with Holland, who lent me a horse to ride in the Park
with.

On Monday evening I drank tea with Stephens ;† his

---

* Founder of the Chair of Zoology at Oxford.
† J. F. Stephens, author of ' A Manual of British Coleoptera,' 1839,
and other works.

cabinet is more magnificent than the most zealous entomologist could dream of; he appears to be a very good-humoured pleasant little man. Whilst in town I went to the Royal Institution, Linnean Society, and Zoological Gardens, and many other places where naturalists are gregarious. If you had been with me, I think London would be a very delightful place; as things were, it was much pleasanter than I could have supposed such a dreary wilderness of houses to be.

I shot whilst in Shrewsbury a Dundiver (female Goosander, as I suppose you know). Shaw has stuffed it, and when I have an opportunity I will send it to Osmaston. There have been shot also five Waxen Chatterers, three of which Shaw has for sale; would you like to purchase a specimen? I have not yet thanked you for your last very long and agreeable letter. It would have been still more agreeable had it contained the joyful intelligence that you were coming up here; my two solitary breakfasts have already made me aware how very very much I shall miss you.

     *   *   *   *   *

> Believe me,
> My dear old Fox,
> Most sincerely yours,
> C. Darwin.

[Later on in the Lent term he writes to Fox :—

"I am leading a quiet everyday sort of a life; a little of Gibbon's History in the morning, and a good deal of *Van John* in the evening; this, with an occasional ride with Simcox and constitutional with Whitley, makes up the regular routine of my days. I see a good deal both of Herbert and Whitley, and the more I see of them increases every day the respect I have for their excellent understandings and dispositions. They have been giving some very gay parties, nearly sixty men there both evenings."]

C. Darwin to W. D. Fox.

Christ's College [Cambridge], April 1 [1829].

MY DEAR FOX,

In your letter to Holden you are pleased to observe "that of all the blackguards you ever met with I am the greatest." Upon this observation I shall make no remarks, excepting that I must give you all due credit for acting on it most rigidly. And now I should like to know in what one particular are you less of a blackguard than I am? You idle old wretch, why have you not answered my last letter, which I am sure I forwarded to Clifton nearly three weeks ago? If I was not really very anxious to hear what you are doing, I should have allowed you to remain till you thought it worth while to treat me like a gentleman. And now having vented my spleen in scolding you, and having told you, what you must know, how very much and how anxiously I want to hear how you and your family are getting on at Clifton, the purport of this letter is finished. If you did but know how often I think of you, and how often I regret your absence, I am sure I should have heard from you long enough ago.

I find Cambridge rather stupid, and as I know scarcely any one that walks, and this joined with my lips not being quite so well, has reduced me to a sort of hybernation. . . . I have caught Mr. Harbour letting —— have the first pick of the beetles; accordingly we have made our final adieus, my part in the affecting scene consisted in telling him he was a d—d rascal, and signifying I should kick him down the stairs if ever he appeared in my rooms again. It seemed altogether mightily to surprise the young gentleman. I have no news to tell you; indeed, when a correspondence has been broken off like ours has been, it is difficult to make the first start again. Last night there was a terrible fire at Linton, eleven miles from Cambridge. Seeing the reflection so plainly in the sky, Hall, Woodyeare, Turner, and myself thought we would ride and see it. We set out at half-past nine, and rode like incarnate devils there, and did not return till two in the morning. Altogether it was a most awful sight. I cannot conclude without telling you, that of all the blackguards I ever met with, you are the greatest and the best.

C. DARWIN.

C. Darwin to W. D. Fox.

[Cambridge, Thursday, April 23, 1829.]

MY DEAR FOX,

I have delayed answering your last letter for these few days, as I thought that under such melancholy circumstances my writing to you would be probably only giving you trouble. This morning I received a letter from Catherine informing me of that event,* which, indeed, from your letter, I had hardly dared to hope would have happened otherwise. I feel most sincerely and deeply for you and all your family; but at the same time, as far as any one can, by his own good principles and religion, be supported under such a misfortune, you, I am assured, will know where to look for such support. And after so pure and holy a comfort as the Bible affords, I am equally assured how useless the sympathy of all friends must appear, although it be as heartfelt and sincere, as I hope you believe me capable of feeling. At such a time of deep distress I will say nothing more, excepting that I trust your father and Mrs. Fox bear this blow as well as, under such circumstances, can be hoped for.

I am afraid it will be a long time, my dear Fox, before we meet; till then, believe me at all times,

Yours most affectionately,
CHARLES DARWIN.

C. Darwin to W. D. Fox.

Shrewsbury, Friday [July 4, 1829].

MY DEAR FOX,

I should have written to you before only that whilst our expedition lasted I was too much engaged, and the conclu-

---

* The death of Fox's sister, Mrs. Bristowe.

II

sion was so unfortunate, that I was too unhappy to write to
you till this week's quiet at home.   The thoughts of Woodhouse next week has at last given me courage to relate my
unfortunate case.

I started from this place about a fortnight ago to take an
entomological trip with Mr. Hope through all North Wales;
and Barmouth was our first destination.   The two first days
I went on pretty well, taking several good insects ; but for
the rest of that week my lips became suddenly so bad,* and
I myself not very well, that I was unable to leave the room,
and on the Monday I retreated with grief and sorrow back
again to Shrewsbury.   The first two days I took some good
insects. . . . But the days that I was unable to go out, Mr.
Hope did wonders . . . . and to-day I have received another
parcel of insects from him, such Colymbetes, such Carabi, and
such magnificent Elaters (two species of the bright scarlet
sort).   I am sure you will properly sympathise with my unfortunate situation : I am determined I will go over the same
ground that he does before autumn comes, and if working
hard will procure insects I will bring home a glorious stock.

    *   *   *   *   *

        My dear Fox,
           Yours most sincerely,
                CHAS. DARWIN.

C. Darwin to W. D. Fox.

                       Shrewsbury, July 18, 1829.

I am going to Maer next week in order to entomologise,
and shall stay there a week, and for the rest of this summer
I intend to lead a perfectly idle and wandering life. . . .
You see I am much in the same state that you are, with this
difference, you make good resolutions and never keep them ;
I never make them, so cannot keep them ; it is all very well
writing in this manner, but I must read for my Little-go.
Graham smiled and bowed so very civilly, when he told me

---

  * Probably with eczema, from which he often suffered.

that he was one of the six appointed to make the examination stricter, and that they were determined this would make it a very different thing from any previous examination, that from all this I am sure it will be the very devil to pay amongst all idle men and entomologists.   Erasmus, we expect home in a few weeks' time : he intends passing next winter in Paris.   Be sure you order the two lists of insects published by Stephens, one printed on both sides, and the other only on one ; you will find them very useful in many points of view.

Dear old Fox, yours,
C. DARWIN.

C. Darwin to W. D. Fox.

Christ's College, Thursday [October 16, 1829].

MY DEAR FOX,

I am afraid you will be very angry with me for not having written during the Music Meeting, but really I was worked so hard that I had no time ; I arrived here on Monday and found my rooms in dreadful confusion, as they have been taking up the floor, and you may suppose that I have had plenty to do for these two days.   The Music Meeting * was the most glorious thing I ever experienced ; and as for Malibran, words cannot praise her enough, she is quite the most charming person I ever saw.   We had extracts out of several of the best operas, acted in character, and you cannot imagine how very superior it made the concerts to any I ever heard before.   J. de Begnis † acted 'Il Fanatico' in character ; being dressed up an extraordinary figure gives a much greater effect to his acting.   He kept the whole theatre in roars of laughter.   I liked Madame Blasis very much, but nothing will do after Malibran, who sung some comic songs, and [a] person's heart must have been made of stone not to have lost it to her.   I lodged very near the Wedgwoods, and lived entirely with them, which was very pleasant, and had you

---

* At Birmingham.   † De Begnis's Christian name was Giuseppe.

been there it would have been quite perfect. It knocked me up most dreadfully, and I will never attempt again to do two things the same day.

*   *   *   *   *

C. Darwin to W. D. Fox.

[Cambridge] Thursday [March, 1830].

MY DEAR FOX,

I am through my Little-Go!!! I am too much exalted to humble myself by apologising for not having written before. But I assure you before I went in, and when my nerves were in a shattered and weak condition, your injured person often rose before my eyes and taunted me with my idleness. But I am through, through, through. I could write the whole sheet full with this delightful word. I went in yesterday, and have just heard the joyful news. I shall not know for a week which class I am in. The whole examination is carried on in a different system. It has one grand advantage—being over in one day. They are rather strict, and ask a wonderful number of questions.

And now I want to know something about your plans; of course you intend coming up here : what fun we will have together; what beetles we will catch; it will do my heart good to go once more together to some of our old haunts. I have two very promising pupils in Entomology, and we will make regular campaigns into the Fens. Heaven protect the beetles and Mr. Jenyns, for we won't leave him a pair in the whole country. My new Cabinet is come down, and a gay little affair it is.

And now for the time—I think I shall go for a few days to town to hear an opera and see Mr. Hope; not to mention my brother also, whom I should have no objection to see. If I go pretty soon, you can come afterwards, but if you will settle your plans definitely, I will arrange mine, so send me a letter by return of post. And I charge you let it be favour-able—that is to say, come directly. Holden has been or-dained, and drove the Coach out on the Monday. I do not think he is looking very well. Chapman wants you and myself to pay him a visit when you come up, and begs to be remembered to you. You must excuse this short letter, as I have no end more to send off by this day's post. I long to see you again, and till then,

My dear good old Fox,
Yours most sincerely,
C. DARWIN.

[In August he was in North Wales and wrote to Fox :—

"I have been intending to write every hour for the last fortnight, but *really* have had no time. I left Shrewsbury this day fortnight ago, and have since that time been working from morning to night in catching fish or beetles. This is literally the first idle day I have had to myself; for on the rainy days I go fishing, on the good ones entomologising. You may recollect that for the fortnight previous to all this, you told me not to write, so that I hope I have made out some sort of defence for not having sooner answered your two long and very agreeable letters."]

C. Darwin to W. D. Fox.

[Cambridge, November 5, 1830.]

MY DEAR FOX,

I have so little time at present, and am so disgusted by reading that I have not the heart to write to anybody. I have only written once home since I came up. This must excuse me for not having answered your three letters, for which I am really very much obliged. . . .

I have not stuck an insect this term, and scarcely opened a case. If I had time I would have sent you the insects which I have so long promised; but really I have not spirits or time to do anything. Reading makes me quite desperate; the plague of getting up all my subjects is next thing to intolerable. Henslow is my tutor, and a most *admirable* one he makes ; the hour with him is the pleasantest in the whole day.

I think he is quite the most perfect man I ever met with. I have been to some very pleasant parties there this term. His good-nature is unbounded.

I am sure you will be sorry to hear poor old Whitley's father is dead. In a worldly point of view it is of great consequence to him, as it will prevent him going to the Bar for some time.—(Be sure answer this :) What did you pay for the iron hoop you had made in Shrewsbury? Because I do not mean to pay the whole of the Cambridge man's bill. You need not trouble yourself about the Phallus, as I have bought up both species. I have heard men say that Henslow has some curious religious opinions. I never perceived anything of it, have you? I am very glad to hear, after all your delays, you have heard of a curacy where you may read all the commandments without endangering your throat. I am also still more glad to hear that your mother continues steadily to improve. I do trust that you will have no further cause for uneasiness. With every wish for your happiness, my dear old Fox,

Believe me yours most sincerely,

CHARLES DARWIN.

C. Darwin to W. D. Fox.

Cambridge, Sunday, January 23, 1831.

MY DEAR FOX,

I do hope you will excuse my not writing before I took my degree. I felt a quite inexplicable aversion to write to anybody. But now I do most heartily congratulate you upon passing your examination, and hope you find your curacy comfortable. If it is my last shilling (I have not many), I will come and pay you a visit.

I do not know why the degree should make one so miserable, both before and afterwards. I recollect you were sufficiently wretched before, and I can assure [you] I am now, and what makes it the more ridiculous is, I know not what about. I believe it is a beautiful provision of nature to make one regret the less leaving so pleasant a place as Cambridge ;

and amongst all its pleasures—I say it for once and for all—none so great as my friendship with you.   I sent you a newspaper yesterday, in which you will see what a good place [10th] I have got in the Poll.   As for Christ's, did you ever see such a college for producing Captains and Apostles? * There are no men either at Emmanuel or Christ's plucked. Cameron is gulfed, together with other three Trinity scholars! My plans are not at all settled.   I think I shall keep this term, and then go and economise at Shrewsbury, return and take my degree.

A man may be excused for writing so much about himself when he has just passed the examination; so you must excuse [me].   And on the same principle do you write a letter brimful of yourself and plans.   I want to know something about your examination.   Tell me about the state of your nerves ; what books you got up, and how perfect.   I take an interest about that sort of thing, as the time will come when I must suffer.   Your tutor, Thompson, begged to be remembered to you, and so does Whitley.   If you will answer this, I will send as many stupid answers as you can desire.

Believe me, dear Fox,
CHAS. DARWIN.

---

* The " Captain " is at the head of the " Poll " : the " Apostles " are the last twelve in the Mathematical Tripos.

CHAPTER V.

THE APPOINTMENT TO THE 'BEAGLE.'

[IN a letter addressed to Captain Fitz-Roy, before the *Beagle* sailed, my father wrote, "What a glorious day the 4th of November * will be to me—my second life will then commence, and it shall be as a birthday for the rest of my life."

The circumstances which led to this second birth—so much more important than my father then imagined—are connected with his Cambridge life, but may be more appropriately told in the present chapter. Foremost in the chain of circumstances which led to his appointment to the *Beagle*, was my father's friendship with Professor Henslow. He wrote in a pocket-book or diary, which contain a brief record of dates, &c., throughout his life :—

"1831. *Christmas.*—Passed my examination for B. A. degree and kept the two following terms.

"During these months lived much with Professor Henslow, often dining with him and walking with him ; became slightly acquainted with several of the learned men in Cambridge, which much quickened the zeal which dinner parties and hunting had not destroyed.

"In the spring paid Mr. Dawes a visit with Ramsay and Kirby, and talked over an excursion to Teneriffe. In the

---

* The *Beagle* did not however make her final and successful start until December 27.

THE BEAGLE LAID ASHORE, RIVER SANTA CRUZ

spring Henslow persuaded me to think of Geology, and introduced me to Sedgwick. During Midsummer geologised a
little in Shropshire.

"*August.*—Went on Geological tour* by Llangollen,
Ruthin, Conway, Bangor, and Capel Curig, where I left Professor Sedgwick, and crossed the mountain to Barmouth."

In a letter to Fox (May, 1831), my father writes :—" I am
very busy . . . and see a great deal of Henslow, whom I do
not know whether I love or respect most." His feeling for
this admirable man is finely expressed in a letter which he
wrote to Rev. L. Blomefield (then Rev. L. Jenyns), when the
latter was engaged in his ' Memoir of Professor Henslow '
(published 1862). The passage † has been made use of in the
first of the memorial notices written for ' Nature,' and Mr.
Romanes points out that my father, "while describing the
character of another, is unconsciously giving a most accurate
description of his own " :—

" I went to Cambridge early in the year 1828, and soon
became acquainted, through some of my brother entomologists, with Professor Henslow, for all who cared for any
branch of natural history were equally encouraged by him.
Nothing could be more simple, cordial, and unpretending
than the encouragement which he afforded to all young
naturalists. I soon became intimate with him, for he had a
remarkable power of making the young feel completely at ease
with him ; though we were all awe-struck with the amount of
his knowledge. Before I saw him, I heard one young man
sum up his attaintments by simply saying that he knew everything. When I reflect how immediately we felt at perfect ease
with a man older, and in every way so immensely our superior,
I think it was as much owing to the transparent sincerity of

---

* Mentioned by Sedgwick in his preface to Salter's 'Catalogue of Cam-
brian and Silurian Fossils,' 1873.
† 'Memoir of the Rev. John Stevens Henslow, M. A ,' by the Rev.
Leonard Jenyns. 8vo. London, 1862, p. 51.

his character as to his kindness of heart ; and, perhaps, even still more, to a highly remarkable absence in him of all self-consciousness.   One perceived at once that he never thought of his own varied knowledge or clear intellect, but solely on the subject in hand.   Another charm, which must have struck every one, was that his manner to old and distinguished persons and to the youngest student was exactly the same : and to all he showed the same winning courtesy.   He would receive with interest the most trifling observation in any branch of natural history ; and however absurd a blunder one might make, he pointed it out so clearly and kindly, that one left him no way disheartened, but only determined to be more accurate the next time.   In short, no man could be better formed to win the entire confidence of the young, and to encourage them in their pursuits.

" His lectures on Botany were universally popular, and as clear as daylight.   So popular were they, that several of the older members of the University attended successive courses. Once every week he kept open house in the evening, and all who cared for natural history attended these parties, which, by thus favouring inter-communication, did the same good in Cambridge, in a very pleasant manner, as the Scientific Societies do in London.   At these parties many of the most distinguished members of the University occasionally attended ; and when only a few were present, I have listened to the great men of those days, conversing on all sorts of subjects, with the most varied and brilliant powers   This was no small advantage to some of the younger men, as it stimulated their mental activity and ambition.   Two or three times in each session he took excursions with his botanical class ; either a long walk to the habitat of some rare plant, or in a barge down the river to the fens, or in coaches to some more distant place, as to Gamlingay, to see the wild lily of the valley, and to catch on the heath the rare natter-jack. These excursions have left a delightful impression on my mind.   He was, on such occasions, in as good spirits as a boy, and laughed as heartily as a boy at the misadventures of those who chased the splendid swallow-tail butterflies across the broken and treacherous fens. He used to pause every now and then to lecture on some plant or other object; and something he could tell us on every insect, shell, or fossil collected, for he had attended to every branch of natural history. After our day's work we used to dine at some inn or house, and most jovial we then were. I believe all who joined these excursions will agree with me that they have left an enduring impression of delight on our minds.

"As time passed on at Cambridge I became very intimate with Professor Henslow, and his kindness was unbounded; he continually asked me to his house, and allowed me to accompany him in his walks. He talked on all subjects, including his deep sense of religion, and was entirely open. I owe more than I can express to this excellent man. . . .

"During the years when I associated so much with Professor Henslow, I never once saw his temper even ruffled. He never took an ill-natured view of any one's character, though very far from blind to the foibles of others. It always struck me that his mind could not be even touched by any paltry feeling of vanity, envy, or jealousy. With all this equability of temper and remarkable benevolence, there was no insipidity of character. A man must have been blind not to have perceived that beneath this placid exterior there was a vigorous and determined will. When principle came into play, no power on earth could have turned him one hair's-breadth. . . .

"Reflecting over his character with gratitude and reverence, his moral attributes rise, as they should do in the highest character, in pre-eminence over his intellect."

In a letter to Rev. L. Blomefield (Jenyns), May 24, 1862, my father wrote with the same feelings that he had expressed in his letters thirty years before:—

"I thank you most sincerely for your kind present of your Memoir of Henslow. I have read about half, and it has interested me much. I did not think that I could have venerated him more than I did; but your book has even exalted his character in my eyes. From turning over the pages of the latter half, I should think your account would be invaluable to any clergyman who wished to follow poor dear Henslow's noble example. What an admirable man he was."

The geological work mentioned in the quotation from my father's pocket-book was doubtless of importance as giving him some practical experience, and perhaps of more importance in helping to give him some confidence in himself. In July of the same year, 1831, he was "working like a tiger" at Geology, and trying to make a map of Shropshire, but not finding it "as easy as I expected."

In writing to Henslow about the same time, he gives some account of his work :—

"I should have written to you some time ago, only I was determined to wait for the clinometer, and I am very glad to say I think it will answer admirably. I put all the tables in my bedroom at every conceivable angle and direction. I will venture to say I have measured them as accurately as any geologist going could do . . . . I have been working at so many things that I have not got on much with geology. I suspect the first expedition I take, clinometer and hammer in hand, will send me back very little wiser and a good deal more puzzled than when I started. As yet I have only indulged in hypotheses, but they are such powerful ones that I suppose, if they were put into action for but one day, the world would come to an end."

He was evidently most keen to get to work with Sedgwick, for he wrote to Henslow : " I have not heard from Professor Sedgwick, so I am afraid he will not pay the Severn formations a visit. I hope and trust you did your best to urge him."

My father has given in his Recollections some account of this Tour.

There too we read of the projected excursion to the Canaries, of which slight mention occurs in letters to Fox and Henslow.

In April 1831 he writes to Fox: "At present I talk, think, and dream of a scheme I have almost hatched of going to the Canary Islands. I have long had a wish of seeing tropical scenery and vegetation, and, according to Humboldt, Teneriffe is a very pretty specimen." And again in May: "As for my Canary scheme, it is rash of you to ask questions; my other friends most sincerely wish me there, I plague them so with talking about tropical scenery, &c. Eyton will go next summer, and I am learning Spanish."

Later on in the summer the scheme took more definite form, and the date seems to have been fixed for June, 1832. He got information in London about passage-money, and in July was working at Spanish and calling Fox "un grandísimo lebron," in proof of his knowledge of the language; which, however, he found "intensely stupid." But even then he seems to have had some doubts about his companions' zeal, for he writes to Henslow (July 27, 1831): "I hope you continue to fan your Canary ardour. I read and re-read Humboldt; do you do the same? I am sure nothing will prevent us seeing the Great Dragon Tree."

Geological work and Teneriffe dreams carried him through the summer, till on returning from Barmouth for the sacred 1st of September, he received the offer of appointment as Naturalist to the *Beagle*.

The following extract from the pocket-book will be a help in reading the letters :—

"Returned to Shrewsbury at end of August. Refused offer of voyage.

"*September.*—Went to Maer, returned with Uncle Jos. to Shrewsbury, thence to Cambridge. London.

"*11th.*—Went with Captain Fitz-Roy in steamer to Plymouth to see the *Beagle*.

"*22nd.*—Returned to Shrewsbury, passing through Cambridge.

"*October* 2*nd.*—Took leave of my home. Stayed in London.

"24*th.*—Reached Plymouth.

"*October and November.*—These months very miserable.

"*December* 10*th.*—Sailed, but were obliged to put back.

"21*st.*—Put to sea again, and were driven back.

"27*th.*—Sailed from England on our Circumnavigation."

George Peacock * *to J. S. Henslow.*

7 Suffolk Street, Pall Mall East.

[1831.]

MY DEAR HENSLOW,

Captain Fitz-Roy is going out to survey the southern coast of Tierra del Fuego, and afterwards to visit many of the South Sea Islands, and to return by the Indian Archipelago. The vessel is fitted out expressly for scientific purposes, combined with the survey; it will furnish, therefore, a rare opportunity for a naturalist, and it would be a great misfortune that it should be lost.

An offer has been made to me to recommend a proper person to go out as a naturalist with this expedition; he will be treated with every consideration. The Captain is a young man of very pleasing manners (a nephew of the Duke of Grafton), of great zeal in his profession, and who is very highly spoken of; if Leonard Jenyns could go, what treasures he might bring home with him, as the ship would be placed at his disposal whenever his inquiries made it necessary or desirable. In the absence of so accomplished a naturalist, is there any person whom you could strongly recommend? he must be such a person as would do credit to our recommendation. Do think of this subject, it would be a serious loss to the cause of natural science if this fine opportunity was lost.

*   *   *   *   *

---

* Formerly Dean of Ely, and Lowndean Professor of Astronomy at Cambridge.

The ship sails about the end of September.

Write immediately, and tell me what can be done.

Believe me,

My dear Henslow,

Most truly yours,

GEORGE PEACOCK.

J. S. Henslow to C. Darwin.

Cambridge, August 24, 1831.

MY DEAR DARWIN,

Before I enter upon the immediate business of this letter, let us condole together upon the loss of our inestimable friend poor Ramsay, of whose death you have undoubtedly heard long before this.

I will not now dwell upon this painful subject, as I shall hope to see you shortly, fully expecting that you will eagerly catch at the offer which is likely to be made you of a trip to Tierra del Fuego, and home by the East Indies. I have been asked by Peacock, who will read and forward this to you from London, to recommend him a Naturalist as companion to Captain Fitz-Roy, employed by Government to survey the southern extremity of America. I have stated that I consider you to be the best qualified person I know of who is likely to undertake such a situation. I state this not in the supposition of your being a *finished* naturalist, but as amply qualified for collecting, observing, and noting, anything worthy to be noted in Natural History. Peacock has the appointment at his disposal, and if he cannot find a man willing to take the office, the opportunity will probably be lost. Captain Fitz-Roy wants a man (I understand) more as a companion than a mere collector, and would not take any one, however good a naturalist, who was not recommended to him likewise as a *gentleman.* Particulars of salary, &c., I know nothing. The voyage is to last two years, and if you take plenty of books with you, anything you please may be done. You will have ample opportunities at command. In short, I suppose there never was a finer chance for a man of zeal and spirit; Captain Fitz-Roy is a young man. What I wish you to do is instantly to come and consult with Peacock (at No. 7 Suffolk Street, Pall Mall East, or else at the University Club), and learn further particulars. Don't put on any modest doubts or fears about your disqualifications, for I assure you I think you are the very man they are in search of; so conceive yourself to be tapped on the shoulder by your bum-bailiff and affectionate friend,

J. S. HENSLOW.

The expedition is to sail on 25th September (at earliest), so there is no time to be lost.

G. Peacock to C. Darwin.

[1831.]

MY DEAR SIR,

I received Henslow's letter last night too late to forward it to you by the post; a circumstance which I do not regret, as it has given me an opportunity of seeing Captain Beaufort at the Admiralty (the Hydrographer), and of stating to him the offer which I have to make to you. He entirely approves of it, and you may consider the situation as at your absolute disposal. I trust that you will accept it, as it is an opportunity which should not be lost, and I look forward with great interest to the benefit which our collections of Natural History may receive from your labors.

The circumstances are these ;—

Captain Fitz-Roy (a nephew of the Duke of Grafton) sails at the end of September, in a ship to survey, in the first instance, the South Coast of Tierra del Fuego, afterwards to visit the South Sea Islands, and to return by the Indian Archipelago to England. The expedition is entirely for scientific purposes, and the ship will generally wait your leisure for researches in Natural History, &c. Captain Fitz-Roy is a public-spirited and zealous officer, of delightful manners, and greatly beloved by all his brother officers. He went with

Captain Beechey,* and spent £1500 in bringing over and educating at his own charge three natives of Patagonia. He engages at his own expense an artist at £200 a year to go with him. You may be sure, therefore, of having a very pleasant companion, who will enter heartily into all your views.

The ship sails about the end of September, and you must lose no time in making known your acceptance to Captain Beaufort, Admiralty Hydrographer. I have had a good deal of correspondence about this matter [with Henslow?], who feels, in common with myself, the greatest anxiety that you should go. I hope that no other arrangements are likely to interfere with it.   *   *   *   *

The Admiralty are not disposed to give a salary, though they will furnish you with an official appointment, and every accommodation. If a salary should be required, however, I am inclined to think that it would be granted.

Believe me, my dear Sir,
Very truly yours,
GEORGE PEACOCK.

C. Darwin to J. S. Henslow.

Shrewsbury, Tuesday [August 30?, 1831].

MY DEAR SIR,

Mr. Peacock's letter arrived on Saturday, and I received it late yesterday evening. As far as my own mind is concerned, I should, I think *certainly*, most gladly have accepted the opportunity which you so kindly have offered me. But my father, although he does not decidedly refuse me, gives such strong advice against going, that I should not be comfortable if I did not follow it.

My father's objections are these: the unfitting me to

---

* For 'Beechey' read 'King.' I do not find the name Fitz-Roy in the list of Beechey's officers. The Fuegians were brought back from Captain King's voyage.

12

settle down as a Clergyman, my little habit of seafaring, *the shortness of the time*, and the chance of my not suiting Captain Fitz-Roy. It is certainly a very serious objection, the very short time for all my preparations, as not only body but mind wants making up for such an undertaking. But if it had not been for my father I would have taken all risks. What was the reason that a Naturalist was not long ago fixed upon? I am very much obliged for the trouble you have had about it; there certainly could not have been a better opportunity.

*   *   ☼   *   *

My trip with Sedgwick answered most perfectly. I did not hear of poor Mr. Ramsay's loss till a few days before your letter. I have been lucky hitherto in never losing any person for whom I had any esteem or affection. My acquaintance, although very short, was sufficient to give me those feelings in a great degree. I can hardly make myself believe he is no more. He was the finest character I ever knew.

Yours most sincerely,
My dear Sir,
CH. DARWIN.

I have written to Mr. Peacock, and I mentioned that I have asked you to send one line in the chance of his not getting my letter. I have also asked him to communicate with Captain Fitz-Roy. Even if I was to go, my father disliking would take away all energy, and I should want a good stock of that. Again I must thank you, it adds a little to the heavy but pleasant load of gratitude which I owe to you.

C. Darwin to R. W. Darwin.

[Maer] August 31, [1831].

MY DEAR FATHER,

I am afraid I am going to make you again very uncomfortable. But, upon consideration, I think you will excuse me once again, stating my opinions on the offer of the voyage. My excuse and reason is the different way all the Wedgwoods view the subject from what you and my sisters do.

I have given Uncle Jos* what I fervently trust is an accurate and full list of your objections, and he is kind enough to give his opinions on all. The list and his answers will be enclosed. But may I beg of you one favour, it will be doing me the greatest kindness, if you will send me a decided answer, yes or no? If the latter, I should be most ungrateful if I did not implicitly yield to your better judgment, and to the kindest indulgence you have shown me all through my life; and you may rely upon it I will never mention the subject again. If your answer should be yes; I will go directly to Henslow and consult deliberately with him, and then come to Shrewsbury.

The danger appears to me and all the Wedgwoods not great. The expense cannot be serious, and the time I do not think, anyhow, would be more thrown away than if I stayed at home. But pray do not consider that I am so bent on going that I would for one *single moment* hesitate, if you thought that after a short period you should continue uncomfortable.

I must again state I cannot think it would unfit me hereafter for a steady life. I do hope this letter will not give you much uneasiness. I send it by the car to-morrow morning; if you make up your mind directly will you send me an answer on the following day by the same means? If this letter should not find you at home, I hope you will answer as soon as you conveniently can.

I do not know what to say about Uncle Jos' kindness; I never can forget how he interests himself about me.

Believe me, my dear father,

Your affectionate son,

CHARLES DARWIN.

---

* Josiah Wedgwood.

[Here follows the list of objections which are referred to in the following letter :—

(1.) Disreputable to my character as a Clergyman hereafter.

(2.) A wild scheme.

(3.) That they must have offered to many others before me the place of Naturalist.

(4.) And from its not being accepted there must be some serious objection to the vessel or expedition.

(5.) That I should never settle down to a steady life hereafter.

(6.) That my accommodations would be most uncomfortable.

(7.) That you [*i.e.* Dr. Darwin] should consider it as again changing my profession.

(8.) That it would be a useless undertaking.]

Josiah Wedgwood to R. W. Darwin.

Maer, August 31, 1831.

[Read this last.]*

MY DEAR DOCTOR,

I feel the responsibility of your application to me on the offer that has been made to Charles as being weighty, but as you have desired Charles to consult me, I cannot refuse to give the result of such consideration as I have been able to [give ?] it.

Charles has put down what he conceives to be your principal objections, and I think the best course I can take will be to state what occurs to me upon each of them.

1. I should not think that it would be in any degree disreputable to his character as a Clergyman. I should on the contrary think the offer honourable to him ; and the pursuit of Natural History, though certainly not professional, is very suitable to a clergyman.

2. I hardly know how to meet this objection, but he would·

---

* In C. Darwin's writing.

have definite objects upon which to employ himself, and might acquire and strengthen habits of application, and I should think would be as likely to do so as in any way in which he is likely to pass the next two years at home.

3. The notion did not occur to me in reading the letters; and on reading them again with that object in my mind I see no ground for it.

4. I cannot conceive that the Admiralty would send out a bad vessel on such a service. As to objections to the expedition, they will differ in each man's case, and nothing would, I think, be inferred in Charles's case, if it were known that others had objected.

5. You are a much better judge of Charles's character than I can be. If on comparing this mode of spending the next two years with the way in which he will probably spend them, if he does not accept this offer, you think him more likely to be rendered unsteady and unable to settle, it is undoubtedly a weighty objection. Is it not the case that sailors are prone to settle in domestic and quiet habits?

6. I can form no opinion on this further than that if appointed by the Admiralty he will have a claim to be as well accommodated as the vessel will allow.

7. If I saw Charles now absorbed in professional studies I should probably think it would not be advisable to interrupt them; but this is not, and, I think, will not be the case with him. His present pursuit of knowledge is in the same track as he would have to follow in the expedition.

8. The undertaking would be useless as regards his profession, but looking upon him as a man of enlarged curiosity, it affords him such an opportunity of seeing men and things as happens to few.

You will bear in mind that I have had very little time for consideration, and that you and Charles are the persons who must decide.   I am,

My dear Doctor,

Affectionately yours,

Josiah Wedgwood.

C. Darwin to J. S. Henslow.

Cambridge, Red Lion [Sept. 2], 1831.

MY DEAR SIR,

I am just arrived ; you will guess the reason. My father has changed his mind. I trust the place is not given away.

I am very much fatigued, and am going to bed.

I dare say you have not yet got my second letter.

How soon shall I come to you in the morning ? Send a verbal answer.

Good-night,
Yours,
C. DARWIN.

C. Darwin to Miss Susan Darwin.

Cambridge, Sunday Morning [September 4].

MY DEAR SUSAN,

As a letter would not have gone yesterday, I put off writing till to-day. I had rather a wearisome journey, but got into Cambridge very fresh. The whole of yesterday I spent with Henslow, thinking of what is to be done, and that I find is a great deal. By great good luck I know a man of the name of Wood, nephew of Lord Londonderry. He is a great friend of Captain Fitz-Roy, and has written to him about me. I heard a part of Captain Fitz-Roy's letter, dated some time ago, in which he says : " I have a right good set of officers, and most of my men have been there before." It seems he has been there for the last few years ; he was then second in command with the same vessel that he has now chosen. He is only twenty-three years old, but [has] seen a deal of service, and won the gold medal at Portsmouth. The Admiralty say his maps are most perfect. He had choice of two vessels, and he chose the smallest. Henslow will give me letters to all travellers in town whom he thinks may assist me.

Peacock has sole appointment of Naturalist. The first

person offered was Leonard Jenyns, who was so near accepting it that he packed up his clothes. But having [a] living, he did not think it right to leave it—to the great regret of all his family. Henslow himself was not very far from accepting it, for Mrs. Henslow most generously, and without being asked, gave her consent; but she looked so miserable that Henslow at once settled the point.

*   *   *   *   *

I am afraid there will be a good deal of expense at first. Henslow is much against taking many things; it is [the] mistake all young travellers fall into. I write as if it was settled, but Henslow tells me *by no means* to make up my mind till I have had long conversations with Captains Beaufort and Fitz-Roy. Good-bye. You will hear from me constantly. Direct 17 Spring Gardens. *Tell nobody* in Shropshire yet. Be sure not.

C. DARWIN.

I was so tired that evening I was in Shrewsbury that I thanked none of you for your kindness half so much as I felt.

Love to my father.

The reason I don't want people told in Shropshire: in case I should not go, it will make it more flat.

C. Darwin to Miss S. Darwin.

17 Spring Gardens, Monday
[September 5, 1831].

I have so little time to spare that I have none to waste in re-writing letters, so that you must excuse my bringing up the other with me and altering it. The last letter was written in the morning. In [the] middle of [the] day, Wood received a letter from Captain Fitz-Roy, which I must say was *most* straightforward and *gentlemanlike*, but so much against my going, that I immediately gave up the scheme; and Henslow did the same, saying that he thought Peacock had acted *very wrong* in misrepresenting things so much.

I scarcely thought of going to town, but here I am ; and now for more details, and much more promising ones. Captain Fitz-Roy is [in] town, and I have seen him; it is no use attempting to praise him as much as I feel inclined to do, for you would not believe me. One thing I am certain, nothing could be more open and kind than he was to me. It seems he had promised to take a friend with him, who is in office and cannot go, and he only received the letter five minutes before I came in ; and this makes things much better for me, as want of room was one of Fitz-Roy's greatest objections. He offers me to go share in everything in his cabin if I like to come, and every sort of accommodation that I can have, but they will not be numerous. He says nothing would be so miserable for him as having me with him if I was uncomfortable, as in a small vessel we must be thrown together, and thought it his duty to state everything in the worst point of view. I think I shall go on Sunday to Plymouth to see the vessel.

There is something most extremely attractive in his manners and way of coming straight to the point. If I live with him, he says I must live poorly—no wine, and the plainest dinners. The scheme is not certainly so good as Peacock describes. Captain Fitz-Roy advises me not [to] make up my mind quite yet, but that, seriously, he thinks it will have much more pleasure than pain for me. The vessel does not sail till the 10th of October. It contains sixty men, five or six officers, &c., but is a small vessel. It will probably be out nearly three years. I shall pay to the mess the same as [the] Captain does himself, £30 per annum ; and Fitz-Roy says if I spend, including my outfitting, £500, it will be beyond the extreme. But now for still worse news. The round the world is not *certain*, but the chance most excellent. Till that point is decided, I will not be so. And you may believe, after the many changes I have made, that nothing but my reason shall decide me.

Fitz-Roy says the stormy sea is exaggerated ; that if I do not choose to remain with them, I can at any time get home to England, so many vessels sail that way, and that during bad weather (probably two months), if I like I shall be left in some healthy, safe and nice country ; that I shall always have assistance ; that he has many books, all instruments, guns, at my service ; that the fewer and cheaper clothes I take the better. The manner of proceeding will just suit me.   They anchor the ship, and then remain for a fortnight at a place.   I have made Captain Beaufort perfectly understand me.   He says if I start and do not go round the world, I shall have good reason to think myself deceived.   I am to call the day after to-morrow, and, if possible, to receive more certain instructions.   The want of room is decidedly the most serious objection ; but Captain Fitz-Roy (probably owing to Wood's letter) seems determined to make me [as] comfortable as he possibly can. I like his manner of proceeding.   He asked me at once, " Shall you bear being told that I want the cabin to myself —when I want to be alone ?   If we treat each other this way, I hope we shall suit ; if not, probably we should wish each other at the devil."

We stop a week at [the] Madeira Islands, and shall see most of [the] big cities in South America.   Captain Beaufort is drawing up the track through the South Sea.   I am writing in [a] great hurry ; I do not know whether you take interest enough to excuse treble postage.   I hope I am judging reasonably, and not through prejudice, about Captain Fitz-Roy ; if so, I am sure we shall suit.   I dine with him to-day. I could write [a] great deal more if I thought you liked it, and I had at present time.   There is indeed a tide in the affairs of man, and I have experienced it, and I had *entirely* given it up till one to-day.

Love to my father.   Dearest Susan, good-bye.

CH. DARWIN.

C. Darwin to J. S. Henslow.

London, Monday, [September 5, 1831].

MY DEAR SIR,

Gloria in excelsis is the most moderate beginning I can think of. Things are more prosperous than I should have thought possible. Captain Fitz-Roy is everything that is delightful. If I was to praise half so much as I feel inclined, you would say it was absurd, only once seeing him. I think he really wishes to have me. He offers me to mess with him, and he will take care I have such room as is possible. But about the cases he says I must limit myself; but then he thinks like a sailor about size. Captain Beaufort says I shall be upon the Boards, and then it will only cost me like other officers. Ship sails 10th of October. Spends a week at Madeira Islands; and then Rio de Janeiro. They all think most extremely probable, home by the Indian archipelago; but till that is decided, I will not be so.

What has induced Captain Fitz-Roy to take a better view of the case is, that Mr. Chester, who was going as a friend, cannot go, so that I shall have his place in every respect.

Captain Fitz-Roy has [a] good stock of books, many of which were in my list, and rifles, &c., so that the outfit will be much less expensive than I supposed.

The vessel will be out three years. I do not object so that my father does not. On Wednesday I have another interview with Captain Beaufort, and on Sunday most likely go with Captain Fitz-Roy to Plymouth. So I hope you will keep on thinking on the subject, and just keep memoranda of what may strike you. I will call most probably on Mr. Burchell and introduce myself. I am in lodgings at 17 Spring Gardens. You cannot imagine anything more pleasant, kind, and open than Captain Fitz-Roy's manners were to me. I am sure it will be my fault if we do not suit.

What changes I have had. Till one to-day I was building

castles in the air about hunting foxes in Shropshire, now llamas in South America.

There is indeed a tide in the affairs of men. If you see Mr. Wood, remember me very kindly to him.

Good-bye.

My dear Henslow,

Your most sincere friend,

CHAS. DARWIN.

Excuse this letter in such a hurry.

C. Darwin to W. D. Fox.

17 Spring Gardens, London,
September 6, 1831.

*   *   *   *   *

Your letter gave me great pleasure. You cannot imagine how much your former letter annoyed and hurt me.* But, thank heaven, I firmly believe that it was my *own entire* fault in so interpreting your letter. I lost a friend the other day, and I doubt whether the moral death (as I then wickedly supposed) of our friendship did not grieve me as much as the real and sudden death of poor Ramsay. We have known each other too long to need, I trust, any more explanations. But I will mention just one thing—that on my death-bed, I think I could say I never uttered one insincere (which at the time I did not fully feel) expression about my regard for you. On thing more—the sending *immediately* the insects, on my honour, was an unfortunate coincidence. I forgot how you naturally would take them. When you look at them now, I hope no unkindly feelings will rise in your mind, and that you will believe that you have always had in me a sincere, and I will add, an obliged friend. The very many pleasant minutes that we spent together in Cambridge rose like departed spirits in judgment against me. May we have

---

* He had misunderstood a letter of Fox's as implying a charge of falsehood.

many more such, will be one of my last wishes in leaving England. God bless you, dear old Fox. May you always be happy.

Yours truly,
CHAS. DARWIN.

I have left your letter behind, so do not know whether I direct right.

C. Darwin to Miss Susan Darwin.

17 Spring Gardens, Tuesday,
[September 6, 1831.]

MY DEAR SUSAN,

Again I am going to trouble you. I suspect, if I keep on at this rate, you will sincerely wish me at Tierra del Fuego, or any other Terra, but England. First I will give my commissions. Tell Nancy to make me some twelve instead of eight shirts. Tell Edward to send me up in my carpet-bag (he can slip the key in the bag tied to some string), my slippers, a pair of lightish walking-shoes, my Spanish books, my new microscope (about six inches long and three or four deep), which must have cotton stuffed inside; my geological compass; my father knows that; a little book, if I have got it in my bedroom—'Taxidermy.' Ask my father if he thinks there would be any objection to my taking arsenic for a little time, as my hands are not quite well, and I have always observed that if I once get them well, and change my manner of living about the same time, they will generally remain well. What is the dose? Tell Edward my gun is dirty. What is Erasmus's direction? Tell me if you think there is time to write and receive an answer before I start, as I should like particularly to know what he thinks about it. I suppose you do not know Sir J. Mackintosh's direction?

I write all this as if it was settled, but it is not more than it was, excepting that from Captain Fitz-Roy wishing me so much to go, and, from his kindness, I feel a predestination I shall start. I spent a very pleasant evening with him yester-

day. He must be more than twenty-three years old; he is
of a slight figure, and a dark but handsome edition of Mr.
Kynaston, and, according to my notions, pre-eminently good
manners. He is all for economy, excepting on one point—
viz., fire-arms. He recommends me strongly to get a case of
pistols like his, which cost £60!! and never to go on shore
anywhere without loaded ones, and he is doubting about a
rifle; he says I cannot appreciate the luxury of fresh meat
here. Of course I shall buy nothing till everything is settled;
but I work all day long at my lists, putting in and striking
out articles. This is the first really cheerful day I have spent
since I received the letter, and it all is owing to the sort of
involuntary confidence I place in my *beau ideal* of a Captain.

We stop at Teneriffe. His object is to stop at as many
places as possible. He takes out twenty chronometers, and
it will be a " sin " not to settle the longitude. He tells me to
get it down in writing at the Admiralty that I have the free
choice to leave as soon and whenever I like. I dare say you
expect I shall turn back at the Madeira; if I have a morsel
of stomach left, I won't give up. Excuse my so often troubling and writing: the one is of great utility, the other a great
amusement to me. Most likely I shall write to-morrow.
Answer by return of post. Love to my father, dearest Susan.

C. DARWIN.

As my instruments want altering, send my things by the
· ' Oxonian ' the same night.

C. Darwin to Miss Susan Darwin.

London, Friday Morning, September 9, 1831.

MY DEAR SUSAN,

I have just received the parcel. I suppose it was not de-
livered yesterday owing to the Coronation. I am very much
obliged to my father, and everybody else. Everything is done
quite right. I suppose by this time you have received my
letter written next day, and I hope will send off the things.
My affairs remain *in statu quo*. Captain Beaufort says I am

on the books for victuals, and he thinks I shall have no difficulty about my collections when I come home. But he is too
deep a fish for me to make him out. The only thing that
now prevents me finally making up my mind, is the want of
certainty about the South Sea Islands; although morally I
have no doubt we should go there whether or no it is put in
the instructions. Captain Fitz-Roy says I do good by plaguing Captain Beaufort, it stirs him up with a long pole. Captain Fitz-Roy says he is sure he has interest enough (particularly if this Administration is not everlasting—I shall soon
turn Tory !), anyhow, even when out, to get the ship ordered
home by whatever track he likes. From what Wood says, I
presume the Dukes of Grafton and Richmond interest themselves about him. By the way, Wood has been of the greatest use to me ; and I am sure his personal introduction of
me inclined Captain Fitz-Roy to have me.

To explain things from the very beginning: Captain Fitz-
Roy first wished to have a Naturalist, and then he seems to
have taken a sudden horror of the chances of having some-
body he should not like on board the vessel. He confesses
his letter to Cambridge was to throw cold water on the scheme.
I don't think we shall quarrel about politics, although Wood
(as might be expected from a Londonderry) solemnly warned
Fitz-Roy that I was a Whig. Captain Fitz-Roy was before
Uncle Jos., he said, " now your friends will tell you a sea-
captain is the greatest brute on the face of the creation. I do
not know how to help you in this case, except by hoping you
will give me a trial." How one does change ! I actually now
wish the voyage was longer before we touch land. I feel my
blood run cold at the quantity I have to do. Everybody
seems ready to assist me. The Zoological want to make me
a corresponding member. All this I can construct without
crossing the Equator. But one friend is quite invaluable, viz.,
a Mr. Yarrell, a stationer, and excellent naturalist.* He goes

---

* William Yarrell, well known for his ' History of British Birds ' and
' History of British Fishes,' was born in 1784. He inherited from his

to the shops with me and bullies about prices (not that I yet buy) : hang me if I give £60 for pistols.

Yesterday all the shops were shut, so that I could do nothing ; and I was child enough to give £1 1s. for an excellent seat to see the Procession.* And it certainly was very well worth seeing. I was surprised that any quantity of gold could make a long row of people quite glitter. It was like only what one sees in picture-books of Eastern processions. The King looked very well, and seemed popular, but there was very little enthusiasm ; so little that I can hardly think there will be a coronation this time fifty years.

The Life Guards pleased me as much as anything—they are quite magnificent ; and it is beautiful to see them clear a crowd. You think that they must kill a score at least, and apparently they really hurt nobody, but most deucedly frighten them. Whenever a crowd was so dense that the people were forced off the causeway, one of these six-feet gentlemen, on a black horse, rode straight at the place, making his horse rear very high, and fall on the thickest spot. You would suppose men were made of sponge to see them shrink away.

In the evening there was an illumination, and much grander than the one on the Reform Bill. All the principal streets were crowded just like a race-ground. Carriages generally being six abreast, and I will venture to say not going one mile an hour. The Duke of Northumberland learnt a lesson last time, for his house was very grand ; much more so than the other great nobility, and in much better taste ; every window in his house was full of straight lines of brilliant lights, and from their extreme regularity and number had a beautiful effect. The paucity of invention was very striking, crowns, anchors, and "W. R.'s" were repeated in endless

---

father a newsagent's business, to which he steadily adhered up to his death, " in his 73rd year." He was a man of a thoroughly amiable and honour-able character, and was a valued office-bearer of several of the learned Societies.

* The Coronation of William IV.

succession. The prettiest were gas-pipes with small holes; they were almost painfully brilliant. I have written so much about the Coronation, that I think you will have no occasion to read the *Morning Herald.*

For about the first time in my life I find London very pleasant; hurry, bustle, and noise are all in unison with my feelings. And I have plenty to do in spare moments. I work at Astronomy, as I suppose it would astound a sailor if one did not know how to find Latitude and Longitude. I am now going to Captain Fitz-Roy, and will keep [this] letter open till evening for anything that may occur. I will give you one proof of Fitz-Roy being a good officer—all the officers are the same as before; two-thirds of his crew and [the] eight marines who went before all offered to come again, so the service cannot be so very bad. The Admiralty have just issued orders for a large stock of canister-meat and lemon-juice, &c. &c. I have just returned from spending a long day with Captain Fitz-Roy, driving about in his gig, and shopping. This letter is too late for to-day's post. You may consider it settled that I go. Yet there is room for change if any untoward accident should happen; this I can see no reason to expect. I feel convinced nothing else will alter my wish of going. I have begun to order things. I have procured a case of good strong pistols and an excellent rifle for £50, there is a saving; a good telescope, with compass, £5, and these are nearly the only expensive instruments I shall want. Captain Fitz-Roy has everything. I never saw so (what I should call, he says not) extravagant a man, as regards himself, but as economical towards me. How he did order things! His fire-arms will cost £400 at least. I found the carpet bag when I arrived all right, and much obliged. I do not think I shall take any arsenic; shall send partridges to Mr. Yarrell; much obliged. Ask Edward to *bargain with* Clemson to make for my gun—*two spare* hammers or cocks, two main-springs, two sere-springs, four nipples or plugs—I mean one for each barrel, except nipples, of which there must be two for each, all of excellent quality, and set

about them immediately ; tell Edward to make inquiries
about prices. I go on Sunday per packet to Plymouth, shall
stay one or two days, then return, and hope to find a letter
from you ; a few days in London ; then Cambridge, Shrewsbury, London, Plymouth, Madeira, is my route. It is a great
bore my writing so much about the Coronation; I could fill
another sheet. I have just been with Captain King, Fitz-
Roy's senior officer last expedition ; he thinks that the expedition will suit me. Unasked, he said Fitz-Roy's temper
was perfect. He sends his own son with him as midshipman. The key of my microscope was forgotten ; it is of no
consequence. Love to all.

Chas. Darwin.

C. Darwin to W. D. Fox.

17 Spring Gardens (and here I shall remain till I start)
[September 19, 1831].

My dear Fox,

I returned from my expedition to see the *Beagle* at Plymouth on Saturday, and found your most welcome letter on
my table. It is quite ridiculous what a very long period
these last twenty days have appeared to me, certainly much
more than as many weeks on ordinary occasions ; this will
account for my not recollecting how much I told you of my
plans.

*   *   *   *   *

But on the whole it is a grand and fortunate opportunity;
there will be so many things to interest me—fine scenery and
an endless occupation and amusement in the different branches
of Natural History ; then again navigation and meteorology
will amuse me on the voyage, joined to the grand requisite of
there being a pleasant set of officers, and, as far as I can
judge, this is certain. On the other hand there is very considerable risk to one's life and health, and the leaving for so
very long a time so many people whom I dearly love, is oftentimes a feeling so painful that it requires all my resolution to
overcome it. But everything is now settled, and before the

13

20th of October I trust to be on the broad sea. My objection to the vessel is its smallness, which cramps one so for room for packing my own body and all my cases, &c., &c. As to its safety, I hope the Admiralty are the best judges; to a landsman's eye she looks very small. She is a ten-gun three-masted brig, but, I believe, an excellent vessel. So much for my future plans, and now for my present. I go to-night by the mail to Cambridge, and from thence, after settling my affairs, proceed to Shrewsbury (most likely on Friday 23rd, or perhaps before); there I shall stay a few days, and be in London by the 1st of October, and start for Plymouth on the 9th.

And now for the principal part of my letter. I do not know how to tell you how very kind I feel your offer of coming to see me before I leave England. Indeed I should like it very much; but I must tell you decidedly that I shall have very little time to spare, and that little time will be almost spoilt by my having so much to think about; and secondly, I can hardly think it worth your while to leave your parish for such a cause. But I shall never forget such generous kindness. Now I know you will act just as you think right; but do not come up for my sake. Any time is the same for me. I think from this letter you will know as much of my plans as I do myself, and will judge accordingly the where and when to write to me. Every now and then I have moments of glorious enthusiasm, when I think of the date and cocoa-trees, the palms and ferns so lofty and beautiful, everything new, everything sublime. And if I live to see years in after life, how grand must such recollections be! Do you know Humboldt? (if you don't, do so directly.) With what intense pleasure he appears always to look back on the days spent in the tropical countries. I hope when you next write to Osmaston, [you will] tell them my scheme, and give them my kindest regards and farewells.

Good-bye, my dear Fox,
Yours ever sincerely,
CHAS. DARWIN.

C. Darwin to R. Fitz-Roy.

17 Spring Gardens [October 17? 1831].

DEAR FITZ-ROY,

Very many thanks for your letter; it has made me most comfortable, for it would have been heart-breaking to have left anything quite behind, and I never should have thought of sending things by some other vessel. This letter will, I trust, accompany some talc. I read your letter without attending to the name. But I have now procured some from Jones, which appears very good, and I will send it this evening by the mail. You will be surprised at not seeing me *propriâ personâ* instead of my handwriting. But I had just found out that the large steam-packet did not intend to sail on Sunday, and I was picturing to myself a small, dirty cabin, with the proportion of 39-40ths of the passengers very sick, when Mr. Earl came in and told me the *Beagle* would not sail till the beginning of November. This, of course, settled the point; so that I remain in London one week more. I shall then send heavy goods by steamer and start myself by the coach on Sunday evening.

Have you a good set of mountain barometers? Several great guns in the scientific world have told me some points in geology to ascertain which entirely depend on their relative height. If you have not a good stock, I will add one more to the list. I ought to be ashamed to trouble you so much, but will you *send one line* to inform me? I am daily becoming more anxious to be off, and, if I am so, you must be in a perfect fever. What a glorious day the 4th of November will be to me! My second life will then commence, and it shall be as a birthday for the rest of my life.

Believe me, dear Fitz-Roy,
Yours most sincerely,
CHAS. DARWIN.

Monday.—I hope I have not put you to much inconvenience by ordering the room in readiness.

C. Darwin to J. S. Henslow.

Devonport, November 15, 1831.

MY DEAR HENSLOW,

The orders are come down from the Admiralty, and everything is finally settled. We positively sail the last day of this month, and I think before that time the vessel will be ready. She looks most beautiful, even a landsman must admire her. *We* all think her the most perfect vessel ever turned out of the Dockyard. One thing is certain, no vessel has been fitted out so expensively, and with so much care. Everything that can be made so is of mahogany, and nothing can exceed the neatness and beauty of all the accommodations. The instructions are very general, and leave a great deal to the Captain's discretion and judgment, paying a substantial as well as a verbal compliment to him.

* * * * *

No vessel ever left England with such a set of Chronometers, viz. twenty-four, all very good ones. In short, everything is well, and I have only now to pray for the sickness to moderate its fierceness, and I shall do very well. Yet I should not call it one of the very best opportunities for natural history that has ever occurred. The absolute want of room is an evil that nothing can surmount. I think L. Jenyns did very wisely in not coming, that is judging from my own feelings, for I am sure if I had left college some few years, or been those years older, I *never* could have endured it. 'The officers (excepting the Captain) are like the freshest freshmen, that is in their manners, in everything else widely different. Remember me most kindly to him, and tell him if ever he dreams in the night of palm-trees, he may in the morning comfort himself with the assurance that the voyage would not have suited him.

I am much obliged for your advice, *de Mathematicis*. I suspect when I am struggling with a triangle, I shall often wish myself in your room, and as for those wicked sulky surds, I do not know what I shall do without you to conjure them.

My time passes away very pleasantly. I know one or two pleasant people, foremost of whom is Mr. Thunder-and-lightning Harris,* whom I dare say you have heard of My chief employment is to go on board the *Beagle*, and try to look as much like a sailor as I can. I have no evidence of having taken in man, woman or child.

I am going to ask you to do one more commission, and I trust it will be the last. When I was in Cambridge, I wrote to Mr. Ash, asking him to send my College account to my father, after having subtracted about £30 for my furniture. This he has forgotten to do, and my father has paid the bill, and I want to have the furniture-money transmitted to my father. Perhaps you would be kind enough to speak to Mr. Ash. I have cost my father so much money, I am quite ashamed of myself.

I will write once again before sailing, and perhaps you will write to me before then.

Remember me to Professor Sedgwick and Mr. Peacock.

Believe me, yours affectionately,

CHAS. DARWIN.

C. Darwin to J. S. Henslow.

Devonport, December 3, 1831.

MY DEAR HENSLOW,

It is now late in the evening, and to-night I am going to sleep on board. On Monday we most certainly sail, so you may guess in what a desperate state of confusion we are all in. If you were to hear the various exclamations of the officers, you would suppose we had scarcely had a week's notice. I am just in the same way taken all *aback*, and in such a bustle I hardly know what to do. The number of things to be done is infinite. · I look forward even to sea-sickness with something like satisfaction, anything must be better than this state of anxiety. I am very much obliged for your

---

* William Snow Harris, the Electrician.

last kind and affectionate letter. I always like advice from you, and no one whom I have the luck to know is more capable of giving it than yourself. Recollect, when you write, that I am a sort of *protégé* of yours, and that it is your bounden duty to lecture me.

I will now give you my direction; it is at first, Rio; but if you will send me a letter on the first Tuesday (when the packet sails) in February, directed to Monte Video, it will give me very great pleasure ; I shall so much enjoy hearing a little Cambridge news. Poor dear old *Alma Mater !* I am a very worthy son in as far as affection goes. I have little more to write about . . . . I cannot end this without telling you how cordially I feel grateful for the kindness you have shown me during my Cambridge life. Much of the pleasure and utility which I may have derived from it is owing to you. I long for the time when we shall again meet, and till then believe me, my dear Henslow,

Your affectionate and obliged friend,

CH. DARWIN.

Remember me most kindly to those who take any interest in me.

CHAPTER VI.

THE VOYAGE.

"THERE is a natural good-humoured energy in his letters just
like himself.' —From a letter of Dr. R. W. Darwin's to Prof. Henslow.

[THE object of the *Beagle* voyage is briefly described in
my father's 'Journal of Researches,' p. 1, as being "to complete the Survey of Patagonia and Tierra del Fuego, commenced under Captain King in 1826 to 1830; to survey the
shores of Chile, Peru, and some island in the Pacific; and
to carry a chain of chronometrical measurements round the
world."

The *Beagle* is described as a well-built little vessel, of
235 tons, rigged as a barque, and carrying six guns. She
belonged to the old class of ten-gun brigs, which were nicknamed "coffins," from their liability to go down in severe
weather. They were very "deep-waisted," that is, their bul-
warks were high in proportion to their size, so that a heavy
sea breaking over them might be highly dangerous. Nevertheless, she lived through the five years' work, in the most
stormy regions in the world, under Commanders Stokes and
Fitz-Roy, without a serious accident. When re-commissioned
in 1831 for her second voyage, she was found (as I learn from
Admiral Sir James Sulivan) to be so rotten that she had
practically to be rebuilt, and it was this that caused the long
delay in refitting. The upper deck was raised, making her
much safer in heavy weather, and giving her far more com-

fortable accommodation below. By these alterations and by
the strong sheathing added to her bottom she was brought
up to 242 tons burthen.   It is a proof of the splendid seaman-
ship of Captain Fitz-Roy and his officers that she returned
without having carried away a spar, and that in only one
of the heavy storms that she encountered was she in great
danger.

She was fitted out for the expedition with all possible care,
being supplied with carefully chosen spars and ropes, six
boats, and a "dinghy;" lightning conductors, "invented by
Mr. Harris, were fixed in all the masts, the bowsprits, and even
in the flying jib-boom."   To quote my father's description,
written from Devonport, November 17, 1831 : "Everybody,
who can judge, says it is one of the grandest voyages that
has almost ever been sent out.   Everything is on a grand
scale.   Twenty-four chronometers.   The whole ship is fitted
up with mahogany ; she is the admiration of the whole place.
In short, everything is as prosperous as human means can
make it."

Owing to the smallness of the vessel, every one on board
was cramped for room, and my father's accommodation seems
to have been small enough : "I have just room to turn round,"
he writes to Henslow, "and that is all."   Admiral Sir James
Sulivan writes to me : "The narrow space at the end of the
chart-table was his only accommodation for working, dress-
ing, and sleeping; the hammock being left hanging over his
head by day, when the sea was at all rough, that he might lie
on it with a book in his hand when he could not any longer
sit at the table.   His only stowage for clothes being several
small drawers in the corner, reaching from deck to deck; the
top one being taken out when the hammock was hung up, without which there was not length for it, so then the foot-clews
took the place of the top drawer.   For specimens he had a
very small cabin under the forecastle."

Yet of this narrow room he wrote enthusiastically, September 17, 1831 :—"When I wrote last I was in great alarm
about my cabin.   The cabins were not then marked out, but

when I left they were, and mine is a capital one, certainly next best to the Captain's and remarkably light. My companion most luckily, I think, will turn out to be the officer whom I shall like best. Captain Fitz-Roy says he will take care that one corner is so fitted up that I shall be comfortable in it and shall consider it my home, but that also I shall have the run of his. My cabin is the drawing one; and in the middle is a large table, on which we two sleep in hammocks. But for the first two months there will be no drawing to be done, so that it will be quite a luxurious room, and good deal larger than the Captain's cabin."

My father used to say that it was the absolute necessity of tidiness in the cramped space of the *Beagle* that helped 'to give him his methodical habits of working.' On the *Beagle*, too, he would say, that he learned what he considered the golden rule for saving time; *i.e.*, taking care of the minutes.

Sir James Sulivan tells me that the chief fault in the outfit of the expedition was the want of a second smaller vessel to act as tender. This want was so much felt by Captain Fitz-Roy that he hired two decked boats to survey the coast of Patagonia, at a cost of £1100, a sum which he had to supply, although the boats saved several thousand pounds to the country. He afterwards bought a schooner to act as a tender, thus saving the country a further large amount. He was ultimately ordered to sell the schooner, and was compelled to bear the loss himself, and it was only after his death that some inadequate compensation was made for all the losses which he suffered through his zeal.

For want of a proper tender, much of the work had to be done in small open whale boats, which were sent away from the ship for weeks together, and this in a climate, where the crews were exposed to severe hardships from the almost constant rains, which sometimes continued for weeks together. The completeness of the equipment was also in other respects largely due to the public spirit of Captain Fitz-Roy. He provided at his own cost an artist, and a skilled instrument-maker to look after the chronometers.* Captain Fitz-Roy's wish was to take "some well-educated and scientific person" as his private guest, but this generous offer was only accepted by my father on condition of being allowed to pay a fair share of the expense of the Captain's table; he was, moreover, on the ship's books for victuals.

In a letter to his sister (July 1832) he writes contentedly of his manner of life at sea:—"I do not think I have ever given you an account of how the day passes. We breakfast at eight o'clock. The invariable maxim is to throw away all politeness—that is, never to wait for each other, and bolt off the minute one has done eating, &c. At sea, when the weather is calm, I work at marine animals, with which the whole ocean abounds. If there is any sea up I am either sick or contrive to read some voyage or travels. At one we dine. You shore-going people are lamentably mistaken about the manner of living on board. We have never yet (nor shall we) dined off salt meat. Rice and peas and *calavanses* are excellent vegetables, and, with good bread, who could want more? Judge Alderson could not be more temperate, as nothing but water comes on the table. At five we have tea. The midshipmen's berth have all their meals an hour before us, and the gun-room an hour afterwards."

The crew of the *Beagle* consisted of Captain Fitz-Roy, "Commander and Surveyor," two lieutenants, one of whom (the first lieutenant) was the late Captain Wickham, Governor of Queensland; the present Admiral Sir James Sulivan, K.C.B., was the second lieutenant. Besides the master and two mates, there was an assistant-surveyor, the present Admiral Lort Stokes. There were also a surgeon, assistant-surgeon, two midshipmen, master's mate, a volunteer (1st class), purser, carpenter, clerk, boatswain, eight marines, thirty-four seamen, and six boys.

There are not now (1882) many survivors of my father's old ship-mates. Admiral Mellersh, Mr. Hamond, and Mr. Philip

---

* Either one or both were on the books for victuals.

King, of the Legislative Council of Sydney, and Mr. Usborne, are among the number. Admiral Johnson died almost at the same time as my father.

He retained to the last a most pleasant recollection of the voyage of the *Beagle*, and of the friends he made on board her. To his children their names were familiar, from his many stories of the voyage, and we caught his feeling of friendship for many who were to us nothing more than names.

It is pleasant to know how affectionately his old companions remembered him.

Sir James Sulivan remained, throughout my father's lifetime, one of his best and truest friends. He writes:—" I can confidently express my belief that during the five years in the *Beagle*, he was never known to be out of temper, or to say one unkind or hasty word *of* or *to* any one. You will therefore readily understand how this, combined with the admiration of his energy and ability, led to our giving him the name of ' the dear old Philosopher.' " * Admiral Mellersh writes to me :—" Your father is as vividly in my mind's eye as if it was only a week ago that I was in the *Beagle* with him ; his genial smile and conversation can never be forgotten by any who saw them and heard them. I was sent on two or three occasions away in a boat with him on some of his scientific excursions, and always looked forward to these trips with great pleasure, an anticipation that, unlike many others, was always realised. I think he was the only man I ever knew against whom I never heard a word said ; and as people when shut up in a ship for five years are apt to get cross with each other, that is saying a good deal. Certainly we were always so hard at work, we had no time to quarrel, but if we had done so, I feel sure your father would have tried (and have been successful) to throw oil on the troubled waters."

---

* His other nickname was " The Flycatcher." I have heard my father tell how he overheard the boatswain of the *Beagle* showing another boatswain over the ship, and pointing out the officers : " That's our first lieutenant ; that's our doctor ; that's our flycatcher."

Admiral Stokes, Mr. King, Mr. Usborne, and Mr. Hamond, all speak of their friendship with him in the same warmhearted way.

Of the life on board and on shore his letters give some idea. Captain Fitz-Roy was a strict officer, and made himself thoroughly respected both by officers and men. The occasional severity of his manner was borne with because every one on board knew that his first thought was his duty, and that he would sacrifice anything to the real welfare of the ship. My father writes, July 1834, "We all jog on very well together, there is no quarrelling on board, which is something to say. The Captain keeps all smooth by rowing every one in turn." The best proof that Fitz-Roy was valued as a commander is given by the fact that many * of the crew had sailed with him in the *Beagle's* former voyage, and there were a few officers as well as seamen and marines, who had served in the *Adventure* or *Beagle* during the whole of that expedition.

My father speaks of the officers as a fine determined set of men, and especially of Wickham, the first lieutenant, as a "glorious fellow." The latter being responsible for the smartness and appearance of the ship strongly objected to his littering the decks, and spoke of specimens as "d—d. beastly devilment," and used to add, "If I were skipper, I would soon have you and all your d—d mess out of the place."

A sort of halo of sanctity was given to my father by the fact of his dining in the Captain's cabin, so that the midshipmen used at first to call him "Sir," a formality, however, which did not prevent his becoming fast friends with the younger officers. He wrote about the year 1861 or 1862 to Mr. P. G. King, M. L. C., Sydney, who, as before stated, was a midshipman on board the *Beagle* :—" The remembrance of old days, when we used to sit and talk on the booms of the *Beagle*, will always, to the day of my death, make me glad to

---

* 'Voyage of the *Adventure* and *Beagle*,' vol. ii. p. 21.

hear of your happiness and prosperity." Mr. King describes the pleasure my father seemed to take " in pointing out to me as a youngster the delights of the tropical nights, with their balmy breezes eddying out of the sails above us, and the sea lighted up by the passage of the ship through the never-ending streams of phosphorescent animalculæ."

It has been assumed that his ill-health in later years was due to his having suffered so much from sea-sickness. This he did not himself believe, but rather ascribed his bad health to the hereditary fault which came out as gout in some of the past generations. I am not quite clear as to how much he actually suffered from sea-sickness; my impression is distinct that, according to his own memory, he was not actually ill after the first three weeks, but constantly uncomfortable when the vessel pitched at all heavily. But, judging from his letters, and from the evidence of some of the officers, it would seem that in later years he forgot the extent of the discomfort from which he suffered. Writing June 3, 1836, from the Cape of Good Hope, he says : " It is a lucky thing for me that the voyage is drawing to its close, for I positively suffer more from sea-sickness now than three years ago." Admiral Lort Stokes wrote to the *Times*, April 25, 1883 :—

"May I beg a corner for my feeble testimony to the marvellous persevering endurance in the cause of science of that great naturalist, my old and lost friend, Mr. Charles Darwin, whose remains are so very justly to be honoured with a resting-place in Westminster Abbey?

"Perhaps no one can better testify to his early and most trying labours than myself. We worked together for several years at the same table in the poop cabin of the *Beagle* during her celebrated voyage, he with his microscope and myself at the charts. It was often a very lively end of the little craft, and distressingly so to my old friend, who suffered greatly from sea-sickness. After perhaps an hour's work he would say to me, ' Old fellow, I must take the horizontal for it,' that being the best relief position from ship motion ; a stretch

out on one side of the table for some time would enable
him to resume his labours for a while, when he had again
to lie down.

"It was distressing to witness this early sacrifice of Mr.
Darwin's health, who ever afterwards seriously felt the ill-
effects of the *Beagle's* voyage."

Mr. A. B. Usborne writes, "He was a dreadful sufferer
from sea-sickness, and at times, when I have been officer of
the watch, and reduced the sails, making the ship more easy,
and thus relieving him, I have been pronounced by him to be
'a good officer,' and he would resume his microscopic observations in the poop cabin."   The amount of work that he
got through on the *Beagle* shows that he was habitually in full
vigour ; he had, however, one severe illness, in South America, when he was received into the house of an Englishman,
Mr. Corfield, who tended him with careful kindness.   I have
heard him say that in this illness every secretion of the body
was affected, and that when he described the symptoms to his
father Dr. Darwin could make no guess as to the nature of
the disease.   My father was sometimes inclined to think that
the breaking up of his health was to some extent due to this
attack.

The *Beagle* letters give ample proof of his strong love of
home, and all connected with it, from his father down to
Nancy, his old nurse, to whom he sometimes sends his love.

His delight in home-letters is shown in such passages as :—
"But if you knew the glowing, unspeakable delight, which I
felt at being certain that my father and all of you were well,
only four months ago, you would not grudge the labour lost
in keeping up the regular series of letters."

Or again—his longing to return in words like these :—
"It is too delightful to think that I shall see the leaves fall
and hear the robin sing next autumn at Shrewsbury.   My
feelings are those of a schoolboy to the smallest point ; I
doubt whether ever boy longed for his holidays as much as
I do to see you all again.   I am at present, although nearly

half the world is between me and home, beginning to arrange what I shall do, where I shall go during the first week."

Another feature in his letters is the surprise and delight with which he hears of his collections and observations being of some use. It seems only to have gradually occurred to him that he would ever be more than a collector of specimens and facts, of which the great men were to make use. And even as to the value of his collections he seems to have had much doubt, for he wrote to Henslow in 1834:—"I really began to think that my collections were so poor that you were puzzled what to say; the case is now quite on the opposite tack, for you are guilty of exciting all my vain feelings to a most comfortable pitch; if hard work will atone for these thoughts, I vow it shall not be spared."

After his return and settlement in London, he began to realise the value of what he had done, and wrote to Captain Fitz-Roy—" However others may look back to the *Beagle's* voyage, now that the small disagreeable parts are well-nigh forgotten, I think it far the *most fortunate circumstance in my life* that the chance afforded by your offer of taking a Naturalist fell on me. I often have the most vivid and delightful pictures of what I saw on board the *Beagle* pass before my eyes. These recollections, and what I learnt on Natural History, I would not exchange for twice ten thousand a year."

In selecting the following series of letters, I have been guided by the wish to give as much personal detail as possible. I have given only a few scientific letters, to illustrate the way in which he worked, and how he regarded his own results. In his ' Journal of Researches ' he gives incidentally some idea of his personal character; the letters given in the present chapter serve to amplify in fresher and more spontaneous words that impression of his personality which the ' Journal ' has given to so many readers.]

C. Darwin to R. W. Darwin.

Bahia, or San Salvador, Brazils
[February 8, 1832].
I find after the first page I have been writing
to my sisters.

MY DEAR FATHER,

I am writing this on the 8th of February, one day's sail past St. Jago (Cape de Verd), and intend taking the chance of meeting with a homeward-bound vessel somewhere about the equator. The date, however, will tell this whenever the opportunity occurs. I will now begin from the day of leaving England, and give a short account of our progress. We sailed, as you know, on the 27th of December, and have been fortunate enough to have had from that time to the present a fair and moderate breeze. It afterwards proved that we had escaped a heavy gale in the Channel, another at Madeira, and another on [the] Coast of Africa. But in escaping the gale, we felt its consequences—a heavy sea. In the Bay of Biscay there was a long and continuous swell, and the misery I endured from sea-sickness is far beyond what I ever guessed at. I believe you are curious about it. I will give you all my dear-bought experience. Nobody who has only been to sea for twenty-four hours has a right to say that sea-sickness is even uncomfortable. The real misery only begins when you are so exhausted that a little exertion makes a feeling of faintness come on. I found nothing but lying in my hammock did me any good. I must especially except your receipt of raisins, which is the only food that the stomach will bear.

On the 4th of January we were not many miles from Madeira, but as there was a heavy sea running, and the island lay to windward, it was not thought worth while to beat up to it. It afterwards has turned out it was lucky we saved ourselves the trouble. I was much too sick even to get up to see the distant outline. On the 6th, in the evening, we sailed into the harbour of Santa Cruz. I now first felt even moderately well, and I was picturing to myself all the delights of fresh fruits growing in beautiful valleys, and reading Humboldt's descriptions of the island's glorious views, when perhaps you may nearly guess at our disappointment, when a small pale man informed us we must perform a strict quarantine of twelve days.   There was a death-like stillness in the ship till the Captain cried "up jib," and we left this long-wished for place.

We were becalmed for a day between Teneriffe and the Grand Canary, and here I first experienced any enjoyment. The view was glorious.   The Peak of Teneriffe was seen amongst the clouds like another world.   Our only drawback was the extreme wish of visiting this glorious island.   *Tell Eyton never to forget either the Canary Islands or South America;* that I am sure it will well repay the necessary trouble, but that he must make up his mind to find a good deal of the latter.   I feel certain he will regret it if he does not make the attempt.   From Teneriffe to St. Jago the voyage was extremely pleasant.   I had a net astern the vessel which caught great numbers of curious animals, and fully occupied my time in my cabin, and on deck the weather was so delightful and clear, that the sky and water together made a picture. On the 16th we arrived at Port Praya, the capital of the Cape de Verds, and there we remained twenty-three days, viz., till yesterday, the 7th of February.   The time has flown away most delightfully, indeed nothing can be pleasanter ; exceedingly busy, and that business both a duty and a great delight. I do not believe I have spent one half-hour idly since leaving Teneriffe.   St. Jago has afforded me an exceedingly rich harvest in several branches of Natural History.   I find the descriptions scarcely 'worth anything of many of the commoner animals that inhabit the Tropics.   I allude, of course, to those of the lower classes.

Geologising in a volcanic country is most delightful ; besides the interest attached to itself, it leads you into most beautiful and retired spots.   Nobody but a person fond of Natural History can imagine the pleasure of strolling under cocoa-nuts in a thicket of bananas and coffee-plants, and an

14

endless number of wild flowers. And this island, that has
given me so much instruction and delight, is reckoned the
most uninteresting place that we perhaps shall touch at dur-
ng our voyage. It certainly is generally very barren, but the
valleys are more exquisitely beautiful, from the very contrast.
It is utterly useless to say anything about the scenery ; it
would be as profitable to explain to a blind man colours, as to
a person who has not been out of Europe, the total dissimi-
larity of a tropical view. Whenever I enjoy anything, I always
either look forward to writing it down, either in my log-book
(which increases in bulk), or in a letter ; so you must excuse
raptures, and those raptures badly expressed. I find my collections are increasing wonderfully, and from Rio I think I
shall be obliged to send a cargo home.

All the endless delays which we experienced at Plymouth
have been most fortunate, as I verily believe no person ever
went out better provided for collecting and observing in the
different branches of Natural History. In a multitude of
counsellors I certainly found good. I find to my great surprise that a ship is singularly comfortable for all sorts of work.
Everything is so close at hand, and being cramped makes one
so methodical, that in the end I have been a gainer. I already
have got to look at going to sea as a regular quiet place, like
going back to home after staying away from it. In short, I
find a ship a very comfortable house, with everything you
want, and if it was not for sea-sickness the whole world would
be sailors. I do not think there is much danger of Erasmus
setting the example, but in case there should be, he may rely
upon it he does not know one-tenth of the sufferings of sea-
sickness.

I like the officers much more than I did at first, especially
Wickham, and young King and Stokes, and indeed all of
them. The Captain continues steadily very kind, and does
everything in his power to assist me. We see very little of
each other when in harbour, our pursuits lead us in such different tracks. I never in my life met with a man who could
endure nearly so great a share of fatigue. He works inces-

santly, and when apparently not employed, he is thinking. If
he does not kill himself, he will during this voyage do a wonderful quantity of work. I find I am very well, and stand
the little heat we have had as yet as well as anybody. We
shall soon have it in real earnest. We are now sailing for
Fernando Noronha, off the coast of Brazil, where we shall not
stay very long, and then examine the shoals between there
and Rio, touching perhaps at Bahia. I will finish this letter
when an opportunity of sending it occurs.

February 26th.—About 280 miles from Bahia. On the
10th we spoke the packet *Lyra*, on her voyage to Rio. I sent
a short letter by her, to be sent to England on [the] first
opportunity. We have been singularly unlucky in not meeting with any homeward-bound vessels, but I suppose [at]
Bahia we certainly shall be able to write to England. Since
writing the first part of [this] letter nothing has occurred
except crossing the Equator, and being shaved. This most
disagreeable operation consists in having your face rubbed
with paint and tar, which forms a lather for a saw which represents the razor, and then being half drowned in a sail filled with
salt water. About 50 miles north of the line we touched at
the rocks of St. Paul; this little speck (about ¼ of a mile
across) in the Atlantic has seldom been visited. It is totally
barren, but is covered by hosts of birds; they were so un-
used to men that we found we could kill plenty with stones
and sticks. After remaining some hours on the island, we
returned on board with the boat loaded with our prey. From
this we went to Fernando Noronha, a small island where the
[Brazilians] send their exiles. The landing there was attended
with so much difficulty owing [to] a heavy surf that the Captain determined to sail the next day after arriving. My one
day on shore was exceedingly interesting, the whole island is
one single wood so matted together by creepers that it is very
difficult to move out of the beaten path. I find the Natural
History of all these unfrequented spots most exceedingly
interesting, especially the geology. I have written this much
in order to save time at Bahia.

Decidedly the most striking thing in the Tropics is the
novelty of the vegetable forms. Cocoa-nuts could well be
imagined from drawings, if you add to them a graceful lightness which no European tree partakes of. Bananas and plan-
tains are exactly the same as those in hothouses, the acacias
or tamarinds are striking from the blueness of their foliage;
but of the glorious orange trees, no description, no drawings,
will give any just idea; instead of the sickly green of our
oranges, the native ones exceed the Portugal laurel in the
darkness of their tint, and infinitely exceed it in beauty of
form. Cocoa-nuts, papaws, the light green bananas, and
oranges, loaded with fruit, generally surround the more luxuriant villages. Whilst viewing such scenes, one feels the impossibility that any description should come near the mark,
much less be overdrawn.

March 1st.—Bahia, or San Salvador. I arrived at this
place on the 28th of February, and am now writing this letter
after having in real earnest strolled in the forests of the new
world. No person could imagine anything so beautiful as the
ancient town of Bahia, it is fairly embosomed in a luxuriant
wood of beautiful trees, and situated on a steep bank, and
overlooks the calm waters of the great bay of All Saints. The
houses are white and lofty, and, from the windows being
narrow and long, have a very light and elegant appearance.
Convents, porticos, and public buildings, vary the uniformity
of the houses; the bay is scattered over with large ships; in
short, and what can be said more, it is one of the finest views
in the Brazils. But the exquisite glorious pleasure of walking
amongst such flowers, and such trees, cannot be comprehended
but by those who have experienced it. Although in so low a
latitude the locality is not disagreeably hot, but at present it
is very damp, for it is the rainy season. I find the climate as
yet agrees admirably with me; it makes me long to live
quietly for some time in such a country. If you really want
to have [an idea] of tropical countries, study Humboldt.
Skip the scientific parts, and commence after leaving Teneriffe. My feelings amount to admiration the more I read him.

Tell Eyton (I find I am writing to my sisters!) how exceedingly I enjoy America, and that I am sure it will be a great
pity if he does not make a start.

This letter will go on the 5th, and I am afraid will be some
time before it reaches you ; it must be a warning how in other
parts of the world you may be a long time without hearing.
A year might by accident thus pass. About the 12th we
start for Rio, but we remain some time on the way in sounding the Albrolhos shoals. Tell Eyton as far as my experience
goes let him study Spanish, French, drawing, and Humboldt.
I do sincerely hope to hear of (if not to see him) in South
America. I look forward to the letters in Rio—till each one
is acknowledged, mention its date in the next.

We have beat all the ships in manœuvring, so much so
that the commanding officer says, we need not follow his
example; because we do everything better than his great
ship. I begin to take great interest in naval points, more
especially now, as I find they all say we are the No. 1 in South
America. I suppose the Captain is a most excellent officer.
It was quite glorious to-day how we beat the *Samarang* in
furling sails. It is quite a new thing for a " sounding ship " to
beat a regular man-of-war; and yet the *Beagle* is not at all a
particular ship. Erasmus will clearly perceive it when he
hears that in the night I have actually sat down in the sacred
precincts of the quarter deck. You must excuse these queer
letters, and recollect they are generally written in the evening
after my day's work. I take more pains over my log-book, so
that eventually you will have a good account of all the places
I visit. Hitherto the voyage has answered *admirably* to me,
and yet I am now more fully aware of your wisdom in throwing cold water on the whole scheme; the chances are so
numerous of turning out quite the reverse ; to such an extent
do I feel this, that if my advice was asked by any person on a
similar occasion, I should be very cautious in encouraging
him. I have not time to write to anybody else, so send to
Maer to let them know, that in the midst of the glorious
tropical scenery, I do not forget how instrumental they were

in placing me there. I will not rapturise again, but I give myself great credit in not being crazy out of pure delight.

Give my love to every soul at home, and to the Owens.

I think one's affections, like other good things, flourish and increase in these tropical regions.

The conviction that I am walking in the New World is even yet marvellous in my own eyes, and I dare say it is little less so to you, the receiving a letter from a son of yours in such a quarter.

Believe me, my dear Father,
Your most affectionate son,
CHARLES DARWIN.

C. Darwin to W. D. Fox.

Botofogo Bay, near Rio de Janeiro,
May, 1832.

MY DEAR FOX,

I have delayed writing to you and all my other friends till I arrived here and had some little spare time. My mind has been, since leaving England, in a perfect *hurricane* of delight and astonishment, and to this hour scarcely a minute has passed in idleness. . . .

At St. Jago my natural history and most delightful labours commenced. During the three weeks I collected a host of marine animals, and enjoyed many a good geological walk. Touching at some islands, we sailed to Bahia, and from thence to Rio, where I have already been some weeks. My collections go on admirably in almost every branch. As for insects, I trust I shall send a host of undescribed species to England. I believe they have no small ones in the collections, and here this morning I have taken minute Hydropori, Noterus, Colymbetes, Hydrophilus, Hydrobius, Gromius, &c., &c., as specimens of fresh-water beetles. I am entirely occupied with land animals, as the beach is only sand. Spiders and the adjoining tribes have perhaps given me, from their novelty, the most pleasure. I think I have already taken several new genera.

But Geology carries the day : it is like the pleasure of gambling. Speculating, on first arriving, what the rocks may be, I often mentally cry out 3 to 1 tertiary against primitive ; but the latter have hitherto won all the bets. So much for the grand end of my voyage ; in other respects things are equally flourishing. My life, when at sea, is so quiet, that to a person who can employ himself, nothing can be pleasanter ; the beauty of the sky and brilliancy of the ocean together make a picture. But when on shore, and wandering in the sublime forests, surrounded by views more gorgeous than even Claude ever imagined, I enjoy a delight which none but those who have experienced it can understand. If it is to be done, it must be by studying Humboldt. At our ancient snug breakfasts, at Cambridge, I little thought that the wide Atlantic would ever separate us; but it is a rare privilege that with the body, the feelings and memory are not divided. On the contrary, the pleasantest scenes in my life, many of which have been in Cambridge, rise from the contrast of the present, the more vividly in my imagination. Do you think any diamond beetle will ever give me so much pleasure as our old friend *crux major* ? . . . . It is one of my most constant amusements to draw pictures of the past ; and in them I often see you and poor little Fan. Oh, Lord, and then old Dash, poor thing ! Do you recollect how you all tormented me about his beautiful tail ?

. . . . Think when you are picking insects off a hawthorn-hedge on a fine May day (wretchedly cold, I have no doubt), think of me collecting amongst pine-apples and orange-trees ; whilst staining your fingers with dirty blackberries, think and be envious of ripe oranges. This is a proper piece of bravado, for I would walk through many a mile of sleet, snow, or rain to shake you by the hand. My dear old Fox, God bless you. Believe me,

Yours very affectionately,

CHAS. DARWIN.

C. Darwin to J. S. Henslow.

Rio de Janeiro, May 18, 1832.

MY DEAR HENSLOW,

*   *   *   *   *

Till arriving at Teneriffe (we did not touch at Madeira) I was scarcely out of my hammock, and really suffered more than you can well imagine from such a cause. At Santa Cruz, whilst looking amongst the clouds for the Peak, and repeating to myself Humboldt's sublime descriptions, it was announced we must perform twelve days' strict quarantine. We had made a short passage, so " Up jib," and away for St. Jago. You will say all this sounds very bad, and so it was ; but from that to the present time it has been nearly one scene of continual enjoyment. A net over the stern kept me at full work till we arrived at St. Jago. Here we spent three most delightful weeks. The geology was pre-eminently interesting, and I believe quite new; there are some facts on a large scale of upraised coast (which is an excellent epoch for all the volcanic rocks to date from), that would interest Mr. Lyell.

One great source of perplexity to me is an utter ignorance whether I note the right facts, and whether they are of sufficient importance to interest others. In the one thing collecting I cannot go wrong. St. Jago is singularly barren, and produces few plants or insects, so that my hammer was my usual companion, and in its company most delightful hours I spent. On the coast I collected many marine animals, chiefly gasteropodous (I think some new). I examined pretty accurately a *Caryopyllia*, and, if my eyes are not bewitched, former descriptions have not the slightest resemblance to the animal. I took several specimens of an Octopus which possessed a most marvellous power of changing its colours, equalling any chameleon, and evidently accommodating the changes to the colour of the ground which it passed over. Yellowish green, dark brown, and red, were the prevailing colours ; this fact appears to be new, as far as I can find out. Geology and the invertebrate animals will be my chief object of pursuit through the whole voyage.

We then sailed for Bahia, and touched at the rock of St. Paul. This is a serpentine formation. Is it not the only island in the Atlantic which is not volcanic? We likewise stayed a few hours at Fernando Noronha ; a tremendous surf was running so that a boat was swamped, and the Captain would not wait. I find my life on board when we are on blue water most delightful, so very comfortable and quiet—it is almost impossible to be idle, and that for me is saying a good deal. Nobody could possibly be better fitted in every respect for collecting than I am ; many cooks have not spoiled the broth this time. Mr. Brown's little hints about microscopes, &c., have been invaluable   I am well off in books, the ' Dictionnaire Classique' *is most useful.* If you should think of any thing or book that would be useful to me, if you would write one line, E. Darwin, Wyndham Club, St. James's Street, he will procure them, and send them with some other things to Monte Video, which for the next year will be my headquarters.

Touching at the Abrolhos, we arrived here on April 4th, when amongst others I received your most kind letter. You may rely on it during the evening I thought of the many most happy hours I have spent with you in Cambridge. I am now living at Botofogo, a village about a league from the city, and shall be able to remain a month longer. The *Beagle* has gone back to Bahia, and will pick me up on its return. There is a most important error in the longitude of South America, to settle which this second trip has been undertaken. Our chronometers, at least sixteen of them, are going superbly ; none on record have ever gone at all like them.

A few days after arriving I started on an expedition of 150 miles to Rio Macao, which lasted eighteen days. Here I first saw a tropical forest in all its sublime grandeur—nothing but the reality can give any idea how wonderful, how magnificent the scene is. If I was to specify any one thing I should give the pre-eminence to the host of parasitical plants. Your

engraving is exactly true, but underrates rather than exag-
gerates the luxuriance.   I never experienced such intense
delight.   I formerly admired Humboldt, I now almost adore
him ; he alone gives any notion of the feelings which are
raised in the mind on first entering the Tropics.   I am now
collecting fresh-water and land animals ; if what was told me
in London is true, viz., that there are no small insects in the
collections from the Tropics, I tell Entomologists to look out
and have their pens ready for describing.   I have taken as
minute (if not more so) as in England, Hydropori, Hygroti,
Hydrobii, Pselaphi, Staphylini, Curculio, &c. &c.   It is exceedingly interesting observing the difference of genera and
species from those which I know; it is however much less
than I had expected.   I am at present red-hot with spiders;
they are very interesting, and if I am not mistaken I have
already taken some new genera.   I shall have a large box to
send very soon to Cambridge, and with that I will mention
some more natural history particulars.

The Captain does everything in his power to assist me,
and we get on very well, but I thank my better fortune he has
not made me a renegade to Whig principles.   I would not be
a Tory, if it was merely on account of their cold hearts about
that scandal to Christian nations—Slavery.   I am very good
friends with all the officers.

I have just returned from a walk, and as a specimen, how
little the insects are known.   Noterus, according to the ' Dictionnaire Classique,' contains solely three European species.
I in one haul of my net took five distinct species ; is this not
quite extraordinary ? . . . .

Tell Professor Sedgwick he does not know how much I
am indebted to him for the Welsh Expedition ; it has given
me an interest in Geology which I would not give up for any
consideration.   I do not think I ever spent a more delightful
three weeks than pounding the North-west Mountains.   I
look forward to the geology about Monte Video as I hear
there are slates there, so I presume in that district I shall find
the junctions of the Pampas, and the enormous granite forma-

tion of Brazils.   At Bahia the pegmatite and gneiss in beds
had the same direction, as observed by Humboldt, prevailing
over Columbia, distant 1300 miles—is it not wonderful?
Monte Video will be for a long time my direction.   I hope
you will write again to me, there is nobody from whom I like
receiving advice so much as from you. . . . Excuse this
almost unintelligible letter, and believe me, my dear Henslow,
with the warmest feelings of respect and friendship,

Yours affectionately,

CHAS. DARWIN.

C. Darwin to J. M. Herbert.

Botofogo Bay, Rio de Janeiro,

June 1832.

MY DEAR OLD HERBERT,

Your letter arrived here when I had given up all hopes of
receiving another, it gave me, therefore, an additional degree
of pleasure.   At such an interval of time and space one does
learn to feel truly obliged to those who do not forget one.
The memory when recalling scenes past by, affords to us
exiles one of the greatest pleasures.   Often and often whilst
wandering amongst these hills do I think of Barmouth, and, I
may add, as often wish for such a companion.   What a contrast does a walk in these two places afford ; here abrupt and
stony peaks are to the very summit enclosed by luxuriant
woods ; the whole surface of the country, excepting where
cleared by man, is one impenetrable forest.   How different
from Wales, with its sloping hills covered with turf, and its
open valleys.   I was not previously aware how intimately
what may be called the moral part is connected with the
enjoyment of scenery.   I mean such ideas, as the history of
the country, the utility of the produce, and more especially
the happiness of the people living with them.   Change the
English labourer into a poor slave, working for another, and
you will hardly recognise the same view.   I am sure you will
be glad to hear how very well every part (Heaven forefend,

except sea-sickness) of the expedition has answered. We
have already seen Teneriffe and the Great Canary ; St. Jago
where I spent three most delightful weeks, revelling in the
delights of first naturalising a tropical volcanic island, and
besides other islands, the two celebrated ports in the Brazils,
viz. Bahia and Rio.

I was in my hammock till we arrived at the Canaries, and
I shall never forget the sublime impression the first view of
Teneriffe made on my mind.   The first arriving into warm
weather was most luxuriously pleasant ; the clear blue sky of
the Tropics was no common change after those accursed south-
west gales at Plymouth.   About the Line it became weltering
hot.   We spent one day at St. Paul's, a little group of rocks
about a quarter of a mile in circumference, peeping up in the
midst of the Atlantic.   There was such a scene here.   Wickham (1st Lieutenant) and I were the only two who landed
with guns and geological hammers, &c.   The birds by myriads
were too close to shoot ; we then tried stones, but at last, *proh
pudor !* my geological hammer was the instrument of death.
We soon loaded the boat with birds and eggs.   Whilst we
were so engaged, the men in the boat were fairly fighting
with the sharks for such magnificent fish as you could not see
in the London market.   Our boat would have made a fine
subject for Snyders, such a medley of game it contained.
We have been here ten weeks, and shall now start for Monte
Video, when I look forward to many a gallop over the Pampas.   I am ashamed of sending such a scrambling letter, but
if you were to see the heap of letters on my table you would
understand the reason. . . .

I am glad to hear music flourishes so well in Cambridge ;
but it [is] as barbarous to talk to me of "celestial concerts"
as to a person in Arabia of cold water.   In a voyage of this
sort, if one gains many new and great pleasures, on the other
side the loss is not inconsiderable.   How should you like to
be suddenly debarred from seeing every person and place,
which you have ever known and loved, for five years ?   I do
assure you I am occasionally "taken aback" by this reflec-

tion ; and then for man or ship it is not so easy to right again.
Remember me most sincerely to the remnant of most excellent fellows whom I have the good luck to know in Cambridge
—I mean Whitley and Watkins. Tell Lowe I am even beneath his contempt. I can eat salt beef and musty biscuits
for dinner. See what a fall man may come to !

My direction for the next year and a half will be Monte
Video.

God bless you, my very dear old Herbert. May you always be happy and prosperous is my most cordial wish.

Yours affectionately,
CHAS. DARWIN.

C. Darwin to F. Watkins.

Monte Video, River Plata,
August 18, 1832.

MY DEAR WATKINS,

I do not feel very sure you will think a letter from one so
far distant will be worth having ; I write therefore on the
selfish principle of getting an answer. In the different countries we visit the entire newness and difference from England
only serves to make more keen the recollection of its scenes
and delights. In consequence the pleasure of thinking of,
and hearing from one's former friends, does indeed become
great. Recollect this, and some long winter's evening sit
down and send me a long account of yourself and our friends ;
both what you have, and what [you] intend doing ; otherwise
in three or four more years when I return you will be all
strangers to me. Considering how many months have passed,
we have not in the *Beagle* made much way round the world.
Hitherto everything has well repaid the necessary trouble and
loss of comfort. We stayed three weeks at the Cape de Verds ;
it was no ordinary pleasure rambling over the plains of lava
under a tropical sun, but when I first entered on and beheld
the luxuriant vegetation in Brazil, it was realizing the visions
in the 'Arabian Nights.' The brilliancy of the scenery

throws one into a delirium of delight, and a beetle hunter is
not likely soon to awaken from it, when whichever way he
turns fresh treasures meet his eye.   At Rio de Janeiro three
months passed away like so many weeks.   I made a most delightful excursion during this time of 150 miles into the country.   I stayed at an estate which is the last of the cleared
ground, behind is one vast impenetrable forest.   It is almost
impossible to imagine the quietude of such a life.   Not a
human being within some miles interrupts the solitude.   To
seat oneself amidst the gloom of such a forest on a decaying
trunk, and then think of home, is a pleasure worth taking
some trouble for.

We are at present in a much less interesting country.
One single walk over the undulatory turf plain shows everything which is to be seen.   It is not at all unlike Cambridgeshire, only that every hedge, tree and hill must be levelled,
and arable land turned into pasture.   All South America is
in such an unsettled state that we have not entered one port
without some sort of disturbance.   At Buenos Ayres a shot
came whistling over our heads ; it is a noise I had never
before heard, but I found I had an instinctive knowledge of
what it meant.   The other day we landed our men here, and
took possession, at the request of the inhabitants, of the central fort.   We philosophers do not bargain for this sort of
work, and I hope there will be no more.   We sail in the
course of a day or two to survey the coast of Patagonia ; as
it is entirely unknown, I expect a good deal of interest.   But
already do I perceive the grievous difference between sailing
on these seas and the Equinoctial ocean.   In the "Ladies'
Gulf," as the Spaniard's call it, it is so luxurious to sit on
deck and enjoy the coolness of the night, and admire the new
constellations of the South. . . . I wonder when we shall ever
meet again ; but be it when it may, few things will give me
greater pleasure than to see you again, and talk over the long
time we have passed together.

If you were to meet me at present I certainly should be
looked at like a wild beast, a great grizzly beard and flushing

jacket would disfigure an angel.   Believe me, my dear Watkins, with the warmest feelings of friendship,

                                        Ever yours,
                                     CHARLES DARWIN.

                C. Darwin to J. S. Henslow.

                                        April 11, 1833.

MY DEAR HENSLOW,

   We are now running up from the Falkland Islands to the
Rio Negro (or Colorado).   The *Beagle* will proceed to Monte
Video; but if it can be managed I intend staying at the
former place.   It is now some months since we have been at
a civilised port; nearly all this time has been spent in the
most southern part of Tierra del Fuego.   It is a detestable
place; gales succeed gales with such short intervals that it is
difficult to do anything.   We were twenty-three days off
Cape Horn, and could by no means get to the westward.
The last and final gale before we gave up the attempt was
unusually severe.   A sea stove one of the boats, and there
was so much water on the decks that every place was afloat;
nearly all the paper for drying plants is spoiled, and half of
this curious collection.

   We at last ran into harbour, and in the boats got to the
west by the inland channels.   As I was one of this party I
was very glad of it.   With two boats we went about 300
miles, and thus I had an excellent opportunity of geologising
and seeing much of the savages.   The Fuegians are in a more
miserable state of barbarism than I had expected ever to
have seen a human being.   In this inclement country they
are absolutely naked, and their temporary houses are like
what children make in summer with boughs of trees.   I do
not think any spectacle can be more interesting than the first
sight of man in his primitive wildness.   It is an interest
which cannot well be imagined until it is experienced.   I
shall never forget this when entering Good Success Bay—

the yell with which a party received us. They were seated
on a rocky point, surrounded by the dark forest of beech; as
they threw their arms wildly round their heads, and their long
hair streaming, they seemed the troubled spirits of another
world. The climate in some respects is a curious mixture
of severity and mildness; as far as regards the animal kingdom, the former character prevails; I have in consequence
not added much to my collections.

The Geology of this part of Tierra del Fuego was, as indeed every place is, to me very interesting. The country is
non-fossiliferous, and a common-place succession of gran-
itic rocks and slates; attempting to make out the relation
of cleavage, strata, &c., &c., was my chief amusement. The
mineralogy, however, of some of the rocks will, I think,
be curious from their resemblance to those of volcanic
origin.

* * * * *

After leaving Tierra del Fuego we sailed to the Falklands.
I forgot to mention the fate of the Fuegians whom we took
back to their country. They had become entirely European
in their habits and wishes, so much so that the younger one
had forgotten his own language, and their countrymen paid
but very little attention to them. We built houses for them
and planted gardens, but by the time we return again on our
passage round the Horn, I think it will be very doubtful how
much of their property will be left unstolen.

. . . When I am sea-sick and miserable, it is one of my
highest consolations to picture the future when we again shall
be pacing together the roads round Cambridge. That day
is a weary long way off. We have another cruise to make to
Tierra del Fuego next summer, and then our voyage round
the world will really commence. Captain Fitz-Roy has purchased a large schooner of 170 tons. In many respects it
will be a great advantage having a consort—perhaps it may
somewhat shorten our cruise, which I most cordially hope it
may. I trust, however, that the Coral Reefs and various animals of the Pacific may keep up my resolution. Remember

me most kindly to Mrs. Henslow and all other friends; I am
a true lover of Alma Mater and all its inhabitants.

　　Believe me, my dear Henslow,

　　　　Your affectionate and most obliged friend,

　　　　　　　　　　　CHARLES DARWIN.

C. Darwin to Miss C. Darwin.

Maldonado, Rio Plata, May 22, 1833.

　. . . The following business piece is to my father. Having a servant of my own would be a really great addition to
my comfort. For these two reasons : as at present the Captain has appointed one of the men always to be with me, but
I do not think it just thus to take a seaman out of the ship ;
and, secondly, when at sea I am rather badly off for any one
to wait on me. The man is willing to be my servant,
and all the expenses would be under £60 per annum. I
have taught him to shoot and skin birds, so that in my main
object he is very useful. I have now left England nearly a
year and a half, and I find my expenses are not above £200
per annum ; so that, it being hopeless (from time) to write
for permission, I have come to the conclusion that you would
allow me this expense. But I have not yet resolved to ask
the Captain, and the chances are even that he would not be
willing to have an additional man in the ship. I have mentioned this because for a long time I have been thinking
about it.

　June.—I have just received a bundle more letters. I do
not know how to thank you all sufficiently. One from Catherine, Feb. 8th, another from Susan, March 3rd, together with
notes from Caroline and from my father ; give my best love
to my father. I almost cried for pleasure at receiving it ; it
was very kind thinking of writing to me. My letters are both
few, short, and stupid in return for all yours ; but I always
ease my conscience by considering the Journal as a long letter. If I can manage it, I will, before doubling the Horn,
send the rest. I am quite delighted to find the hide of the

15

Megatherium has given you all some little interest in my
employments. These fragments are not, however, by any
means the most valuable of the geological relics. I trust
and believe that the time spent in this voyage, if thrown away
for all other respects, will produce its full worth in Natural
History; and it appears to me the doing what *little* we can
to increase the general stock of knowledge is as respectable
an object of life as one can in any likelihood pursue. It is
more the result of such reflections (as I have already said)
than much immediate pleasure which now makes me continue the voyage, together with the glorious prospect of the
future, when passing the Straits of Magellan, we have in
truth the world before us. Think of the Andes, the luxuriant
forest of Guayaquil, the islands of the South Sea, and New
South Wales. How many magnificent and characteristic
views, how many and curious tribes of men we shall see!
What fine opportunities for geology and for studying the infinite host of living beings! Is not this a prospect to keep
up the most flagging spirit? If I was to throw it away, I
don't think I should ever rest quiet in my grave. I certainly
should be a ghost and haunt the British Museum.

How famously the Ministers appear to be going on. I
always much enjoy political gossip and what you at home
think will, &c., &c., take place. I steadily read up the weekly
paper, but it is not sufficient to guide one's opinion; and I
find it a very painful state not to be as obstinate as a pig in
politics. I have watched how steadily the general feeling,
as shown at elections, has been rising against Slavery. What
a proud thing for England if she is the first European nation
which utterly abolishes it! I was told before leaving England
that after living in slave countries all my opinions would be
altered; the only alteration I am aware of is forming a much
higher estimate of the negro character. It is impossible to
see a negro and not feel kindly towards him; such cheerful,
open, honest expressions and such fine muscular bodies. I
never saw any of the diminutive Portuguese, with their mur-
derous countenances, without almost wishing for Brazil to

follow the example of Hayti; and, considering the enormous healthy-looking black population, it will be wonderful if, at some future day, it does not take place. There is at Rio a man (I know not his title) who has a large salary to prevent (I believe) the landing of slaves; he lives at Botofogo, and yet that was the bay where, during my residence, the greater number of smuggled slaves were landed. Some of the Anti-Slavery people ought to question about his office; it was the subject of conversation at Rio amongst the lower English. . . .

C. Darwin to J. M. Herbert.

Maldonado, Rio Plata, June 2, 1833.

MY DEAR HERBERT,

I have been confined for the last three days to a miserable dark room, in an old Spanish house, from the torrents of rain: I am not, therefore, in very good trim for writing; but, defying the blue devils, I will send you a few lines, if it is merely to thank you very sincerely for writing to me. I received your letter, dated December 1st, a short time since. We are now passing part of the winter in the Rio Plata, after having had a hard summer's work to the south. Tierra del Fuego is indeed a miserable place; the ceaseless fury of the gales is quite tremendous. One evening we saw old Cape Horn, and three weeks afterwards we were only thirty miles to windward of it. It is a grand spectacle to see all nature thus raging; but Heaven knows every one in the *Beagle* has seen enough in this one summer to last them their natural lives.

The first place we landed at was Good Success Bay. It was here Banks and Solander met such disasters on ascending one of the mountains. The weather was tolerably fine, and I enjoyed some walks in a wild country, like that behind Barmouth. The valleys are impenetrable from the entangled woods, but the higher parts, near the limits of perpetual snow, are bare. From some of these hills the scenery, from its savage, solitary character, was most sublime. The only inhabitant of these heights is the guanaco, and with its shrill neighing it often breaks the stillness. The consciousness that no European foot had ever trod much of this ground added to the delight of these rambles. How often and how vividly have many of the hours spent at Barmouth come before my mind ! I look back to that time with no common pleasure : at this moment I can see you seated on the hill behind the inn, almost as plainly as if you were really there. It is necessary to be separated from all which one has been accustomed to, to know how properly to treasure up such recollections, and at this distance, I may add, how properly to esteem such as yourself, my dear old Herbert. I wonder when I shall ever see you again. I hope it may be, as you say, surrounded with heaps of parchment ; but then there must be, sooner or later, a dear little lady to take care of you and your house. Such a delightful vision makes me quite envious. This is a curious life for a regular shore-going person such as myself; the worst part of it is its extreme length. There is certainly a great deal of high enjoyment, and on the contrary a tolerable share of vexation of spirit. Everything, however, shall bend to the pleasure of grubbing up old bones, and captivating new animals. By the way, you rank my Natural History labours far too high. I am nothing more than a lions' provider : I do not feel at all sure that they will not growl and finally destroy me.

It does one's heart good to hear how things are going on in England. Hurrah for the honest Whigs ! I trust they will soon attack that monstrous stain on our boasted liberty, Colonial Slavery. I have seen enough of Slavery and the dispositions of the negroes, to be thoroughly disgusted with the lies and nonsense one hears on the subject in England. Thank God, the cold-hearted Tories, who, as J. Mackintosh used to say, have no enthusiasm, except against enthusiasm, have for the present run their race. I am sorry, by your letter, to hear you have not been well, and that you partly attribute it to want of exercise. I wish you were here amongst the green plains ; we would take walks which would rival the Dolgelly ones, and you should tell stories, which I would be-

lieve, even to a *cubic fathom of pudding*. Instead I must take
my solitary ramble, think of Cambridge days, and pick up
snakes, beetles and toads. Excuse this short letter (you
know I never studied 'The Complete Letter-writer'), and believe me, my dear Herbert,

Your affectionate friend,
CHARLES DARWIN.

C. Darwin to J. S. Henslow.

East Falkland Island, March, 1834.

. . . . . I am quite charmed with Geology, but like the
wise animal between two bundles of hay, I do not know which
to like the best; the old crystalline group of rocks, or the
softer and fossiliferous beds. When puzzling about stratifi-
cations, &c., I feel inclined to cry "a fig for your big oysters,
and your bigger megatheriums." But then when digging out
some fine bones, I wonder how any man can tire his arms
with hammering granite. By the way I have not one clear
idea about cleavage, stratification, lines of upheaval. I have
no books which tell me much, and what they do I cannot
apply to what I see. In consequence I draw my own conclusions, and most gloriously ridiculous ones they are, I sometimes fancy. . . . Can you throw any light into my mind by
telling me what relation cleavage and planes of deposition
bear to each other?

And now for my second *section*, Zoology. I have chiefly
been employed in preparing myself for the South Sea by
examining the polypi of the smaller Corallines in these lati-
tudes. Many in themselves are very curious, and I think are
quite undescribed; there was one appalling one, allied to a
Flustra, which I dare say I mentioned having found to the
northward, where the cells have a movable organ (like a vult-
ure's head, with a dilatable beak), fixed on the edge. But
what is of more general interest is the unquestionable (as it
appears to me) existence of another species of ostrich, besides
the *Struthio rhea*. All the Gauchos and Indians state it is
the case, and I place the greatest faith in their observations.

I have the head, neck, piece of skin, feathers, and legs of one. The differences are chiefly in the colour of the feathers and scales on legs, being feathered below the knees, nidification, and geographical distribution. So much for what I have lately done ; the prospect before me is full of sunshine, fine weather, glorious scenery, the geology of the Andes, plains abounding with organic remains (which perhaps I may have the good luck to catch in the very act of moving), and lastly, an ocean, its shores abounding with life, so that, if nothing unforeseen happens, I will stick to the voyage, although for what I can see this may last till we return a fine set of white-headed old gentlemen. I have to thank you most cordially for sending me the books. I am now reading the Oxford ' Report ; ' * the whole account of your proceedings is most glorious ; you remaining in England cannot well imagine how excessively interesting I find the reports. I am sure from my own thrilling sensations when reading them, that they cannot fail to have an excellent effect upon all those residing in distant colonies, and who have little opportunity of seeing the periodicals. My hammer has flown with redoubled force on the devoted blocks ; as I thought over the eloquence of the Cambridge President, I hit harder and harder blows. I hope to give my arms strength for the Cordilleras. You will send me through Capt. Beaufort a copy of the Cambridge ' Report.'

I have forgotten to mention that for some time past, and for the future, I will put a pencil cross on the pill-boxes containing insects, as these alone will require being kept particularly dry ; it may perhaps save you some trouble. When this letter will go I do not know, as this little seat of discord has lately been embroiled by a dreadful scene of murder, and at present there are more prisoners than inhabitants. If a merchant vessel is chartered to take them to Rio, I will send some specimens (especially my few plants and seeds). Re-

---

* The second meeting of the British Association was held at Oxford in 1832, the following year it was at Cambridge.

member me to all my Cambridge friends. I love and treasure up every recollection of dear old Cambridge. I am much obliged to you for putting my name down to poor Ramsay's monument; I never think of him without the warmest admiration. Farewell, my dear Henslow.

Believe me your most obliged and affectionate friend,

CHARLES DARWIN.

C. Darwin to Miss C. Darwin.

East Falkland Island, April 6, 1834.

MY DEAR CATHERINE,

When this letter will reach you I know not, but probably some man-of-war will call here before, in the common course of events, I should have another opportunity of writing.

* * * * *

After visiting some of the southern islands, we beat up through the magnificent scenery of the Beagle Channel to Jemmy Button's * country. We could hardly recognise poor Jemmy. Instead of the clean, well-dressed stout lad we left him, we found him a naked, thin, squalid savage. York and Fuegia had moved to their own country some months ago, the former having stolen all Jemmy's clothes. Now he had nothing except a bit of blanket round his waist. Poor Jemmy was very glad to see us, and, with his usual good feeling, brought several presents (otter-skins, which are most valuable to themselves) for his old friends. The Captain offered to take him to England, but this, to our surprise, he at once refused. In the evening his young wife came alongside and showed us the reason. He was quite contented. Last year, in the height of his indignation, he said "his country people no *sabe* nothing—damned fools "—now they were very good people, with *too* much to eat, and all the luxuries of life. Jemmy and his wife paddled away in their

---

* Jemmy Button, York Minster, and Fuegia Basket, were natives of Tierra del Fuego, brought to England by Captain Fitz-Roy in his former voyage, and restored to their country by him in 1832.

canoe loaded with presents, and very happy. The most curious thing is, that Jemmy, instead of recovering his own language, has taught all his friends a little English. "J. Button's canoe" and "Jemmy's wife come," "Give me knife," &c., was said by several of them.

We then bore away for this island—this little miserable seat of discord. We found that the Gauchos, under pretence of a revolution, had murdered and plundered all the Englishmen whom they could catch, and some of their own countrymen. All the economy at home makes the foreign movements of England most contemptible. How different from old Spain. Here we, dog-in-the-manger fashion, seize an island, and leave to protect it a Union Jack ; the possessor has, of course, been murdered ; we now send a lieutenant with four sailors, without authority or instructions. A man-of-war, however, ventured to leave a party of marines, and by their assistance, and the treachery of some of the party, the murderers have all been taken, there being now as many prisoners as inhabitants. This island must some day become a very important halting-place in the most turbulent sea in the world. It is mid-way between Australia and the South Sea to England ; between Chili, Peru, &c., and the Rio Plata and the Rio de Janeiro. There are fine harbours, plenty of fresh water, and good beef. It would doubtless produce the coarser vegetables. In other respects it is a wretched place. A little time since, I rode across the island, and returned in four days. My excursion would have been longer, but during the whole time it blew a gale of wind, with hail and snow. There is no firewood bigger than heath, and the whole country is, more or less, an elastic peat-bog. Sleeping out at night was too miserable work to endure it for all the rocks in South America.

We shall leave this scene of iniquity in two or three days, and go to the Rio de la Sta. Cruz. One of the objects is to look at the ship's bottom. We struck rather heavily on an unknown rock off Port Desire, and some of her copper is torn off. After this is repaired the Captain has a glorious scheme ;

it is to go to the very head of this river, that is probably to the
Andes. It is quite unknown; the Indians tell us it is two
or three hundred yards broad, and horses can nowhere ford it.
I cannot imagine anything more interesting. Our plans then
are to go to Fort Famine, and there we meet the *Adventure*,
who is employed in making the Chart of the Falklands. This
will be in the middle of winter, so I shall see Tierra del Fuego
in her white drapery. We leave the straits to enter the
Pacific by the Barbara Channel, one very little known, and
which passes close to the foot of Mount Sarmiento (the highest mountain in the south, excepting Mt. ! ! Darwin! !). We
then shall scud away for Concepcion in Chili. I believe the
ship must once again steer southward, but if any one catches
me there again, I will give him leave to hang me up as a
scarecrow for all future naturalists. I long to be at work in
the Cordilleras, the geology of this side, which I understand
pretty well is so intimately connected with periods of violence
in that great chain of mountains. The future is, indeed, to
me a brilliant prospect. You say its very brilliancy frightens
you; but really I am very careful; I may mention as a proof,
in all my rambles I have never had any one accident or
scrape. . . . Continue in your good custom of writing plenty
of gossip; I much like hearing all about all things. Remember me most kindly to Uncle Jos, and to all the Wedgwoods.
Tell Charlotte (their married names sound downright unnatural) I should like to have written to her, to have told her
how well everything is going on; but it would only have been
a transcript of this letter, and I have a host of animals at this
minute surrounding me which all require embalming and
numbering. I have not forgotten the comfort I received that
day at Maer, when my mind was like a swinging pendulum.
Give my best love to my father. I hope he will forgive all
my extravagance, but not as a Christian, for then I suppose
he would send me no more money.

Good-bye, dear, to you, and all your goodly sisterhood.

Your affectionate brother,

CHAS. DARWIN.

My love to Nancy; * tell her, if she was now to see me with my great beard, she would think I was some worthy Solomon, come to sell the trinkets.

C. Darwin to C. Whitley.

Valparaiso, July 23, 1834.

MY DEAR WHITLEY,

I have long intended writing, just to put you in mind that there is a certain hunter of beetles, and pounder of rocks still in existence. Why I have not done so before I know not, but it will serve me right if you have quite forgotten me. It is a very long time since I have heard any Cambridge news; I neither know where you are living or what you are doing. I saw your name down as one of the indefatigable guardians of the eighteen hundred philosophers. I was delighted to see this, for when we last left Cambridge you were at sad variance with poor science; you seemed to think her a public prostitute working for popularity. If your opinions are the same as formerly, you would agree most admirably with Captain Fitz-Roy,—the object of his most devout abhorrence is one of the d—d scientific Whigs. As captains of men-of-war are the greatest men going, far greater than kings or schoolmasters, I am obliged to tell him everything in my own favour. I have often said I once had a very good friend, an out-and-out Tory, and we managed to get on very well together. But he is very much inclined to doubt if ever I really was so much honoured; at present we hear scarcely anything about politics; this saves a great deal of trouble, for we all stick to our former opinions rather more obstinately than before, and can give rather fewer reasons for doing so.

I do hope you will write to me: ('H. M. S. *Beagle*, S. American Station' will find me). I should much like to hear in what state you are both in body and mind. ¿ *Quién Sabe?* as the people say here (and God knows they well may, for

---

* His old nurse.

they do know little enough), if you are not a married man,
and may be nursing, as Miss Austen says, little olive branches,
little pledges of mutual affection.   Eheu!. Eheu! this puts
me in mind of former visions of glimpses into futurity, where
I fancied I saw retirement, green cottages, and white petticoats.   What will become of me hereafter I know not; I feel
like a ruined man, who does not see or care how to extricate
himself.   That this voyage must come to a conclusion my
reason tells me, but otherwise I see no end to it.   It is impossible not bitterly to regret the friends and other sources of
pleasure one leaves behind in England; in place of it there
is much solid enjoyment, some present, but more in anticipation, when the ideas gained during the voyage can be compared to fresh ones.   I find in Geology a never-failing interest,
as it has been remarked, it creates the same grand ideas respecting this world which Astronomy does for the universe.
We have seen much fine scenery; that of the Tropics in its
glory and luxuriance exceeds even the language of Humboldt
to describe.   A Persian writer could alone do justice to it,
and if he succeeded he would in England be called the 'Grandfather of all liars.'"

But I have seen nothing which more completely astonished me than the first sight of a savage.   It was a naked
Fuegian, his long hair blowing about, his face besmeared
with paint.   There is in their countenances an expression
which I believe, to those who have not seen it, must be in-
conceivably wild.   Standing on a rock he uttered tones and
made gesticulations, than which the cries of domestic animals
are far more intelligible.

When I return to England, you must take me in hand
with respect to the fine arts.   I yet recollect there was a
man called Raffaelle Sanctus.   How delightful it will be
once again to see, in the Fitzwilliam, Titian's Venus.   How
much more than delightful to go to some good concert or
fine opera.   These recollections will not do.   I shall not be
able to-morrow to pick out the entrails of some small animal
with half my usual gusto.   Pray tell me some news about

Cameron, Watkins, Marindin the two Thompsons of Trinity, Lowe, Heaviside, Matthew. Herbert I have heard from. How is Henslow getting on? and all other good friends of dear Cambridge? Often and often do I think over those past hours, so many of which have been passed in your company. Such can never return, but their recollection can never die away.

God bless you, my dear Whitley,

Believe me, your most sincere friend,

CHAS. DARWIN.

C. Darwin to Miss C. Darwin.

Valparaiso, November 8, 1834.

MY DEAR CATHERINE,

My last letter was rather a gloomy one, for I was not very well when I wrote it. Now everything is as bright as sunshine. I am quite well again after being a second time in bed for a fortnight. Captain Fitz-Roy very generously has delayed the ship ten days on my account, and without at the time telling me for what reason.

We have had some strange proceedings on board the *Beagle*, but which have ended most capitally for all hands. Captain Fitz-Roy has for the last two months been working *extremely* hard, and at the same time constantly annoyed by interruptions from officers of other ships; the selling the schooner and its consequences were very vexatious; the cold manner the Admiralty (solely I believe because he is a Tory) have treated him, and a thousand other, &c. &c.'s, has made him very thin and unwell. This was accompanied by a morbid depression of spirits, and a loss of all decision and resolution. . . . All that Bynoe [the Surgeon] could say, that it was merely the effect of bodily health and exhaustion after such application, would not do; he invalided, and Wickham was appointed to the command. By the instructions Wickham could only finish the survey of the southern part, and would then have been obliged to return direct to England. The grief on board the *Beagle* about the Captain's decision was universal and deeply felt ; one great source of his annoyment was the feeling it impossible to fulfil the whole instructions; from his state of mind it never occurred to him that the very instructions ordered him to do as much of the West coast *as he has time for*, and then proceed across the Pacific.

Wickham (very disinterestedly giving up his own promotion) urged this most strongly, stated that when he took the command nothing should induce him to go to Tierra del Fuego again ; and then asked the Captain what would be gained by his resignation? why not do the more useful part, and return as commanded by the Pacific. The Captain at last, to every one's joy, consented, and the resignation was withdrawn.

Hurrah ! hurrah ! it is fixed the *Beagle* shall not go one mile south of Cape Tres Montes (about 200 miles south of Chiloe), and from that point to Valparaiso will be finished in about five months. We shall examine the Chonos Archipelago, entirely unknown, and the curious inland sea behind Chiloe. For me it is glorious. Cape Tres Montes is the most southern point where there is much geological interest, as there the modern beds end. The Captain then talks of crossing the Pacific; but I think we shall persuade him to finish the Coast of Peru, where the climate is delightful, the country hideously sterile, but abounding with the highest interest to a geologist. For the first time since leaving England I now see a clear and not so distant prospect of returning to you all : crossing the Pacific, and from Sydney home, will not take much time.

As soon as the Captain invalided I at once determined to leave the *Beagle*, but it was quite absurd what a revolution in five minutes was effected in all my feelings. I have long been grieved and most sorry at the interminable length of the voyage (although I never would have quitted it) ; but the minute it was all over, I could not make up my mind to return. I could not give up all the geological castles in the air which

I had been building up for the last two years. One whole night I tried to think over the pleasure of seeing Shrewsbury again, but the barren plains of Peru gained the day. I made the following scheme (I know you will abuse me, and perhaps if I had put it in execution, my father would have sent a mandamus after me); it was to examine the Cordilleras of Chili during this summer, and in winter go from port to port on the coast of Peru to Lima, returning this time next year to Valparaiso, cross the Cordilleras to Buenos Ayres, and take ship to England. Would not this have been a fine excursion, and in sixteen months I should have been with you all? To have endured Tierra del Fuego and not seen the Pacific would have been miserable. . . .

I go on board to-morrow; I have been for the last six weeks in Corfield's house. You cannot imagine what a kind friend I have found him. He is universally liked, and re-spected by the natives and foreigners. Several Chileno Sig-noritas are very obligingly anxious to become the signoras of this house. Tell my father I have kept my promise of being extravagant in Chili. I have drawn a bill of £100 (had it not better be notified to Messrs. Robarts & Co.); £50 goes to the Captain for the ensuing year, and £30 I take to sea for the small ports; so that *bonâ fide* I have not spent £180 during these last four months. I hope not to draw another bill for six months. All the foregoing particulars were only settled yesterday. It has done me more good than a pint of medi-cine, and I have not been so happy for the last year. If it had not been for my illness, these four months in Chili would have been very pleasant. I have had ill luck, however, in only one little earthquake having happened. I was lying in bed when there was a party at dinner in the house; on a sudden I heard such a hubbub in the dining-room; without a word being spoken, it was devil take the hindmost who should get out first; at the same moment I felt my bed *slightly* vibrate in a lateral direction. The party were old stagers, and heard the noise which always precedes a shock; and no old stager looks at an earthquake with philosophical eyes. . . .

Good-bye to you all; you will not have another letter for some time.

My dear Catherine,

Yours affectionately,

CHAS. DARWIN.

My best love to my father, and all of you.   Love to Nancy.

C. Darwin to Miss S. Darwin.

Valparaiso, April 23, 1835.

MY DEAR SUSAN,

I received, a few days since, your letter of November; the three letters which I before mentioned are yet missing, but I do not doubt they will come to life.   I returned a week ago from my excursion across the Andes to Mendoza.   Since leaving England I have never made so successful a journey; it has, however, been very expensive.   I am sure my father would not regret it, if he could know how deeply I have enjoyed it: it was something more than enjoyment; I cannot express the delight which I felt at such a famous winding-up of all my geology in South America.   I literally could hardly sleep at nights for thinking over my day's work.   The scenery was so new, and so majestic; everything at an elevation of 12,000 feet bears so different an aspect from that in a lower country.   I have seen many views more beautiful, but none with so strongly marked a character.   To a geologist, also, there are such manifest proofs of excessive violence; the strata of the highest pinnacles are tossed about like the crust of a broken pie.

I crossed by the Portillo Pass, which at this time of the year is apt to be dangerous, so could not afford to delay there.   After staying a day in the stupid town of Mendoza, I began my return by Uspallate, which I did very leisurely. My whole trip only took up twenty-two days.   I travelled with, for me, uncommon comfort, as I carried a *bed!*   My party consisted of two Peons and ten mules, two of which were with baggage, or rather food, in case of being snowed up.   Everything, however, favoured me; not even a speck of

this year's snow had fallen on the road. I do not suppose
any of you can be much interested in geological details, but
I will just mention my principal results :—Besides understanding to a certain extent the description and manner of
the force which has elevated this great line of mountains,
I can clearly demonstrate that one part of the double line is
of an age long posterior to the other. In the more ancient
line, which is the true chain of the Andes, I can describe the
sort and order of the rocks which compose it. These are
chiefly remarkable by containing a bed of gypsum nearly
2000 feet thick—a quantity of this substance I should think
unparalleled in the world. What is of much greater consequence, I have procured fossil shells (from an elevation of
12,000 feet). I think an examination of these will give an
approximate age to these mountains, as compared to the
strata of Europe. In the other line of the Cordilleras there
is a strong presumption (in my own mind, conviction) that
the enormous mass of mountains, the peaks of which rise to
13,000 and 14,000 feet, are so very modern as to be contemporaneous with the plains of Patagonia (or about with
the *upper* strata of the Isle of Wight). If this result shall be
considered as proved,* it is a very important fact in the theory
of the formation of the world ; because, if such wonderful
changes have taken place so recently in the crust of the globe,
there can be no reason for supposing former epochs of excessive violence. These modern strata are very remarkable
by being threaded with metallic veins of silver, gold, copper,
&c. ; hitherto these have been considered as appertaining to
older formations. In these same beds, and close to a gold-
mine, I found a clump of petrified trees, standing upright,
with layers of fine sandstone deposited round them, bearing
the impression of their bark. These trees are covered by
other sandstones and streams of lava to the thickness of several thousand feet. These rocks have been deposited be-

---

* The importance of these results has been fully recognized by geologists.

neath water; yet it is clear the spot where the trees grew must once have been above the level of the sea, so that it is certain the land must have been depressed by at least as many thousand feet as the superincumbent subaqueous deposits are thick. But I am afraid you will tell me I am prosy with my geological descriptions and theories. . . .

Your account of Erasmus' visit to Cambridge has made me long to be back there. I cannot fancy anything more delightful than his Sunday round of King's, Trinity, and those talking giants, Whewell and Sedgwick; I hope your musical tastes continue in due force. I shall be ravenous for the pianoforte. . . .

I have not quite determined whether I will sleep at the 'Lion' the first night when I arrive per 'Wonder,' or disturb you all in the dead of the night; everything short of that is absolutely planned. Everything about Shrewsbury is growing in my mind bigger and more beautiful; I am certain the acacia and copper beech are two superb trees; I shall know every bush, and I will trouble you young ladies, when each of you cut down your tree, to spare a few. As for the view behind the house, I have seen nothing like it. It is the same with North Wales; Snowdon, to my mind, looks much higher and much more beautiful than any peak in the Cordilleras. So you will say, with my benighted faculties, it is time to return, and so it is, and I long to be with you. Whatever the trees are, I know what I shall find all you. I am writing nonsense, so farewell. My most affectionate love to all, and I pray forgiveness from my father.

Yours most affectionately,
CHARLES DARWIN.

C. Darwin to W. D. Fox.

Lima, July, 1835.

MY DEAR FOX,

I have lately received two of your letters, one dated June and the other November, 1834 (they reached me, however, in an inverted order). I was very glad to receive a history

16

of this most important year in your life. Previously I had
only heard the plain fact that you were married. You are a
true Christian and return good for evil, to send two such letters to so bad a correspondent as I have been. God bless
you for writing so kindly and affectionately ; if it is a pleasure to have friends in England, it is doubly so to think and
know that one is not forgotten because absent. This voyage
is terribly long. I do so earnestly desire to return, yet I dare
hardly look forward to the future, for I do not know what
will become of me. Your situation is above envy: I do not
venture even to frame such happy visions. To a person fit to
take the office, the life of a clergyman is a type of all that is
respectable and happy. You tempt me by talking of your
fireside, whereas it is a sort of scene I never ought to think
about. I saw the other day a vessel sail for England; it was
quite dangerous to know how easily I might turn deserter.
As for an English lady, I have almost forgotten what she is—
something very angelic and good. As for the women in these
countries, they wear caps and petticoats, and a very few have
pretty faces, and then all is said. But if we are not wrecked
on some unlucky reef, I will sit by that same fireside in Vale
Cottage and tell some of the wonderful stories, which you
seem to anticipate and, I presume, are not very ready to believe. *Gracias a dios*, the prospect of such times is rather
shorter than formerly.

From this most wretched· ' City of the Kings ' we sail in
a fortnight, from thence to Guayaquil, Galapagos, Marquesas,
Society Islands, &c., &c. I look forward to the Galapagos
with more interest than any other part of the voyage. They
abound with active volcanoes, and, I should hope, contain
Tertiary strata. I am glad to hear you have some thoughts
of beginning Geology. I hope you will ; there is so much
larger a field for thought than in the other branches of Natural History. I am become a zealous disciple of Mr. Lyell's
views, as known in his admirable book. Geologising in South
America, I am tempted to carry parts to a greater extent
even than he does. Geology is a capital science to begin, as

it requires nothing but a little reading, thinking, and hammering. I have a considerable body of notes together; but it is
a constant subject of perplexity to me, whether they are of
sufficient value for all the time I have spent about them,
or whether animals would not have been of more certain
value.

I shall indeed be glad once again to see you and tell you
how grateful I feel for your steady friendship. God bless
you, my very dear Fox.

　　　　　　　　Believe me,
　　　　　　　　　　Yours affectionately,
　　　　　　　　　　　　CHAS. DARWIN.

C. Darwin to J. S. Henslow.

　　　　　　　　　　　Sydney, January, 1836.

MY DEAR HENSLOW,

This is the last opportunity of communicating with you
before that joyful day when I shall reach Cambridge. I have
very little to say: but I must write if it is only to express
my joy that the last year is concluded, and that the present
one, in which the *Beagle* will return, is gliding onwards. We
have all been disappointed here in not finding even a single
letter; we are, indeed, rather before our expected time,
otherwise, I dare say, I should have seen your handwriting.
I must feed upon the future, and it is beyond bounds delightful to feel the certainty that within eight months I shall
be residing once again most quietly in Cambridge. Certainly, I never was intended for a traveller; my thoughts
are always rambling over past or future scenes; I cannot
enjoy the present happiness for anticipating the future, which
is about as foolish as the dog who dropped the real bone for
its shadow.

　　　*　　　*　　　*　　　*　　　*

In our passage across the Pacific we only touched at
Tahiti and New Zealand; at neither of these places or at sea
had I much opportunity of working. Tahiti is a most charming spot. Everything which former navigators have written

is true. 'A new Cytheræa has risen from the ocean.' Delicious scenery, climate, manners of the people are all in harmony. It is, moreover, admirable to behold what the missionaries both here and at New Zealand have effected. I
firmly believe they are good men working for the sake of a
good cause. I much suspect that those who have abused or
sneered at the missionaries have generally been such as were
not very anxious to find the natives moral and intelligent
beings. During the remainder of our voyage we shall only
visit places generally acknowledged as civilised, and nearly
all under the British flag. These will be a poor field for
Natural History, and without it I have lately discovered that
the pleasure of seeing new places is as nothing. I must
return to my old resource and think of the future, but that I
may not become more prosy, I will say farewell till the day
arrives, when I shall see my Master in Natural History,
and can tell him how grateful I feel for his kindness and
friendship.

   Believe me, dear Henslow,
     Ever yours, most faithfully,
       CHAS. DARWIN.

C. Darwin to Miss S. Darwin.

        Bahia, Brazil, August 4 [1836].

MY DEAR SUSAN,

 I will just write a few lines to explain the cause of this
letter being dated on the coast of South America. Some
singular disagreements in the longitudes made Captain Fitz-
Roy anxious to complete the circle in the southern hemisphere, and then retrace our steps by our first line to England.
This zigzag manner of proceeding is very grievous; it has
put the finishing stroke to my feelings. I loathe, I abhor the
sea and all ships which sail on it. But I yet believe we shall
reach England in the latter half of October. At Ascension
I received Catherine's letter of October, and yours of November; the letter at the Cape was of a later date, but letters of
all sorts are inestimable treasures, and I thank you both for

them. The desert, volcanic rocks, and wild sea of Ascension, as soon as I knew there was news from home, suddenly wore a pleasing aspect, and I set to work with a good-will at my old work of Geology. You would be surprised to know how entirely the pleasure in arriving at a new place depends on letters. We only stayed four days at Ascension, and then made a very good passage to Bahia.

I little thought to have put my foot on South American coast again. It has been almost painful to find how much good enthusiasm has been evaporated during the last four years. I can now walk soberly through a Brazilian forest; not but what it is exquisitely beautiful, but now, instead of seeking for splendid contrasts, I compare the stately mango trees with the horse-chestnuts of England. Although this zigzag has lost us at least a fortnight, in some respects I am glad of it. I think I shall be able to carry away one vivid picture of inter-tropical scenery. We go from hence to the Cape de Verds; that is, if the winds or the Equatorial calms will allow us. I have some faint hopes that a steady foul wind might induce the Captain to proceed direct to the Azores. For which most untoward event I heartily pray.

Both your letters were full of good news; especially the expressions which you tell me Professor Sedgwick used about my collections. I confess they are deeply gratifying—I trust one part at least will turn out true, and that I shall act as I now think—as a man who dares to waste one hour of time has not discovered the value of life. Professor Sedgwick mentioning my name at all gives me hopes that he will assist me with his advice, of which, in my geological questions, I stand much in need. It is useless to tell you from the shameful state of this scribble that I am writing against time, having been out all morning, and now there are some strangers on board to whom I must go down and talk civility. Moreover, as this letter goes by a foreign ship, it is doubtful whether it will ever arrive. Farewell, my very dear Susan and all of you. Good-bye.

C. DARWIN.

C. Darwin to J. S. Henslow.

St. Helena, July 9, 1836.

MY DEAR HENSLOW,

I am going to ask you to do me a favour. I am very
anxious to belong to the Geological Society. I do not know,
but I suppose it is necessary to be proposed some time before being ballotted for; if such is the case, would you be
good enough to take the proper preparatory steps? Professor
Sedgwick very kindly offered to propose me before leaving
England, if he should happen to be in London. I dare say
he would yet do so.

I have very little to write about. We have neither seen,
done, or heard of anything particular for a long time past;
and indeed if at present the wonders of another planet could
be displayed before us, I believe we should unanimously
exclaim, what a consummate plague. No schoolboys ever
sung the half sentimental and half jovial strain of 'dulce
domum' with more fervour, than we all feel inclined to do.
But the whole subject of 'dulce domum,' and the delight of
seeing one's friends, is most dangerous, it must infallibly make
one very prosy or very boisterous. Oh, the degree to which
I long to be once again living quietly with not one single
novel object near me! No one can imagine it till he has
been whirled round the world during five long years in a
ten-gun-brig. I am at present living in a small house (amongst
the clouds) in the centre of the island, and within stone's
throw of Napoleon's tomb. It is blowing a gale of wind with
heavy rain and wretchedly cold; if Napoleon's ghost haunts
his dreary place of confinement, this would be a most excellent night for such wandering spirits. If the weather chooses
to permit me, I hope to see a little of the Geology (so often
partially described) of the island. I suspect that differently
from most volcanic islands its structure is rather complicated.
It seems strange that this little centre of a distinct creation
should, as is asserted, bear marks of recent elevation.

The *Beagle* proceeds from this place to Ascension, then to

the Cape de Verds (wh.t miserable places!) to the Azores to
Plymouth, and then to home.   That most glorious of all days
in my life will not, however, arrive till the middle of October.
Some time in that month you will see me at Cambridge,
where I must directly come to report myself to you, as my
first Lord of the Admiralty.   At the Cape of Good Hope we
all on board suffered a bitter disappointment in missing nine
months' letters, which are chasing us from one side of the
globe to the other.   I dare say amongst them there was a
letter from you; it is long since I have seen your hand-
writing, but I shall soon see you yourself, which is far better.
As I am your pupil, you are bound to undertake the task of
criticising and scolding me for all the things ill done and not
done at all, which I fear I shall need much; but I hope for
the best, and I am sure I have a good if not too easy task-
master.

At the Cape Captain Fitz-Roy and myself enjoyed a memorable piece of good fortune in meeting Sir J. Herschel.   We
dined at his house and saw him a few times besides.   He
was exceedingly good natured, but his manners at first appeared to me rather awful.   He is living in a very comfortable country house, surrounded by fir and oak trees, which
alone in so open a country, give a most charming air of seclu-
sion and comfort.   He appears to find time for everything;
he showed us a pretty garden full of Cape bulbs of his own
collecting, and I afterwards understood that everything was
the work of his own hands. . . . I am very stupid, and I have
nothing more to say; the wind is whistling so mournfully
over the bleak hills, that I shall go to bed and dream of
England.

Good night, my dear Henslow,

Yours most truly obliged and affectionately,

CHAS. DARWIN.

C. Darwin to J. S. Henslow.

Shrewsbury, Thursday, October 6. [1836].

MY DEAR HENSLOW,

I am sure you will congratulate me on the delight of once again being home. The *Beagle* arrived at Falmouth on Sunday evening, and I reached Shrewsbury yesterday morning. I am exceedingly anxious to see you, and as it will be necessary in four or five days to return to London to get my goods and chattels out of the *Beagle*, it appears to me my best plan to pass through Cambridge. I want your advice on many points; indeed I am in the clouds, and neither know what to do or where to go. My chief puzzle is about the geological specimens—who will have the charity to help me in describing their mineralogical nature? Will you be kind enough to write to me one line by *return of post*, saying whether you are now at Cambridge? I am doubtful till I hear from Captain Fitz-Roy whether I shall not be obliged to start before the answer can arrive, but pray try the chance. My dear Henslow, I do long to see you; you have been the kindest friend to me that ever man possessed. I can write no more, for I am giddy with joy and confusion.

Farewell for the present,

Yours most truly obliged,

CHARLES DARWIN.

C. Darwin to R. Fitz-Roy.

Shrewsbury, Thursday morning, October 6, [1836].'

MY DEAR FITZ-ROY,

I arrived here yesterday morning at breakfast-time, and, thank God, found all my dear good sisters and father quite well. My father appears more cheerful and very little older than when I left. My sisters assure me I do not look the least different, and I am able to return the compliment. Indeed, all England appears changed excepting the good old

town of Shrewsbury and its inhabitants, which, for all I can
see to the contrary, may go on as they now are to Doomsday.
I wish with all my heart I was writing to you amongst your
friends instead of at that horrid Plymouth. But the day will
soon come, and you will be as happy as I now am. I do
assure you I am a very great man at home; the five years'
voyage has certainly raised me a hundred per cent. I fear
such greatness must experience a fall.

I am thoroughly ashamed of myself in what a dead-and-
half-alive state I spent the few last days on board; my only
excuse is that certainly I was not quite well. The first day
in the mail tired me, but as I drew nearer to Shrewsbury
everything looked more beautiful and cheerful. In passing
Gloucestershire and Worcestershire I wished much for you
to admire the fields, woods, and orchards. The stupid people
on the coach did not seem to think the fields one bit greener
than usual; but I am sure we should have thoroughly agreed
that the wide world does not contain so happy a prospect
as the rich cultivated land of England.

I hope you will not forget to send me a note telling me
how you go on. I do indeed hope all your vexations and
trouble with respect to our voyage, which we now know HAS
an end, have come to a close. If you do not receive much
satisfaction for all the mental and bodily energy you have
expended in His Majesty's service, you will be most hardly
treated. I put my radical sisters into an uproar at some of
the prudent (if they were not honest Whigs, I would say
shabby) proceedings of our Government. By the way, I must
tell you for the honour and glory of the family that my father
has a large engraving of King George IV. put up in his
sitting-room. But I am no renegade, and by the time we
meet my politics will be as firmly fixed and as wisely founded
as ever they were.

I thought when I began this letter I would convince you
what a steady and sober frame of mind I was in. But I find
I am writing most precious nonsense. Two or three of our
labourers yesterday immediately set to work and got most

excessively drunk in honour of the arrival of Master Charles.
Who then shall gainsay if Master Charles himself chooses to
make himself a fool.   Good-bye.   God bless you !   I hope
you are as happy, but much wiser, than your most sincere but
unworthy philosopher,

CHAS. DARWIN.

CHAPTER VII.

[THE period illustrated by the following letters includes the years between my father's return from the voyage of the *Beagle* and his settling at Down. It is marked by the gradual appearance of that weakness of health which ultimately forced him to leave London and take up his abode for the rest of his life in a quiet country house. In June, 1841, he writes to Lyell: "My father scarcely seems to expect that I shall become strong for some years; it has been a bitter mortification for me to digest the conclusion that the 'race is for the strong,' and that I shall probably do little more but be content to admire the strides others make in science."

There is no evidence of any intention of entering a profession after his return from the voyage, and early in 1840 he wrote to Fitz-Roy: "I have nothing to wish for, excepting stronger health to go on with the subjects to which I have joyfully determined to devote my life."

These two conditions—permanent ill-health and a passionate love of scientific work for its own sake—determined thus early in his career, the character of his whole future life. They impelled him to lead a retired life of constant labour, carried on to the utmost limits of his physical power, a life which signally falsified his melancholy prophecy.

The end of the last chapter saw my father safely arrived

at Shrewsbury on October 4, 1836, "after an absence of five years and two days." He wrote to Fox: "You cannot imagine how gloriously delightful my first visit was at home; is was worth the banishment." But it was a pleasure that he could not long enjoy, for in the last days of October he was at Greenwich unpacking specimens from the *Beagle*. As to the destination of the collections he writes, somewhat despondingly, to Henslow :—

"I have not made much progress with the great men. I find, as you told me, that they are all overwhelmed with their own business. Mr. Lyell has entered, in the *most* good-natured manner, and almost without being asked, into all my plans. He tells me, however, the same story, that I must do all myself. Mr. Owen seems anxious to dissect some of the animals in spirits, and, besides these two, I have scarcely met any one who seems to wish to possess any of my specimens. I must except Dr. Grant, who is willing to examine some of the corallines. I see it is quite unreasonable to hope for a minute that any man will undertake the examination of a whole order. It is clear the collectors so much outnumber the real naturalists that the latter have no time to spare.

"I do not even find that the Collections care for receiving the unnamed specimens. The Zoological Museum * is nearly full, and upwards of a thousand specimens remain unmounted. I dare say the British Museum would receive them, but I cannot feel, from all I hear, any great respect even for the present state of that establishment. Your plan will be not only the best, but the only one, namely, to come down to Cambridge, arrange and group together the different families, and then wait till people, who are already working in different branches, may want specimens. But it appears to me [that] to do this it will be almost necessary to reside in London. As far as I can yet see my best plan will be to spend several months in Cambridge, and then when, by your assistance, I

---

* The Museum of the Zoological Society, then at 33 Bruton Street The collection was some years later broken up and dispersed.

know on what ground I stand, to emigrate to London, where I can complete my Geology and try to push on the Zoology. I assure you I grieve to find how many things make me see the necessity of living for some time in this dirty, odious London. For even in Geology I suspect much assistance and communication will be necessary in this quarter, for instance, in fossil bones, of which none excepting the fragments of Megatherium have been looked at, and I clearly see that without my presence they never would be. . . .

"I only wish I had known the Botanists cared so much for specimens * and the Zoologists so little ; the proportional number of specimens in the two branches should have had a very different appearance. I am out of patience with the Zoologists, not because they are overworked, but for their mean, quarrelsome spirit. I went the other evening to the Zoological Society, where the speakers were snarling at each other in a manner anything but like that of gentlemen. Thank Heavens ! as long as I remain in Cambridge there will not be any danger of falling into any such contemptible quarrels, whilst in London I do not see how it is to be avoided. Of the Naturalists, F. Hope is out of London ; Westwood I have not seen, so about my insects I know nothing. I have seen Mr. Yarrell twice, but he is so evidently oppressed with business that it is too selfish to plague him with my concerns. He has asked me to dine with the Linnean on Tuesday, and on Wednesday I dine with the Geological, so that I shall see all the great men. Mr. Bell, I hear, is so much occupied that there is no chance of his wishing for specimens of rep-

---

* A passage in a subsequent letter shows that his plants also gave him some anxiety. "I met Mr. Brown a few days after you had called on him ; he asked me in rather an ominous manner what I meant to do with my plants. In the course of conversation Mr. Broderip, who was present, remarked to him, 'You forget how long it is since Captain King's expedition.' He answered, 'Indeed, I have something in the shape of Captain Kings's undescribed plants to make me recollect it.' Could a better reason be given, if I had been asked, by me, for not giving the plants to the British Museum?"

tiles. I have forgotten to mention Mr. Lonsdale,* who gave me a most cordial reception, and with whom I had much most interesting conversation. If I was not much more inclined for geology than the other branches of Natural History, I am sure Mr. Lyell's and Lonsdale's kindness ought to fix me. You cannot conceive anything more thoroughly good-natured than the heart-and-soul manner in which he put himself in my place and thought what would be best to do. At first he was all for London versus Cambridge, but at last I made him confess that, for some time at least, the latter would be for me much the best. There is not another soul whom I could ask, excepting yourself, to wade through and criticise some of those papers which I have left with you. Mr. Lyell owned that, second to London, there was no place in England so good for a Naturalist as Cambridge. Upon my word I am ashamed of writing so many foolish details; no young lady ever described her first ball with more particularity."

A few days later he writes more cheerfully : " I became acquainted with Mr. Bell, † who to my surprise expressed a good deal of interest about my crustacea and reptiles, and seems willing to work at them. I also heard that Mr. Broderip would be glad to look over the South American shells, so that things flourish well with me."

About his plants he writes with characteristic openness as to his own ignorance : " You have made me known amongst the botanists, but I felt very foolish when Mr. Don remarked on the beautiful appearance of some plant with an astounding long name, and asked me about its habitation. Some one else seemed quite surprised that I knew nothing about a Carex

---

* William Lonsdale, b 1794, d. 1871, was originally in the army, and served at the battles of Salamanca and Waterloo. After the war he left the service and gave himself up to science. He acted as assistant secretary to the Geological Society from 1829–42, when he resigned, owing to ill health.

† T. Bell, F.R.S., formerly Prof. of Zoology in King's College, London, and sometime secretary to the Royal Society. He afterwards described the reptiles for the zoology of the voyage of the *Beagle*.

from I do not know where. I was at last forced to plead most entire innocence, and that I knew no more about the plants which I had collected than the man in the moon."

As to part of his Geological Collection he was soon able to write : " I [have] disposed of the most important part [of] my collections, by giving all the fossil bones to the College of Surgeons, casts of them will be distributed, and descriptions published. They are very curious and valuable ; one head belonged to some gnawing animal, but of the size of a Hippopotamus! Another to an ant-eater of the size of a horse ! "

It is worth noting that at this time the only extinct mammalia from South America, which had been described, were Mastodon (three species) and Megatherium. The remains of the other extinct Edentata from Sir Woodbine Parish's collection had not been described. My father's specimens included (besides the above-mentioned Toxodon and Scelidotherium) the remains of Mylodon, Glossotherium, another gigantic animal allied to the ant-eater, and Macrauchenia. His discovery of these remains is a matter of interest in itself, but it has a special importance as a point in his own life, since it was the vivid impression produced by excavating them with his own hands * that formed one of the chief starting-points of his speculation on the origin of species. This is shown in the following extract from his Pocket Book for this year (1837) : " In July opened first note-book on Transmutation of Species. Had been greatly struck from about the month of previous March on character of South American fossils, and species on Galapagos Archipelago. These facts (especially latter), origin of all my views."]

* I have often heard him speak of the despair with which he had to break off the projecting extremity of a huge, partly excavated bone, when the boat waiting for him would wait no longer.

1836–1837.

C. Darwin to W. D. Fox.

43 Great Marlborough Street,
November 6th [1836].

MY DEAR FOX,

I have taken a shamefully long time in answering your letter. But the busiest time of the whole voyage has been tranquillity itself to this last month. After paying Henslow a short but very pleasant visit, I came up to town to wait for the *Beagle's* arrival. At last I have removed all my property from on board, and sent the specimens of Natural History to Cambridge, so that I am now a free man. My London visit has been quite idle as far as Natural History goes, but has been passed in most exciting dissipation amongst the Dons in science. All my affairs, indeed, are most prosperous ; I find there are plenty who will undertake the description of whole tribes of animals, of which I know nothing. So that about this day month I hope to set to work tooth and nail at the Geology, which I shall publish by itself.

It is quite ridiculous what an immensely long period it appears to me since landing at Falmouth. The fact is I have talked and laughed enough for years instead of weeks, so [that] my memory is quite confounded with the noise. I am delighted to hear you are turned geologist : when I pay the Isle of Wight a visit, which I am determined shall somehow come to pass, you will be a capital cicerone to the famous line of dislocation. I really suppose there are few parts of the world more interesting to a geologist than your island. Amongst the great scientific men, no one has been nearly so friendly and kind as Lyell. I have seen him several times, and feel inclined to like him much. You cannot imagine how good-naturedly he entered into all my plans. I speak now only of the London men, for Henslow was just like his former self, and therefore a most cordial and affectionate friend. When you pay London a visit I shall be very proud to take you to the Geological Society, for be it known, I was proposed to be a F. G. S. last Tuesday. It is, however, a great pity that these and the other letters, especially F. R. S., are so very expensive.

I do not scruple to ask you to write to me in a week's time in Shrewsbury, for you are a good letter writer, and if people will have such good characters they must pay the penalty. Good-bye, dear Fox.

Yours,

C. D.

[His affairs being thus so far prosperously managed he was able to put into execution his plan of living at Cambridge, where he settled on December 10th, 1836. He was at first a guest in the comfortable home of the Henslows, but afterwards, for the sake of undisturbed work, he moved into lodgings. He thus writes to Fox, March 13th, 1837, from London :—

"My residence at Cambridge was rather longer than I expected, owing to a job which I determined to finish there, namely, looking over all my geological specimens. Cambridge yet continues a very pleasant, but not half so merry a place as before. To walk through the courts of Christ's College, and not know an inhabitant of a single room, gave one a feeling half melancholy. The only evil I found in Cambridge was its being too pleasant: there was some agreeable party or another every evening, and one cannot say one is engaged with so much impunity there as in this great city."

A trifling record of my father's presence in Cambridge occurs in the book kept in Christ's College combination-room, where fines and bets were recorded, the earlier entries giving a curious impression of the after-dinner frame of mind of the fellows. The bets were not allowed to be made in money, but were, like the fines, paid in wine. The bet which my father made and lost is thus recorded :—

"*Feb.* 23, 1837.—Mr. Darwin *v.* Mr. Baines, that the combination-room measures from the ceiling to the floor more than (x) feet.   1 Bottle paid same day.

17

"N. B. Mr. Darwin may measure at any part of the room he pleases."

Besides arranging the geological and mineralogical specimens, he had his 'Journal of Researches' to work at, which occupied his evenings at Cambridge. He also read a short paper at the Zoological Society,* and another at the Geological Society,† on the recent elevation of the coast of Chili.

Early in the spring of 1837 (March 6th) he left Cambridge for London, and a week later he was settled in lodgings at 36 Great Marlborough Street; and except for a "short visit to Shrewsbury" in June, he worked on till September, being almost entirely employed on his 'Journal.' He found time, however, for two papers at the Geological Society.‡

He writes of his work to Fox (March, 1837):—

"In your last letter you urge me to get ready *the* book. I am now hard at work and give up everything else for it. Our plan is as follows: Captain Fitz-Roy writes two volumes out of the materials collected during the last voyage under Capt. King to Tierra del Fuego, and during our circumnavigation. I am to have the third volume, in which I intend giving a kind of journal of a naturalist, not following, however, always the order of time, but rather the order of position. The habits of animals will occupy a large portion, sketches of the geology, the appearance of the country, and personal details will make the hodge-podge complete. Afterwards I shall write an account of the geology in detail, and draw up some zoological papers. So that I have plenty of work for the next year or two, and till that is finished I will have no holidays."

---

* "Notes upon Rhea Americana," 'Zool. Soc. Proc.' v. 1837, pp. 35, 36.

† 'Geol. Soc. Proc.' ii. 1838, pp. 446-449.

‡ "A sketch of the deposits containing extinct mammalia in the neighbourhood of the Plata," 'Geol. Soc. Proc.' ii. 1838, pp. 542-544 ; and "On certain areas of elevation and subsidence in the Pacific and Indian oceans, as deduced from the study of coral formations," 'Geol. Soc. Proc.' ii. 1838, pp. 552-554.

Another letter to Fox (July) gives an account of the progress of his work :—

"I gave myself a holiday and a visit to Shrewsbury [in June], as I had finished my Journal. I shall now be very busy in filling up gaps and getting it quite ready for the press by the first of August. I shall always feel respect for every one who has written a book, let it be what it may, for I had no idea of the trouble which trying to write common English could cost one. And, alas, there yet remains the worst part of all, correcting the press. As soon as ever that is done I must put my shoulder to the wheel and commence at the Geology. I have read some short papers to the Geological Society, and they were favourably received by the great guns, and this gives me much confidence, and I hope not a very great deal of vanity, though I confess I feel too often like a peacock admiring his tail. I never expected that my Geology would ever have been worth the consideration of such men as Lyell, who has been to me, since my return, a most active friend. My life is a very busy one at present, and I hope may ever remain so ; though Heaven knows there are many serious drawbacks to such a life, and chief amongst them is the little time it allows one for seeing one's natural friends. For the last three years, I have been longing and longing to be living at Shrewsbury, and after all now in the course of several months, I see my dear good people at Shrewsbury for a week. Susan and Catherine have, however, been staying with my brother here for some weeks, but they had returned home before my visit."

Besides the work already mentioned he had much to busy him in making arrangements for the publication of the 'Zoology of the Voyage of the *Beagle*.' The following letters illustrate this subject.]

*C. Darwin to L. Jenyns.**

36 Great Marlborough Street,
April 10th, 1837.

DEAR JENYNS,

During the last week several of the zoologists of this place
have been urging me to consider the possibility of publishing
the 'Zoology of the *Beagle's* Voyage' on some uniform plan.
Mr. Macleay † has taken a great deal of interest in the subject, and maintains that such a publication is very desirable,
because it keeps together a series of observations made respecting animals inhabiting the same part of the world, and
allows any future traveller taking them with him.   How far
this facility of reference is of any consequence I am very
doubtful ; but if such is the case, it would be more satisfactory to myself to see the gleanings of my hands, after having passed through the brains of other naturalists, collected
together in one work.   But such considerations ought not to
have much weight.   The whole scheme is at present merely
floating in the air ; but I was determined to let you know, as
I should much like to know what you think about it, and
whether you would object to supply descriptions of the fish
to such a work instead of to 'Transactions.'   I apprehend
the whole will be impracticable, without Government will aid
in engraving the plates, and this I fear is a mere chance, only
I think I can put in a strong claim, and get myself well
backed by the naturalists of this place, who nearly all take a

* Now Rev. L. Blomefield.

† William Sharp Macleay was the son of Alexander Macleay, formerly
Colonial Secretary of New South Wales, and for many years Secretary of
the Linnean Society.   The son, who was a most zealous Naturalist, and
had inherited from his father a very large general collection of insects,
made Entomology his chief study, and gained great notoriety by his now
forgotten *Quinary System*, set forth in the Second Part of his ' Horæ En-
tomologicæ,' published in 1821.—[I am indebted to Rev. L. Blomefield
for the foregoing note.]

good deal of interest in my collections. I mean to-morrow
to see Mr. Yarrell; if he approves, I shall begin and take
more active steps; for I hear he is most prudent and most
wise. It is scarcely any use speculating about any plan, but
I thought of getting subscribers and publishing the work in
parts (as long as funds would last, for I myself will not lose
money by it). In such case, whoever had his own part ready
on any order might publish it separately (and ultimately the
parts might be sold separately), so that no one should be delayed by the other. The plan would resemble, on a humble
scale, Ruppel's 'Atlas,' or Humboldt's 'Zoologie,' where
Latreille, Cuvier, &c., wrote different parts. I myself should
have little to do with it; excepting in some orders adding
habits and ranges, &c., and geographical sketches, and perhaps afterwards some descriptions of invertebrate animals . . . .

I am working at my Journal; it gets on slowly, though I
am not idle. I thought Cambridge a bad place from good
dinners and other temptations, but I find London no better,
and I fear it may grow worse. I have a capital friend in
Lyell, and see a great deal of him, which is very advantageous to me in discussing much South American geology. I
miss a walk in the country very much; this London is a vile
smoky place, where a man loses a great part of the best en-
joyments in life. But I see no chance of escaping, even for
a week, from this prison for a long time to come. I fear it
will be some time before we shall meet; for I suppose you
will not come up here during the spring, and I do not think
I shall be able to go down to Cambridge. How I should
like to have a good walk along the Newmarket road to-
morrow, but Oxford Street must do instead. I do hate the
streets of London. Will you tell Henslow to be careful with
the *edible* fungi from Tierra del Fuego, for I shall want some
specimens for Mr. Brown, who seems *particularly* interested
about them. Tell Henslow, I think my silicified wood has
unflintified Mr. Brown's heart, for he was very gracious to me,
and talked about the Galapagos plants; but before he never

would say a word. It is just striking twelve o'clock; so I will wish you a very good night.

My dear Jenyns,
Yours most truly,
C. DARWIN.

[A few weeks later the plan seems to have been matured, and the idea of seeking Government aid to have been adopted.]

C. Darwin to J. S. Henslow.

36 Great Marlborough Street,
[18th May, 1837].

MY DEAR HENSLOW,

I was very glad to receive your letter. I wanted much to hear how you were getting on with your manifold labours. Indeed I do not wonder your head began to ache; it is almost a wonder you have any head left. Your account of the Gamlingay expedition was cruelly tempting, but I cannot anyhow leave London. I wanted to pay my good, dear people at Shrewsbury a visit of a few days, but I found I could not manage it; at present I am waiting for the signatures of the Duke of Somerset, as President of the Linnean, and of Lord Derby and Whewell, to a statement of the value of my collection; the instant I get this I shall apply to Government for assistance in engraving, and so publish the 'Zoology' on some uniform plan. It is quite ridiculous the time any operation requires which depends on many people.

I have been working very steadily, but have only got two-thirds through the Journal part alone. I find, though I remain daily many hours at work, the progress is very slow: it is an awful thing to say to oneself, every fool and every clever man in England, if he chooses, may make as many ill-natured remarks as he likes on this unfortunate sentence.

*   *   *   *   *

[In August he writes to Henslow to announce the success of the scheme for the publication of the 'Zoology of the

Voyage of the *Beagle*,' through the promise of a grant of £1000 from the Treasury: "I have delayed writing to you, to thank you most sincerely for having so effectually managed my affair. I waited till I had an interview with the Chancellor of the Exchequer.* He appointed to see me this morning, and I had a long conversation with him, Mr. Peacock being present. Nothing could be more thoroughly obliging and kind than his whole manner. He made no sort of restriction, but only told me to make the most of [the] money, which of course I am right willing to do.

"I expected rather an awful interview, but I never found anything less so in my life. It will be my fault if I do not make a good work; but I sometimes take an awful fright that I have not materials enough. It will be excessively satisfactory at the end of some two years to find all materials made the most they were capable of."

Later in the autumn he wrote to Henslow: "I have not been very well of late, with an uncomfortable palpitation of the heart, and my doctors urge me *strongly* to knock off all work, and go and live in the country for a few weeks." He accordingly took a holiday of about a month at Shrewsbury and Maer, and paid Fox a visit in the Isle of Wight. It was, I believe, during this visit, at Mr. Wedgwood's house at Maer, that he made his first observations on the work done by earthworms, and late in the autumn he read a paper on the subject at the Geological Society.† During these two months he was also busy preparing the scheme of the 'Zoology of the Voyage of the *Beagle*,' and in beginning to put together the Geological results of his travels.

The following letter refers to the proposal that he should take the Secretaryship of the Geological Society.]

---

* T. Spring Rice.

† "On the formation of mould," 'Geol. Soc. Proc.' ii. 1838, pp. 574–576.

C. Darwin to J. S. Henslow.

October 14th, [1837].

MY DEAR HENSLOW,

. . . I am much obliged to you for your message about the Secretaryship. I am exceedingly anxious for you to hear my side of the question, and will you be so kind as afterwards to give me your fair judgment. The subject has haunted me all summer. I am unwilling to undertake the office for the following reasons : First, my entire ignorance of English Geology, a knowledge of which would be almost necessary in order to shorten many of the papers before reading them before the Society, or rather to know what parts to skip. Again, my ignorance of all languages, and not knowing how to pronounce a *single* word of French—a language so perpetually quoted. It would be disgraceful to the Society to have a Secretary who could not read French. Secondly, the loss of time ; pray consider that I should have to look after the artists, superintend and furnish materials for the Government work, which will come out in parts, and which must appear regularly. All my Geological notes are in a very rough state ; none of my fossil shells worked up ; and I have much to read. I have had hopes, by giving up society and not wasting an hour, that I should finish my Geology in a year and a half, by which time the description of the higher animals by others would be completed, and my whole time would then necessarily be required to complete myself the description of the invertebrate ones. If this plan fails, as the Government work must go on, the Geology would necessarily be deferred till probably at least three years from this time. In the present state of the science, a great part of the utility of the little I have done would be lost, and all freshness and pleasure quite taken from me.

I know from experience the time required to make abstracts *even* of my own papers for the 'Proceedings.' If I was Secretary, and had to make double abstracts of each paper, studying them before reading, and attendance would *at least* cost me three days (and often more) in the fortnight. There are likewise other accidental and contingent losses of time: I know Dr. Royle found the office consumed much of his time. If by merely giving up any amusement, or by working harder than I have done, I could save time, I would undertake the Secretaryship ; but I appeal to you whether, with my slow manner of writing, with two works in hand, and with the certainty, if I cannot complete the Geological part within a fixed period, that its publication must be retarded for a very long time,—whether any Society whatever has any claim on me for three days' disagreeable work every fortnight. I cannot agree that it is a duty on my part, as a follower of science, as long as I devote myself to the completion of the work I have in hand, to delay that, by undertaking what may be done by any person who happens to have more spare time than I have at present. Moreover, so early in my scientific life, with so very much as I have to learn, the office, though no doubt a great honour, &c., for me, would be the more burdensome. Mr. Whewell (I know very well), judging from himself, will think I exaggerate the time the Secretaryship would require ; but I absolutely know the time which with me the simplest writing consumes. I do not at all like appearing so selfish as to refuse Mr. Whewell, more especially as he has always shown, in the kindest manner, an interest in my affairs. But I cannot look forward with even tolerable comfort to undertaking an office without entering on it heart and soul, and that would be impossible with the Government work and the Geology in hand.

My last objection is, that I doubt how far my health will stand the confinement of what I have to do, without any additional work. I merely repeat, that you may know I am not speaking idly, that when I consulted Dr. Clark in town, he at first urged me to give up entirely all writing and even correcting press for some weeks. Of late anything which flurries me completely knocks me up afterwards, and brings on a violent palpitation of the heart. Now the Secretaryship would be a periodical source of more annoying trouble to me than all the rest of the fortnight put together.   In fact, till I return to town, and see how I get on, if I wished the office ever so much, I *could* not say I would positively undertake it.   I beg of you to excuse this very long prose all about myself, but the point is one of great interest.   I can neither bear to think myself very selfish and sulky, nor can I see the possibility of my taking the Secretaryship without making a sacrifice of all my plans and a good deal of comfort.

If you see Whewell, would you tell him the substance of this letter ; or, if he will take the trouble, he may read it.   My dear Henslow, I appeal to you *in loco parentis.*   Pray tell me what you think?   But do not judge me by the activity of mind which you and a few others possess, for in that case the more difficult things in hand the pleasanter the work ; but, though I hope I never shall be idle, such is not the case with me.

Ever, dear Henslow,
Yours most truly,
C. DARWIN.

[He ultimately accepted the post, and held it for three years—from February 16, 1838, to February 19, 1841.

After being assured of the Grant for the publication of the 'Zoology of the Voyage of the *Beagle*,' there was much to be done in arranging the scheme of publication, and this occupied him during part of October and November.]

C. Darwin to J. S. Henslow.

[4th November, 1837.]

MY DEAR HENSLOW,   .

. . . Pray tell Leonard* that my Government work is going on smoothly, and I hope will be prosperous.   He will see in the Prospectus his name attached to the fish ; I set my shoulders to the work with a good heart.   I am very much better than I was during the last month before my Shrews-

---

* Rev. L. Jenyns.

bury visit. I fear the Geology will take me a great deal of time; I was looking over one set of notes, and the quantity I found I had to read, for that one place was frightful. If I live till I am eighty years old I shall not cease to marvel at finding myself an author; in the summer before I started, if any one had told me that I should have been an angel by this time, I should have thought it an equal impossibility. This marvellous transformation is all owing to you.

I am sorry to find that a good many errata are left in the part of my volume, which is printed. During my absence Mr. Colburn employed some goose to revise, and he has multiplied, instead of diminishing my oversights; but for all that, the smooth paper and clear type has a charming appearance, and I sat the other evening gazing in silent admiration at the first page of my own volume, when I received it from the printers !

Good-bye, my dear Henslow,

C. DARWIN.

1838.

[From the beginning of this year to nearly the end of June, he was busily employed on the zoological and geological results of his voyage. This spell of work was interrupted only by a visit of three days to Cambridge, in May; and even this short holiday was taken in consequence of failing health, as we may assume from the entry in his diary: "May 1st, unwell," and from a letter to his sister (May 16, 1838), when he wrote :—

"My trip of three days to Cambridge has done me such wonderful good, and filled my limbs with such elasticity, that I must get a little work out of my body before another holiday." This holiday seems to have been thoroughly enjoyed; he wrote to his sister :—

"Now for Cambridge: I stayed at Henslow's house and enjoyed my visit extremely. My friends gave me a most cordial welcome. Indeed, I was quite a lion there. Mrs. Henslow unfortunately was obliged to go on Friday for a visit in the country. That evening we had at Henslow's a brilliant party of all the geniuses in Cambridge, and a most remarkable set of men they most assuredly are. On Saturday I rode over to L. Jenyns', and spent the morning with him. I found him very cheerful, but bitterly complaining of his solitude. On Saturday evening dined at one of the Colleges, played at bowls on the College Green after dinner, and was deafened with nightingales singing. Sunday, dined in Trinity ; capital dinner, and was very glad to sit by Professor Lee* . . .; I find him a very pleasant chatting man, and in high spirits like a boy, at having lately returned from a living or a curacy, for seven years in Somersetshire, to civilised society and oriental manuscripts. He had exchanged his living to one within fourteen miles of Cambridge, and seemed perfectly happy. In the evening attended Trinity Chapel, and heard 'The Heavens are telling the Glory of God,' in magnificent style ; the last chorus seemed to shake the very walls of the College. After chapel a large party in Sedgwick's rooms. So much for my Annals."

He started, towards the end of June, on his expedition to Glen Roy, of which he writes to Fox : " I have not been very well of late, which has suddenly determined me to leave London earlier than I had anticipated. I go by the steam-packet to Edinburgh,—take a solitary walk on Salisbury Craigs, and call up old thoughts of former times, then go on to Glasgow and the great valley of Inverness, near which I intend stopping a week to geologise the parallel roads of Glen Roy, thence to Shrewsbury, Maer for one day, and London for smoke, ill-health and hard work."

He spent "eight good days" over the Parallel Roads. His Essay on this subject was written out during the same summer, and published by the Royal Society.† He wrote in his Pocket Book : "September 6 [1838]. Finished the paper

---

* Samuel Lee, of Queens', was Professor of Arabic from 1819 to 1831, and Regius Professor of Hebrew from 1831 to 1848.

† 'Phil. Trans.' 1839, pp. 39–82.

on 'Glen Roy,' one of the most difficult and instructive tasks
I was ever engaged on." It will be remembered that in his
'Recollections' he speaks of this paper as a failure, of which
he was ashamed.

At the time at which he wrote, the latest theory of the formation of the Parallel Roads was that of Sir Lauder Dick
and Dr. Macculloch, who believed that lakes had anciently
existed in Glen Roy, caused by dams of rock or allu-
vium. In arguing against this theory he conceived that
he had disproved the admissibility of any lake theory,
but in this point he was mistaken. He wrote (Glen Roy
paper, p. 49) "the conclusion is inevitable, that no hypothesis founded on the supposed existence of a sheet of
water confined by *barriers*, that is a lake, can be admitted
as solving the problematical origin of the parallel roads of
Lochaber."

Mr. Archibald Geikie has been so good as to allow me to
quote a passage from a letter addressed to me (Nov. 19, 1884)
in compliance with my request for his opinion on the character of my father's Glen Roy work :—

"Mr. Darwin's 'Glen Roy' paper, I need not say, is
marked by all his characteristic acuteness of observation and
determination to consider all possible objections. It is a
curious example, however, of the danger of reasoning by a
method of exclusion in Natural Science. Finding that the
waters which formed the terraces in the Glen Roy region
could not possibly have been dammed back by barriers of
rock or of detritus, he saw no alternative but to regard them
as the work of the sea. Had the idea of transient barriers
of glacier-ice occurred to him, he would have found the difficulties vanish from the lake-theory which he opposed, and he
would not have been unconsciously led to minimise the altogether overwhelming objections to the supposition that the
terraces are of marine origin."

It may be added that the idea of the barriers being formed
by glaciers could hardly have occurred to him, considering
what was the state of knowledge at the time, and bearing in

mind his want of opportunities of observing glacial action on a large scale.

, The latter half of July was passed at Shrewsbury and Maer. The only entry of any interest is one of being "very idle" at Shrewsbury, and of opening "a note-book connected with metaphysical inquiries." In August he records that he read "a good deal of various amusing books, and paid some attention to metaphysical subjects."

The work done during the remainder of the year comprises the book on coral reefs (begun in October), and some work on the phenomena of elevation in S. America.]

C. Darwin to C. Lyell.

36 Great Marlborough Street,
August 9th [1838].

MY DEAR LYELL,

I did not write to you at Norwich, for I thought I should have more to say, if I waited a few more days. Very many thanks for the present of your 'Elements,' which I received (and I believe the *very first* copy distributed) together with your note. I have read it through every word, and am full of admiration of it, and, as I now see no geologist, I must talk to you about it. There is no pleasure in reading a book if one cannot have a good talk over it; I repeat, I am full of admiration of it, it is as clear as daylight, in fact I felt in many parts some mortification at thinking how geologists have laboured and struggled at proving what seems, as you have put it, so evidently probable. I read with much interest your sketch of the secondary deposits; you have contrived to make it quite "juicy," as we used to say as children of a good story. There was also much new to me, and I have to copy out some fifty notes and references. It must do good, the heretics against common sense must yield. . . . By the way, do you recollect my telling you how much I disliked the manner ——— referred to his other works, as much as to say, "You must, ought, and shall buy everything I have written." To my mind, you have somehow quite avoided this; your references only seem to say, "I can't tell you all in this work, else I would, so you must go to the 'Principles'"; and many a one, I trust, you will send there, and make them, like me, adorers of the good science of rock-breaking. You will see I am in a fit of enthusiasm, and good cause I have to be, when I find you have made such infinitely more use of my Journal than I could have anticipated. I will say no more about the book, for it is all praise. I must, however, admire the elaborate honesty with which you quote the words of all living and dead geologists.

My Scotch expedition answered brilliantly; my trip in the steam-packet was absolutely pleasant, and I enjoyed the spectacle, wretch that I am, of two ladies, and some small children quite sea-sick, I being well. Moreover, on my return from Glasgow to Liverpool, I triumphed in a similar manner over some full-grown men. I stayed one whole day in Edinburgh, or more truly on Salisbury Craigs; I want to hear some day what you think about that classical ground,—the structure was to me new and rather curious,—that is, if I understand it right. I crossed from Edinburgh in gigs and carts (and carts without springs, as I never shall forget) to Loch Leven. I was disappointed in the scenery, and reached Glen Roy on Saturday evening, one week after leaving Marlborough Street. Here I enjoyed five [?] days of the most beautiful weather with gorgeous sunsets, and all nature looking as happy as I felt. I wandered over the mountains in all directions, and examined that most extraordinary district. I think, without any exceptions, not even the first volcanic island, the first elevated beach, or the passage of the Cordillera, was so interesting to me as this week. It is far the most remarkable area I ever examined. I have fully convinced myself (after some doubting at first) that the shelves are sea-beaches, although I could not find a trace of a shell; and I think I can explain away most, if not all, the difficulties. I found a piece of a road in another valley, not hitherto observed, which is important; and I have some curious facts about erratic blocks, one of which was perched up on

a peak 2200 feet above the sea.   I am now employed in
writing a paper on the subject, which I find very amusing
work, excepting that I cannot anyhow condense it into reasonable limits.   At some future day I hope to talk over
some of the conclusions with you, which the examination of
Glen Roy has led me to.   Now I have had my talk out, I
am much easier, for I can assure you Glen Roy has astonished me.

I am living very quietly, and therefore pleasantly, and am
crawling on slowly but steadily with my work.   I have come
to one conclusion, which you will think proves me to be
a very sensible man, namely, that whatever you say proves
right ; and as a proof of this, I am coming into your way of
only working about two hours at a spell ; I then go out and
do my business in the streets, return and set to work again,
and thus make two separate days out of one.   The new plan
answers capitally ; after the second half day is finished I go
and dine at the Athenæum like a gentleman, or rather like a
lord, for I am sure the first evening I sat in that great drawing-
room, all on a sofa by myself, I felt just like a duke.   I am
full of admiration at the Athenæum, one meets so many people
there that one likes to see.   The very first time I dined there
(*i.e.* last week) I met Dr. Fitton * at the door, and he got together quite a party—Robert Brown, who is gone to Paris and
Auvergne, Macleay [?] and Dr. Boott.† Your helping me into

---

* W. H. Fitton (b. 1780, d. 1861) was a physician and geologist, and
sometime president of the Geological Society.   He established the ' Proceedings,' a mode of publication afterwards adopted by other societies.

† Francis Boott (b. 1792, d. 1863) is chiefly known as a botanist through
his work on the genus Carex.   He was also well known in connection with
the Linnean Society of which he was for many years an office-bearer.   He
is described (in a biographical sketch published in the *Gardeners' Chronicle*,
1864) as having been one of the first physicians in London who gave up
the customary black coat, knee-breeches and silk stockings, and adopted
the ordinary dress of the period, a blue coat with brass buttons, and a buff
waistcoat, a costume which he continued to wear to the last.   After giving
up practice, which he did early in life, he spent much of his time in acts of
unpretending philanthropy.

the Athenæum has not been thrown away, and I enjoy it the
more because I fully expected to detest it.

I am writing you a most unmerciful letter, but I shall get
Owen to take it to Newcastle. If you have a mind to be a
very generous man you will write to me from Kinnordy,* and
tell me some Newcastle news, as well as about the Craig, and
about yourself and Mrs. Lyell, and everything else in the
world. I will send by Hall the 'Entomological Transactions,'
which I have borrowed for you ; you will be disappointed in
——'s papers, that is if you suppose my dear friend has a
single clear idea upon any one subject. He has so involved
recent insects and true fossil insects in one table that I fear
you will not make much out of it, though it is a subject which
ought I should think to come into the 'Principles.' You will
be amused at some of the ridiculo-sublime passages in the
papers, and no doubt will feel acutely a sneer there is at yourself. I have heard from more than one quarter that quarrelling is expected at Newcastle ; † I am sorry to hear it. I met
old —— this evening at the Athenæum, and he muttered
something about writing to you or some one on the subject ;
I am however all in the dark. I suppose, however, I shall be
illuminated, for I am going to dine with him in a few days, as
my inventive powers failed in making any excuse. A friend
of mine dined with him the other day, a party of four, and
they finished ten bottles of wine—a pleasant prospect for me ;
but I am determined not even to taste his wine, partly for the
fun of seeing his infinite disgust and surprise. . . .

I pity you the infliction of this most unmerciful letter.
Pray remember me most kindly to Mrs. Lyell when you arrive
at Kinnordy. I saw her name in the landlord's book of In-
verorum. Tell Mrs. Lyell to read the second series of 'Mr.
Slick of Slickville's Sayings.' . . . He almost beats "Samivel,"
that prince of heroes. Good night, my dear Lyell ; you will
think I have been drinking some strong drink to write so

---

*The house of Lyell's father.
† At the meeting of the British Association.

much nonsense, but I did not even taste Minerva's small beer to-day.   Yours most sincerely,

CHAS. DARWIN.

C. Darwin to C. Lyell.

Friday night, September 13th [1838].

MY DEAR LYELL,

I was astonished and delighted at your gloriously long letter, and I am sure I am very much obliged to Mrs. Lyell for having taken the trouble to write so much.*   I mean to have a good hour's enjoyment and scribble away to you, who have so much geological sympathy that I do not care how egotistically I write. . . .

I have got so much to say about all sorts of trifling things that I hardly know what to begin about.   I need not say how pleased I am to hear that Mr. Lyell † likes my Journal. To hear such tidings is a kind of resurrection, for I feel towards my first-born child as if it had long since been dead, buried, and forgotten ; but the past is nothing and the future everything to us geologists, as you show in your capital motto to the ' Elements.'   By the way, have you read the article, in the ' Edinburgh Review,' on M. Comte, ' Cours de la Philosophie ' (or some such title) ?   It is capital ; there are some fine sentences about the very essence of science being prediction, which reminded me of " its law being progress."

I will now begin and go through your letter *seriatim*.   I dare say your plan of putting the Elie de Beaumont's chapter separately and early will be very good ; anyhow, it is showing a bold front in the first edition which is to be translated into French.   It will be a curious point to geologists hereafter to note how long a man's name will support a theory so completely exposed as that of De Beaumont's has been by you ; you say you " begin to hope that the great principles there insisted on will stand the test of time."   *Begin to hope :* why,

---

* Lyell dictated much of his correspondence.
† Father of the geologist.

the *possibility* of a doubt has never crossed my mind for many a day. This may be very unphilosophical, but my geological salvation is staked on it. After having just come back from Glen Roy, and found how difficulties smooth away under your principles, it makes me quite indignant that you should talk of *hoping*. With respect to the question, how far my coral theory bears on De Beaumont's theory, I think it would be prudent to quote me with great caution until my whole account is published, and then you (and others) can judge how far there is foundation for such generalisation. Mind, I do not doubt its truth ; but the extension of any view over such large spaces, from comparatively few facts, must be received with much caution. I do not myself the least doubt that within the recent (or as you, much to my annoyment, would call it, "New Pliocene") period, tortuous bands—not all the bands parallel to each other—have been elevated and corresponding ones subsided, though within the same period some parts probably remained for a time stationary, or even subsided. I do not believe a more utterly false view could have been invented than great straight lines being suddenly thrown up.

When my book on Volcanoes and Coral Reefs will be published I hardly know ; I fear it will be at least four or five months ; though, mind, the greater part is written. I find so much time is lost in correcting details and ascertaining their accuracy. The Government Zoological work is a millstone round my neck, and the Glen Roy paper has lost me six weeks. I will not, however, say lost ; for, supposing I can prove to others' satisfaction what I have convinced myself is the case, the inference I think you will allow to be important. I cannot doubt that the molten matter beneath the earth's crust possesses a high degree of fluidity, almost like the sea beneath the block ice. By the way, I hope you will give me some Swedish case to quote, of shells being preserved on the surface, but not in contemporaneous beds of gravel. . . .

Remember what I have often heard you say : the country

is very bad for the intellects; the Scotch mists will put out some volcanic speculations.   You see I am affecting to become very Cockneyfied, and to despise the poor country-folk, who breathe fresh air instead of smoke, and see the goodly fields instead of the brick houses in Marlborough Street, the very sight of which I confess I abhor.   I am glad to hear what a favourable report you give of the British Association.   I am the more pleased because I have been fighting its battles with Basil Hall, Stokes, and several others, having made up my mind, from the report in the *Athenæum*, that it must have been an excellent meeting.   I have been much amused with an account I have received of the wars of Don Roderick * and Babbage.   What a grievous pity it is that the latter should be so implacable. . . . This is a most rigmarole letter, for after each sentence I take breath, and you will have need of it in reading it. . . .

I wish with all my heart that my Geological book was out. I have every motive to work hard, and will, following your steps, work just that degree of hardness to keep well.   I should like my volume to be out before your new edition of 'Principles' appears.   Besides the Coral theory, the volcanic chapters will. I think, contain some new facts.   I have lately been sadly tempted to be idle—that is, as far as pure geology is concerned—by the delightful number of new views which have been coming in thickly and steadily,—on the classification and affinities and instincts of animals—bearing on the question of species.   Note-book after note-book has been filled with facts which begin to group themselves *clearly* under sub-laws.

Good night, my dear Lyell.   I have filled my letter and enjoyed my talk to you as much as I can without having you *in propriâ personâ*.   Think of the bad effects of the country—so once more good night.   Ever yours,

CHAS. DARWIN.

Pray again give my best thanks to Mrs. Lyell.

---

* Murchison.

[The record of what he wrote during the year does not
give a true index of the most important work that was in
progress,—the laying of the foundation-stones of what was to
be the achievement of his life. This is shown in the foregoing letter to Lyell, where he speaks of being "idle," and
the following extract from a letter to Fox, written in June, is
of interest in this point of view:

"I am delighted to hear you are such a good man as not
to have forgotten my questions about the crossing of animals.
It is my prime hobby, and I really think some day I shall be
able to do something in that most intricate subject, species
and varieties."]

1839 to 1841.

[In the winter of 1839 (Jan. 29) my father was married to
his cousin, Emma Wedgwood.* The house in which they
lived for the first few years of their married life, No. 12
Upper Gower Street, was a small common-place London
house, with a drawing-room in front, and a small room behind, in which they lived for the sake of quietness. In later
years my father used to laugh over the surpassing ugliness of
the furniture, carpets, &c., of the Gower Street house. The
only redeeming feature was a better garden than most London houses have, a strip as wide as the house, and thirty
yards long. Even this small space of dingy grass made their
London house more tolerable to its two country-bred inhabitants.

Of his life in London he writes to Fox (October 1839):
"We are living a life of extreme quietness; Delamere itself,
which you describe as so secluded a spot, is, I will answer
for it, quite dissipated compared with Gower Street. We
have given up all parties, for they agree with neither of us;
and if one is quiet in London, there is nothing like its quiet-

---

* Daughter of Josiah Wedgwood of Maer, and grand-daughter of the
founder of the Etruria Pottery Works.

ness—there is a grandeur about its smoky fogs, and the dull distant sounds of cabs and coaches; in fact you may perceive I am becoming a thorough-paced Cockney, and I glory in thoughts that I shall be here for the next six months."

The entries of ill health in the Diary increase in number during these years, and as a consequence the holidays become longer and more frequent.   From April 26 to May 13, 1839, he was at Maer and Shrewsbury.   Again, from August 23 to October 2 he was away from London at Maer, Shrewsbury, and at Birmingham for the meeting of the British Association.

The entry under August 1839 is: "During my visit to Maer, read a little, was much unwell and scandalously idle. I have derived this much good, that *nothing* is so intolerable as idleness."

At the end of 1839 his eldest child was born, and it was then that he began his observations ultimately published in the 'Expression of the Emotions.'   His book on this subject, and the short paper published in 'Mind,'* show how closely he observed his child.   He seems to have been surprised at his own feelings for a young baby, for he wrote to Fox (July 1840): "He [*i. e.* the baby] is so charming that I cannot pretend to any modesty.   I defy anybody to flatter us on our baby, for I defy any one to say anything in its praise of which we are not fully conscious. . . . I had not the smallest conception there was so much in a five-month baby.   You will perceive by this that I have a fine degree of paternal fervour."

During these years he worked intermittently at 'Coral Reefs,' being constantly interrupted by ill health.   Thus he speaks of "recommencing" the subject in February 1839, and again in the October of the same year, and once more in July 1841, "after more than thirteen months' interval."   His other scientific work consisted of a contribution to the Geo-

---

* July 1877.

logical Society,* on the boulders and "till" of South America,
as well as a few other minor papers on geological subjects.
He also worked busily at the ornithological part of the Zoology of the *Beagle, i. e.* the notice of the habits and ranges of
the birds which were described by Gould.]

C. Darwin to C. Lyell.

Wednesday morning [February 1840].

MY DEAR LYELL,

Many thanks for your kind note. I will send for the
Scotsman. Dr. Holland thinks he has found out what is the
matter with me, and now hopes he shall be able to set me
going again. Is it not mortifying, it is now nine weeks since
I have done a whole day's work, and not more than four half
days. But I won't grumble any more, though it is hard work
to prevent doing so. Since receiving your note I have read
over my chapter on Coral, and find I am prepared to stand by
almost everything ; it is much more cautiously and accurately
written than I thought. I had set my heart upon having my
volume completed before your new edition, but not, you may
believe me, for you to notice anything new in it (for there is
very little besides details), but you are the one man in Europe
whose opinion of the general truth of a toughish argument I
should be always most anxious to hear. My MS. is in such
confusion, otherwise I am sure you should most willingly, if it
had been worth your while, have looked at any part you
choose.

    *   *   *   *   *

[In a letter to Fox (January 1841) he shows that his
"Species work" was still occupying his mind :—

"If you attend at all to Natural History I send you this
P.S. as a memento, that I continue to collect all kinds of facts
about 'Varieties and Species,' for my some-day work to be so
entitled ; the smallest contributions thankfully accepted ; descriptions of offspring of all crosses between all domestic birds

* 'Geol. Soc. Proc.' iii. 1842, and 'Geol. Soc. Trans.' vi.

and animals, dogs, cats, &c., &c., very valuable.   Don't forget, if your half-bred African cat should die that I should be
very much obliged for its carcase sent up in a little hamper
for the skeleton ; it, or any cross-bred pigeons, fowl, duck,
&c., &c., will be more acceptable than the finest haunch of
venison, or the finest turtle."

Later in the year (September) he writes to Fox about his
health, and also with reference to his plan of moving into the
country :—

"I have steadily been gaining ground, and really believe
now I shall some day be quite strong.   I write daily for a
couple of hours on my Coral volume, and take a little walk or
ride every day.   I grow very tired in the evenings, and am
not able to go out at that time, or hardly to receive my nearest relations ; but my life ceases to be burdensome now that
I can do something.   We are taking steps to leave London,
and live about twenty miles from it on some railway."]

1842.

[The record of work includes his volume on 'Coral
Reefs,'* the manuscript of which was at last sent to the
printers in January of this year, and the last proof corrected
in May.   He thus writes of the work in his diary :—

"I commenced this work three years and seven months
ago.   Out of this period about twenty months (besides work
during Beagle's voyage) has been spent on it, and besides it,
I have only compiled the Bird part of Zoology ; Appendix
to Journal, paper on Boulders, and corrected papers on Glen
Roy and earthquakes, reading on species, and rest all lost by
illness."

In May and June he was at Shrewsbury and Maer, whence
he went on to make the little tour in Wales, of which he spoke
in his 'Recollections,' and of which the results were published
as "Notes on the effects produced by the ancient glaciers of

---

* A notice of the Coral Reef work appeared in the Geograph. Soc. Journal, xii., p. 115.

Caernarvonshire, and on the Boulders transported by floating Ice." *

Mr. Archibald Geikie speaks of this paper as standing "almost at the top of the long list of English contributions to the history of the Ice Age." †

The latter part of this year belongs to the period including the settlement at Down, and is therefore dealt with in another chapter.]

---

* ' Philosophical Magazine,' 1842, p. 352.
† Charles Darwin, ' Nature ' Series, p. 23.

CHAPTER VIII.

RELIGION.

[The history of this part of my father's life may justly include some mention of his religious views. For although, as he points out, he did not give continuous systematic thought to religious questions, yet we know from his own words that about this time (1836–39) the subject was much before his mind.

In his published works he was reticent on the matter of religion, and what he has left on the subject was not written with a view to publication.*

I believe that his reticence arose from several causes. He felt strongly that a man's religion is an essentially private matter, and one concerning himself alone. This is indicated by the following extract from a letter of 1879 :—†

"What my own views may be is a question of no consequence to any one but myself. But, as you ask, I may state that my judgment often fluctuates . . . In my most extreme fluctuations I have never been an Atheist in the sense of denying the existence of a God. I think that generally (and more and more as I grow older), but not always, that an Agnostic would be the more correct description of my state of mind."

---

* As an exception may be mentioned, a few words of concurrence with Dr. Abbot's 'Truths for the Times,' which my father allowed to be published in the *Index*.

† Addressed to Mr. J. Fordyce, and published by him in his 'Aspects of Scepticism,' 1883.

He naturally shrank from wounding the sensibilities of others in religious matters, and he was also influenced by the consciousness that a man ought not to publish on a subject to which he has not given special and continuous thought. That he felt this caution to apply to himself in the matter of religion is shown in a letter to Dr. F. E. Abbot, of Cambridge, U. S. (Sept. 6, 1871). After explaining that the weakness arising from his bad health prevented him from feeling "equal to deep reflection, on the deepest subject which can fill a man's mind," he goes on to say: "With respect to my former notes to you, I quite forget their contents. I have to write many letters, and can reflect but little on what I write; but I fully believe and hope that I have never written a word, which at the time I did not think; but I think you will agree with me, that anything which is to be given to the public ought to be maturely weighed and cautiously put. It never occurred to me that you would wish to print any extract from my notes: if it had, I would have kept a copy. I put private' from habit, only as yet partially acquired, from some hasty notes of mine having been printed, which were not in the least degree worth printing, though otherwise unobjectionable. It is simply ridiculous to suppose that my former note to you would be worth sending to me, with any part marked which you desire to print; but if you like to do so, I will at once say whether I should have any objection. I feel in some degree unwilling to express myself publicly on religious subjects, as I do not feel that I have thought deeply enough to justify any publicity."

I may also quote from another letter to Dr. Abbot (Nov. 16, 1871), in which my father gives more fully his reasons for not feeling competent to write on religious and moral subjects :—

"I can say with entire truth that I feel honoured by your request that I should become a contributor to the *Index*, and am much obliged for the draft. I fully, also, subscribe to the proposition that it is the duty of every one to spread what he believes to be the truth; and I honour you for doing so, with so much devotion and zeal. But I cannot comply with your request for the following reasons ; and excuse me for giving them in some detail, as I should be very sorry to appear in your eyes ungracious. My health is very weak : I *never* pass 24 hours without many hours of discomfort, when I can do nothing whatever. I have thus, also, lost two whole consecutive months this season. Owing to this weakness, and my head being often giddy, I am unable to master new subjects requiring much thought, and can deal only with old materials. At no time am I a quick thinker or writer : whatever I have done in science has solely been by long pondering, patience and industry.

"Now I have never systematically thought much on religion in relation to science, or on morals in relation to society ; and without steadily keeping my mind on such subjects for a *long* period, I am really incapable of writing anything worth sending to the *Index*."

He was more than once asked to give his views on religion, and he had, as a rule, no objection to doing so in a private letter. Thus in answer to a Dutch student he wrote (April 2, 1873) :—

"I am sure you will excuse my writing at length, when I tell you that I have long been much out of health, and am now staying away from my home for rest.

"It is impossible to answer your question briefly ; and I am not sure that I could do so, even if I wrote at some length. But I may say that the impossibility of conceiving that this grand and wondrous universe, with our conscious selves, arose through chance, seems to me the chief argument for the existence of God ; but whether this is an argument of real value, I have never been able to decide. I am aware that if we admit a first cause, the mind still craves to know whence it came, and how it arose. Nor can I overlook the difficulty from the immense amount of suffering through the world. I am, also, induced to defer to a certain extent to the judgment of the many able men who have fully believed in God ; but here again I see how poor an argument this is. The

safest conclusion seems to me that the whole subject is beyond the scope of man's intellect ; but man can do his duty."

Again in 1879 he was applied to by a German student, in
a similar manner. The letter was answered by a member of
my father's family, who wrote :—

"Mr. Darwin begs me to say that he receives so many letters, that he cannot answer them all.

"He considers that the theory of Evolution is quite compatible with the belief in a God ; but that you must remember
that different persons have different definitions of what they
mean by God."

This, however, did not satisfy the German youth, who
again wrote to my father, and received from him the following reply :—

"I am much engaged, an old man, and out of health, and
I cannot spare time to answer your questions fully,—nor indeed can they be answered. Science has nothing to do with
Christ, except in so far as the habit of scientific research
makes a man cautious in admitting evidence. For myself, I
do not believe that there ever has been any revelation. As
for a future life, every man must judge for himself between
conflicting vague probabilities."

The passages which here follow are extracts, somewhat
abbreviated, from a part of the Autobiography, written in
1876, in which my father gives the history of his religious
views :—

"During these two years * I was led to think much about
religion. Whilst on board the *Beagle* I was quite orthodox,
and I remember being heartily laughed at by several of the
officers (though themselves orthodox) for quoting the Bible
as an unanswerable authority on some point of morality. I
suppose it was the novelty of the argument that amused them.
But I had gradually come by this time, *i.e.* 1836 to 1839, to
see that the Old Testament was no more to be trusted than
the sacred books of the Hindoos. The question then con-

* Oct. 1836 to Jan. 1839.

tinually rose before my mind and would not be banished,—
is it credible that if God were now to make a revelation to
the Hindoos, he would permit it to be connected with the
belief in Vishnu, Siva, &c., as Christianity is connected with
the Old Testament? This appeared to me utterly incredible.

"By further reflecting that the clearest evidence would be
requisite to make any sane man believe in the miracles by
which Christianity is supported,—and that the more we know
of the fixed laws of nature the more incredible do miracles
become,—that the men at that time were ignorant and credu-
lous to a degree almost incomprehensible by us,—that the
Gospels cannot be proved to have been written simultaneously with the events,—that they differ in many important details, far too important, as it seemed to me, to be admitted as
the usual inaccuracies of eye-witnesses;—by such reflections
as these, which I give not as having the least novelty or value,
but as they influenced me, I gradually came to disbelieve in
Christianity as a divine revelation. The fact that many false
religions have spread over large portions of the earth like
wild-fire had some weight with me.

"But I was very unwilling to give up my belief; I feel
sure of this, for I can well remember often and often inventing day-dreams of old letters between distinguished Romans,
and manuscripts being discovered at Pompeii or elsewhere,
which confirmed in the most striking manner all that was
written in the Gospels. But I found it more and more difficult, with free scope given to my imagination, to invent evidence which would suffice to convince me. Thus disbelief
crept over me at a very slow rate, but was at last complete.
The rate was so slow that I felt no distress.

"Although I did not think much about the existence of
a personal God until a considerably later period of my life,
I will here give the vague conclusions to which I have been
driven. The old argument from design in Nature, as given
by Paley, which formerly seemed to me so conclusive, fails,
now that the law of natural selection has been discovered.

We can no longer argue that, for instance, the beautiful hinge of a bivalve shell must have been made by an intelligent being, like the hinge of a door by man. There seems to be no more design in the variability of organic beings, and in the action of natural selection, than in the course which the wind blows. But I have discussed this subject at the end of my book on the 'Variations of Domesticated Animals and Plants,'* and the argument there given has never, as far as I can see, been answered.

"But passing over the endless beautiful adaptations which we everywhere meet with, it may be asked how can the generally beneficent arrangement of the world be accounted for? Some writers indeed are so much impressed with the amount of suffering in the world, that they doubt, if we look to all sentient beings, whether there is more of misery or of happiness; whether the world as a whole is a good or bad one. According to my judgment happiness decidedly prevails, though this would be very difficult to prove. If the truth of this conclusion be granted, it harmonizes well with the effects which we might expect from natural selection. If all the individuals of any species were habitually to suffer to an extreme degree, they would neglect to propagate their kind; but we have no reason to believe that this has ever, or at least often occurred. Some other considerations, moreover, lead to the belief that all sentient beings have been formed so as to enjoy, as a general rule, happiness.

---

* My father asks whether we are to believe that the forms are preordained ôf the broken fragments of rock tumbled from a precipice which are fitted together by man to build his houses. If not, why should we believe that the variations of domestic animals or plants are preordained for the sake of the breeder? "But if we give up the principle in one case, . . . no shadow of reason can be assigned for the belief that variations, alike in nature and the result of the same general laws, which have been the groundwork through natural selection of the formation of the most perfectly adapted animals in the world, man included, were intentionally and specially guided."—' The Variation of Animals and Plants,' 1st Edit. vol. ii. p. 431.—F. D.

"Every one who believes, as I do, that all the corporeal
and mental organs (excepting those which are neither advantageous nor disadvantageous to the possessor) of all beings
have been developed through natural selection, or the survival
of the fittest, together with use or habit, will admit that these
organs have been formed so that their possessors may compete successfully with other beings, and thus increase in number. Now an animal may be led to pursue that course of
action which is most beneficial to the species by suffering,
such as pain, hunger, thirst, and fear ; or by pleasure, as in
eating and drinking, and in the propagation of the species,
&c. ; or by both means combined, as in the search for food.
But pain or suffering of any kind, if long continued, causes
depression and lessens the power of action, yet is well adapted
to make a creature guard itself against any great or sudden
evil.   Pleasurable sensations, on the other hand, may be long
continued without any depressing effect ; on the contrary,
they stimulate the whole system to increased action.   Hence
it has come to pass that most or all sentient beings have been
developed in such a manner, through natural selection, that
pleasurable sensations serve as their habitual guides. We see
this in the pleasure from exertion, even occasionally from
great exertion of the body or mind,—in the pleasure of our
daily meals, and especially in the pleasure derived from socia-
bility, and from loving our families.   The sum of such pleasures as these, which are habitual or frequently recurrent, give,
as I can hardly doubt, to most sentient beings an excess of
happiness over misery, although many occasionally suffer
much.   Such suffering is quite compatible with the belief in
Natural Selection, which is not perfect in its action, but tends
only to render each species as successful as possible in the
battle for life with other species, in wonderfully complex and
changing circumstances.

"That there is much suffering in the world no one dis-
putes.   Some have attempted to explain this with reference
to man by imagining that it serves for his moral improvement.
But the number of men in the world is as nothing compared

with that of all other sentient beings, and they often suffer greatly without any moral improvement. This very old argument from the existence of suffering against the existence of an intelligent First Cause seems to me a strong one ; whereas, as just remarked, the presence of much suffering agrees well with the view that all organic beings have been developed through variation and natural selection.

"At the present day the most usual argument for the existence of an intelligent God is drawn from the deep inward conviction and feelings which are experienced by most persons.

"Formerly I was led by feelings such as those just referred to (although I do not think that the religious sentiment was ever strongly developed in me), to the firm conviction of the existence of God, and of the immortality of the soul. In my Journal I wrote that whilst standing in the midst of the grandeur of a Brazilian forest, "it is not possible to give an adequate idea of the higher feelings of wonder, admiration, and devotion, which fill and elevate the mind." I well remember my conviction that there is more in man than the mere breath of his body. But now the grandest scenes would not cause any such convictions and feelings to rise in my mind. It may be truly said that I am like a man who has become colour-blind, and the universal belief by men of the existence of redness makes my present loss of perception of not the least value as evidence. This argument would be a valid one if all men of all races had the same inward conviction of the existence of one God ; but we know that this is very far from being the case. Therefore I cannot see that such inward convictions and feelings are of any weight as evidence of what really exists. The state of mind which grand scenes formerly excited in me, and which was intimately connected with a belief in God, did not essentially differ from that which is often called the sense of sublimity ; and however difficult it may be to explain the genesis of this sense, it can hardly be advanced as an argument for the existence of God, any more than the powerful though vague and similar feelings excited by music.

"With respect to immortality, nothing shows me [so clearly] how strong and almost instinctive a belief it is, as the consideration of the view now held by most physicists, namely, that the sun with all the planets will in time grow too cold for life, unless indeed some great body dashes into the sun, and thus gives it fresh life. Believing as I do that man in the distant future will be a far more perfect creature than he now is, it is an intolerable thought that he and all other sentient beings are doomed to complete annihilation after such long-continued slow progress. To those who fully admit the immortality of the human soul, the destruction of our world will not appear so dreadful.

"Another source of conviction in the existence of God, connected with the reason, and not with the feelings, impresses me as having much more weight. This follows from the extreme difficulty or rather impossibility of conceiving this immense and wonderful universe, including man with his capacity of looking far backwards and far into futurity, as the result of blind chance or necessity. When thus reflecting I feel compelled to look to a First Cause having an intelligent mind in some degree analogous to that of man; and I deserve to be called a Theist. This conclusion was strong in my mind about the time, as far as I can remember, when I wrote the 'Origin of Species;' and it is since that time that it has very gradually, with many fluctuations, become weaker. But then arises the doubt, can the mind of man, which has, as I fully believe, been developed from a mind as low as that possessed by the lowest animals, be trusted when it draws such grand conclusions?

"I cannot pretend to throw the least light on such abstruse problems. The mystery of the beginning of all things is insoluble by us; and I for one must be content to remain an Agnostic."

The following letters repeat to some extent what has been given from the Autobiography. The first one refers to 'The Boundaries of Science, a Dialogue,' published in 'Macmillan's Magazine,' for July 1861.]

C. Darwin to Miss Julia Wedgwood.

July 11 [1861].

Some one has sent us 'Macmillan'; and I must tell you how much I admire your Article; though at the same time I must confess that I could not clearly follow you in some parts, which probably is in main part due to my not being at all accustomed to metaphysical trains of thought. I think that you understand my book * perfectly, and that I find a very rare event with my critics. The ideas in the last page have several times vaguely crossed my mind. Owing to several correspondents I have been led lately to think, or rather to try to think over some of the chief points discussed by you. But the result has been with me a maze—something like thinking on the origin of evil, to which you allude. The mind refuses to look at this universe, being what it is, without having been designed; yet, where one would most expect design, viz. in the structure of a sentient being, the more I think on the subject, the less I can see proof of design. Asa Gray and some others look at each variation, or at least at each beneficial variation (which A. Gray would compare with the rain drops † which do not fall on the sea, but on to the land to fertilize it) as having been providentially designed. Yet when I ask him whether he looks at each variation in the rock-pigeon, by which man has made by accumulation a pouter or fantail pigeon, as providentially designed for man's

---

* The ' Origin 'of Species.'

† Dr. Gray's rain-drop metaphor occurs in the Essay 'Darwin and his Reviewers' ('Darwiniana,' p. 157): "The whole animate life of a country depends absolutely upon the vegetation, the vegetation upon the rain. The moisture is furnished by the ocean, is raised by the sun's heat from the ocean's surface, and is wafted inland by the winds. But what multitudes of rain-drops fall back into the ocean—are as much without a final cause as the incipient varieties which come to nothing! Does it therefore follow that the rains which are bestowed upon the soil with such rule and average regularity were not designed to support vegetable and animal life?"

amusement, he does not know what to answer; and if he, or any one, admits [that] these variations are accidental, as far as purpose is concerned (of course not accidental as to their cause or origin); then I can see no reason why he should rank the accumulated variations by which the beautifully adapted woodpecker has been formed, as providentially designed. For it would be easy to imagine the enlarged crop of the pouter, or tail of the fantail, as of some use to birds, in a state of nature, having peculiar habits of life. These are the considerations which perplex me about design; but whether you will care to hear them, I know not.

*   *   *   *   *

[On the subject of design, he wrote (July 1860) to Dr. Gray: "One word more on 'designed laws' and 'undesigned results.' I see a bird which I want for food, take my gun and kill it, I do this *designedly*. An innocent and good man stands under a tree and is killed by a flash of lightning. Do you believe (and I really should like to hear) that God *designedly* killed this man? Many or most persons do believe this; I can't and don't. If you believe so, do you believe that when a swallow snaps up a gnat that God designed that that particular swallow should snap up that particular gnat at that particular instant? I believe that the man and the gnat are in the same predicament. If the death of neither man nor gnat are designed, I see no good reason to believe that their *first* birth or production should be necessarily designed."]

C. Darwin to W. Graham.

Down, July 3rd, 1881.

DEAR SIR,

I hope that you will not think it intrusive on my part to thank you heartily for the pleasure which I have derived from reading your admirably written 'Creed of Science,' though I have not yet quite finished it, as now that I am old I read very slowly. It is a very long time since any other book has interested me so much. The work must have cost you several years and much hard labour with full leisure for work. You would not probably expect any one fully to agree with you on so many abstruse subjects ; and there are some points in your book which I cannot digest. The chief one is that the existence of so-called natural laws implies purpose. I cannot see this. Not to mention that many expect that the several great laws will some day be found to follow inevitably from some one single law, yet taking the laws as we now know them, and look at the moon, where the law of gravitation—and no doubt of the conservation of energy—of the atomic theory, &c. &c., hold good, and I cannot see that there is then necessarily any purpose. Would there be purpose if the lowest organisms alone, destitute of consciousness existed in the moon ? But I have had no practice in abstract reasoning, and I may be all astray. Nevertheless you have expressed my inward conviction, though far more vividly and clearly than I could have done, that the Universe is not the result of chance.* But then with me the horrid doubt always arises whether the convictions of man's mind, which has been developed from the mind of the lower animals, are of any value or at all trustworthy. Would any one trust in the convictions of a monkey's mind, if there are any convictions in such a mind ? Secondly, I think that I could make somewhat of a case against the enormous importance which you attribute to our greatest men ; I have been accustomed to think, second, third, and fourth rate men of very high importance, at least in the case of Science. Lastly, I could show fight on natural selection having done and doing more

---

* The Duke of Argyll ('Good Words,' Ap. 1885, p. 244) has recorded a few words on this subject, spoken by my father in the last year of his life. " . . . in the course of that conversation I said to Mr. Darwin, with reference to some of his own remarkable works on the 'Fertilization of Orchids,' and upon 'The Earthworms,' and various other observations he made of the wonderful contrivances for certain purposes in nature—I said it was impossible to look at these without seeing that they were the effect and the expression of mind. I shall never forget Mr. Darwin's answer. He looked at me very hard and said, 'Well, that often comes over me with overwhelming force ; but at other times,' and he shook his head vaguely, adding, 'it seems to go away.'"

for the progress of civilization than you seem inclined to
admit. Remember what risk the nations of Europe ran, not
so many centuries ago of being overwhelmed by the Turks,
and how ridiculous such an idea now is ! The more civilized
so-called Caucasian races have beaten the Turkish hollow in
the struggle for existence. Looking to the world at no very
distant date, what an endless number of the lower races will
have been eliminated by the higher civilized races throughout the world. But I will write no more, and not even mention the many points in your work which have much interested me. I have indeed cause to apologise for troubling
you with my impressions, and my sole excuse is the excitement in my mind which your book has aroused.

　　　　I beg leave to remain,
　　　　　　Dear Sir,
　　　　　　　　Yours faithfully and obliged,
　　　　　　　　　　CHARLES DARWIN.

[My father spoke little on these subjects, and I can contribute nothing from my own recollection of his conversation
which can add to the impression here given of his attitude
towards Religion. Some further idea of his views may, however, be gathered from occasional remarks in his letters.] *

---

* Dr. Aveling has published an account of a conversation with my
father. I think that the readers of this pamphlet ('The Religious Views
of Charles Darwin,' Free Thought Publishing Company, 1883) may be
misled into seeing more resemblance than really existed between the po-
sitions of my father and Dr. Aveling : and I say this in spite of my conviction that Dr. Aveling gives quite fairly his impressions of my father's
views. Dr. Aveling tried to show that the terms "Agnostic" and "Atheist"
were practically equivalent—that an atheist is one who, without denying
the existence of God, is without God, inasmuch as he is unconvinced of
the existence of a Deity. My father's replies implied his preference for
the unaggressive attitude of an Agnostic. Dr. Aveling seems (p. 5) to
regard the absence of aggressiveness in my father's views as distinguishing
them in an unessential manner from his own. But, in my judgment, it is
precisely differences of this kind which distinguish him so completely from
the class of thinkers to which Dr. Aveling belongs.

CHAPTER IX.

LIFE AT DOWN.

1842–1854.

"My life goes on like clockwork, and I am fixed on the spot where I shall end it."

Letter to Captain Fitz-Roy, October, 1846.

[WITH the view of giving in the following chapters a connected account of the growth of the 'Origin of Species,' I have taken the more important letters bearing on that subject out of their proper chronological position here, and placed them with the rest of the correspondence bearing on the same subject; so that in the present group of letters we only get occasional hints of the growth of my father's views, and we may suppose ourselves to be looking at his life, as it might have been looked at by those who had no knowledge of the quiet development of his theory of evolution during this period.

On Sept. 14, 1842, my father left London with his family and settled at Down.* In the Autobiographical chapter, his motives for taking this step in the country are briefly given. He speaks of the attendance at scientific societies, and ordinary social duties, as suiting his health so "badly that we

---

* I must not omit to mention a member of the household who accompanied him. This was his butler, Joseph Parslow, who remained in the family, a valued friend and servant, for forty years, and became, as Sir Joseph Hooker once remarked to me, "an integral part of the family, and felt to be such by all visitors at the house."

resolved to live in the country, which we both preferred and
have never repented of." His intention of keeping up with
scientific life in London is expressed in a letter to Fox (Dec.,
1842):—

"I hope by going up to town for a night every fortnight
or three weeks, to keep up my communication with scientific
men and my own zeal, and so not to turn into a complete
Kentish hog."

Visits to London of this kind were kept up for some years
at the cost of much exertion on his part. I have often heard
him speak of the wearisome drives of ten miles to or from
Croydon or Sydenham—the nearest stations—with an old
gardener acting as coachman, who drove with great caution
and slowness up and down the many hills. In later years,
all regular scientific intercourse with London became, as before mentioned, an impossibility.

The choice of Down was rather the result of despair than
of actual preference; my father and mother were weary of
house-hunting, and the attractive points about the place thus
seemed to them to counterbalance its somewhat more obvious
faults. It had at least one desideratum, namely quietness.
Indeed it would have been difficult to find a more retired
place so near to London. In 1842 a coach drive of some
twenty miles was the only means of access to Down; and
even now that railways have crept closer to it, it is singularly
out of the world, with nothing to suggest the neighbourhood of London, unless it be the dull haze of smoke that
sometimes clouds the sky. The village stands in an angle
between two of the larger high-roads of the country, one
leading to Tunbridge and the other to Westerham and Eden-
bridge. It is cut off from the Weald by a line of steep chalk
hills on the south, and an abrupt hill, now smoothed down
by a cutting and embankment, must formerly have been
something of a barrier against encroachments from the side
of London. In such a situation, a village, communicating
with the main lines of traffic, only by stony tortuous lanes,
may well have been enabled to preserve its retired character.

Nor is it hard to believe in the smugglers and their strings
of pack-horses making their way up from the lawless old
villages of the Weald, of which the memory still existed
when my father settled in Down. The village stands on
solitary upland country, 500 to 600 feet above the sea,—a
country with little natural beauty, but possessing a certain
charm in the shaws, or straggling strips of wood, capping the
chalky banks and looking down upon the quiet ploughed
lands of the valleys. The village, of three or four hundred
inhabitants, consists of three small streets of cottages meeting
in front of the little flint-built church. It is a place where
new-comers are seldom seen, and the names occurring far
back in the old church registers are still well known in the
village. The smock-frock is not yet quite extinct, though
chiefly used as a ceremonial dress by the "bearers" at funer-
als : but as a boy I remember the purple or green smocks of
the men at church.

The house stands a quarter of a mile from the village, and
is built, like so many houses of the last century, as near as
possible to the road—a narrow lane winding away to the
Westerham high-road. In 1842, it was dull and unattractive
enough : a square brick building of three storeys, covered
with shabby whitewash and hanging tiles. The garden
had none of the shrubberies or walls that now give shelter ;
it was overlooked from the lane, and was open, bleak, and
desolate. One of my father's first undertakings was to lower
the lane by about two feet, and to build a flint wall along that
part of it which bordered the garden. The earth thus excavated was used in making banks and mounds round the
lawn : these were planted with evergreens, which now give
to the garden its retired and sheltered character.

The house was made to look neater by being covered with
stucco, but the chief improvement effected was the building
of a large bow extending up through three storeys. This
bow became covered with a tangle of creepers, and pleasantly
varied the south side of the house. The drawing-room, with
its verandah opening into the garden, as well as the study in

which my father worked during the later years of his life, were added at subsequent dates.

Eighteen acres of land were sold with the house, of which twelve acres on the south side of the house formed a pleasant field, scattered with fair-sized oaks and ashes. From this field a strip was cut off and converted into a kitchen garden, in which the experimental plot of ground was situated, and where the greenhouses were ultimately put up.

The following letter to Mr. Fox (March 28th, 1843) gives among other things my father's early impressions of Down :—

"I will tell you all the trifling particulars about myself that I can think of. We are now exceedingly busy with the first brick laid down yesterday to an addition to our house ; with this, with almost making a new kitchen garden and sundry other projected schemes, my days are very full. I find all this very bad for geology, but I am very slowly progressing with a volume, or rather pamphlet, on the volcanic islands which we visited : I manage only a couple of hours per day and that not very regularly. It is uphill work writing books, which cost money in publishing, and which are not read even by geologists. I forget whether I ever described this place : it is a good, very ugly house with 18 acres, situated on a chalk flat, 560 feet above sea. There are peeps of far distant country and the scenery is moderately pretty : its chief merit is its extreme rurality. I think I was never in a more perfectly quiet country. Three miles south of us the great chalk escarpment quite cuts us off from the low country of Kent, and between us and the escarpment there is not a village or gentleman's house, but only great woods and arable fields (the latter in sadly preponderant numbers), so that we are absolutely at the extreme verge of the world. The whole country is intersected by foot-paths ; but the surface over the chalk is clayey and sticky, which is the worst feature in our purchase. The dingles and banks often remind me of Cambridgeshire and walks with you to Cherry Hinton, and other places, though the general aspect of the country is very different. I was looking over my arranged cabinet (the only remnant I

have preserved of all my English insects), and was admiring
Panagæus Crux-major : it is curious the vivid manner in
which this insect calls up in my mind your appearance, with
little Fan trotting after, when I was first introduced to you.
Those entomological days were very pleasant ones. I am *very*
much stronger corporeally, but am little better in being able
to stand mental fatigue, or rather excitement, so that I cannot
dine out or receive visitors, except relations with whom I can
pass some time after dinner in silence."

I could have wished to give here some idea of the position
which, at this period of his life, my father occupied among
scientific men and the reading public generally. But contemporary notices are few and of no particular value for my
purpose,—which therefore must, in spite of a good deal of
pains, remain unfulfilled.

His ' Journal of Researches ' was then the only one of his
books which had any chance of being commonly known. But
the fact that it was published with the ' Voyages ' of Captains
King and Fitz-Roy probably interfered with its general popularity. Thus Lyell wrote to him in 1838 (' Lyell's Life,' ii' p-
43), " I assure you my father is quite enthusiastic about
your journal . . . . and he agrees with me that it would have
a large sale if published separately. He was disappointed
at hearing that it was to be fettered by the other volumes, for,
although he should equally buy it, he feared so many of the
public would be checked from doing so." In a notice of the
three voyages in the ' Edinburgh Review ' (July, 1839), there
is nothing leading a reader to believe that he would find it
more attractive than its fellow-volumes. And, as a fact, it
did not become widely known until it was separately published in 1845. It may be noted, however, that the ' Quarterly Review' (December, 1839) called the attention of its
readers to the merits of the ' Journal ' as a book of travels.
The reviewer speaks of the " charm arising from the freshness of heart which is thrown over these virgin pages of a
strong intellectual man and an acute and deep observer."

The German translation (1844) of the ' Journal ' received

a favourable notice in No. 12 of the 'Heidelberger Jahr-
bücher der Literatur,' 1847—where the Reviewer speaks of
the author's "varied canvas, on which he sketches in lively
colours the strange customs of those distant regions with their
remarkable fauna, flora and geological peculiarities." Alluding
to the translation, my father writes—"Dr. Dieffenbach . . .
has translated my 'Journal' into German, and I must, with
unpardonable vanity, boast that it was at the instigation of
Liebig and Humboldt."

The geological work of which he speaks in the above letter
to Mr. Fox occupied him for the whole of 1843, and was published in the spring of the following year. It was entitled
'Geological Observations on the Volcanic Islands, visited
during the voyage of H. M. S. *Beagle*, together with some brief
notices on the geology of Australia and the Cape of Good
Hope': it formed the second part of the 'Geology of the
Voyage of the *Beagle*,' published "with the Approval of the
Lords Commissioners of Her Majesty's Treasury." The
volume on 'Coral Reefs' forms Part I. of the series, and was
published, as we have seen, in 1842. For the sake of the
non-geological reader, I may here quote Professor Geikie's
words * on these two volumes—which were up to this time
my father's chief geological works. Speaking of the 'Coral
Reefs,' he says :—p. 17, "This well-known treatise, the most
original of all its author's geological memoirs, has become
one of the classics of geological literature. The origin of
those remarkable rings of coral-rock in mid-ocean has given
rise to much speculation, but no satisfactory solution of the
problem has been proposed. After visiting many of them,
and examining also coral reefs that fringe islands and continents, he offered a theory which for simplicity and grandeur
strikes every reader with astonishment. It is pleasant, after
the lapse of many years, to recall the delight with which one
first read the 'Coral Reefs'; how one watched the facts being
marshalled into their places, nothing being ignored or passed

---

* Charles Darwin, 'Nature' Series, 1882.

lightly over; and how, step by step, one was led to the grand conclusion of wide oceanic subsidence. No more admirable example of scientific method was ever given to the world, and even if he had written nothing else, the treatise alone would have placed Darwin in the very front of investigators of nature."

It is interesting to see in the following extract from one of Lyell's letters * how warmly and readily he embraced the theory. The extract also gives incidentally some idea of the theory itself.

"I am very full of Darwin's new theory of Coral Islands, and have urged Whewell to make him read it at our next meeting. I must give up my volcanic crater theory for ever, though it cost me a pang at first, for it accounted for so much, the annular form, the central lagoon, the sudden rising of an isolated mountain in a deep sea; all went so well with the notion of submerged, crateriform, and conical volcanoes, . . . and then the fact that in the South Pacific we had scarcely any rocks in the regions of coral islands, save two kinds, coral limestone and volcanic! Yet spite of all this, the whole theory is knocked on the head, and the annular shape and central lagoon have nothing to do with volcanoes, nor even with a crateriform bottom. Perhaps Darwin told you when at the Cape what he considers the true cause? Let any mountain be submerged gradually, and coral grow in the sea in which it is sinking, and there will be a ring of coral, and finally only a lagoon in the centre. Why? For the same reason that a barrier reef of coral grows along certain coasts : Australia, &c. Coral islands are the last efforts of drowning continents to lift their heads above water. Regions of elevation and subsidence in the ocean may be traced by the state of the coral reefs." There is little to be said as to published contemporary criticism. The book was not reviewed in the 'Quarterly Review' till 1847, when a favourable notice was

* To Sir John Herschel, May 24, 1837. 'Life of Sir Charles Lyell,' vol. ii. p. 12.

given. The reviewer speaks of the "bold and startling" character of the work, but seems to recognize the fact that the views are generally accepted by geologists. By that time the minds of men were becoming more ready to receive geology of this type. Even ten years before, in 1837, Lyell * says, "people are now much better prepared to believe Darwin when he advances proofs of the slow rise of the Andes, than they were in 1830, when I first startled them with that doctrine." This sentence refers to the theory elaborated in my father's geological observations on South America (1846), but the gradual change in receptivity of the geological mind must have been favourable to all his geological work. Nevertheless, Lyell seems at first not to have expected any ready acceptance of the Coral theory; thus he wrote to my father in 1837:—"I could think of nothing for days after your lesson on coral reefs, but of the tops of submerged continents. It is all true, but do not flatter yourself that you will be believed till you are growing bald like me, with hard work and vexation at the incredulity of the world."

The second part of the 'Geology of the Voyage of the Beagle,' i.e. the volume on Volcanic Islands, which specially concerns us now, cannot be better described than by again quoting from Professor Geikie (p. 18):—

"Full of detailed observations, this work still remains the best authority on the general geological structure of most of the regions it describes. At the time it was written the 'crater of elevation theory,' though opposed by Constant Prévost, Scrope, and Lyell, was generally accepted, at least on the Continent. Darwin, however, could not receive it as a valid explanation of the facts; and though he did not share the view of its chief opponents, but ventured to propose a hypothesis of his own, the observations impartially made and described by him in this volume must be regarded as having contributed towards the final solution of the difficulty." Professor Geikie continues (p. 21): "He is one of the earliest

* 'Life of Sir Charles Lyell,' vol. ii. p. 6.

writers to recognize the magnitude of the denudation to which even recent geological accumulations have been· subjected. One of the most impressive lessons to be learnt from his account of 'Volcanic Islands' is the prodigious extent to which they have been denuded. . . . He was disposed to attribute more of this work to the sea than most geologists would now admit; but he lived himself to modify his original views, and on this subject his latest utterances are quite abreast of the time."

An extract from a letter of my father's to Lyell shows his estimate of his own work. "You have pleased me much by saying that you intend looking through my 'Volcanic Islands': it cost me eighteen months! ! ! and I have heard of very few who have read it. Now I shall feel, whatever little (and little it is) there is confirmatory of old work, or new, will work its effect and not be lost."

The third of his geological books, 'Geological Observations on South America,' may be mentioned here, although it was not published until 1846. "In this work the author embodied all the materials collected by him for the illustration of South American Geology, save some which have been published elsewhere. One of the most important features of the book was the evidence which it brought forward to prove the slow interrupted elevation of the South American Continent during a recent geological period."*

Of this book my father wrote to Lyell :—" My volume will be about 240 pages, dreadfully dull, yet much condensed. I think whenever you have time to look through it, you will think the collection of facts on the elevation of the land and on the formation of terraces pretty good."

Of his special geological work as a whole, Professor Geikie, while pointing out that it was not "of the same epoch-making kind as his biological researches," remarks that he "gave a powerful impulse to" the general reception of Lyell's teaching "by the way in which he gathered from all parts of the world facts in its support."

---

* Geikie, *loc. cit.*

WORK OF THE PERIOD 1842 TO 1854.

The work of these years may be roughly divided into a period of geology from 1842 to 1846, and one of zoology from 1846 onwards.

I extract from his diary notices of the time spent on his geological books and on his ' Journal.'

' Volcanic Islands.'   Summer of 1842 to January, 1844.

' Geology of South America.'   July, 1844, to April, 1845.

Second Edition of ' The Journal,' October, 1845, to October, 1846.

The time between October, 1846, and October, 1854, was practically given up to working at the Cirripedia (Barnacles) ; the results were published in two volumes by the Ray Society in 1851 and 1854.   His volumes on the Fossil Cirripedes were published by the Palæontographical Society in 1851 and 1854.

Some account of these volumes will be given later.

The minor works may be placed together, independently of subject matter.

" Observations on the Structure, &c., of the genus Sagitta," Ann. Nat. Hist. xiii., 1844, pp. 1–6.

" Brief Descriptions of several Terrestrial Planariæ, &c.," Ann. Nat. Hist. xiv., 1844, pp. 241–251.

" An Account of the Fine Dust * which often Falls on Vessels in the Atlantic Ocean," Geol. Soc. Journ. ii., 1846, pp. 26–30.

" On the Geology of the Falkland Islands," Geol. Soc. Journ. ii., 1846, pp. 267–274.

" On the Transportal of Erratic Boulders, &c.," Geol. Soc. Journ. iv., 1848, pp. 315–323.†

---

* A sentence occurs in this paper of interest, as showing that the author was alive to the importance of all means of distribution :—" The fact that particles of this size have been brought at least 330 miles from the land is interesting as bearing on the distribution of Cryptogamic plants."

† An extract from a letter to Lyell, 1847, is of interest in connection with this essay :—" Would you be so good (if you know it) as to put Maclaren's

The article "Geology," in the Admiralty Manual of Scientific Enquiry (1849), pp. 156–195. This was written in the spring of 1848.

"On British Fossil Lepadidæ," 'Geol. Soc. Journ.' vi., 1850, pp. 439–440.

"Analogy of the structure of some Volcanic Rocks with that of Glaciers," 'Edin. Roy. Soc. Proc.' ii., 1851, pp. 17–18.

Professor Geikie has been so good as to give me (in a letter dated Nov. 1885) his impressions of my father's article in the 'Admiralty Manual.' He mentions the following points as characteristic of the work :—

" 1. Great breadth of view. No one who had not practically studied and profoundly reflected on the questions discussed could have written it.

" 2. The insight so remarkable in all that Mr. Darwin ever did. The way in which he points out lines of enquiry that would elucidate geological problems is eminently typical of him. Some of these lines have never yet been adequately followed; so with regard to them he was in advance of his time.

" 3. Interesting and sympathetic treatment. The author at once puts his readers into harmony with him. He gives them enough of information to show how delightful the field is to which he invites them, and how much they might accomplish in it. There is a broad sketch of the subject

---

address on the enclosed letter and post it. It is chiefly to enquire in what paper he has described the Boulders on Arthur's Seat. Mr. D. Milne in the last Edinburgh 'New Phil. Journal' [1847], has a long paper on it. He says: 'Some glacialists have ventured to explain the transportation of boulders even in the situation of those now referred to, by imagining that they were transported on ice floes,' &c. He treats this view, and the scratching of rocks by icebergs, as almost absurd . . . he has finally stirred me up so, that (without you would answer him) I think I will send a paper in opposition to the same Journal. I can thus introduce some old remarks of mine, and some new, and will insist on your capital observations in N. America. It is a bore to stop one's work, but he has made me quite wroth."

20

which everybody can follow, and there is enough of detail to instruct and guide a beginner and start him on the right track.

"Of course, geology has made great strides since 1849, and the article, if written now, would need to take notice of other branches of enquiry, and to modify statements which are not now quite accurate ; but most of the advice Mr. Darwin gives is as needful and valuable now as when it was given. It is curious to see with what unerring instinct he seems to have fastened on the principles that would stand the test of time."

In a letter to Lyell (1853) my father wrote, "I went up for a paper by the Arctic Dr. Sutherland, on ice action, read only in abstract, but I should think with much good matter. It was very pleasant to hear that it was written owing to the Admiralty Manual."

To give some idea of the retired life which now began for my father at Down, I have noted from his diary the short periods during which he was away from home between the autumn of 1842, when he came to Down, and the end of 1854.

1843, *July.*—Week at Maer and Shrewsbury.

  „   *October.*—Twelve days at Shrewsbury.

1844, *April.*—Week at Maer and Shrewsbury.

  „   *July.*—Twelve days at Shrewsbury.

1845, *September* 15.—Six weeks, "Shrewsbury, Lincolnshire, York, the Dean of Manchester, Waterton, Chatsworth."

1846, *February.*—Eleven days at Shrewsbury.

  „   *July.*—Ten days at Shrewsbury.

  „   *September.*—Ten days at Southampton, &c., for the British Association.

1847, *February.*—Twelve days at Shrewsbury.

  „   *June.*—Ten days at Oxford, &c., for the British Association.

  „   *October.*—Fortnight at Shrewsbury.

1848, *May.*—Fortnight at Shrewsbury.

„ *July.*—Week at Swanage.

„ *October.*—Fortnight at Shrewsbury.

„ *November.*—Eleven days at Shrewsbury.

1849, *March to June.*—Sixteen weeks at Malvern.

„ *September.*—Eleven days at Birmingham for the British Association.

1850, *June.*—Week at Malvern.

„ *August.*—Week at Leith Hill, the house of a relative.

„ *October.*—Week at the house of another relative.

1851, *March.*—Week at Malvern.

„ *April.*—Nine days at Malvern.

„ *July.*—Twelve days in London.

1852, *March.*—Week at Rugby and Shrewsbury.

„ *September.*—Six days at the house of a relative.

1853, *July.*—Three weeks at Eastbourne.

„ *August.*—Five days at the military Camp at Chobham.

1854, *March.*—Five days at the house of a relative.

„ *July.*—Three days at the house of a relative.

„ *October.*—Six days at the house of a relative.

It will be seen that he was absent from home sixty weeks in twelve years. But it must be remembered that much of the remaining time spent at Down was lost through ill-health.]

LETTERS.

C. Darwin to R. Fitz-Roy.

Down [March 31st, 1843].

DEAR FITZ-ROY,—I read yesterday with surprise and the greatest interest, your appointment as Governor of New Zealand. I do not know whether to congratulate you on it, but I am sure I may the Colony, on possessing your zeal and energy. I am most anxious to know whether the report is true, for I cannot bear the thoughts of your leaving the country without seeing you once again ; the past is often in

my memory, and I feel that I owe to you much bygone enjoyment, and the whole destiny of my life, which (had my health
been stronger) would have been one full of satisfaction to me.
During the last three months I have never once gone up to
London without intending to call in the hopes of seeing Mrs.
Fitz-Roy and yourself; but I find, most unfortunately for
myself, that the little excitement of breaking out of my most
quiet routine so generally knocks me up, that I am able to do
scarcely anything when in London, and I have not even been
able to attend one evening meeting of the Geological Society.
Otherwise, I am very well, as are, thank God, my wife and
two children. The extreme retirement of this place suits us
all very well, and we enjoy our country life much. But I am
writing trifles about myself, when your mind and time must
be fully occupied. My object in writing is to beg of you or
Mrs. Fitz-Roy to have the kindness to send me one line to
say whether it is true, and whether you sail soon. I shall
come up next week for one or two days; could you see me
for even five minutes, if I called early on Thursday morning,
viz. at nine or ten o'clock, or at whatever hour (if you keep
early ship hours) you finish your breakfast. Pray remember
me very kindly to Mrs. Fitz-Roy, who I trust is able to look
at her long voyage with boldness.

Believe me, dear Fitz-Roy,

Your ever truly obliged,

CHARLES DARWIN.

[A quotation from another letter (1846) to Fitz-Roy may
be worth giving, as showing my father's affectionate remembrance of his old Captain.

"Farewell, dear Fitz-Roy, I often think of your many
acts of kindness to me, and not seldomest on the time, no
doubt quite forgotten by you, when, before making Madeira,
you came and arranged my hammock with your own hands,
and which, as I afterwards heard, brought tears into my
father's eyes."]

C. Darwin to W. D. Fox.

[Down, September 5, 1843.]
Monday morning.

My DEAR Fox,—When I sent off the glacier paper, I was just going out and so had no time to write. I hope your friend will enjoy (and I wish you were going there with him) his tour as much as I did. It was a kind of geological novel. But your friend must have patience, for he will not get a good *glacial eye* for a few days. Murchison and Count Keyserling *rushed* through North Wales the same autumn and could see nothing except the effects of rain trickling over the rocks! I cross-examined Murchison a little, and evidently saw he had looked carefully at nothing. I feel *certain* about the glacier-effects in North Wales. Get up your steam, if this weather lasts, and have a ramble in Wales; its glorious scenery must do every one's heart and body good. I wish I had energy to come to Delamere and go with you; but as you observe, you might as well ask St. Paul's. Whenever I give myself a trip, it shall be, I think, to Scotland, to hunt for more parallel roads. My marine theory for these roads was for a time knocked on the head by Agassiz ice-work, but it is now reviving again. . . .

Farewell,—we are getting nearly finished—almost all the workmen gone, and the gravel laying down on the walks. Ave Maria! how the money does go. There are twice as many temptations to extravagance in the country compared with London. Adios.

Yours,
C. DARWIN.

C. Darwin to J. D. Hooker.

Down [1844 ?].

. . . . I have also read the 'Vestiges,' * but have been somewhat less amused at it than you appear to have been:

---

* 'The Vestiges of the Natural History of Creation' was published anonymously in 1844, and is confidently believed to have been written by

the writing and arrangement are certainly admirable, but his geology strikes me as bad, and his zoology far worse. I should be very much obliged, if at any future or leisure time you could tell me on what you ground your doubtful belief in imagination of a mother affecting her offspring.* I have attended to the several statements scattered about, but do not believe in more than accidental coincidences. W. Hunter told my father, then in a lying-in hospital, that in many thousand cases, he had asked the mother, *before her confinement*, whether anything had affected her imagination, and recorded the answers; and absolutely not one case came right, though, when the child was anything remarkable, they afterwards made the cap to fit. Reproduction seems governed by such similar laws in the whole animal kingdom, that I am most loth [to believe]. . . .

C. Darwin to J. M. Herbert.

Down [1844 or 1845].

MY DEAR HERBERT,—I was very glad to see your handwriting and hear a bit of news about you   Though you cannot come here this autumn, I do hope you and Mrs. Herbert will come in the winter, and we will have lots of talk of old times, and lots of Beethoven.

---

the late Robert Chambers. My father's copy gives signs of having been carefully read, a long list of marked passages being pinned in at the end. One useful lesson he seems to have learned from it. He writes : " The idea of a fish passing into a reptile, monstrous. I will not specify any genealogies—much too little known at present." He refers again to the book in a letter to Fox, February, 1845 : " Have you read that strange, unphilosophical, but capitally-written book, the ' Vestiges ' : it has made more talk than any work of late, and has been by some attributed to me— at which I ought to be much flattered and unflattered "

* This refers to the case of a relative of Sir J. Hooker's, who insisted that a mole, which appeared on one of her children, was the effect of fright upon herself on having, before the birth of the child, blotted with sepia a copy of Turner's ' Liber Studiorum ' that had been lent to her with special injunctions to be careful.

I have little or rather nothing to say about myself ; we live like clock-work, and in what most people would consider the dullest possible manner. I have of late been slaving extra hard, to the great discomfiture of wretched digestive organs, at South America, and thank all the fates, I have done three-fourths of it. Writing plain English grows with me more and more difficult, and never attainable. As for your pretending that you will read anything so dull as my pure geological descriptions, lay not such a flattering unction on my soul * for it is incredible. I have long discovered that geologists never read each other's works, and that the only object in writing a book is a proof of earnestness, and that you do not form your opinions without undergoing labour of some kind. Geology is at present very oral, and what I here say is to a great extent quite true. But I am giving you a discussion as long as a chapter in the odious book itself.

I have lately been to Shrewsbury, and found my father surprisingly well and cheerful.

Believe me, my dear old friend, ever yours,

C. DARWIN.

C. Darwin to J. D. Hooker.

Down, Monday [February 10th, 1845].

MY DEAR HOOKER,—I am much obliged for your very agreeable letter ; it was very good-natured, in the midst of your scientific and theatrical dissipation, to think of writing so long a letter to me. I am astonished at your news, and I must condole with you in your *present* view of the Professor-ship,† and most heartily deplore it on my own account. There

---

* On the same subject he wrote to Fitz-Roy : " I have sent my ' South American Geology ' to Dover Street, and you will get it, no doubt, in the course of time. You do not know what you threaten when you propose to read it—it is purely geological. I said to my brother, ' You will of course read it,' and his answer was, ' Upon my life, I would sooner even buy it.' "

† Sir J. D. Hooker was a candidate for the Professorship of Botany at Edinburgh University.

is something so chilling in a separation of so many hundred
miles, though we did not see much of each other when nearer.
You will hardly believe how deeply I regret for *myself* your
present prospects.   I had looked forward to [our] seeing
much of each other during our lives.   It is a heavy disappointment; and in a mere selfish point of view, as aiding me
in my work, your loss is indeed irreparable.   But, on the
other hand, I cannot doubt that you take at present a de-
sponding, instead of bright, view of your prospects : surely
there are great advantages, as well as disadvantages.   The
place is one of eminence; and really it appears to me there
are so many indifferent workers, and so few readers, that it
is a high advantage, in a purely scientific point of view, for a
good worker to hold a position which leads others to attend
to his work.   I forget whether you attended Edinburgh, as a
student, but in my time there was a knot of men who were
far from being the indifferent and dull listeners which you
expect for your audience.   Reflect what a satisfaction and
honour it would be to *make* a good botanist—with your disposition you will be to many what Henslow was at Cambridge
to me and others, a most kind friend and guide.   Then what
a fine garden, and how good a Public Library ! why, Forbes
always regrets the advantages of Edinburgh for work : think
of the inestimable advantage of getting within a short walk of
those noble rocks and hills and sandy shores near Edinburgh !
Indeed, I cannot pity you much, though I pity myself exceedingly in your loss.   Surely lecturing will, in a year or
two, with your *great* capacity for work (whatever you may be
pleased to say to the contrary) become easy, and you will
have a fair time for your Antarctic Flora and general views
of distribution.   If I thought your Professorship would stop
your work, I should wish it and all the good worldly consequences at *el Diavolo*.   I know I shall live to see you the
first authority in Europe on that grand subject, that almost
keystone of the laws of creation, Geographical Distribution.
Well, there is one comfort, you will be at Kew, no doubt,
every year, so I shall finish by forcing down your throat my

sincere congratulations.   Thanks for all your news.   I grieve
to hear Humboldt is failing ; one cannot help feeling, though
unrightly, that such an end is humiliating : even when I saw
him he talked beyond all reason.   If you see him again, pray
give him my most respectful and kind compliments, and say
that I never forget that my whole course of life is due to
having read and re-read as a youth his ' Personal Narrative.'
How true and pleasing are all your remarks on his kindness ;
think how many opportunities you will have, in your new
place, of being a Humboldt to others.   Ask him about the
river in N. E. Europe, with the Flora very different on its
opposite banks.   I have got and read your Wilkes ; what a
feeble book in matter and style, and how splendidly got up !
Do write me a line from Berlin.   Also thanks for the proof-
sheets.   I did not, however, mean proof plates ; I value them,
as saving me copying extracts.   Farewell, my dear Hooker,
with a heavy heart I wish you joy of your prospects.

Your sincere friend,

C. DARWIN.

[The second edition of the ' Journal,' to which the following letter refers, was completed between April 25th and August 25th.   It was published by Mr. Murray in the ' Colonial
and Home Library,' and in this more accessible form soon
had a large sale.

Up to the time of his first negotiations with Mr. Murray
for its publication in this form, he had received payment only
in the form of a large number of presentation copies, and he
seems to have been glad to sell the copyright of the second
edition to Mr. Murray for 150*l.*

The points of difference between it and the first edition
are of interest chiefly in connection with the growth of the
author's views on evolution, and will be considered later.]

C. Darwin to C. Lyell.

Down [July, 1845].

MY DEAR LYELL,—I send you the first part * of the new edition [of the ' Journal of Researches '], which I so entirely owe to you.   You will see that I have ventured to dedicate it to you,† and I trust that this cannot be disagreeable.   I have long wished, not so much for your sake, as for my own feelings of honesty, to acknowledge more plainly than by mere refer- ence, how much I geologically owe you.   Those authors, how- ever, who like you, educate people's minds as well as teach them special facts, can never, I should think, have full justice done them except by posterity, for the mind thus insensibly improved can hardly perceive its own upward ascent.   I had intended putting in the present acknowledgment in the third part of my Geology, but its sale is so exceedingly small that I should not have had the satisfaction of thinking that as far as lay in my power I had owned, though imperfectly, my debt. Pray do not think that I am so silly, as to suppose that my dedication can any ways gratify you, except so far as I trust you will receive it, as a most sincere mark of my gratitude and friendship.   I think I have improved this edition, espe- cially the second part, which I have just finished.   I have added a good deal about the Fuegians, and cut down into half the mercilessly long discussion on climate and glaciers, &c.   I do not recollect anything added to the first part, long enough to call your attention to; there is a page of descrip- tion of a very curious breed of oxen in Banda Oriental.   I should like you to read the few last pages; there is a little discussion on extinction, which will not perhaps strike you

---

* No doubt proof-sheets.

† The dedication of the second edition of the ' Journal of Researches,' is as follows :—" To Charles Lyell, Esq., F. R. S., this second edition is dedicated with grateful pleasure—as an acknowledgment that the chief part of whatever scientific merit this Journal and the other works of the Author may possess, has been derived from studying the well-known and admirable ' Principles of Geology.' "

as new, though it has so struck me, and has placed in my
mind all the difficulties with respect to the causes of extinction, in the same class with other difficulties which are generally quite overlooked and undervalued by naturalists; I ought,
however, to have made my discussion longer and shewn by
facts, as I easily could, how steadily every species must be
checked in its numbers.

I received your Travels * yesterday; and I like exceedingly its external and internal appearance; I read only about
a dozen pages last night (for I was tired with hay-making),
but I saw quite enough to perceive how *very* much it will interest ·me, and how many passages will be scored.   I am
pleased to find a good sprinkling of Natural History; I shall
be astonished if it does not sell very largely. . . .

How sorry I am to think that we shall not see you here
again for so long; I wish you may knock yourself a little bit
up before you start and require a day's fresh air, before the
ocean breezes blow on you. . . .

Ever yours,
C. DARWIN.

C. Darwin to C. Lyell.

Down, Saturday [August 1st, 1845].

MY DEAR LYELL,—I have been wishing to write to you for
a week past, but every five minutes' worth of strength has
been expended in getting out my second part.†   Your note
pleased me a good deal more I dare say than my dedication
did you, and I thank you much for it.   Your work has interested me much, and I will give you my impressions,
though, as I never thought you would care to hear what I
thought of the non-scientific parts, I made no notes, nor
took pains to remember any particular impression of two-
thirds of the first volume.   The first impression I should say

---

* 'Travels in North America,' 2 vols., 1845.
† Of the second edition of the 'Journal of Researches.'

would be with most (though I have literally seen not one
soul since reading it) regret at there not being more of the
non-scientific [parts].   I am not a good judge, for I have
read nothing, *i. e.* non-scientific about North America, but the
whole struck me as very new, fresh, and interesting.   Your
discussions bore to my mind the evident stamp of matured
thought, and of conclusions drawn from facts observed by
yourself, and not from the opinions of the people whom you
met; and this I suspect is comparatively rare.

Your slave discussion disturbed me much; but as you
would care no more for my opinion on this head than for the
ashes of this letter, I will say nothing except that it gave me
some slee, less, most uncomfortable hours.   Your account of
the religious state of the States particularly interested me; I
am surprised throughout at your very proper boldness against
the Clergy.   In your University chapter the Clergy, and not
the State of Education, are most severely and justly handled,
and, this I think is very bold, for I conceive you might crush
a leaden-headed old Don, as a Don, with more safety, than
touch the finger of that Corporate Animal, the Clergy.   What
a contrast in Education does England shew itself!   Your
apology (using the term, like the old religionists who meant
anything but an apology) for lectures, struck me as very
clever; but all the arguments in the world on your side, are
not equal to one course of Jamieson's Lectures on the other
side, which I formerly for my sins experienced.   Although
I had read about the 'Coalfields in North America,' I never
in the smallest degree really comprehended their area, their
thickness and favourable position; nothing hardly astounded
me more in your book.

Some few parts struck me as rather heterogeneous, but I do
not know whether to an extent that at all signified.   I missed
however, a good. deal, some general heading to the chapters,
such as the two or three principal places visited.   One has
no right to expect an author to write down to the zero of geographical ignorance of the reader; but I not knowing a single
place, was occasionally rather plagued in tracing your course.

Sometimes in the beginning of a chapter, in one paragraph your course was traced through a half dozen places; anyone, as ignorant as myself, if he could be found, would prefer such a disturbing paragraph left out. I cut your map loose, and I found that a great comfort; I could not follow your engraved track. I think in a second edition, interspaces here and there of one line open, would be an improvement. By the way, I take credit to myself in giving my Journal a less scientific air in having printed all names of species and genera in Romans; the printing looks, also, better. All the illustrations strike me as capital, and the map is an admirable volume in itself. If your 'Principles' had not met with such universal admiration, I should have feared there would have been too much geology in this for the general reader; certainly all that the most clear and light style could do, has been done. To myself the geology was an excellent, well-condensed, well-digested *résumé* of all that has been made out in North America, and every geologist ought to be grateful to you. The summing up of the Niagara chapter appeared to me the grandest part; I was also deeply interested by your discussion on the origin of the Silurian formations. I have made scores of *scores* marking passages hereafter useful to me.

All the coal theory appeared to me very good; but it is no use going on enumerating in this manner. I wish there had been more Natural History; I liked *all* the scattered fragments. I have now given you an exact transcript of my thoughts, but they are hardly worth your reading. . . .

C. Darwin to C. Lyell.

Down, August 25th [1845].

MY DEAR LYELL,—This is literally the first day on which I have had any time to spare; and I will amuse myself by beginning a letter to you. . . .

I was delighted with your letter in which you touch on Slavery; I wish the same feelings had been apparent in your published discussion. But I will not write on this subject, I should perhaps annoy you, and most certainly myself. I have exhaled myself with a paragraph or two in my Journal on the sin of Brazilian slavery; you perhaps will think that it is in answer to you; but such is not the case. I have remarked on nothing which I did not hear on the coast of South America. My few sentences, however, are merely an explosion of feeling. How could you relate so placidly that atrocious sentiment * about separating children from their parents; and in the next page speak of being distressed at the whites not having prospered; I assure you the contrast made me exclaim out. But I have broken my intention, and so no more on this odious deadly subject.

There is a favourable, but not strong enough review on you, in the *Gardeners' Chronicle.* I am sorry to see that Lindley abides by the carbonic acid gas theory. By the way, I was much pleased by Lindley picking out my extinction paragraphs and giving them uncurtailed. To my mind, putting the comparative rarity of existing species in the same category with extinction has removed a great weight; though of course it does not explain anything, it shows that until we can explain comparative rarity, we ought not to feel any surprise at not explaining extinction. . . .

I am much pleased to hear of the call for a new edition of the 'Principles': what glorious good that work has done. I fear this time you will not be amongst the old rocks; how I shall rejoice to live to see you publish and discover another stage below the Silurian—it would be the grandest step possible, I think. I am very glad to hear what progress Bunbury is making in fossil Botany; there is a fine hiatus for him to fill up in this country. I will certainly call on him this winter. . . . From what little I saw of him, I can quite believe everything which you say of his talents. . . .

---

* In the passage referred to, Lyell does not give his own views, but those of a planter.

C. *Darwin to J. D. Hooker.*

MY DEAR HOOKER,—I have just received your note, which has astonished me, and has most truly grieved me. I never for one minute doubted of your success, for I most erroneously imagined, that merit was sure to gain the day. I feel most sure that the day will come soon, when those who have voted against you, if they have any shame or conscience in them, will be ashamed at having allowed politics to blind their eyes to your qualifications, and those qualifications vouched for by Humboldt and Brown ! Well, those testimonials must be a consolation to you. *Proh pudor!* I am vexed and indignant by turns. I cannot even take comfort in thinking that I shall see more of you, and extract more knowledge from your well-arranged stock. I am pleased to think, that after having read a few of your letters, I never once doubted the position you will ultimately hold amongst European Botanists. I can think about nothing else, otherwise I should like [to] discuss ' Cosmos ' * with you. I trust you will pay me and my wife a visit this autumn at Down. I shall be at Down on the 24th, and till then moving about.

My dear Hooker, allow me to call myself

Your very true friend,

C. DARWIN.

C. *Darwin to C. Lyell.*

October 8th [1845], Shrewsbury.

. . . I have lately been taking a little tour to see a farm I have purchased in Lincolnshire,† and then to York, where I

---

* A translation of Humboldt's ' Kosmos.'

† He speaks of his Lincolnshire farm in a letter to Henslow (July 4th) :—" I have bought a farm in Lincolnshire, and when I go there this autumn, I mean to see what I can do in providing any cottage on my small estate with gardens. It is a hopeless thing to look to, but I believe few things would do this country more good in future ages than the destruction

visited the Dean of Manchester,* the great maker of Hybrids, who gave me much curious information. I also visited Waterton at Walton Hall, and was extremely amused with my visit there. He is an amusing strange fellow; at our early dinner, our party consisted of two Catholic priests and two Mulattresses! He is past sixty years old, and the day before ran down and caught a leveret in a turnip-field. It is a fine old house, and the lake swarms with water-fowl. I then saw Chatsworth, and was in transport with the great hothouse; it is a perfect fragment of a tropical forest, and the sight made me think with delight of old recollections. My little ten-day tour made me feel wonderfully strong at the time, but the good effects did not last. My wife, I am sorry to say, does not get very strong, and the children are the hope of the family, for they are all happy, life, and spirits. I have been much interested with Sedgwick's review;† though I find it far from popular with our scientific readers. I think some few passages savour of the dogmatism of the pulpit, rather than of the philosophy of the Professor's Chair; and some of the wit strikes me as only worthy of —— in the 'Quarterly.' Nevertheless, it is a grand piece of argument against mutability of species, and I read it with fear and trembling, but was well pleased to find that I had not overlooked any of the arguments, though I had put them to myself as feebly as

---

of primogeniture, so as to lessen the difference in land-wealth, and make more small freeholders. How atrociously unjust are the stamp laws, which render it so expensive for the poor man to buy his quarter of an acre; it makes one's blood burn with indignation."

* Hon. and Rev. W. Herbert. The visit is mentioned in a letter to Dr. Hooker:—"I have been taking a little tour, partly on business, and visited the Dean of Manchester, and had very much interesting talk with him on hybrids, sterility, and variation, &c., &c. He is full of self-gained knowledge, but knows surprisingly little what others have done on the same subjects. He is very heterodox on 'species': not much better. as most naturalists would esteem it, than poor Mr. Vestiges."

† Sedgwick's review of the 'Vestiges of Creation' in the 'Edinburgh Review,' July, 1845.

milk and water.   Have you read ' Cosmos' yet?   The English translation is wretched, and the semi-metaphysico-politico
descriptions in the first part are barely intelligible; but I
think the volcanic discussion well worth your attention, it has
astonished me by its vigour and information.   I grieve to find
Humboldt an adorer of Von Buch, with his classification of
volcanos, craters of elevation, &c., &c., and carbonic acid gas
atmosphere.   He is indeed a wonderful man.

I hope to get home in a fortnight and stick to my weary-
ful South America till I finish it.   I shall be very anxious to
hear how you get on from the Horners, but you must not
think of wasting your time by writing to me.   We shall miss,
indeed, your visits to Down, and I shall feel a lost man
in London without my morning "house of call" at Hart
Street. . . .

Believe me, my dear Lyell, ever yours,

C. DARWIN.

C. Darwin to J. D. Hooker.

Down, Farnborough, Kent.
Thursday, September, 1846.

MY DEAR HOOKER,—I hope this letter will catch you at
Clifton, but I have been prevented writing by being unwell,
and having had the Horners here as visitors, which, with my
abominable press-work, has fully occupied my time.   It is,
indeed, a long time since we wrote to each other; though, I
beg to tell you, that I wrote last, but what about I cannot
remember, except, I know, it was after reading your last
numbers,* and I sent you a uniquely laudatory epistle, considering it was from a man who hardly knows a Daisy from
a Dandelion to a professed Botanist. . . .

I cannot remember what papers have given me the impression, but I have that, which you state to be the case,
firmly fixed on my mind, namely, the little chemical importance of the soil to its vegetation.   What a strong fact it is,

---

* Sir J. D. Hooker's Antarctic Botany.

21

as R. Brown once remarked to me, of certain plants being calcareous ones here, which are not so under a more favourable climate on the Continent, or the reverse, for I forget which; but you, no doubt, will know to what I refer. By-the-way, there are some such cases in Herbert's paper in the 'Horticultural Journal.' * Have you read it: it struck me as extremely original, and bears *directly* on your present researches.† To a *non-botanist* the chalk has the most peculiar aspect of any flora in England; why will you not come here to make your observations? *We* go to Southampton, if my courage and stomach do not fail, for the Brit. Assoc. (Do you not consider it your duty to be there?) And why cannot you come here afterward and *work?* . . . .

The Monograph of the Cirripedia,
October 1846 *to October* 1854.

[Writing to Sir J. D. Hooker in 1845, my father says : "I hope this next summer to finish my South American Geology, then to get out a little Zoology, and hurrah for my species work. . . ." This passage serves to show that he had at this time no intention of making an exhaustive study of the Cirripedes. Indeed it would seem that his original intention was, as I learn from Sir J. D. Hooker, merely to work out one special problem. This is quite in keeping with the following passage in the Autobiography : "When on the coast of Chile, I found a most curious form, which burrowed into the shells of Concholepas, and which differed so much from all other Cirripedes that I had to form a new sub-order for its sole reception. . . . To understand the structure of my new Cirripede I had to examine and dissect many of the common forms; and this gradually led me on to take up the whole group." In later years he seems to have felt some doubt as to the value of these eight years of work,—for instance when

---

* 'Journal of the Horticultural Society,' 1846.
  † Sir J. D. Hooker was at this time attending to polymorphism, variability, &c.

he wrote in his Autobiography—"My work was of considerable use to me, when I had to discuss in the 'Origin of Species,' the principles of a natural classification. Nevertheless I doubt whether the work was worth the consumption of so much time." Yet I learn from Sir J. D. Hooker that he certainly recognised at the time its value to himself as systematic training. Sir Joseph writes to me: "Your father recognised three stages in his career as a biologist: the mere collector at Cambridge; the collector and observer in the *Beagle*, and for some years afterwards; and the trained naturalist after, and only after the Cirripede work. That he was a thinker all along is true enough, and there is a vast deal in his writings previous to the Cirripedes that a trained naturalist could but emulate. . . . He often alluded to it as a valued discipline, and added that even the 'hateful' work of digging out synonyms, and of describing, not only improved his methods but opened his eyes to the difficulties and merits of the works of the dullest of cataloguers. One result was that he would never allow a depreciatory remark to pass unchallenged on the poorest class of scientific workers, provided that their work was honest, and good of its kind. I have always regarded it as one of the finest traits of his character,—this generous appreciation of the hod-men of science, and of their labours . . . and it was monographing the Barnacles that brought it about."

Professor Huxley allows me to quote his opinion as to the value of the eight years given to the Cirripedes:—

"In my opinion your sagacious father never did a wiser thing than when he devoted himself to the years of patient toil which the Cirripede-book cost him.

"Like the rest of us, he had no proper training in biological science, and it has always struck me as a remarkable instance of his scientific insight, that he saw the necessity of giving himself such training, and of his courage, that he did not shirk the labour of obtaining it.

"The great danger which besets all men of large speculative faculty, is the temptation to deal with the accepted statements of facts in natural science, as if they were not only correct, but exhaustive; as if they might be dealt with deductively, in the same way as propositions in Euclid may be dealt with. In reality, every such statement, however true it may be, is true only relatively to the means of observation and the point of view of those who have enunciated it. So far it may be depended upon. But whether it will bear every speculative conclusion that may be logically deduced from it, is quite another question.

"Your father was building a vast superstructure upon the foundations furnished by the recognised facts of geological and biological science. In Physical Geography, in Geology proper, in Geographical Distribution, and in Palæontology, he had acquired an extensive practical training during the voyage of the *Beagle*. He knew of his own knowledge the way in which the raw materials of these branches of science are acquired, and was therefore a most competent judge of the speculative strain they would bear. That which he needed, after his return to England, was a corresponding acquaintance with Anatomy and Development, and their relation to Taxonomy—and he acquired this by his Cirripede work.

"Thus, in my apprehension, the value of the Cirripede monograph lies not merely in the fact that it is a very admirable piece of work, and constituted a great addition to positive knowledge, but still more in the circumstance that it was a piece of critical self-discipline, the effect of which manifested itself in everything your father wrote afterwards, and saved him from endless errors of detail.

"So far from such work being a loss of time, I believe it would have been well worth his while, had it been practicable, to have supplemented it by a special study of embryology and physiology. His hands would have been greatly strengthened thereby when he came to write out sundry chapters of the 'Origin of Species.' But of course in those days it was almost impossible for him to find facilities for such work."

No one can look at the two volumes on the recent Cirripedes, of 399 and 684 pages respectively (not to speak of the
volumes on the fossil species), without being struck by the
immense amount of detailed work which they contain. The
forty plates, some of them with thirty figures, and the fourteen pages of index in the two volumes together, give some
rough idea of the labour spent on the work.* The state of
knowledge, as regards the Cirripedes, was most unsatisfactory
at the time that my father began to work at them. As an
illustration of this fact, it may be mentioned that he had
even to re-organise the nomenclature of the group, or, as he
expressed it, he "unwillingly found it indispensable to give
names to several valves, and to some few of the softer parts
of Cirripedes."† It is interesting to learn from his diary the
amount of time which he gave to different genera. Thus
the genus Chthamalus, the description of which occupies
twenty-two pages, occupied him for thirty-six days; Coronula took nineteen days, and is described in twenty-seven
pages. Writing to Fitz-Roy, he speaks of being "for the
last half-month daily hard at work in dissecting a little animal about the size of a pin's head, from the Chonos archipelago, and I could spend another month, and daily see more
beautiful structure."

Though he became excessively weary of the work before
the end of the eight years, he had much keen enjoyment in
the course of it. Thus he wrote to Sir J. D. Hooker (1847 ?):
—"As you say, there is an extraordinary pleasure in pure
observation; not but what I suspect the pleasure in this case
is rather derived from comparisons forming in one's mind
with allied structures. After having been so long employed
in writing my old geological observations, it is delightful to
use one's eyes and fingers again." It was, in fact, a return to

---

* The reader unacquainted with Zoology will find some account of the
more interesting results in Mr. Romanes' article on "Charles Darwin"
('Nature' Series, 1882).

† Vol. i. p. 3.

the work which occupied so much of his time when at sea
during his voyage.   His zoological notes of that period give
an impression of vigorous work, hampered by ignorance and
want of appliances ; and his untiring industry in the dissection of marine animals, especially of Crustacea, must have
been of value to him as training for his Cirripede work.
Most of his work was done with the simple dissecting microscope—but it was the need which he found for higher powers
that induced him, in 1846, to buy a compound microscope.
He wrote to Hooker :—" When I was drawing with L., I
was so delighted with the appearance of the objects, especially
with their perspective, as seen through the weak powers of a
good compound microscope, that I am going to order one ;
indeed, I often have structures in which the $\frac{1}{30}$ is not power
enough."

During part of the time covered by the present chapter,
my father suffered perhaps more from ill-health than at any
other time of his life.   He felt severely the depressing influence of these long years of illness ; thus as early as 1840 he
wrote to Fox : " I am grown a dull, old, spiritless dog to what
I used to be.   One gets stupider as one grows older I think."
It is not wonderful that he should so have written, it is rather
to be wondered at that his spirit withstood so great and
constant a strain.   He wrote to Sir J. D. Hooker in 1845 :
" You are very kind in your enquiries about my health ; I
have nothing to say about it, being always much the same,
some days better and some worse.   I believe I have not
had one whole day, or rather night, without my stomach
having been greatly disordered, during the last three years,
and most days great prostration of strength : thank you for
your kindness ; many of my friends, I believe, think me a
hypochondriac."

Again, in 1849, he notes in his diary :—" January 1st to
March 10th.—Health very bad, with much sickness and failure of power.   Worked on all well days."   This was written
just before his first visit to Dr. Gully's Water-Cure Establishment at Malvern.   In April of the same year he wrote :—" I

believe I am going on very well, but I am rather weary of my
present inactive life, and the water-cure has the most extraordinary effect in producing indolence and stagnation of
mind : till experiencing it, I could not have believed it possible. I now increase in weight, have escaped sickness for
thirty days." He returned in June, after sixteen weeks' absence, much improved in health, and, as already described (p.
108), continued the water-cure at home for some time.]

C. Darwin to J. D. Hooker.

Down [October, 1846].

MY DEAR HOOKER,—I have not heard from Sulivan *
lately ; when he last wrote he named from 8th to 10th as the
most likely time. Immediately that I hear, I will fly you a
line, for the chance of your being able to come. I forget
whether you know him, but I suppose so ; he is a real good
fellow. Anyhow, if you do not come then, I am very glad
that you propose coming soon after. . . .

I am going to begin some papers on the lower marine
animals, which will last me some months, perhaps a year, and
then I shall begin looking over my ten-year-long accumulation of notes on species and varieties, which, with writing, I dare say will take me five years, and then, when published, I dare say I shall stand infinitely low in the opinion
of all sound Naturalists—so this is my prospect for the future.

Are you a good hand at inventing names. I have a quite
new and curious genus of Barnacle, which I want to name,
and how to invent a name completely puzzles me.

By the way, I have told you nothing about Southampton.
We enjoyed (wife and myself) our week beyond measure :
the papers were all dull, but I met so many friends and
made so many new acquaintances (especially some of the
Irish Naturalists), and took so many pleasant excursions. I

* Admiral Sir B. J. Sulivan, formerly an officer of the *Beagle.*

wish you had been there. On Sunday we had so pleasant an excursion to Winchester with Falconer,* Colonel Sabine,† and Dr. Robinson,‡ and others. I never enjoyed a day more in my life. I missed having a look at H. Watson.# I suppose you heard that he met Forbes and told him he had a severe article in the Press. I understood that Forbes explained to him that he had no cause to complain, but as the article was printed, he would not withdraw it, but offered it to Forbes for him to append notes to it, which Forbes naturally declined. . . .

C. Darwin to J. D. Hooker.

Down, April 7th [1847 ?].

MY DEAR HOOKER,—I should have written before now, had I not been almost continually unwell, and at present I am suffering from four boils and swellings, one of which hardly allows me the use of my right arm, and has stopped all my work, and damped all my spirits. I was much disappointed at missing my trip to Kew, and the more so, as I had forgotten you would be away all this month ; but I had no choice, and was in bed nearly all Friday and Saturday. I congratulate

---

* Hugh Falconer, born 1809, died 1865. Chiefly known as a palæontologist, although employed as a botanist during his whole career in India, where he was also a medical officer in H. E. I. C. Service ; he was superintendent of the Company's garden, first at Saharunpore, and then at Calcutta. He was one of the first botanical explorers of Kashmir. Falconer's discoveries of Miocene mammalian remains in the Sewalik Hills, were, at the time, perhaps the greatest "finds" which had been made. His book on the subject, 'Fauna Antiqua Sivalensis,' remained unfinished at the time of his death.

† The late Sir Edward Sabine, formerly President of the Royal Society, and author of a long series of memoirs on Terrestrial Magnetism.

‡ The late Dr. Thomas Romney Robinson, of the Armagh Observatory.

The late Hewett Cottrell Watson, author of the 'Cybele Britannica,' one of a most valuable series of works on the topography and geographical distribution of the plants of the British Islands.

you over your improved prospects about India,* but at the same time must sincerely groan over it. I shall feel quite lost without you to discuss many points with, and to point out (ill-luck to you) difficulties and objections to my species hypotheses. It will be a horrid shame if money stops your expedition ; but Government will surely help you˜to some extent. . . . . Your present trip, with your new views, amongst the coal-plants, will be very interesting. If you have spare time, *but not without*, I should enjoy having some news of your progress. Your present trip will work well in, if you go to any of the coal districts in India. Would this not be a good object to parade before Government; the utilitarian souls would comprehend this. By the way, I will get some work out of you, about the domestic races of animals in India. . . .

C. Darwin to L. Jenyns (Blomefield).

Down [1847].

DEAR JENYNS,—I am very much obliged for the capital little Almanack ; † it so happened that I was wishing for one to keep in my portfolio. I had never seen this kind before, and shall certainly get one for the future. I think it is very amusing to have a list before one's eyes of the order of ap-

---

* Sir J. Hooker left England on November 11, 1847, for his Himalayan and Tibetan journey. The expedition was supported by a small grant from the Treasury, and thus assumed the character of a Government mission.

† "This letter relates to a small Almanack first published in 1843, under the name of 'The Naturalists' Pocket Almanack,' by Mr. Van Voorst, and which I edited for him. It was intended especially for those who interest themselves in the periodic phenomena of animals and plants, of which a select list was given under each month of the year.

"The Pocket Almanack contained, moreover, miscellaneous information relating to Zoology and Botany ; to Natural History and other scientific societies; to public Museums and Gardens, in addition to the ordinary celestial phenomena found in most other Almanacks. It continued to be issued till 1847, after which year the publication was abandoned."— From a letter from Rev. L. Blomefield to F. Darwin.

pearance of the plants and animals around one; it gives a fresh interest to each fine day. There is one point I should like to see a little improved, viz., the correction for the clock at shorter intervals. Most people, I suspect, who like myself have dials, will wish to be more precise than with a margin of three minutes. I always buy a shilling almanack for this *sole* end. By the way, *yours, i. e.,* Van Voorst's Almanack, is very dear; it ought, at least, to be advertised post-free for the shilling. Do you not think a table (not rules) of conversion of French into English measures, and perhaps weights, would be exceedingly useful; also centigrade into Fahrenheit,—magnifying powers according to focal distances?—in fact you might make it the most useful publication of the age. I know what I should like best of all, namely, current meteorological remarks for each month, with statement of average course of winds and prediction of weather, in accordance with movements of barometer. People, I think, are always amused at knowing the extremes and means of temperature for corresponding times in other years.

I hope you will go on with it another year. With many thanks, my dear Jenyns,

Yours very truly,

CHARLES DARWIN.

C. Darwin to J. D. Hooker.

Down, Sunday [April 18th, 1847].

MY DEAR HOOKER,—I return with many thanks Watson's letter, which I have had copied. It is a capital one, and I am extremely obliged to you for obtaining me such valuable information. Surely he is rather in a hurry when he says intermediate varieties must almost be necessarily rare, otherwise they would be taken as the types of the species; for he overlooks numerical frequency as an element. Surely if A, B, C were three varieties, and if A were a good deal the commonest (therefore, also, first known), it would be taken as the type, without regarding whether B was quite intermediate or not, or whether it was rare or not. What capital essays W.

would write ; but I suppose he has written a good deal in the ' Phytologist.' You ought to encourage him to publish on variation ; it is a shame that such facts as those in his let-- ter should remain unpublished. I must get you to introduce me to him ; would he be a good and sociable man for Drop- more ? * though if he comes, Forbes must not (and I think you talked of inviting Forbes), or we shall have a glorious bat- tle. I should like to see sometime the war correspondence. Have you the ' Phytologist,' and could you sometime spare it ? I would go through it quickly. . . . I have read your last five numbers,† and as usual have been much interested in several points, especially with your discussions on the beech and potato. I see you have introduced several sentences against us Transmutationists. I have also been looking through the latter volumes of the ' Annals of Natural History,' and have read two such soulless, pompous papers of ——, quite worthy of the author . . . . The contrast of the papers in the *Annals* with those in the *Annales* is rather humiliating ; so many papers in the former, with short descriptions of species, with- out one word on their affinities, internal structure, range or habits. I am now reading ——, and I have picked out some things which have interested me ; but he strikes me as rather dullish, and with all his Materia Medica smells of the doctor's shop. I shall ever hate the name of the Materia Medica, since hearing Duncan's lectures at eight o'clock on a winter's morning—a whole, cold, breakfastless hour on the properties of rhubarb !

I hope your journey will be very prosperous. Believe me, my dear Hooker,

Ever yours,
C. DARWIN.

P.S.—I think I have only made one new acquaintance of late, that is, R. Chambers ; and I have just received a

---

* A much enjoyed expedition made from Oxford—when the British Association met there in 1847.

† Of the Botany of Hooker's ' Antarctic Voyage.'

presentation copy of the sixth edition of the 'Vestiges.' Somehow I now feel perfectly convinced he is the author. He is
in France, and has written to me thence.

C. Darwin to J. D. Hooker.

Down [1847 ?].

. . . I am delighted to hear that Brongniart thought
Sigillaria aquatic, and that Binney considers coal a sort of
submarine peat. I would bet 5 to 1 that in twenty years this
will be generally admitted; * and I do not care for whatever
the botanical difficulties or impossibilities may be. If I could
but persuade myself that Sigillaria and Co. had a good range
of depth, *i. e.*, could live from 5 to 100 fathoms under water,
all difficulties of nearly all kinds would be removed (for the
simple fact of muddy ordinary shallow sea implies proximity
of land). [N.B.—I am chuckling to think how you are
sneering all this time.] It is not much of a difficulty, there not
being shells with the coal, considering how unfavourable deep
mud is for most Mollusca, and that shells would probably
decay from the humic acid, as seems to take place in peat
and in the *black* moulds (as Lyell tells me) of the Mississippi.
So coal question settled—Q. E. D.   Sneer away!

Many thanks for your welcome note from Cambridge, and
I am glad you like my *alma mater*, which I despise heartily
as a place of education, but love from many most pleasant
recollections. . . .

Thanks for your offer of the 'Phytologist;' I shall be
very much obliged for it, for I do not suppose I should be
able to borrow it from any other quarter. I will not be set
up too much by your praise, but I do not believe I ever lost
a book or forgot to return it during a long lapse of time.
Your 'Webb' is well wrapped up, and with your name in
large letters *outside*.

My new microscope is come home (a "splendid play-

---

* An unfulfilled prophecy.

thing," as old R. Brown called it), and I am delighted with it; it really is a splendid plaything. I have been in London for three days, and saw many of our friends. I was extremely sorry to hear a not very good account of Sir William. Farewell, my dear Hooker, and be a good boy, and make Sigillaria a submarine sea-weed.

Ever yours,

C. DARWIN.

C. Darwin to J. D. Hooker.

Down [May 6th, 1847].

MY DEAR HOOKER,—You have made a savage onslaught, and I must try to defend myself. But, first, let me say that I never write to you except for my own good pleasure; now I fear that you answer me when busy and without inclination (and I am sure I should have none if I was as busy as you). Pray do not do so, and if I thought my writing entailed an answer from you *nolens volens*, it would destroy all my pleasure in writing. Firstly, I did not consider my letter as *reasoning*, or even as *speculation*, but simply as mental rioting; and as I was sending Binney's paper, I poured out to you the result of reading it. Secondly, you are right, indeed, in thinking me mad, if you suppose that I would class any ferns as marine plants ; but surely there is a wide distinction between the plants found upright in the coal-beds and those not upright, and which might have been drifted. Is it not possible that the same circumstances which have preserved the vegetation *in situ*, should have preserved drifted plants? I know Calamites is found upright ; but I fancied its affinities were very obscure, like Sigillaria. As for Lepidodendron, I forgot its existence, as happens when one goes riot, and now know neither what it is, or whether upright. If these plants, *i. e.* Calamites and Lepidodendron, have *very clear relations* to terrestrial vegetables, like the ferns have, and are found upright *in situ*, of course I must give up the ghost. But surely Sigillaria is the main upright plant, and on its obscure affinities I have heard you enlarge.

Thirdly, it never entered my head to undervalue botanical relatively to zoological evidence; except in so far as I thought it was admitted that the vegetative structure seldom yielded any evidence of affinity nearer than that of families, and not always so much. And is it not in plants, as certainly it is in animals, dangerous to judge of habits without very near affinity. Could a Botanist tell from structure alone that the Mangrove family, almost or quite alone in Dicotyledons, could live in the sea, and the Zostera family almost alone among the Monocotyledons? Is it a safe argument, that because algæ are almost the only, or the only submerged sea-plants, that formerly other groups had not members with such habits? With animals such an argument would not be conclusive, as I could illustrate by many examples; but I am forgetting myself; I want only to some degree to defend myself, and not burn my fingers by attacking you. The foundation of my letter, and what is my deliberate opinion, though I dare say you will think it absurd, is that I would rather trust, *cæteris paribus*, pure geological evidence than either zoological or botanical evidence. I do not say that I would sooner trust *poor* geological evidence than *good* organic. I think the basis of pure geological reasoning is simpler (consisting chiefly of the action of water on the crust of the earth, and its up and down movements) than a basis drawn from the difficult subject of affinities and of structure in relation to habits. I can hardly analyze the facts on which I have come to this conclusion; but I can illustrate it. Pallas's account would lead any one to suppose that the Siberian strata, with the frozen carcasses, had been quickly deposited, and hence that the embedded animals had lived in the neighbourhood; but our zoological knowledge of thirty years ago led every one falsely to reject this conclusion.

Tell me that an upright fern *in situ* occurs with Sigillaria and Stigmaria, or that the affinities of Calamites and Lepidodendron (supposing that they are found *in situ* with Sigillaria) are so *clear*, that they could not have been marine, like, but in a greater degree, than the mangrove and sea-wrack, and I will humbly apologise to you and all Botanists for having let my mind run riot on a subject on which assuredly I know nothing. But till I hear this, I shall keep privately to my own opinion with the same pertinacity and, as you will think, with the same philosophical spirit with which Koenig maintains that Cheirotherium-footsteps are fuci.

Whether this letter will sink me still lower in your opinion, or put me a little right, I know not, but hope the latter. Anyhow, I have revenged myself with boring you with a very long epistle. Farewell, and be forgiving. Ever yours,

C. DARWIN.

P.S.—When will you return to Kew? I have forgotten one main object of my letter, to thank you *much* for your offer of the 'Hort. Journal,' but I have ordered the two numbers.

[The two following extracts [1847] give the continuation and conclusion of the coal battle.

"By the way, as submarine coal made you so wrath, I thought I would experimentise on Falconer and Bunbury* together, and it made [them] even more savage; 'such infernal nonsense ought to be thrashed out of me.' Bunbury was more polite and contemptuous. So I now know how to stir up and show off any Botanist. I wonder whether Zoologists and Geologists have got their tender points; I wish I could find out."

"I cannot resist thanking you for your most kind note. Pray do not think that I was annoyed by your letter: I perceived that you had been thinking with animation, and accordingly expressed yourself strongly, and so I understood it. Forfend me from a man who weighs every expression with Scotch prudence. I heartily wish you all success in your noble problem, and I shall be very curious to have some talk with you and hear your ultimatum."]

* The late Sir C. Bunbury, well known as a palæobotanist.

*C. Darwin to J. D. Hooker.**

Down [October, 1847].

I congratulate you heartily on your arrangements being completed, with some prospect for the future. It will be a noble voyage and journey, but I wish it was over, I shall miss you selfishly and all ways to a dreadful extent . . . I am in great perplexity how we are to meet . . . I can well understand how dreadfully busy you must be. If you *cannot* come here, you *must* let me come to you for a night; for I must have one more chat and one more quarrel with you over the coal.

By the way, I endeavoured to stir up Lyell (who has been staying here some days with me) to theorise on the coal : his oolitic *upright* Equisetums are dreadful for my submarine flora. I should die much easier if some one would solve me the coal question. I sometimes think it could not have been formed at all. Old Sir Anthony Carlisle once said to me gravely, that he supposed Megatherium and such cattle were just sent down from heaven to see whether the earth would support them; and I suppose the coal was rained down to puzzle mortals. You must work the coal well in India.

Ever yours,

C. DARWIN.

C. Darwin to J. D. Hooker.

[November 6th, 1847.]

MY DEAR HOOKER,—I have just received your note with sincere grief : there is no help for it. I shall always look at your intention of coming here, under such circumstances, as the greatest proof of friendship I ever received from mortal man. My conscience would have upbraided me in not having come to you on Thursday, but, as it turned out, I could not, for I was quite unable to leave Shrewsbury before that

---

* Parts of two letters.

day, and I reached home only last night, much knocked up. Without I hear to-morrow (which is hardly possible), and if I am feeling pretty well, I will drive over to Kew on Monday morning, just to say farewell. I will stay only an hour. . . .

C. Darwin to J. D. Hooker.

[November, 1847.]

MY DEAR HOOKER,—I am very unwell, and incapable of doing anything. I do hope I have not inconvenienced you. I was so unwell all yesterday, that I was rejoicing you were not here; for it would have been a bitter mortification to me to have had you here and not enjoyed your last day. I shall not now see you. Farewell, and God bless you.

Your affectionate friend,

C. DARWIN.

I will write to you in India.

[In 1847 appeared a paper by Mr. D. Milne,* in which my father's Glen Roy work is criticised, and which is referred to in the following characteristic extract from a letter to Sir J. Hooker:] "I have been bad enough for these few last days, having had to think and write too much about Glen Roy. . . . Mr. Milne having attacked my theory, which made me horribly sick." I have not been able to find any published reply to Mr. Milne, so that I imagine the "writing" mentioned was confined to letters. Mr. Milne's paper was not destructive to the Glen Roy paper, and this my father recognises in the following extract from a letter to Lyell (March, 1847). The reference to Chambers is explained by the fact that he accompanied Mr. Milne in his visit to Glen Roy. "I got R. Chambers to give me a sketch of Milne's Glen Roy views, and I have re-read my paper, and am, now that I have heard what is to be said, not even staggered. It is provoking and humiliating to find that Chambers not only had not read

---

* Now Mr. Milne Home. The essay was published in Transactions of the Edinburgh Royal Society, vol. xvi.

with any care my paper on this subject, or even looked at the coloured map, so that the new shelf described by me had not been searched for, and my arguments and facts of detail not in the least attended to. I entirely gave up the ghost, and was quite chicken-hearted at the Geological Society, till you reassured and reminded me of the main facts in the whole case."

The two following letters to Lyell, though of later date (June, 1848), bear on the same subject :—

" I was at the evening meeting [of the Geological Society], but did not get within hail of you. What a fool (though I must say a very amusing one) —— did make of himself. Your speech was refreshing after it, and was well characterized by Fox (my cousin) in three words—' What a contrast ! ' That struck me as a capital speculation about the Wealden Continent going down. I did not hear what you settled at the Council; I was quite wearied out and bewildered. I find Smith, of Jordan Hill, has a much worse opinion of R. Chambers's book than even I have. Chambers has piqued me a little; * he says I ' propound ' and ' profess my belief ' that Glen Roy is marine, and that the idea was accepted because the ' mobility of the land was the ascendant idea of the day.' He adds some very faint *upper* lines in Glen Spean (seen, by the way, by Agassiz), and has shown that Milne and Kemp are right in there being horizontal aqueous markings (*not* at coincident levels with those of Glen Roy) in other parts of Scotland at great heights, and he adds several other cases. This is the whole of his addition to the data. He not only takes my line of argument from the buttresses and terraces below the lower shelf and some other arguments (without acknowledgment), but he sneers at all his predecessors not having perceived the importance of the short portions of lines intermediate between the chief ones in Glen Roy; whereas

---

* ' Ancient Sea Margins, 1848.'   The words quoted by my father should be " the mobility of the land was an ascendant idea."

I commence the description of them with saying, that 'perceiving their importance, I examined them with scrupulous care,' and expatiate at considerable length on them.   I have indirectly told him I do not think he has quite claims to consider that he alone (which he pretty directly asserts) has solved the problem of Glen Roy.   With respect to the terraces at lower levels coincident in height all round Scotland and England, I am inclined to believe he shows some little probability of there being some leading ones coincident, but much more exact evidence is required.   Would you believe it credible? he advances as a probable solution to account for the rise of Great Britain that in some great ocean one-twentieth of the bottom of the whole aqueous surface of the globe has sunk in (he does not say where he puts it) for a thickness of half a mile, and this he has calculated would make an apparent rise of 130 feet."

C. Darwin to C. Lyell.

Down [June, 1848].

MY DEAR LYELL,—Out of justice to Chambers I must trouble you with one line to say, as far as I am personally concerned in Glen Roy, he has made the amende honorable, and pleads guilty through inadvertency of taking my two lines of arguments and facts without acknowledgment. He concluded by saying he "came to the same point by an independent course of inquiry, which in a small degree excuses this inadvertency." His letter altogether shows a very good disposition, and says he is "much gratified with the *measured* approbation which you bestow, &c." I am heartily glad I was able to say in truth that I thought he had done good service in calling more attention to the subject of the terraces. He protests it is unfair to call the sinking of the sea his theory, for that he with care always speaks of mere change of level, and this is quite true; but the one section in which he shows how he conceives the sea might sink is so astonishing, that I believe it will with others, as with me, more than counterbalance his previous caution. I hope that you may think better of the book than I do.

Yours most truly,

C. DARWIN.

C. Darwin to J. D. Hooker.

October 6th, 1848.

. . . I have lately been trying to get up an agitation (but I shall not succeed, and indeed doubt whether I have time and strength to go on with it), against the practice of Naturalists appending for perpetuity the name of the *first* describer to species. I look at this as a direct premium to hasty work, to *naming* instead of *describing*. A species ought to have a name so well known that the addition of the author's name would be superfluous, and a [piece] of empty vanity.* At present, it would not do to give mere specific names; but I think Zoologists might open the road to the omission, by referring to good systematic writers instead of to first describers. Botany, I fancy, has not suffered so much as Zoology from mere *naming ;* the characters, fortunately, are

---

* His contempt for the self-regarding spirit in a naturalist is illustrated by an anecdote, for which I am indebted to Rev. L. Blomefield. After speaking of my father's love of Entomology at Cambridge, Mr. Blomefield continues :—" He occasionally came over from Cambridge to my Vicarage at Swaffham Bulbeck, and we went out together to collect insects in the woods at Bottisham Hall, close at hand, or made longer excursions in the Fens. On one occasion he captured in a large bag net, with which he used vigorously to sweep the weeds and long grass, a rare coleopterous insect, one of the *Lepturidæ*, which I myself had never taken in Cambridgeshire. He was pleased with his capture, and of course carried it home in triumph. Some years afterwards, the voyage of the *Beagle* having been made in the interim, talking over old times with him, I reverted to this circumstance, and asked if he remembered it. ' Oh yes,' (he said,) ' I remember it well ; and I was selfish enough to keep the specimen, when you were collecting materials for a Fauna of Cambridgeshire, and for a local museum in the Philosophical Society.' He followed this up with some remarks on the pettiness of collectors, who aimed at nothing beyond filling their cabinets with rare things."

more obscure. Have you ever thought on this point? Why should Naturalists append their own names to new species, when Mineralogists and Chemists do not do so to new substances? When you write to Falconer pray remember me affectionately to him. I grieve most sincerely to hear that he has been ill. My dear Hooker, God bless you, and fare you well.　　　　　Your sincere friend,

　　　　　　　　　　　　　　　　　C. DARWIN.

*C. Darwin to Hugh Strickland.**

Down, Jan. 29th [1849].

　. . . . What a labour you have undertaken ; I do *honour* your devoted zeal in the good cause of Natural Science. Do you happen to have a *spare* copy of the Nomenclature rules published in the 'British Association Transactions?' if you

---

* Hugh Edwin Strickland, M. A., F. R. S., was born 2nd of March, 1811, and educated at Rugby, under Arnold, and at Oriel College, Oxford. In 1835 and 1836 he travelled through Europe to the Levant with W. J. Hamilton, the geologist, wintering in Asia Minor. In 1841 he brought the subject of Natural History Nomenclature before the British Association, and prepared the Code of Rules for Zoological Nomenclature, now known by his name—the principles of which are very generally adopted. In 1843 he was one of the founders (if not the original projector) of the Ray Society. In 1845 he married the second daughter of Sir William Jardine, Bart. In 1850 he was appointed, in consequence of Buckland's illness, Deputy Reader in Geology at Oxford. His promising career was suddenly cut short on September 14, 1853, when, while geologizing in a railway cutting between Retford and Gainsborough, he was run over by a train and instantly killed. A memoir of him and a reprint of his principal contributions to journals was published by Sir William Jardine in 1858 ; but he was also the author of 'The Dodo and its Kindred' (1848) ; 'Bibliographia Zoologiæ' (the latter in conjunction with Louis Agassiz, and issued by the Ray Society) ; 'Ornithological Synonyms' (one volume only published, and that posthumously). A catalogue of his ornithological collection, given by his widow to the University of Cambridge, was compiled by Mr. Salvin, and published in 1882. (I am indebted to Prof. Newton for the above note.)

have, and would give it to me, I should be truly obliged, for I grudge buying the volume for it.   I have found the rules very useful, it is quite a comfort to have something to rest on in the turbulent ocean of nomenclature (and am accordingly grateful to you), though I find it very difficult to obey always. Here is a case (and I think it should have been noticed in the rules), Coronula, Cineras and Otion, are names adopted by Cuvier, Lamarck, Owen, and almost *every* well-known writer, but I find that all three names were anticipated by a German : now I believe if I were to follow the strict rule of priority, more harm would be done than good, and more especially as I feel sure that the newly fished-up names would not be adopted.   I have almost made up my mind to reject the rule of priority in this case ; would you grudge the trouble to send me your opinion ?   I have been led of late to reflect much on the subject of naming, and I have come to a fixed opinion that the plan of the first describer's name, being appended for perpetuity to a species, had been the greatest curse to Natural History.   Some months since, I wrote out the en-closed badly drawn-up paper, thinking that perhaps I would agitate the subject ; but the fit has passed, and I do not sup-pose I ever shall ; I send it you for the *chance* of your caring to see my notions.   I have been surprised to find in con-versation that several naturalist were of nearly my way of thinking.   I feel sure as long as species-mongers have their vanity tickled by seeing their own names appended to a species, because they miserably described it in two or three lines, we shall have the same *vast* amount of bad work as at present, and which is enough to dishearten any man who is willing to work out any branch with care and time.   I find every genus of Cirripedia has half-a-dozen names, and not one careful description of any one species in any one genus. I do not believe that this would have been the case if each man knew that the memory of his own name depended on his doing his work well, and not upon merely appending a name with a few wretched lines indicating only a few prominent external characters.   But I will not weary you with any

longer tirade. Read my paper or *not*, just as you like, and
return it whenever you please.

Yours most sincerely,
C. DARWIN.

Hugh Strickland to C. Darwin.

The Lodge, Tewkesbury, Jan. 31st, 1849.

. . . . I have next to notice your second objection—that
retaining the name of the *first* describer in *perpetuum* along
with that of the species, is a premium on hasty and careless
work. This is quite a different question from that of the law
of priority itself, and it never occurred to me before, though it
seems highly probable that the general recognition of that law
may produce such a result. We must try to conteract this
evil in some other way.

The object of appending the name of a man to the name
of a species is not to gratify the vanity of the man, but to indicate more precisely the species. Sometimes two men will,
by accident, give the same name (independently) to two species of the same genus. More frequently a later author will
misapply the specific name of an older one. Thus the *Helix
putris* of Montagu is not *H. putris* of Linnæus, though Mon-
tague supposed it to be so. In such a case we cannot define
the species by *Helix putris* alone, but must append the name
of the author whom we quote. But when a species has never
borne but one name (as *Corvus frugilegus*), and no other species of Corvus has borne the same name, it is, of course, un-
necessary to add the author's name. Yet even here I like
the form *Corvus frugilegus, Linn.*, as it reminds us that this is
one of the old species, long known, and to be found in the
'Systema Naturæ,' &c. I fear, therefore, that (at least until
our nomenclature is more definitely settled) it will be impossible to indicate species with scientific accuracy, without adding the name of their first author. You may, indeed, do it as
you propose, by saying *in Lam. An. Invert., &c*, but then this
would be incompatible with the law of priority, for where

Lamarck has violated that law, one cannot adopt his name. It is, nevertheless, highly conducive to accurate indication to append to the (oldest) specific name *one* good reference to a standard work, especially to a *figure*, with an accompanying synonym if necessary. This method may be cumbrous, but cumbrousness is a far less evil than uncertainty.

It, moreover, seems hardly possible to carry out the *priority* principle, without the historical aid afforded by appending the author's name to the specific one. If I, a *priority man*, called a species C. D., it implies that C. D. is the oldest name that I know of ; but in order that you and others may judge of the propriety of that name, you must ascertain when, and by whom, the name was first coined. Now, if to the specific name C. D., I append the name A. B., of its first describer, I at once furnish you with the clue to the dates when, and the book in which, this description was given, and I thus assist you in determining whether C. D. be really the oldest, and therefore the correct, designation.

I do, however, admit that the priority principle (excellent as it is) has a tendency, when the author's name is added, to encourage vanity and slovenly work. I think, however, that much might be done to discourage those obscure and unsatisfactory definitions of which you so justly complain, by *writing down* the practice. Let the better disposed naturalists combine to make a formal protest against all vague, loose, and inadequate definitions of (supposed) new species. Let a committee (say of the British Association) be appointed to prepare a sort of *Class List* of the various modern works in which new species are described, arranged in order of merit. The lowest class would contain the worst examples of the kind, and their authors would thus be exposed to the obloquy which they deserve, and be gibbeted *in terrorem* for the edification of those who may come after.

I have thus candidly stated my views (I hope intelligibly) of what seems best to be done in the present transitional and dangerous state of systematic zoology. Innumerable labourers, many of them crotchety and half-educated, are rushing

into the field, and it depends, I think, on the present generation whether the science is to descend to posterity a chaotic
mass, or possessed of some traces of law and organisation. If
we could only get a congress of deputies from the chief scientific bodies of Europe and America, something might be done,
but, as the case stands, I confess I do not clearly see my way,
beyond humbly endeavouring to reform *Number One*.

Yours ever,

H. E. STRICKLAND.

C. Darwin to Hugh Strickland.

Down, Sunday [Feb. 4th, 1849].

MY DEAR STRICKLAND,—I am, in truth, *greatly* obliged to
you for your long, most interesting, and clear letter, and the
Report. I will consider your arguments, which are of the
greatest weight, but I confess I cannot yet bring myself to
reject very *well-known* names, not in *one* country, but over the
world, for obscure ones,—simply on the ground that I do not
believe I should be followed. Pray believe that I should
break the law of priority only in rare cases ; will you read the
enclosed (and return it), and tell me whether it does not
stagger you? (N. B. I *promise* that I will not give you any
more trouble.) I want simple answers, and not for you to
waste your time in reasons ; I am curious for your answer in
regard to Balanus. I put the case of Otion, &c., to W.
Thompson, who is fierce for the law of priority, and he gave
it up in such well-known names. I am in a perfect maze of
doubt on nomenclature. In not one large genus of Cirripedia
has *any one* species been correctly defined ; it is pure guess-
work (being guided by range and commonness and habits) to
recognise any species : thus I can make out, from plates or
descriptions, hardly any of the British sessile cirripedes. I
cannot bear to give new names to all the species, and yet I
shall perhaps do wrong to attach old names by little better
than guess ; I cannot at present tell the least which of two
species all writers have meant by the common *Anatifera*

lævis; I have, therefore, given that name to the one which is rather the commonest. Literally, not one species is properly defined ; not one naturalist has ever taken the trouble to open the shell of any species to describe it scientifically, and yet all the genera have half-a-dozen synonyms. For *argument's* sake, suppose I do my work thoroughly well, any one who happens to have the original specimens named, I will say by Chenu, who has figured and named hundreds of species, will be able to upset all my names according to the law of priority (for he may maintain his descriptions are sufficient), do you think it advantageous to science that this should be done : I think not, and that convenience and high merit (here put as mere argument) had better come into some play. The subject is heart-breaking.

I hope you will occasionally turn in your mind my argument of the evil done by the "mihi" attached to specific names ; I can most clearly see the *excessive* evil it has caused ; in mineralogy I have myself found there is no rage to merely name ; a person does not take up the subject without he intends to work it out, as he knows that his *only* claim to merit rests on his work being ably done, and has no relation whatever to *naming*. I give up one point, and grant that reference to first describer's name should be given in all systematic works, but I think something would be gained if a reference was given without the author's name being actually appended as part of the binomial name, and I think, except in systematic works, a reference, such as I propose, would damp vanity much. I think a very wrong spirit runs through all Natural History, as if some merit was due to a man for merely naming and defining a species ; I think scarcely any, or none, is due ; if he works out *minutely* and anatomically any one species, or systematically a whole group, credit is due, but I must think the mere defining a species is nothing, and that no *injustice* is done him if it be overlooked, though a great inconvenience to Natural History is thus caused. I do not think more credit is due to a man for defining a species, than to a carpenter for making a box. But I am foolish and rabid against species-mongers, or rather against their vanity ; it is useful and necessary work which must be done ; but they act as if they had actually made the species, and it was their own property.

I use Agassiz's nomenclator ; at least two-thirds of the dates in the Cirripedia are grossly wrong.

I shall do what I can in fossil Cirripedia, and should be very grateful for specimens ; but I do not believe that species (and hardly genera) can be defined by single valves ; as in every recent species yet examined their forms vary greatly : to describe a species by valves alone, is the same as to describe a crab from *small* portions of its carapace alone, these portions being highly variable, and not, as in Crustacea, modelled over viscera. I sincerely apologise for the trouble which I have given you, but indeed I will give no more.

Yours most sincerely,
C. DARWIN.

P. S.—In conversation I found Owen and Andrew Smith much inclined to throw over the practice of attaching authors' names ; I believe if I agitated I could get a large party to join. W. Thompson agreed some way with me, but was not prepared to go nearly as far as I am.

C. Darwin to Hugh Strickland.

Down, Feb. 10th [1849].

MY DEAR STRICKLAND,—I have again to thank you cordially for your letter. Your remarks shall fructify to some extent, and I will try to be more faithful to rigid virtue and priority ; but as for calling Balanus " Lepas " (which I did not think of), I cannot do it, my pen won't write it—it is *impossible*. I have great hopes some of my difficulties will disappear, owing to wrong dates in Agassiz, and to my having to run several genera into one, for I have as yet gone, in but few cases, to original sources. With respect to adopting my

own notions in my Cirripedia book, I should not like to do
so without I found others approved, and in some public
way—nor, indeed, is it well adapted, as I can never recognise a species without I have the original specimen, which,
fortunately, I have in many cases in the British Museum.
Thus far I mean to adopt my notion, as never putting mihi
or " Darwin " after my own species, and in the anatomical
text giving no authors' names at all, as the systematic Part
will serve for those who want to know the History of a
species as far as I can imperfectly work it out. . . .

C. Darwin to J. D. Hooker.

[The Lodge, Malvern,
March 28th, 1849.]

MY DEAR HOOKER,—Your letter of the 13th of October
has remained unanswered till this day ! What an ungrateful
return for a letter which interested me so much, and which
contained so much and curious information. But I have
had a bad winter.

On the 13th of November, my poor dear father died, and
no one who did not know him would believe that a man
above eighty-three years old could have retained so tender
and affectionate a disposition, with all his sagacity unclouded
to the last. I was at the time so unwell, that I was unable to
travel, which added to my misery. Indeed, all this winter I
have been bad enough . . . and my nervous system began to
be affected, so that my hands trembled, and head was often
swimming. I was not able to do anything one day out of
three, and was altogether too dispirited to write to you, or to
do anything but what I was compelled. I thought I was
rapidly going the way of all flesh. Having heard, accident-
ally, of two persons who had received much benefit from the
water-cure, I got Dr. Gully's book, and made further enquiries, and at last started here, with wife, children, and all
our servants. We have taken a house for two months, and
have been here a fortnight. I am already a little stronger.

. . . Dr. Gully feels pretty sure he can do me good, which most certainly the regular doctors could not. . . . I feel certain that the water-cure is no quackery.

How I shall enjoy getting back to Down with renovated health, if such is to be my good fortune, and resuming the beloved Barnacles. Now I hope that you will forgive me for my negligence in not having sooner answered your letter. I was uncommonly interested by the sketch you give of your intended grand expedition, from which I suppose you will soon be returning. How earnestly I hope that it may prove in every way successful. . . .

[When my father was at the Water-cure Establishment at Malvern he was brought into contact with clairvoyance, of which he writes in the following extract from a letter to Fox, September, 1850.

"You speak about Homœopathy, which is a subject which makes me more wrath, even than does Clairvoyance. Clairvoyance so transcends belief, that one's ordinary faculties are put out of the question, but in homœopathy common sense and common observation come into play, and both these must go to the dogs, if the infinitesimal doses have any effect whatever. How true is a remark I saw the other day by Quetelet, in respect to evidence of curative processes, viz., that no one knows in disease what is the simple result of nothing being done, as a standard with which to compare homœopathy, and all other such things. It is a sad flaw, I cannot but think, in my beloved Dr. Gully, that he believes in everything. When Miss —— was very ill, he had a clairvoyant girl to report on internal changes, a mesmerist to put her to sleep—an homœopathist, viz. Dr. ——, and himself as hydropathist ! and the girl recovered."

A passage out of an earlier letter to Fox (December, 1844) shows that he was equally sceptical on the subject of mesmerism : "With respect to mesmerism, the whole country resounds with wonderful facts or tales . . . I have just heard of a child, three or four years old (whose parents and self I well knew) mesmerised by his father, which is the first fact which has staggered me. I shall not believe fully till I see or hear from good evidence of animals (as has been stated is possible) not drugged, being put to stupor; of course the impossibility would not prove mesmerism false; but it is the only clear *experimentum crucis*, and I am astonished it has not been systematically tried. If mesmerism was investigated, like a science, this could not have been left till the present day to be *done satisfactorily*, as it has been I believe left. Keep some cats yourself, and do get some mesmeriser to attempt it. One man told me he had succeeded, but his experiments were most vague, as was likely from a man who said cats were more easily done than other animals, because they were so electrical ! "]

C. Darwin to C. Lyell.

Down, December 4th [1849].

MY DEAR LYELL,—This letter requires no answer, and I write from exuberance of vanity. Dana has sent me the Geology of the United States Expedition, and I have just read the Coral part. To begin with a modest speech, *I am astonished at my own accuracy !!* If I were to rewrite now my Coral book there is hardly a sentence I should have to alter, except that I ought to have attributed more effect to recent volcanic action in checking growth of coral. When I say all this I ought to add that the *consequences* of the theory on areas of subsidence are treated in a separate chapter to which I have not come, and in this, I suspect, we shall differ more. Dana talks of agreeing with my theory *in most points ;* I can find out not one in which he differs. Considering how infinitely more he saw of Coral Reefs than I did, this is wonderfully satisfactory to me. He treats me most courteously. There now, my vanity is pretty well satisfied. . .

C. Darwin to J. D. Hooker.

Malvern, April 9th, 1849.

MY DEAR HOOKER,—The very next morning after posting my last letter (I think on 23rd of March), I received your two interesting gossipaceous and geological letters; and the latter I have since exchanged with Lyell for his. I will write higglety-pigglety just as subjects occur. I saw the Review in the 'Athenæum,' it was written in an ill-natured spirit'; but the whole virus consisted in saying that there was not novelty enough in your remarks for publication. No one, nowadays, cares for reviews. I may just mention that my Journal got some *real good* abuse, "presumption," &c.—ended with saying that the volume appeared "made up of the scraps and rubbish of the author's portfolio." I most truly enter into what you say, and quite believe you that you care only for the review with respect to your father; and that this *alone* would make you like to see extracts from your letters more properly noticed in this same periodical. I have considered to the very best of my judgment whether any portion of your present letters are adapted for the 'Athenæum' (in which I have no interest; the beasts not having even *noticed* my three geological volumes which I had sent to them), and I have come to the conclusion it is better not to send them. I feel sure, considering all the circumstances, that without you took pains and wrote *with care*, a condensed and finished sketch of some striking feature in your travels, it is better not to send anything. These two letters are, moreover, rather too geological for the 'Athenæum,' and almost require woodcuts. On the other hand, there are hardly enough details for a communication to the Geological Society. I have not the *smallest doubt* that your facts are of the highest interest with regard to glacial action in the Himalaya; but it struck both Lyell and myself that your evidence ought to have been given more distinctly. . . .

I have written so lately that I have nothing to say about myself; my health prevented me going on with a crusade against " mihi " and " nobis," of which you warn me of the dangers. I showed my paper to three or four Naturalists, and they all agreed with me to a certain extent : with health and vigour, I would not have shown a white feather, [and] with aid of half-a-dozen really good Naturalists, I believe something might have been done against the miserable and degrading passion of mere species naming. In your letter you wonder what " Ornamental Poultry " has to do with Barnacles ; but do not flatter yourself that I shall not yet live to finish the Barnacles, and then make a fool of myself on the subject of species, under which head ornamental Poultry are very interesting. . . .

C. Darwin to C. Lyell.

The Lodge, Malvern [June, 1849].

. . . I have got your book,* and have read all the first and a small part of the second volume (reading is the hardest work allowed here), and greatly I have been interested by it. It makes me long to be a Yankee. E. desires me to say that she quite " gloated " over the truth of your remarks on religious progress . . . I delight to think how you will disgust some of the bigots and educational dons. As yet there has not been *much* Geology or Natural History, for which I hope you feel a little ashamed. Your remarks on all social subjects strike me as worthy of the author of the ' Principles.' And yet (I know it is prejudice and pride) if I had written the Principles, I never would have written any travels; but I believe I am more jealous about the honour and glory of the Principles than you are yourself. . . .

C. Darwin to C. Lyell.

September 14th, 1849.

. . . I go on with my aqueous processes, and very steadily but slowly gain health and strength. Against all rules, I dined

---

* ' A Second Visit to the United States.'

at Chevening with Lord Mahon, who did me the great honour of calling on me, and how he heard of me I can't guess. I was charmed with Lady Mahon, and any one might have been proud at the pieces of agreeableness which came from her beautiful lips with respect to you. I like old Lord Stanhope very much; though he abused Geology and Zoology heartily. "To suppose that the Omnipotent God made a world, found it a failure, and broke it up, and then made it again, and again broke it up, as the Geologists say, is all fiddld faddle. Describing Species of birds and shells, &c., is all fiddle faddle. . . ."

I am heartily glad we shall meet at Birmingham, as I trust we shall, if my health will but keep up. I work now every day at the Cirripedia for 2½ hours, and so get on a little, but very slowly. I sometimes, after being a whole week employed and having described perhaps only two species, agree mentally with Lord Stanhope, that it is all fiddle faddle; however, the other day I got a curious case of a unisexual, instead of hermaphrodite cirripede, in which the female had the common cirripedial character, and in two valves of her shell had two little pockets, in *each* of which she kept a little husband; I do not know of any other case where a female invariably has two husbands. I have one still odder fact, common to several species, namely, that though they are hermaphrodite, they have small additional, or as I shall call them, complemental males, one specimen itself hermaphrodite had no less than *seven*, of these complemental males attached to it. Truly the schemes and wonders of Nature are illimitable. But I am running on as badly about my cirripedia as about Geology; it makes me groan to think that probably I shall never again have the exquisite pleasure of making out some new district, of evolving geological light out of some troubled dark region. So I must make the best of my Cirripedia. . . .

C. Darwin to J. D. Hooker.

Down, October 12th, 1849.

. . . By the way, one of the pleasantest parts of the British Association was my journey down to Birmingham with Mrs. Sabine, Mrs. Reeve, and the Colonel ; also Col. Sykes and Porter. Mrs. Sabine and myself agreed wonderfully on many points, and in none more sincerely than about you. We spoke about your letters from the Erebus ; and she quite agreed with me, that you and the *author*,* of the description of the cattle hunting in the Falklands, would have made a capital book together ! A very nice woman she is, and so is her sharp and sagacious mother. . . . Birmingham was very flat compared to Oxford, though I had my wife with me. We saw a good deal of the Lyells and Horners and Robinsons (the President) ; but the place was dismal, and I was prevented, by being unwell, from going to Warwick, though that, *i. e.*, the party, by all accounts, was wonderfully inferior to Blenheim, not to say anything of that heavenly day at Dropmore. One gets weary of all the spouting. . . .

You ask about my cold-water cure ; I am going on very well, and am certainly a little better every month, my nights mend much slower than my days. I have built a douche, and am to go on through all the winter, frost or no frost. My treatment now is lamp five times per week, and shallow bath for five minutes afterwards ; douche daily for five minutes, and dripping sheet daily. The treatment is wonderfully tonic, and I have had more better consecutive days this month than on any previous ones. . . . I am allowed to work now two and a half hours daily, and I find it as much as I can do ; for the cold-water cure, together with three short walks, is curiously exhausting ; and I am actually *forced* to go to bed at eight o'clock completely tired. I steadily gain in weight,

---

* Sir J. Hooker wrote the spirited description of cattle hunting in Sir J. Ross's ' Voyage of Discovery in the Southern Regions,' 1847, vol. ii., p. 245.

and eat immensely, and am never oppressed with my food. I have lost the involuntary twitching of the muscle, and all the fainting feelings, &c —black spots before eyes, &c. Dr. Gully thinks he shall quite cure me in six or nine months more.

The greatest bore, which I find in the water-cure, is the having been compelled to give up all reading, except the newspapers ; for my daily two and a half hours at the Barnacles is fully as much as I can do of anything which occupies the mind ; I am consequently terribly behind in all scientific books. I have of late been at work at mere species describing, which is much more difficult than I expected, and has much the same sort of interest as a puzzle has ; but I confess I often feel wearied with the work, and cannot help sometimes asking myself what is the good of spending a week or fortnight in ascertaining that certain just perceptible differences blend together and constitute varieties and not species. As long as I am on anatomy I never feel myself in that disgusting, horrid, *cui bono*, inquiring, humour. What miserable work, again, it is searching for priority of names. I have just finished two species, which possess seven generic, and twenty-four specific names! My chief comfort is, that the work must be sometime done, and I may as well do it, as any one else.

I have given up my agitation against *mihi* and *nobis ;* my paper is too long to send to you, so you must see it, if you care to do so, on your return. By-the-way, you say in your letter that you care more for my species work than for the Barnacles ; now this is too bad of you, for I declare your decided approval of my plain Barnacle work over theoretic species work, had very great influence in deciding me to go on with the former, and defer my species paper. . . .

[The following letter refers to the death of his little daughter, which took place at Malvern on April 24, 1851 :]

C. Darwin to W. D. Fox.

Down, April 29th [1851].

MY DEAR FOX,—I do not suppose you will have heard of our bitter and cruel loss. Poor dear little Annie, when going on very well at Malvern, was taken with a vomiting attack, which was at first thought of the smallest importance; but it rapidly assumed the form of a low and dreadful fever, which carried her off in ten days. Thank God, she suffered hardly at all, and expired as tranquilly as a little angel. Our only consolation is that she passed a short, though joyous life She was my favourite child; her cordiality, openness, buoyant joyousness and strong affections made her most lovable. Poor dear little soul. Well it is all over. . . .

C. Darwin to W. D. Fox.

Down, March 7th [1852].

MY DEAR FOX,—It is indeed an age since we have had any communication, and very glad I was to receive your note. Our long silence occurred to me a few weeks since, and I had then thought of writing, but was idle. I congratulate and condole with you on your *tenth* child; but please to observe when I have a tenth, send only condolences to me. We have now seven children, all well, thank God, as well as their mother; of these seven, five are boys; and my father used to say that it was certain that a boy gave as much trouble as three girls; so that *bonâ fide* we have seventeen children. It makes me sick whenever I think of professions; all seem hopelessly bad, and as yet I cannot see a ray of light. I should very much like to talk over this (by the way, my three bugbears are Californian and Australian gold, beggaring me by making my money on mortgage worth nothing; the French coming by the Westerham and Sevenoaks roads, and therefore enclosing Down; and thirdly, professions for my boys), and I should like to talk about education, on which you ask me what we are doing. No one can more truly despise the old stereotyped stupid classical education than I do; but yet I have not had courage to break through the trammels. After many doubts we have just sent our eldest boy to Rugby, where for his age he has been very well placed. . . . I honour, admire, and envy you for educating your boys at home. What on earth shall you do with your boys? Towards the end of this month we go to see W. at Rugby, and thence for five or six days to Susan * at Shrewsbury; I then return home to look after the babies, and E. goes to F. Wedgwood's of Etruria for a week. Very many thanks for your most kind and large invitation to Delamere, but I fear we can hardly compass it. I dread going anywhere, on account of my stomach so easily failing under any excitement. I rarely even now go to London; not that I am at all worse, perhaps rather better, and lead a very comfortable life with my three hours of daily work, but it is the life of a hermit. My nights are *always* bad, and that stops my becoming vigourous. You ask about water-cure. I take at intervals of two or three months, five or six weeks of *moderately* severe treatment, and always with good effect. Do you come here, I pray and beg whenever you can find time; you cannot tell how much pleasure it would give me and E. I have finished the 1st vol. for the Ray Society of Pedunculated Cirripedes, which, as I think you are a member, you will soon get. Read what I describe on the sexes of Ibla and Scalpellum. I am now at work on the Sessile Cirripedes, and am wonderfully tired of my job: a man to be a systematic naturalist ought to work at least eight hours per day. You saw through me, when you said that I must have wished to have seen the effects of the [word illegible] Debacle, for I was saying a week ago to E., that had I been as I was in old days, I would have been certainly off that hour. You ask after Erasmus; he is much as usual, and constantly more or less unwell. Susan * is much better, and very flourishing and happy. Catherine * is at Rome, and has enjoyed it in a degree that is quite astonish-

---

* His sisters.

ing to my old dry bones. And now I think I have told you
enough, and more than enough about the house of Darwin;
so my dear old friend, farewell. What pleasant times we had
in drinking coffee in your rooms at Christ's College, and think
of the glories of Crux major.* Ah, in those days there were
no professions for sons, no ill-health to fear for them, no Californian gold, no French invasions. How paramount the
future is to the present when one is surrounded by children. My dread is hereditary ill-health. Even death is better for them.   My dear Fox, your sincere friend,

C. DARWIN.

P. S.—Susan has lately been working in a way which I
think truly heroic about the scandalous violation of the Act
against children climbing chimneys. We have set up a little
Society in Shrewsbury to prosecute those who break the law.
It is all Susan's doing. She has had very nice letters from
Lord Shaftesbury and the Duke of Sutherland, but the brutal
Shropshire squires are as hard as stones to move. The Act
out of London seems most commonly violated. It makes one
shudder to fancy one of one's own children at seven years
old being forced up a chimney—to say nothing of the conse-
quent loathsome disease and ulcerated limbs, and utter moral
degradation. If you think strongly on this subject, do make
some enquiries; add to your many good works, this other
one, and try to stir up the magistrates. There are several
people making a stir in different parts of England on this
subject. It is not very likely that you would wish for such,
but I could send you some essays and information if you so
liked, either for yourself or to give away.

C. Darwin to W. D. Fox.

Down [October 24th, 1852].

MY DEAR FOX,—I received your long and most welcome
letter this morning, and will answer it this evening, as I shall
be very busy with an artist, drawing Cirripedia, and much

---

* The beetle *Panagæus crux-major.*

overworked for the next fortnight.   But first you deserve to
be well abused—and pray consider yourself well abused—for
thinking or writing that I could for one minute be bored by
any amount of detail about yourself and belongings. It is
just what I like hearing; believe me that I often think of old
days spent with you, and sometimes can hardly believe what a
jolly careless individual one was in those old days.   A bright
autumn evening often brings to mind some shooting excursion
from Osmaston.   I do indeed regret that we live so far off
each other, and that I am so little locomotive.   I have been
unusually well of late (no water-cure), but I do not find that
I can stand any change better than formerly. . . The other
day I went to London and back, and the fatigue, though so
trifling, brought on my bad form of vomiting.   I grieve to
hear that your chest has been ailing, and most sincerely do
I hope that it is only the muscles ; how frequently the voice
fails with the clergy.   I can well understand your reluctance
to break up your large and happy party and go abroad ; but
your life is very valuable, so you ought to be very cautious in
good time.   You ask about all of us, now five boys (oh ! the
professions ; oh ! the gold ; and oh ! the French—these three
oh's all rank as dreadful bugbears) and two girls . . . but
another and the worst of my bugbears is hereditary weakness.
All my sisters are well except Mrs. Parker, who is much out of
health ; and so is Erasmus at his poor average : he has lately
moved into Queen Anne Street.   I had heard of the intended
marriage * of your sister Frances.   I believe I have seen her
since, but my memory takes me back some twenty-five years,
when she was lying down.   I remember well the delightful
expression of her countenance.   I most sincerely wish her all
happiness.

I see I have not answered half your queries.   We like very
well all that we have seen and heard of Rugby, and have
never repented of sending [W.] there.   I feel sure schools
have greatly improved since our days ; but I hate schools and

---

* To the Rev. J. Hughes.

the whole system of breaking through the affections of the family by separating the boys so early in life; but I see no help, and dare not run the risk of a youth being exposed to the temptations of the world without having undergone the milder ordeal of a great school.

I see you even ask after our pears. We have lots of Beurrées d'Aremberg, Winter Nelis, Marie Louise, and "Ne plus Ultra," but all off the wall; the standard dwarfs have borne a few, but I have no room for more trees, so their names would be useless to me. You really must make a holiday and pay us a visit sometime; nowhere could you be more heartily welcome. I am at work at the second volume of the Cirripedia, of which creatures I am wonderfully tired. I hate a Barnacle as no man ever did before, not even a sailor in a slow-sailing ship. My first volume is out; the only part worth looking at is on the sexes of Ibla and Scalpellum. I hope by next summer to have done with my tedious work. Farewell,—do come whenever you can possibly manage it.

I cannot but hope that the carbuncle may possibly do you good: I have heard of all sorts of weaknesses disappearing after a carbuncle. I suppose the pain is dreadful. I agree most entirely, what a blessed discovery is chloroform. When one thinks of one's children, it makes quite a little difference in one's happiness. The other day I had five grinders (two by the elevator) out at a sitting under this wonderful substance, and felt hardly anything.

My dear old friend, yours very affectionately,

CHARLES DARWIN.

C. *Darwin to W. D. Fox.*

Down, January 29th [1853].

MY DEAR FOX,—Your last account some months ago was so little satisfactory that I have often been thinking of you, and should be really obliged if you would give me a few lines, and tell me how your voice and chest are. I most sincerely hope that your report will be good. . . . Our second lad has a strong mechanical turn, and we think of making him an engineer. I shall try and find out for him some less classical school, perhaps Bruce Castle. I certainly should like to see more diversity in education than there is in any ordinary school—no exercising of the observing or reasoning faculties, no general knowledge acquired—I must think it a wretched system. On the other hand, a boy who has learnt to stick at Latin and conquer its difficulties, ought to be able to stick at any labour. I should always be glad to hear anything about schools or education from you. I am at my old, never-ending subject, but trust I shall really go to press in a few months with my second volume on Cirripedes. I have been much pleased by finding some odd facts in my first volume believed by Owen and a few others, whose good opinion I regard as final. . . . Do write pretty soon, and tell me all you can about yourself and family ; and I trust your report of yourself may be much better than your last.

. . . I have been very little in London of late, and have not seen Lyell since his return from America; how lucky he was to exhume with his own hand parts of three skeletons of reptiles out of the *Carboniferous* strata, and out of the inside of a fossil tree, which had been hollow within.

Farewell, my dear Fox, yours affectionately,
CHARLES DARWIN.

C. Darwin to W. D. Fox.

13 Sea Houses, Eastbourne,
[July 15th ? 1853].

MY DEAR FOX,—Here we are in a state of profound idleness, which to me is a luxury; and we should all, I believe, have been in a state of high enjoyment, had it not been for the detestable cold gales and much rain, which always gives much *ennui* to children away from their homes. I received your letter of 13th June, when working like a slave with Mr. Sowerby at drawing for my second volume, and so put off answering it till when I knew I should be at leisure. I was

extremely glad to get your letter. I had intended a couple
of months ago sending you a savage or supplicating jobation
to know how you were, when I met Sir P. Egerton, who told
me you were well, and, as usual, expressed his admiration of
your doings, especially your farming, and the number of animals, including children, which you kept on your land.
Eleven children, ave Maria! it is a serious look-out for you.
Indeed, I look at my five boys as something awful, and hate
the very thoughts of professions, &c. If one could insure
moderate health for them it would not signify so much, for I
cannot but hope, with the enormous emigration, professions
will somewhat improve. But my bugbear is hereditary weakness. I particularly like to hear all that you can say about
education, and you deserve to be scolded for saying "you did
not mean to *torment* me with a long yarn." You ask about
Rugby. I like it very well, on the same principle as my
neighbour, Sir J. Lubbock, likes Eton, viz., that it is not
worse than any other school ; the expense, *with all &c., &c.,*
including some clothes, travelling expenses, &c., is from £110
to £120 per annum. I do not think schools are so wicked as
they were, and far more industrious. The boys, I think, live
too secluded in their separate studies ; and I doubt whether
they will get so much knowledge of character as boys used to
do; and this, in my opinion, is the *one* good of public schools
over small schools. I should think the only superiority of a
small school over home was forced regularity in their work,
which your boys perhaps get at your home, but which I do
not believe my boys would get at my home. Otherwise, it is
quite lamentable sending boys so early in life from their home.
    . . . To return to schools. My main objection to them,
as places of education, is the enormous proportion of time
spent over classics. I fancy (though perhaps it is only fancy)
that I can perceive the ill and contracting effect on my eldest
boy's mind, in checking interest in anything in which reasoning and observation come into play. Mere memory seems to
be worked. I shall certainly look out for some school with
more diversified studies for my younger boys. I was talking

lately to the Dean of Hereford, who takes most strongly this view; and he tells me that there is a school at Hereford commencing on this plan; and that Dr. Kennedy at Shrewsbury is going to begin vigorously to modify that school. . . .

I am *extremely* glad to hear that you approved of my cirripedial volume. I have spent an almost ridiculous amount of labour on the subject, and certainly would never have undertaken it had I foreseen what a job it was. I hope to have finished by the end of the year. Do write again before a very long time; it is a real pleasure to me to hear from you. Farewell, with my wife's kindest remembrances to yourself and Mrs. Fox.

My dear old friend, yours affectionately,

C. DARWIN.

C. Darwin to W. D. Fox.

Down, August 10th [1853].

MY DEAR FOX,—I thank you sincerely for writing to me so soon after your most heavy misfortune. Your letter affected me so much. We both most truly sympathise with you and Mrs. Fox. We too lost, as you may remember, not so very long ago, a most dear child, of whom I can hardly yet bear to think tranquilly; yet, as you must know from your own most painful experience, time softens and deadens, in a manner truly wonderful, one's feelings and regrets. At first it is indeed bitter. I can only hope that your health and that of poor Mrs. Fox may be preserved, and that time may do its work softly, and bring you all together, once again, as the happy family, which, as I can well believe, you so lately formed.

My dear Fox, your affectionate friend,

CHARLES DARWIN.

[The following letter refers to the Royal Society's Medal, which was awarded to him in November, 1853:]

C. Darwin to J. D. Hooker.

Down, November 5th [1853].

MY DEAR HOOKER,—Amongst my letters received this morning, I opened first one from Colonel Sabine; the contents certainly surprised me very much, but, though the letter was a *very kind one,* somehow, I cared very little indeed for the announcement it contained. I then opened yours, and such is the effect of warmth, friendship, and kindness from one that is loved, that the very same fact, told as you told it, made me glow with pleasure till my very heart throbbed. Believe me, I shall not soon forget the pleasure of your letter. Such hearty, affectionate sympathy is worth more than all the medals that ever were or will be coined.   Again, my dear Hooker, I thank you.   I hope Lindley * will never hear that he was a competitor against me ; for really it is almost *ridiculous* (of course you would never repeat that I said this, for it would be thought by others, though not, I believe, by you, to be affectation) his not having the medal long before me ; I must feel *sure* that you did quite right to propose him ;

---

* John Lindley (b. 1799, d. 1865) was the son of a nurseryman near Norwich, through whose failure in business he was thrown at the age of twenty on his own resources.   He was befriended by Sir W. Hooker, and employed as assistant librarian by Sir J. Banks.   He seems to have had enormous capacity of work, and is said to have translated Richard's 'Analyse du Fruit' at one sitting of two days and three nights.   He became Assistant-Secretary to the Horticultural Society, and in 1829 was appointed Professor of Botany at University College, a post which he held for upwards of thirty years.   His writings are numerous : the best known being perhaps his 'Vegetable Kingdom,' published in 1846.   His influence in helping to introduce the natural system of classification was considerable, and he brought "all the weight of his teaching and all the force of his controversial powers to support it," as against the Linnean system universally taught in the earlier part of his career.   Sachs points out (Geschichte der Botanik, 1875, p. 161), that though Lindley adopted in the main a sound classification of plants, he only did so by abandoning his own theoretical principle that the physiological importance of an organ is a measure of its classificatory value.

and what a good, dear, kind fellow you are, nevertheless, to rejoice in this honour being bestowed on me.

What *pleasure* I have felt on the occasion, I owe almost entirely to you.

Farewell, my dear Hooker, yours affectionately,

C. DARWIN.

P. S.—You may believe what a surprise it was, for I had never heard that the medals could be given except for papers in the 'Transactions.' All this will make me work with better heart at finishing the second volume.

C. Darwin to C. Lyell.

Down, February 18th [1854].

MY DEAR LYELL,—I should have written before, had it not seemed doubtful whether you would go on to Teneriffe, but now I am extremely glad to hear your further progress is certain ; not that I have much of any sort to say, as you may well believe when you hear that I have only once been in London since you started. I was particularly glad to see, two days since, your letter to Mr. Horner, with its geological news ; how fortunate for you that your knees are recovered. I am astonished at what you say of the beauty, though I had fancied it great. It really makes me quite envious to think of your clambering up and down those steep valleys. And what a pleasant party on your return from your expeditions. I often think of the delight which I felt when examining volcanic islands, and I can remember even particular rocks which I struck, and the smell of the hot, black, scoriaceous cliffs ; but of those *hot* smells you do not seem to have had much. I do quite envy you. How I should like to be with you, and speculate on the deep and narrow valleys.

How very singular the fact is which you mention about the inclination of the strata being greater round the circumference than in the middle of the island ; do you suppose the elevation has had the form of a flat dome? I remember in the

Cordillera being *often* struck with the greater abruptness of the strata in the *low extreme* outermost ranges, compared with the great mass of inner mountains.   I dare say you will have thought of measuring exactly the width of any dikes at the top and bottom of any great cliff (which was done by Mr. Searle [?] at St. Helena), for it has often struck me as *very odd* that the cracks did not die out *oftener* upwards.   I can think of hardly any news to tell you, as I have seen no one since being in London, when I was delighted to see Forbes looking so well, quite big and burly.   I saw at the Museum some of the surprisingly rich gold ore from North Wales.   Ramsay also told me that he has lately turned a good deal of New Red Sandstone into Permian, together with the Labyrinthodon.   No doubt you see newspapers, and know that E. de Beaumont is perpetual Secretary, and will, I suppose, be more powerful than ever ; and Le Verrier has Arago's place in the Observatory.   There was a meeting lately at the Geological Society, at which Prestwich (judging from what R. Jones told me) brought forward your exact theory, viz. that the whole red clay and flints over the chalk plateau hereabouts is the residuum from the slow dissolution of the chalk !

As regards ourselves, we have no news, and are all well. The Hookers, sometime ago, stayed a fortnight with us, and, to our extreme delight, Henslow came down, and was most quiet and comfortable here.   It does one good to see so composed, benevolent, and intellectual a countenance.   There have been great fears that his heart is affected ; but, I hope to God, without foundation.   Hooker's book * is out, and *most beautifully* got up.   He has honoured me beyond measure by dedicating it to me !   As for myself, I am got to the page 112 of the Barnacles, and that is the sum total of my history.   By-the-way, as you care so much about North America, I may mention that I had a long letter from a shipmate in Australia, who says the Colony is getting decidedly

---

* Sir J. Hooker's ' Himalayan Journal.'

republican from the influx of Americans, and that all the
great and novel schemes for working the gold are planned
and executed by these men.   What a go-a-head nation it is!
Give my kindest remembrances to Lady Lyell, and to Mrs.
Bunbury, and to Bunbury.   I most heartily wish that the
Canaries may be ten times as interesting as Madeira, and
that everything may go on most prosperously with your
whole party.

My dear Lyell,
Yours most truly and affectionately,
C. DARWIN.

C. Darwin to J. D. Hooker.

Down, March 1st [1854].

MY DEAR HOOKER,—I finished yesterday evening the
first volume, and I very sincerely congratulate you on having produced a *first-class* book *—a book which certainly will
last.   I cannot doubt that it will take its place as a standard,
not so much because it contains real solid matter, but that it
gives a picture of the whole country.   One can feel that one
has seen it (and desperately uncomfortable I felt in going
over some of the bridges and steep slopes), and one *realises*
all the great Physical features.   You have in truth reason to
be proud ; consider how few travellers there have been with
a profound knowledge of one subject, and who could in
addition make a map (which, by-the-way, is one of the most
distinct ones I ever looked at, wherefore blessings alight on
your head), and study geology and meteorology!   I thought
I knew you very well, but I had not the least idea that your
Travels were your hobby ; but I am heartily glad of it, for I
feel sure that the time will never come when you and Mrs.
Hooker will not be proud to look back at the labour bestowed on these beautiful volumes.

Your letter, received this morning, has interested me *ex-*

* 'Himalayan Journal.'

tremely, and I thank you sincerely for telling me your old thoughts and aspirations. All that you say makes me even more deeply gratified by the Dedication; but you, bad man, do you remember asking me how I thought Lyell would like the work to be dedicated to him? I remember how strongly I answered, and I presume you wanted to know what I should feel; whoever would have dreamed of your being so crafty? I am glad you have shown a little bit of ambition about your Journal, for you must know that I have often abused you for not caring more about fame, though, at the same time, I must confess, I have envied and honoured you for being so free (too free, as I have always thought) of this "last infirmity of, &c." Do not say, "there never was a past hitherto to me— the phantom was always in view," for you will soon find other phantoms in view. How well I know this feeling, and did formerly still more vividly; but I think my stomach has much deadened my former pure enthusiasm for science and knowledge.

I am writing an unconscionably long letter, but I must return to the Journals, about which I have hardly said any-thing in detail. Imprimis, the illustrations and maps appear to me the best I have ever seen; the style seems to me everywhere perfectly clear (how rare a virtue), and some pas-sages really eloquent. How excellently you have described the upper valleys, and how detestable their climate; I felt quite anxious on the slopes of Kinchin that dreadful snowy night. Nothing has astonished me more than your physical strength; and all those devilish bridges! Well, thank good-ness! it is not *very* likely that I shall ever go to the Hima-laya. Much in a scientific point of view has interested me, especially all about those wonderful moraines. I certainly think I quite realise the valleys, more vividly perhaps from having seen the valleys of Tahiti. I cannot doubt that the Himalaya owe almost all their contour to running water, and that they have been subjected to such action longer than any mountains (as yet described) in the world. What a contrast with the Andes!

Perhaps you would like to hear the very little that I can say *per contra*, and this only applied to the beginning, in which (as it struck me) there was not *flow* enough till you get to Mirzapore on the Ganges (but the Thugs were *most* interesting), where the stream seemed to carry you on more equably with longer sentences and longer facts and discussions, &c. In another edition (and 1 am delighted to hear that Murray has sold all off), I would consider whether this part could not be condensed. Even if the meteorology was put in foot-notes, I think it would be an improvement. All the world is against me, but it makes me very unhappy to see the Latin names all in Italics, and all mingled with English names in Roman type ; but I must bear this burden, for all men of Science seem to think it would corrupt the Latin to dress it up in the same type as poor old English. Well, I am very proud of *my* book ; but there is one bore, that I do not much like asking people whether they have seen it, and how they like it, for I feel so much identified with it, that such questions become rather personal. Hence, I cannot tell you the opinion of others. You will have seen a fairly good review in the 'Athenæum.'

What capital news from Tasmania : it really is a very remarkable and creditable fact to the Colony.* I am always building veritable castles in the air about emigrating, and Tasmania has been my head-quarters of late ; so that I feel very proud of my adopted country : it is really a very singular and delightful fact, contrasted with the slight appreciation of science in the old country. I thank you heartily for your letter this morning, and for all the gratification your Dedication has given me; I could not help thinking how much —— would despise you for not having dedicated it to some great man, who would have done you and it some good in the eyes of the world. Ah, my dear Hooker, you were very soft on this head, and justify what I say about not caring enough for

---

* This refers to an unsolicited grant by the Colonial Government towards the expenses of Sir J. Hooker's 'Flora of Tasmania.'

your own fame.   I wish I was in every way more worthy of your good opinion.   Farewell.   How pleasantly Mrs. Hooker and you must rest from one of your many labours. . . .

Again farewell: I have written a wonderfully long letter. Adios, and God bless you.

My dear Hooker, ever yours,

C. DARWIN.

P.S.—I have just looked over my rambling letter; I see that I have not at all expressed my strong admiration at the amount of scientific work, in so many branches, which you have effected.   It is really grand.   You have a right to rest on your oars; or even to say, if it so pleases you, that "your meridian is past;" but well assured do I feel that the day of your reputation and general recognition has only just begun to dawn.

[In September, 1854, his Cirripede work was practically finished, and he wrote to Dr. Hooker:

"I have been frittering away my time for the last several weeks in a wearisome manner, partly idleness, and odds and ends, and sending ten thousand Barnacles out of the house all over the world.   But I shall now in a day or two begin to look over my old notes on species.   What a deal I shall have to discuss with you; I shall have to look sharp that I do not 'progress' into one of the greatest bores in life, to the few like you with lots of knowledge."]

CHAPTER X.

[ON page 67, the growth of the 'Origin of Species' has
been briefly described in my father's words. The letters
given in the present and following chapters will illustrate and
amplify the history thus sketched out.

It is clear that in the early·part of the voyage of the
Beagle he did not feel it inconsistent with his views to express
himself in thoroughly orthodox language as to the genesis of
new species. Thus in 1834 he wrote* at Valparaiso: "I
have already found beds of recent shells yet retaining their
colour at an elevation of 1300 feet, and beneath, the level
country is strewn with them. It seems not a very improbable
conjecture that the want of animals may be owing to none
having been created since this country was raised from the
sea."

This passage does not occur in the published 'Journal,'
the last proof of which was finished in 1837 ; and this fact
harmonizes with the change we know to have been proceeding in his views. But in the published 'Journal' we find passages which show a point of view more in accordance with
orthodox theological natural history than with his later views.
Thus, in speaking of the birds Synallaxis and Scytalopus (1st
edit. p. 353 ; 2nd edit. p. 289), he says : "When finding, as
in this case, any animal which seems to play so insignificant

---

a part in the great scheme of nature, one is apt to wonder why a distinct species should have been created."

A comparison of the two editions of the 'Journal' is instructive, as giving some idea of the development of his views on evolution. It does not give us a true index of the mass of conjecture which was taking shape in his mind, but it shows us that he felt sure enough of the truth of his belief to allow a stronger tinge of evolution to appear in the second edition. He has mentioned in the Autobiography (p. 68) that it was not until he read Malthus that he got a clear view of the potency of natural selection. This was in 1838—a year after he finished the first edition (it was not published until 1839), and five years before the second edition was written (1845). Thus the turning-point in the formation of his theory took place between the writing of the two editions.

I will first give a few passages which are practically the same in the two editions, and which are, therefore, chiefly of interest as illustrating his frame of mind in 1837.

The case of the two species of Molothrus (1st edit. p. 61; 2nd edit. p. 53) must have been one of the earliest instances noticed by him of the existence of representative species—a phenomenon which we know ('Autobiography,' p. 68) struck him deeply. The discussion on introduced animals (1st edit. p. 139; 2nd edit. p. 120) shows how much he was impressed by the complicated interdependence of the inhabitants of a given area.

An analogous point of view is given in the discussion (1st edit. p. 98; 2nd edit. p. 85) of the mistaken belief that large animals require, for their support, a luxuriant vegetation; the incorrectness of this view is illustrated by the comparison of the fauna of South Africa and South America, and the vegetation of the two continents. The interest of the discussion is that it shows clearly our *à priori* ignorance of the conditions of life suitable to any organism.

There is a passage which has been more than once quoted as bearing on the origin of his views. It is where he discusses the striking difference between the species of mice on the east and west of the Andes (1st edit. p. 399): "Unless we suppose the same species to have been created in two different countries, we ought not to expect any closer similarity between the organic beings on the opposite sides of the Andes than on shores separated by a broad strait of the sea." In the 2nd edit. p. 327, the passage is almost verbally identical, and is practically the same.

There are other passages again which are more strongly evolutionary in the 2nd edit., but otherwise are similar to the corresponding passages in the 1st edition. Thus, in describing the blind Tuco-tuco (1st edit. p. 60; 2nd edit. p. 52), in the first edition he makes no allusion to what Lamarck might have thought, nor is the instance used as an example of modification, as in the edition of 1845.

A striking passage occurs in the 2nd edit. (p. 173) on the relationship between the "extinct edentata and the living sloths, ant-eaters, and armadillos."

"This wonderful relationship in the same continent between the dead and the living, will, I do not doubt, hereafter throw more light on the appearance of organic beings on our earth, and their disappearance from it, than any other class of facts."

This sentence does not occur in the 1st edit., but he was evidently profoundly struck by the disappearance of the gigantic forerunners of the present animals. The difference between the discussions in the two editions is most instructive. In both, our ignorance of the conditions of life is insisted on, but in the second edition, the discussion is made to lead up to a strong statement of the intensity of the struggle for life. Then follows a comparison between rarity * and extinction, which introduces the idea that the preservation and dominance of existing species depend on the degree in which they are adapted to surrounding conditions. In the first edition,

---

* In the second edition, p. 146, the destruction of Niata cattle by droughts is given as a good example of our ignorance of the causes of rarity or extinction. The passage does not occur in the first edition.

he is merely "tempted to believe in such simple relations as variation of climate and food, or introduction of enemies, or the increased number of other species, as the cause of the succession of races." But finally (1st edit.) he ends the chapter by comparing the extinction of a species to the exhaustion and disappearance of varieties of fruit-trees: as if he thought that a mysterious term of life was impressed on each species at its creation.

The difference of treatment of the Galapagos problem is of some interest. In the earlier book, the American type of the productions of the islands is noticed, as is the fact that the different islands possess forms specially their own, but the importance of the whole problem is not so strongly put forward. Thus, in the first edition, he merely says :—

"This similarity of type between distant islands and continents, while the species are distinct, has scarcely been sufficiently noticed. The circumstance would be explained, according to the views of some authors, by saying that the creative power had acted according to the same law over a wide area."—(1st edit. p. 474.)

This passage is not given in the second edition, and the generalisations on geographical distribution are much wider and fuller. Thus he asks :—

"Why were their aboriginal inhabitants, associated . . . in different proportions both in kind and number from those on the Continent, and therefore acting on each other in a different manner—why were they created on American types of organisation?"—(2nd edit. p. 393.)

The same difference of treatment is shown elsewhere in this chapter. Thus the gradation in the form of beak presented by the thirteen allied species of finch is described in the first edition (p. 461) without comment. Whereas in the second edition (p. 380) he concludes :—

"One might really fancy that from an original paucity of birds in this Archipelago, one species has been taken and modified for different ends."

On the whole it seems to me remarkable that the difference

between the two editions is not greater; it is another proof of the author's caution and self-restraint in the treatment of his theory. After reading the second edition of the ' Journal,' we find with a strong sense of surprise how far developed were his views in 1837. We are enabled to form an opinion on this point from the note-books in which he wrote down detached thoughts and queries. I shall quote from the first note-book, completed between July 1837 and February 1838 : and this is the more worth doing, as it gives us an insight into the condition of his thoughts before the reading of Malthus. The notes are written in his most hurried style, so many words being omitted, that it is often difficult to arrive at the meaning. With a few exceptions (indicated by square brackets) * I have printed the extracts as written; the punctuation, however, has been altered, and a few obvious slips corrected where it seemed necessary. The extracts are not printed in order, but are roughly classified.†

" Propagation explains why modern animals same type as extinct, which is law, almost proved."

" We can see why structure is common in certain countries when we can hardly believe necessary, but if it was necessary to one forefather, the result would be as it is. Hence antelopes at Cape of Good Hope; marsupials at Australia."

" Countries longest separated greatest differences—if separated from immersage, possibly two distinct types, but each having its representatives—as in Australia."

" Will this apply to whole organic kingdom when our planet first cooled ? "

The two following extracts show that he applied the theory

---

* In the extracts from the note-book ordinary brackets represent my father's parentheses.

† On the first page of the note-book, is written " Zoonomia "; this seems to refer to the first few pages in which reproduction by gemmation is discussed, and where the " Zoonomia " is mentioned. Many pages have been cut out of the note-book, probably for use in writing the Sketch of 1844, and these would have no doubt contained the most interesting extracts.

368 THE GROWTH OF THE 'ORIGIN OF SPECIES.'

of evolution to the "whole organic kingdom" from plants to man.

"If we choose to let conjecture run wild, then animals, our fellow brethren in pain, disease, death, suffering and famine—our slaves in the most laborious works, our companions in our amusements—they may partake [of?] our origin in one common ancestor—we may be all melted together."

"The different intellects of man and animals not so great as between living things without thought (plants), and living things with thought (animals)."

The following extracts are again concerned with an *à priori* view of the probability of the origin of species by descent ["propagation," he called it].

"The tree of life should perhaps be called the coral of life, base of branches dead; so that passages cannot be seen."

"There never may have been grade between pig and tapir, yet from some common progenitor. Now if the intermediate ranks had produced infinite species, probably the series would have been more perfect."

At another place, speaking of intermediate forms he says :—

"Cuvier objects to propagation of species by saying, why have not some intermediate forms been discovered between Palæotherium, Megalonyx, Mastodon, and the species now living? Now according to my view (in S. America) parent of all Armadilloes might be brother to Megatherium—uncle now dead."

Speaking elsewhere of intermediate forms, he remarks :—

"Opponents will say—*show them me*. I will answer yes, if you will show me every step between bulldog and greyhound."

Here we see that the case of domestic animals was already present in his mind as bearing on the production of natural species. The disappearance of intermediate forms naturally leads up to the subject of extinction, with which the next extract begins.

"It is a wonderful fact, horse, elephant, and mastodon, dying out about same time in such different quarters.

"Will Mr. Lyell say that some [same?] circumstance killed it over a tract from Spain to South America?—(Never).

"They die, without they change, like golden pippins; it is a *generation of species* like generation *of individuals*.

"Why does individual die? To perpetuate certain peculiarities (therefore adaptation), and obliterate accidental varieties, and to accommodate itself to change (for, of course, change, even in varieties, is accommodation). Now this argument applies to species.

"If individual cannot propagate he has no issue—so with species.

"If *species* generate other *species*, their race is not utterly cut off :—like golden pippins, if produced by seed, go on—otherwise all die.

"The fossil horse generated, in South Africa, zebra—and continued—perished in America.

"All animals of same species are bound together just like buds of plants, which die at one time, though produced either sooner or later. Prove animals like plants—trace gradation between associated and non-associated animals—and the story will be complete."

Here we have the view already alluded to of a term of life impressed on a species.

But in the following note we get extinction connected with unfavourable variation, and thus a hint is given of natural selection :

"With respect to extinction, we can easily see that [a] variety of [the] ostrich (Petise), may not be well adapted, and thus perish out; or, on the other hand, like Orpheus [a Galapagos bird], being favourable, many might be produced. This requires [the] principle that the permanent variations produced by confined breeding and changing circumstances are continued and produced according to the adaptation of such circumstance, and therefore that death of species is a consequence (contrary to what would appear from America) of non-adaptation of circumstances."

The first part of the next extract has a similar bearing. The end of the passage is of much interest, as showing that he had at this early date visions of the far-reaching character of the theory of evolution :—

"With belief of transmutation and geographical grouping, we are led to endeavour to discover *causes* of change ; the manner of adaptation (wish of parents ? ?), instinct and struct-ure becomes full of speculation and lines of observation. View of generation being condensation,* test of highest or-ganisation intelligible . . . . My theory would give zest to recent and fossil comparative anatomy ; it would lead to the study of instincts, heredity, and mind-heredity, whole [of] metaphysics.

"It would lead to closest examination of hybridity and generation, causes of change in order to know what we have come from and to what we tend—to what circumstances favour crossing and what prevents it—this, and direct exam-ination of direct passages of structure in species, might lead to laws of change, which would then be [the] main object of study, to guide our speculations."

The following two extracts have a similar interest ; the second is especially interesting, as it contains the germ of concluding sentence of the 'Origin of Species' : †—

"Before the attraction of gravity discovered it might have been said it was as great a difficulty to account for the movement of all [planets] by one law, as to account for each separate one ; so to say that all mammalia were born from

---

* I imagine him to mean that each generation is "condensed" to a small number of the best organized individuals.

† 'Origin of Species' (edit. i.), p. 490 :—" There is a grandeur in this view of life, with its several powers, having been originally breathed into a few forms or into one : and that whilst this planet has gone cycling on according to the fixed law of gravity, from so simple a beginning endless forms most beautiful and most wonderful have been, and are being evolved."

one stock, and since distributed by such means as we can recognise, may be thought to explain nothing.

"Astronomers might formerly have said that God fore-ordered each planet to move in its particular destiny. In the same manner God orders each animal created with certain forms in certain countries, but how much more simple and sublime [a] power—let attraction act according to certain law, such are inevitable consequences—let animals be created, then by the fixed laws of generation, such will be their successors.

"Let the powers of transportal be such, and so will be the forms of one country to another—let geological changes go at such a rate, so will be the number and distribution of the species !! "

The three next extracts are of miscellaneous interest :—

"When one sees nipple on man's breast, one does not say some use, but sex not having been determined—so with use-less wings under elytra of beetles—born from beetles with wings, and modified—if simple creation merely, would have been born without them."

"In a decreasing population at any one moment fewer closely related (few species of genera); ultimately few genera (for otherwise the relationship would converge sooner), and lastly, perhaps, some one single one. Will not this account for the odd genera with few species which stand between great groups, which we are bound to consider the increasing ones ? "

The last extract which I shall quote gives the germ of his theory of the relation between alpine plants in various parts of the world, in the publication of which he was forestalled. by E. Forbes (see vol. i. p. 72). He says, in the 1837 note-book, that alpine plants, "formerly descended lower, there-fore [they are] species of lower genera altered, or northern plants."

When we turn to the Sketch of his theory, written in 1844 (still therefore before the second edition of the 'Journal' was completed), we find an enormous advance made on the note-book of 1837. The Sketch is in fact a surprisingly complete presentation of the argument afterwards familiar to us in the 'Origin of Species.' There is some obscurity as to the date of the short Sketch which formed the basis of the 1844 Essay. We know from his own words (vol. i., p. 68), that it was in June 1842 that he first wrote out a short sketch of his views.* This statement is given with so much circumstance that it is almost impossible to suppose that it contains an error of date. It agrees also with the following extract from his Diary.

1842. May 18th. Went to Maer.

"June 15th to Shrewsbury, and on 18th to Capel Curig. During my stay at Maer and Shrewsbury (five years after commencement) wrote pencil-sketch of species theory."

Again in the introduction to the 'Origin,' p. 1, he writes, "after an interval of five years' work" [from 1837, i. e. in 1842], "I allowed myself to speculate on the subject, and drew up some short notes."

Nevertheless in the letter signed by Sir C. Lyell and Sir J. D. Hooker, which serves as an introduction to the joint paper of Messrs. C. Darwin and A. Wallace on the 'Tendency of Species to form Varieties,'† the essay of 1844 (extracts from which form part of the paper) is said to have been "sketched in 1839, and copied in 1844." This statement is obviously made on the authority of a note written in my father's hand across the Table of Contents of the 1844 Essay. It is to the following effect: "This was sketched in 1839, and copied out in full, as here written and read by you in 1844." I conclude that this note was added in 1858, when the MS. was sent to Sir J. D. Hooker (see Letter of June 29, 1858, p. 476). There is also some further evidence on this side of the question. Writing to Mr. Wallace (Jan. 25, 1859) my father says :—" Every one whom I have seen has thought

---

* This version I cannot find, and it was probably destroyed, like so much of his MS., after it had been enlarged and re-copied in 1844.

† 'Linn. Soc. Journal,' 1858, p. 45.

your paper very well written and interesting. It puts my extracts (written in 1839, now just twenty years ago !), which .I must say in apology were never for an instant intended for publication, into the shade." The statement that the earliest sketch was written in 1839 has been frequently made in bio-graphical notices of my father, no doubt on the authority of the 'Linnean Journal,' but it must, I think, be considered as erroneous. The error may possibly have arisen in this way. In writing on the Table of Contents of the 1844 MS. that it was sketched in 1839, I think my father may have intended to imply that the framework of the theory was clearly thought out by him at that date. In the Autobiography (p. 71) he speaks of the time, " about 1839, when the theory was clearly conceived," meaning, no doubt, the end of 1838 and begin-ning of 1839, when the reading of Malthus had given him the key to the idea of natural selection. But this explanation does not apply to the letter to Mr. Wallace ; and with regard to the passage * in the 'Linnean Journal' it is difficult to understand how it should have been allowed to remain as it now stands, conveying, as it clearly does, the impression that 1839 was the date of his earliest written sketch.

The sketch of 1844 is written in a clerk's hand, in two hundred and thirty-one pages folio, blank leaves being alter-nated with the MS. with a view to amplification. The text has been revised and corrected, criticisms being pencilled by himself on the margin. It is divided into two parts : I. "On the variation of Organic Beings under Domestication and in their Natural State." II. "On the Evidence favourable and opposed to the view that Species are naturally formed races descended from common Stocks." The first part contains the main argument of the 'Origin of Species.' It is founded, as is the argument of that work, on the study of domestic animals, and both the Sketch and the 'Origin' open with a

---

* My father certainly saw the proofs of the paper, for he added a foot-note apologising for the style of the extracts, on the ground that the "work was never intended for publication."

chapter on variation under domestication and on artificial
selection. This is followed, in both essays, by discussions on
variation under nature, on natural selection, and on the
struggle for life. Here, any close resemblance between the
two essays with regard to arrangement ceases. Chapter III.
of the Sketch, which concludes the first part, treats of the
variations which occur in the instincts and habits of animals,
and thus corresponds to some extent with Chapter VII. of
the 'Origin' (1st edit.). It thus forms a complement to the
chapters which deal with variation in structure. It seems to
have been placed thus early in the Essay to prevent the hasty
rejection of the whole theory by a reader to whom the idea of
natural selection acting on instincts might seem impossible.
This is the more probable, as the Chapter on Instinct in the
'Origin' is specially mentioned (Introduction, p. 5) as one of
the "most apparent and gravest difficulties on the theory."
Moreover the chapter in the Sketch ends with a discussion,
"whether any particular corporeal structures . . . . . are so
wonderful as to justify the rejection *primâ facie* of our theory." Under this heading comes the discussion of the eye,
which in the 'Origin' finds its place in Chapter VI. under
"Difficulties of the Theory." The second part seems to have
been planned in accordance with his favourite point of view
with regard to his theory. This is briefly given in a letter to
Dr. Asa Gray, November 11th, 1859 : "I cannot possibly believe that a false theory would explain so many classes of
facts, as I think it certainly does explain. On these grounds
I drop my anchor, and believe that the difficulties will
slowly disappear." On this principle, having stated the
theory in the first part, he proceeds to show to what extent various wide series of facts can be explained by its
means.

Thus the second part of the Sketch corresponds roughly
to the nine concluding Chapters of the First Edition of the
'Origin.' But we must exclude Chapter VII. ('Origin')
on Instinct, which forms a chapter in the first part of the
Sketch, and Chapter VIII. ('Origin') on Hybridism, a subject

treated in the Sketch with 'Variation under Nature' in the first part.

The following list of the chapters of the second part of the Sketch will illustrate their correspondence with the final chapters of the 'Origin.'

Chapter I. "On the kind of intermediateness necessary, and the number of such intermediate forms."

This includes a geological discussion, and corresponds to parts of Chapters VI. and IX. of the 'Origin.'

Chapter II. "The gradual appearance and disappearance of organic beings." Corresponds to Chapter X. of the 'Origin.'

Chapter III. "Geographical Distribution." Corresponds to Chapters XI. and XII. of the 'Origin.'

Chapter IV. "Affinities and Classification of Organic beings."

Chapter V. "Unity of Type," Morphology, Embryology.

Chapter VI. Rudimentary Organs.

These three chapters correspond to Chapter XII. of the 'Origin.'

Chapter VII. Recapitulation and Conclusion. The final sentence of the Sketch, which we saw in its first rough form in the Note Book of 1837, closely resembles the final sentence of the 'Origin,' much of it being identical. The 'Origin' is not divided into two "Parts," but we see traces of such a division having been present in the writer's mind, in this resemblance between the second part of the Sketch and the final chapters of the 'Origin.' That he should speak * of the chapters on transition, on instinct, on hybridism, and on the geological record, as forming a group, may be due to the division of his early MS. into two parts.

Mr. Huxley, who was good enough to read the Sketch at my request, while remarking that the "main lines of argument," and the illustrations employed are the same, points out that in the 1844 Essay, "much more weight is attached

---

* 'Origin,' Introduction, p. 5.

to the influence of external conditions in producing variation, and to the inheritance of acquired habits than in the 'Origin.'"

It is extremely interesting to find in the Sketch the first mention of principles familiar to us in the 'Origin of Species.' Foremost among these may be mentioned the principle of Sexual Selection, which is clearly enunciated. The important form of selection known as "unconscious," is also given. Here also occurs a statement of the law that peculiarities tend to appear in the offspring at an age corresponding to that at which they occurred in the parent.

Professor Newton, who was so kind as to look through the 1844 Sketch, tells me that my father's remarks on the migration of birds, incidentally given in more than one passage, show that he had anticipated the views of some later writers.

With regard to the general style of the Sketch, it is not to be expected that it should have all the characteristics of the 'Origin,' and we do not, in fact, find that balance and control, that concentration and grasp, which are so striking in the work of 1859.

In the Autobiography (p. 68, vol. 1) my father has stated what seemed to him the chief flaw of the 1844 Sketch; he had overlooked "one problem of great importance," the problem of the divergence of character. This point is discussed in the 'Origin of Species,' but, as it may not be familiar to all readers, I will give a short account of the difficulty and its solution. The author begins by stating that varieties differ from each other less than species, and then goes on: "Nevertheless, according to my view, varieties are species in process of formation. . . . . How then does the lesser difference between varieties become augmented into the greater difference between species?"* He shows how an analogous divergence takes place under domestication where an originally uniform stock of horses has been split up into race-horses,

---

* 'Origin,' 1st edit. p. 111.

dray-horses, &c., and then goes on to explain how the same principle applies to natural species. "From the simple circumstance that the more diversified the descendants from any one species become in structure, constitution, and habits, by so much will they be better enabled to seize on many and widely diversified places in the polity of nature, and so be enabled to increase in numbers."

The principle is exemplified by the fact that if on one plot of ground a single variety of wheat be sown, and on to another a mixture of varieties, in the latter case the produce is greater. More individuals have been able to exist because they were not all of the same variety. An organism becomes more perfect and more fitted to survive when by division of labour the different functions of life are performed by different organs. In the same way a species becomes more efficient and more able to survive when different sections of the species become differentiated so as to fill different stations.

In reading the Sketch of 1844, I have found it difficult to recognise the absence of any definite statement of the principle of divergence as a flaw in the Essay. Descent with modification implies divergence, and we become so habituated to a belief in descent, and therefore in divergence, that we do not notice the absence of proof that divergence is in itself an advantage. As shown in the Autobiography, my father in 1876 found it hardly credible that he should have overlooked the problem and its solution.

The following letter will be more in place here than its chronological position, since it shows what was my father's feeling as to the value of the Sketch at the time of its completion.]

C. Darwin to Mrs. Darwin.

Down, July 5, 1844.

I have just finished my sketch of my species theory. If, as I believe, my theory in time be accepted even by one competent judge, it will be a considerable step in science.

25

I therefore write this in case of my sudden death, as my most solemn and last request, which I am sure you will consider the same as if legally entered in my will, that you will devote £400 to its publication, and further, will yourself, or through Hensleigh,* take trouble in promoting it. I wish that my sketch be given to some competent person, with this sum to induce him to take trouble in its improvement and enlargement. I give to him all my books on Natural History, which are either scored or have references at the end to the pages, begging him carefully to look over and consider such passages as actually bearing, or by possibility bearing, on this subject. I wish you to make a list of all such books as some temptation to an editor. I also request that you will hand over [to] him all those scraps roughly divided in eight or ten brown paper portfolios. The scraps, with copied quotations from various works, are those which may aid my editor. I also request that you, or some amanuensis, will aid in deciphering any of the scraps which the editor may think possibly of use. I leave to the editor's judgment whether to interpolate these facts in the text, or as notes, or under appendices. As the looking over the references and scraps will be a long labour, and as the *correcting* and enlarging and altering my sketch will also take considerable time, I leave this sum of £400 as some remuneration, and any profits from the work. I consider that for this the editor is bound to get the sketch published either at a publisher's or his own risk. Many of the scrap in the portfolios contains mere rude suggestions and early views, now useless, and many of the facts will probably turn out as having no bearing on my theory.

With respect to editors, Mr. Lyell would be the best if he would undertake it; I believe he would find the work pleasant, and he would learn some facts new to him. As the editor must be a geologist as well as a naturalist, the next best editor would be Professor Forbes of London. The next best (and quite best in many respects) would be Professor Hens-

* Mr. H. Wedgwood.

low. Dr. Hooker would be *very* good. The next, Mr. Strick-land.* If none of these would undertake it, I would request you to consult with Mr. Lyell, or some other capable man for some editor, a geologist and naturalist. Should one other hundred pounds make the difference of procuring a good editor, request earnestly that you will raise £500.

My remaining collections in Natural History may be given to any one or any museum where it would be accepted. . . .

[The following note seems to have formed part of the original letter, but may have been of later date :

" Lyell, especially with the aid of Hooker (and of any good zoological aid), would be best of all. Without an editor will pledge himself to give up time to it, it would be of no use paying such a sum.

" If there should be any difficulty in getting an editor who would go thoroughly into the subject, and think of the bear-ing of the passages marked in the books and copied out of scraps of paper, then let my sketch be published as it is, stating that it was done several years ago † and from memory without consulting any works, and with no intention of pub-lication in its present form."

The idea that the Sketch of 1844 might remain, in the event of his death, as the only record of his work, seems to have been long in his mind, for in August 1854, when he had finished with the Cirripedes, and was thinking of beginning his " species work," he added on the back of the above letter, " Hooker by far best man to edit my species volume. August 1854."]

---

* After Mr. Strickland's name comes the following sentence, which has been erased but remained legible. " Professor Owen would be very good ; but I presume he would not undertake such a work."

† The words " several years ago and," seem to have been added at a later date.

CHAPTER XI.

THE GROWTH OF THE 'ORIGIN OF SPECIES.'
LETTERS, 1843–1856.

[THE history of my father's life is told more completely in his correspondence with Sir J. D. Hooker than in any other series of letters ; and this is especially true of the history of the growth of the 'Origin of Species.' This, therefore, seems an appropriate place for the following notes, which Sir Joseph Hooker has kindly given me. They give, moreover, an interesting picture of his early friendship with my father :—

"My first meeting with Mr. Darwin was in 1839, in Trafalgar Square. I was walking with an officer who had been his shipmate for a short time in the *Beagle* seven years before, but who had not, I believe, since met him. I was introduced ; the interview was of course brief, and the memory of him that I carried away and still retain was that of a rather tall and rather broad-shouldered man, with a slight stoop, an agreeable and animated expression when talking, beetle brows, and a hollow but mellow voice ; and that his greeting of his old acquaintance was sailor-like—that is, delightfully frank and cordial. I observed him well, for I was already aware of his attainments and labours, derived from having read various proof-sheets of his then unpublished ' Journal.' These had been submitted to Mr. (afterwards Sir Charles) Lyell by Mr. Darwin, and by him sent to his father, Ch. Lyell, Esq., of Kinnordy, who (being a very old friend of my father, and taking a kind interest in my projected career as a naturalist) had allowed me to peruse them. At this time I was hurrying on my studies, so as to take my degree before volunteering to accompany Sir James Ross in the Antarctic Expedition, which had just been determined on by the Admiralty; and so pressed for time was I, that I used to sleep with the sheets of the 'Journal' under my pillow, that I might read them between waking and rising. They impressed me profoundly, I might say despairingly, with the variety of acquirements, mental and physical, required in a naturalist who should follow in Darwin's footsteps, whilst they stimulated me to enthusiasm in the desire to travel and observe.

"It has been a permanent source of happiness to me that I knew so much of Mr. Darwin's scientific work so many years before that intimacy began which ripened into feelings as near to those of reverence for his life, works, and character as is reasonable and proper. It only remains to add to this little episode that I received a copy of the 'Journal' complete,—a gift from Mr. Lyell,—a few days before leaving England.

"Very soon after the return of the Antarctic Expedition my correspondence with Mr. Darwin began (December, 1843) by his sending me a long letter, warmly congratulating me on my return to my family and friends, and expressing a wish to hear more of the results of the expedition, of which he had derived some knowledge from private letters of my own (written to or communicated through Mr. Lyell). Then, plunging at once into scientific matters, he directed my attention to the importance of correlating the Fuegian Flora with that of the Cordillera and of Europe, and invited me to study the botanical collections which he had made in the Galapagos Islands, as well as his Patagonian and Fuegian plants.

"This led to me sending him an outline of the conclusions I had formed regarding the distribution of plants in the southern regions, and the necessity of assuming the destruction of considerable areas of land to account for the relations of the flora of the so-called Antarctic Islands. I do not suppose that any of these ideas were new to him, but they led to an animated and lengthy correspondence full of instruction."

Here follows the letter (1843) to Sir J. D. Hooker above referred to.]

MY DEAR SIR,—I had hoped before this time to have had the pleasure of seeing you and congratulating you on your safe return from your long and glorious voyage. But as I seldom go to London, we may not yet meet for some time—without you are led to attend the Geological Meetings.

I am anxious to know what you intend doing with all your materials—I had so much pleasure in reading parts of some of your letters, that I shall be very sorry if I, as one of the public, have no opportunity of reading a good deal more. I suppose you are very busy now and full of enjoyment: how well I remember the happiness of my first few months of England—it was worth all the discomforts of many a gale ! But I have run from the subject, which made me write, of expressing my pleasure that Henslow (as he informed me a few days since by letter) has sent to you my small collection of plants. You cannot think how much pleased I am, as I feared they would have been all lost, and few as they are, they cost me a good deal of trouble. There are a very few notes, which I believe Henslow has got, describing the habitats, &c., of some few of the more remarkable plants. I paid particular attention to the Alpine flowers of Tierra del Fuego, and I am sure I got every plant which was in flower in Patagonia at the seasons when we were there. I have long thought that some general sketch of the Flora of the point of land, stretching so far into the southern seas, would be very curious. Do make comparative remarks on the species allied to the European species, for the advantage of botanical ignoramuses like myself. It has often struck me as a curious point to find out, whether there are many European genera in T. del Fuego which are not found along the ridge of the Cordillera; the separation in such case would be so enormous. Do point out in any sketch you draw up, what genera are

American and what European, and how great the differences of the species are, when the genera are European, for the sake of the ignoramuses.

I hope Henslow will send you my Galapagos plants (about which Humboldt even expressed to me considerable curiosity) —I took much pains in collecting all I could. A Flora of this archipelago would, I suspect, offer a nearly parallel case to that of St. Helena, which has so long excited interest. Pray excuse this long rambling note, and believe me, my dear sir, yours very sincerely,   C. DARWIN.

Will you be so good as to present my respectful compliments to Sir W. Hooker.

[Referring to Sir J. D. Hooker's work on the Galapagos Flora, my father wrote in 1846 :

"I cannot tell you how delighted and astonished I am at the results of your examination ; how wonderfully they support my assertion on the differences in the animals of the different islands, about which I have always been fearful."

Again he wrote (1849) :—

"I received a few weeks ago your Galapagos papers,* and I have read them since being here. I really cannot express too strongly my admiration of the geographical discussion : to my judgment it is a perfect model of what such a paper should be; it took me four days to read and think over. How interesting the Flora of the Sandwich Islands appears to be, how I wish there were materials for you to treat its flora as you have done the Galapagos. In the Systematic paper I was rather disappointed in not finding general remarks on affinities, structures, &c., such as you often give in conversation, and such as De Candolle and St. Hilaire introduced

---

* These papers include the results of Sir J. D. Hooker's examination of my father's Galapagos plants, and were published by the Linnean Society in 1849.

in almost all their papers, and which make them interesting even to a non-Botantist."

"Very soon afterwards [continues Sir J. D. Hooker] in a letter dated January 1844, the subject of the '.Origin of Species' was brought forward by him, and I believe that I was the first to whom he communicated his then new ideas on the subject, and which being of interest as a contribution to the history of Evolution, I here copy from his letter" :—]

C. Darwin to J. D. Hooker.

[January 11th, 1844.]

Besides a general interest about the southern lands, I have been now ever since my return engaged in a very presumptuous work, and I know no one individual who would not say a very foolish one. I was so struck with the distribution of the Galapagos organisms, &c. &c., and with the character of the American fossil mammifers, &c. &c., that I determined to collect blindly every sort of fact, which could bear any way on what are species. I have read heaps of agricultural and horticultural books, and have never ceased collecting facts. At last gleams of light have come, and I am almost convinced (quite contrary to the opinion I started with) that species are not (it is like confessing a murder) immutable. Heaven forfend me from Lamarck nonsense of a "tendency to progression," "adaptations from the slow willing of animals," &c.! But the conclusions I am led to are not widely different from his ; though the means of change are wholly so. I think I have found out (here's presumption !) the simple way by which species become exquisitely adapted to various ends. You will now groan, and think to yourself, "on what a man have I been wasting my time and writing to." I should, five years ago, have thought so. . . .

[The following letter written on February 23, 1844, shows that the acquaintanceship with Sir J. D. Hooker was then fast ripening into friendship. The letter is chiefly of interest as showing the sort of problems then occupying my father's mind :]

DEAR HOOKER,—I hope you will excuse the freedom of my address, but I feel that as co-circum-wanderers and as fellow labourers (though myself a very weak one) we may throw aside some of the old-world formality. . . . I have just finished a little volume on the volcanic islands which we visited. I do not know how far you care for dry simple geology, but I hope you will let me send you a copy. I suppose I can send it from London by common coach conveyance.

. . . I am going to ask you some *more* questions, though I daresay, without asking them, I shall see answers in your work, when published, which will be quite time enough for my purposes. First for the Galapagos, you will see in my Journal, that the Birds, though peculiar species, have a most obvious S. American aspect : I have just ascertained the same thing holds good with the sea-shells. It is so with those plants which are peculiar to this archipelago ; you state that their numerical proportions are continental (is not this a very curious fact?) but are they related in forms to S. America. Do you know of any other case of an archipelago, with the separate islands possessing distinct representative species? I have always intended (but have not yet done so) to examine Webb and Berthelot on the Canary Islands for this object. Talking with Mr. Bentham, he told me that the separate islands of the Sandwich Archipelago possessed distinct representative species of the same genera of Labiatæ : would not this be worth your enquiry? How is it with the Azores ; to be sure the heavy western gales would tend to diffuse the same species over that group.

I hope you will (I dare say my hope is quite superfluous) attend to this general kind of affinity in isolated islands, though I suppose it is more difficult to perceive this sort of relation in plants, than in birds or quadrupeds, the groups of

which are, I fancy, rather more confined.   Can St. Helena be
classed, though remotely, either with Africa or S. America?
From some facts, which I have collected, I have been led to
conclude that the fauna of mountains are *either* remarkably
similar (sometimes in the presence of the same species and at
other times of same genera), *or* that they are remarkably dis-
similar ; and it has occurred to me that possibly part of this
peculiarity of the St. Helena and Galapagos floras may be
attributed to a great part of these two Floras being mountain Floras.   I fear my notes will hardly serve to distinguish
much of the habitats of the Galapagos plants, but they may
in some cases ; most, if not all, of the green, leafy plants
come from the summits of the islands, and the thin brown
leafless plants come from the lower arid parts : would you be
so kind as to bear this remark in mind, when examining my
collection.

I will trouble you with only one other question.   In discussion with Mr. Gould, I found that in most of the genera
of birds which range over the whole or greater part of the
world, the individual species have wider ranges, thus the Owl
is mundane, and many of the species have very wide ranges.
So I believe it is with land and fresh-water shells—and I
might adduce other cases.   Is it not so with Cryptogamic
plants ; have not most of the species wide ranges, in those
genera which are mundane?   I do not suppose that the
converse holds, viz.—that when a species has a wide range,
its genus also ranges wide.   Will you so far oblige me by
occasionally thinking over this?   It would cost me vast
trouble to get a list of mundane phanerogamic genera and
then search how far the species of these genera are apt to
range wide in their several countries; but you might occasionally, in the course of your pursuits, just bear this in mind,
though perhaps the point may long since have occurred to
you or other Botanists.   Geology is bringing to light interesting facts, concerning the ranges of shells; I think it is pretty
well established, that according as the geographical range of
a species is wide, so is its persistence and duration in time.   I

hope you will try to grudge as little as you can the trouble of my letters, and pray believe me very truly yours,

C. DARWIN.

P. S. I should feel extremely obliged for your kind offer of the sketch of Humboldt; I venerate him, and after having had the pleasure of conversing with him in London, I shall still more like to have any portrait of him.

[What follows is quoted from Sir J. Hooker's notes.

"The next act in the drama of our lives opens with personal intercourse. This began with an invitation to breakfast with him at his brother's (Erasmus Darwin's) house in Park Street; which was shortly afterwards followed by an invitation to Down to meet a few brother Naturalists. In the short intervals of good health that followed the long illnesses which oftentimes rendered life a burthen to him, between 1844 and 1847, I had many such invitations, and delightful they were. A more hospitable and more attractive home under every point of view could not be imagined—of Society there were most often Dr. Falconer, Edward Forbes, Professor Bell, and Mr. Waterhouse—there were long walks, romps with the children on hands and knees, music that haunts me still. Darwin's own hearty manner, hollow laugh, and thorough enjoyment of home life with friends; strolls with him all together, and interviews with us one by one in his study, to discuss questions in any branch of biological or physical knowledge that we had followed; and which I at any rate always left with the feeling that I had imparted nothing and carried away more than I could stagger under. Latterly, as his health became more seriously affected, I was for days and weeks the only visitor, bringing my work with me and enjoying his society as opportunity offered. It was an established rule that he every day pumped me, as he called it, for half an hour or so after breakfast in his study, when he first brought out a heap of slips with questions botanical, geographical, &c., for me to answer, and concluded by telling

me of the progress he had made in his own work, asking my
opinion on various points.   I saw no more of him till about
noon, when I heard his mellow ringing voice calling my
name under my window—this was to join him in his daily
forenoon walk round the sand-walk.*   On joining him I
found him in a rough grey shooting-coat in summer, and
thick cape over his shoulders in winter, and a stout staff in
his hand; away we trudged through the garden, where there
was always some experiment to visit, and on to the sand-
walk, round which a fixed number of turns were taken, during
which our conversation usually ran on foreign lands and seas,
old friends, old books, and things far off to both mind and
eye.

"In the afternoon there was another such walk, after which
he again retired till dinner if well enough to join the family;
if not, he generally managed to appear in the drawing-room,
where seated in his high chair, with his feet in enormous carpet shoes, supported on a high stool—he enjoyed the music
or conversation of his family."

Here follows a series of letters illustrating the growth of
my father's views, and the nature of his work during this
period.]

C. Darwin to J. D. Hooker.

Down [1844].

. . . The conclusion, which I have come at is, that those
areas, in which species are most numerous, have oftenest been
divided and isolated from other areas, united and again divided ; a process implying antiquity and some changes in the
external conditions. This will justly sound very hypothetical.
I cannot give my reasons in detail ; but the most general conclusion, which the geographical distribution of all organic
beings, appears to me to indicate, is that isolation is the chief
concomitant or cause of the appearance of *new* forms (I well

---

* See p. 93.

know there are some staring exceptions). Secondly, from seeing how often the plants and animals swarm in a country, when introduced into it, and from seeing what a vast number of plants will live, for instance in England, if kept *free from weeds, and native plants*, I have been led to consider that the spreading and number of the organic beings of any country depend less on its external features, than on the number of forms, which have been there originally created or produced. I much doubt whether you will find it possible to explain the number of forms by proportional differences of exposure; and I cannot doubt if half the species in any country were destroyed or had not been created, yet that country would appear to us fully peopled. With respect to original creation or production of new forms, I have said that isolation appears the chief element. Hence, with respect to terrestrial productions, a tract of country, which had oftenest within the late geological periods subsided and been converted into islands, and reunited, I should expect to contain most forms.

But such speculations are amusing only to one self, and in this case useless, as they do not show any direct line of observation : if I had seen how hypothetical [is] the little, which I have unclearly written, I would not have troubled you with the reading of it. Believe me,—at last not hypothetically, Yours very sincerely,

C. DARWIN.

C. Darwin to J. D. Hooker.

Down, 1844.

. . . I forget my last letter, but it must have been a very silly one, as it seems I gave my notion of the number of species being in great degree governed by the degree to which the area had been·often isolated and divided ; I must have been cracked to have written it, for I have no evidence, without a person be willing to admit all my views, and then it does follow ; but in my most sanguine moments, all I expect, is that I shall be able to show even to sound Naturalists, that there are two sides to the question of the immu-

tability of species;—that facts can be viewed and grouped
under the notion of allied species having descended from
common stocks. With respect to books on this subject, I
do not know of any systematical ones, except Lamarck's,
which is veritable rubbish; but there are plenty, as Lyell,
Pritchard, &c., on the view of the immutability. Agassiz
lately has brought the strongest argument in favour of immutability. Isidore G. St. Hilaire has written some good Essays,
tending towards the mutability-side, in the ' Suites à Buffon,'
entitled " Zoolog. Générale." Is it not strange that the author,
of such a book as the ' Animaux sans Vertèbres,' should have
written that insects, which never see their eggs, should *will*
(and plants, their seeds) to be of particular forms, so as to
become attached to particular objects. The other, common
(specially Germanic) notion is hardly less absurd, viz. that
climate, food, &c., should make a Pediculus formed to climb
hair, or wood-pecker, to climb trees. I believe all these
absurd views arise, from no one having, as far as I know,
approached the subject on the side of variation under domestication, and having studied all that is known about domestication. I was very glad to hear your criticism on island-floras
and on non-diffusion of plants : the subject is too long for a
letter: I could defend myself to some considerable extent,
but I doubt whether successfully in your eyes, or indeed in
my own. . . .

C. Darwin to J. D. Hooker.

Down [July, 1844].

. . . I am now reading a wonderful book for facts on
variation—Bronn, ' Geschichte der Natur.' It is stiff German :
it forestalls me, sometimes I think delightfully, and sometimes cruelly. You will be ten times hereafter more horrified
at me than at H. Watson. I hate arguments from results,
but on my views of descent, really Natural History becomes
a sublimely grand result-giving subject (**now you** may quiz
me for so foolish an escape of mouth). . . . I must leave this

letter till to-morrow, for I am tired ; but I so enjoy writing to you, that I must inflict a little more on you.

Have you any good evidence for absence of insects in small islands ?   I found thirteen species in Keeling Atoll. Flies are good fertilizers, and I have seen a microscopic Thrips and a Cecidomya take flight from a flower in the direction of another with pollen adhering to them.   In Arctic countries a bee seems to go as far N. as any flower. . . . .

C. Darwin to J. D. Hooker.

Shrewsbury [September, 1845].

MY DEAR HOOKER,—I write a line to say that Cosmos * arrived quite safely [N.B. One sheet came loose in Pt. I.], and to thank you for your nice note.   I have just begun the introduction, and groan over the style, which in such parts is full half the battle.   How true many of the remarks are (i. e. as far as I can understand the wretched English) on the scenery; it is an exact expression of one's own thoughts.

I wish I ever had any books to lend you in return for the many you have lent me. . . .

All of what you kindly say about my species work does not alter one iota my long self-acknowledged presumption in accumulating facts and speculating on the subject of variation, without having worked out my due share of species.   But now for nine years it has been anyhow the greatest amusement to me.

Farewell, my dear Hooker, I grieve more than you can well believe, over our prospect of so seldom meeting.

I have never perceived but one fault in you, and that you have grievously, viz. modesty ; you form an exception to Sydney Smith's aphorism, that merit and modesty have no other connection, except in their first letter. Farewell,

C. DARWIN.

---

* A translation of Humboldt's ' Kosmos.'

C. Darwin to L. Jenyns (Blomefield).

Down, Oct. 12th, [1845].

MY DEAR JENYNS,—Thanks for your note.   I am sorry to say I have not even the tail-end of a fact in English Zoology to communicate.   I have found that even trifling observations require, in my case, some leisure and energy, both of which ingredients I have had none to spare, as writing my Geology thoroughly expends both.   I had always thought that I would keep a journal and record everything, but in the way I now live I find I observe nothing to record.   Looking after my garden and trees, and occasionally a very little walk in an idle frame of mind, fills up every afternoon in the same manner.   I am surprised that with all your parish affairs, you have had time to do all that which you have done.   I shall be very glad to see your little work * (and proud should I have been if I could have added a single fact to it).   My work on the species question has impressed me very forcibly with the importance of all such works as your intended one, containing what people are pleased generally to call trifling facts.   These are the facts which make one understand the working or economy of nature.   There is one subject, on which I am very curious, and which perhaps you may throw some light on, if you have ever thought on it; namely, what are the checks and what the periods of life,—by which the increase of any given species is limited.   Just calculate the increase of any bird, if you assume that only half the young are reared, and these breed : within the *natural* (*i. e.*, if free from accidents) life of the parents the number of individuals will become enormous, and I have been much surprised to think how great destruction *must* annually or occasionally be falling

---

* Mr. Jenyns' 'Observations in Natural History.'   It is prefaced by an Introduction on "Habits of observing as connected with the study of Natural History," and followed by a "Calendar of Periodic Phenomena in Natural History," with "Remarks on the importance of such Registers." My father seems to be alluding to this Register in the P.S. to the letter dated Oct. 17, 1846.

on every species, yet the means and period of such destruction is scarcely perceived by us.

I have continued steadily reading and collecting facts on variation of domestic animals and plants, and on the question of what are species. I have a grand body of facts, and I think I can draw some sound conclusions. The general conclusions at which I have slowly been driven from a directly opposite conviction, is that species are mutable, and that allied species are co-descendants from common stocks. I know how much I open myself to reproach for such a conclusion, but I have at least honestly and deliberately come to it. I shall not publish on this subject for several years. At present I am on the Geology of South America. I hope to pick up from your book some facts on slight variations in structure or instincts in the animals of your acquaintance.

Believe me, ever yours,
C. DARWIN.

*C. Darwin to L. Jenyns.**

Down, [1845 ?].

MY DEAR JENYNS,—I am very much obliged to you for the trouble you have taken in having written me so long a note. The question of where, when, and how the check to the increase of a given species falls appears to me particularly interesting, and our difficulty in answering it shows how really ignorant we are of the lives and habits of our most familiar species. I was aware of the bare fact of old birds driving away their young, but had never thought of the effect you so clearly point out, of local gaps in number being thus immediately filled up. But the original difficulty remains; for if your farmers had not killed your sparrows and rooks, what would have become of those which now immigrate into your parish? in the middle of England one is too far distant from the natural limits of the rook and sparrow to suppose

---

that the young are thus far expelled from Cambridgeshire. The check must fall heavily at some time of each species' life ; for, if one calculates that only half the progeny are reared and bred, how enormous is the increase ! One has, however, no business to feel so much surprise at one's ignorance, when one knows how impossible it is without statistics to conjecture the duration of life and percentage of deaths to births in mankind. If it could be shown that apparently the birds of passage *which breed here* and increase, return in the succeeding years in about the same number, whereas those that come here for their winter and non-breeding season annually, come here with the same numbers, but return with greatly decreased numbers, one would know (as indeed seems probable) that the check fell chiefly on full-grown birds in the winter season, and not on the eggs and very young birds, which has appeared to me often the most probable period. If at any time any remarks on this subject should occur to you, I should be most grateful for the benefit of them.

With respect to my far distant work on species, I must have expressed myself with singular inaccuracy if I led you to suppose that I meant to say that my conclusions were inevitable. They have become so, after years of weighing puzzles, to myself *alone ;* but in my wildest day-dream, I never expect more than to be able to show that there are two sides to the question of the immutability of species, *i. e.* whether species are *directly* created or by intermediate laws (as with the life and death of individuals). I did not approach the subject on the side of the difficulty in determining what are species and what are varieties, but (though, why I should give you such a history of my doings it would be hard to say) from such facts as the relationship between the living and extinct mammifers in South America, and between those living on the Continent and on adjoining islands, such as the Galapagos. It occurred to me that a collection of all such analogous facts would throw light either for or against the view of related species being co-descendants from a common

stock. A long searching amongst agricultural and horticultural books and people makes me believe (I well know how
absurdly presumptuous this must appear) that I see the way
in which new varieties become exquisitely adapted to the
external conditions of life and to other surrounding beings.
I am a bold man to lay myself open to being thought a complete fool, and a most deliberate one. From the nature of
the grounds which make me believe that species are mutable
in form, these grounds cannot be restricted to the closest-
allied species ; but how far they extend I cannot tell, as my
reasons fall away by degrees, when applied to species more
and more remote from each other. Pray do not think that I
am so blind as not to see that there are numerous immense
difficulties in my notions, but they appear to me less than on
the common view. I have drawn up a sketch and had it
copied (in 200 pages) of my conclusions; and if I thought at
some future time that you would think it worth reading, I
should, of course, be most thankful to have the criticism of
so competent a critic. Excuse this very long and egotistical
and ill-written letter, which by your remarks you had led me
into, and believe me,   Yours very truly,

                                        C. DARWIN.

C. Darwin to L. Jenyns.

Down, Oct. 17th, 1846.

DEAR JENYNS,—I have taken a most ungrateful length
of time in thanking you for your very kind present of your
'Observations.' But I happened to have had in hand several
other books, and have finished yours only a few days ago. I
found it very pleasant reading, and many of your facts interested me much. I think I was more interested, which is odd,
with your notes on some of the lower animals than on the
higher ones. The introduction struck me as very good; but
this is what I expected, for I well remember being quite delighted with a preliminary essay to the first number of the
'Annals of Natural History.' I missed one discussion, and

think myself ill-used, for I remember your saying you would make some remarks on the weather and barometer, as a guide for the ignorant in prediction. I had also hoped to have perhaps met with some remarks on the amount of variation in our common species. Andrew Smith once declared he would get some hundreds of specimens of larks and sparrows from all parts of Great Britain, and see whether, with finest measurements, he could detect any proportional variations in beaks or limbs, &c. This point interests me from having lately been skimming over the absurdly opposite conclusions of Gloger and Brehm; the one making half-a-dozen species out of every common bird, and the other turning so many reputed species into one. Have you ever done anything of this kind, or have you ever studied Gloger's or Brehm's works? I was interested in your account of the martins, for I had just before been utterly perplexed by noticing just such a proceeding as you describe: I counted seven, one day lately, visiting a single nest and sticking dirt on the adjoining wall. I may mention that I once saw some squirrels eagerly splitting those little semi-transparent spherical galls on the back of oak-leaves for the maggot within; so that they are insectivorous. A *Cychrus rostratus* once squirted into my eyes and gave me extreme pain; and I must tell you what happened to me on the banks of the Cam, in my early entomological days: under a piece of bark I found two *Carabi* (I forget which), and caught one in each hand, when lo and behold I saw a sacred *Panagæus crux major!* I could not bear to give up either of my *Carabi*, and to lose *Panagæus* was out of the question; so that in despair I gently seized one of the *Carabi* between my teeth, when to my unspeakable disgust and pain the little inconsiderate beast squirted his acid down my throat, and I lost both *Carabi* and *Panagæus!* I was quite astonished to hear of a terrestrial *Planaria*; for about a year or two ago I described in the 'Annals of Natural History' several beautifully coloured terrestrial species of the Southern Hemisphere, and thought it quite a new fact. By the way, you speak of a sheep with a broken leg not having flukes: I have heard my

father aver that a fever, or any *serious accident*, as a broken
limb, will cause in a man all the intestinal worms to be evacu-
ated. Might not this possibly have been the case with the
flukes in their early state?

I hope you were none the worse for Southampton ; * I wish
I had seen you looking rather fatter. I enjoyed my week
extremely, and it did me good. I missed you the last few
days, and we never managed to see much of each other ; but
there were so many people there, that I for one hardly saw
anything of any one. Once again I thank you very cordially
for your kind present, and the pleasure it has given me, and
believe me,   Ever most truly yours,

C. DARWIN.

P.S.—I have quite forgotten to say how greatly interested
I was with your discussion on the statistics of animals : when
will Natural History be so perfect that such points as you
discuss will be perfectly known about any one animal?

C. Darwin to J. D. Hooker.

Malvern, June 13 [1849].

. . . At last I am going to press with a small poor first-
fruit of my confounded Cirripedia, viz. the fossil pedunculate
cirripedia. You ask what effect studying species has had on
my variation theories; I do not think much—I have felt
some difficulties more. On the other hand, I have been
struck (and probably unfairly from the class) with the variability of every part in some slight degree of every species.
When the same organ is *rigorously* compared in many individuals, I always find some slight variability, and consequently that the diagnosis of species from minute differences
is always dangerous. I had thought the same parts of the
same species more resemble (than they do anyhow in Cirripedia) objects cast in the same mould. Systematic work

---

* The meeting of the British Association.

would be easy were it not for this confounded variation, which, however, is pleasant to me as a speculatist, though odious to me as a systematist. Your remarks on the distinctness (so unpleasant to me) of the Himalayan Rubi, willows, &c., compared with those of northern [Europe?], &c., are very interesting; if my rude species-sketch had any *small* share in leading you to these observations, it has already done good and ample service, and may lay its bones in the earth in peace. I never heard anything so strange as Falconer's neglect of your letters; I am extremely glad you are cordial with him again, though it must have cost you an effort. Falconer is a man one must love. . . . May you prosper in every way, my dear Hooker.

Your affectionate friend,
C. DARWIN.

C. Darwin to J. D. Hooker.

Down, Wednesday [September, n. d.].

. . . Many thanks for your letter received yesterday, which, as always, set me thinking: I laughed at your attack at my stinginess in changes of level towards Forbes,* being so liberal towards myself; but I must maintain, that I have never let down or upheaved our mother-earth's surface, for the sake of explaining any one phenomenon, and I trust I have very seldom done so without some distinct evidence. So I must still think it a bold step (perhaps a very true one)

---

* Edward Forbes, born in the Isle of Man 1815, died 1854. His best known work was his Report on the distribution of marine animals at different depths in the Mediterranean. An important memoir of his is referred to in my father's 'Autobiography,' p. 72. . He held successively the posts of Curator to the Geological Society's Museum, and Professor of Natural History in the Museum of Practical Geology; shortly before he died he was appointed Professor of Natural History in the University of Edinburgh. He seems to have impressed his contemporaries as a man of strikingly versatile and vigorous mind. The above allusion to changes of level refers to Forbes's tendency to explain the facts of geographical distribution by means of an active geological imagination.

to sink into the depths of ocean, within the period of existing species, so large a tract of surface. But there is no amount or extent of change of level, which I am not fully prepared to admit, but I must say I should like better evidence, than the identity of a few plants, which *possibly* (I do not say probably) might have been otherwise transported. Particular thanks for your attempt to get me a copy of 'L'Espèce,'* and almost equal thanks for your criticisms on him : I rather misdoubted him, and felt not much inclined to take as gospel his facts. I find this one of my greatest difficulties with foreign authors, viz. judging of their credibility. How painfully (to me) true is your remark, that no one has hardly a right to examine the question of species who has not minutely described many. I was, however, pleased to hear from Owen (who is vehemently opposed to any mutability in species), that he thought it was a very fair subject, and that there was a mass of facts to be brought to bear on the question, not hitherto collected. My only comfort is (as I mean to attempt the subject), that I have dabbled in several branches of Natural History, and seen good specific men work out my species, and know something of geology (an indispensable union); and though I shall get more kicks than half-pennies, I will, life serving, attempt my work. Lamarck is the only exception, that I can think of, of an accurate describer of species at least in the Invertebrate Kingdom, who has disbelieved in permanent species, but he in his absurd though clever work has done the subject harm, as has Mr. Vestiges, and, as (some future loose naturalist attempting the same speculations will perhaps say) has Mr. D. . . .

C. DARWIN.

---

* Probably Godron's essay, published by the Academy of Nancy in 1848–49, and afterwards as a separate book in 1859.

C. Darwin to J. D. Hooker.

Down, September 25th [1853].

MY DEAR HOOKER,—I have read your paper with great interest; it seems all very clear, and will form an admirable introduction to the New Zealand Flora, or to any Flora in the world. How few generalizers there are among systematists; I really suspect there is something absolutely opposed to each other and hostile in the two frames of mind required for systematising and reasoning on large collections of facts. Many of your arguments appear to me very well put, and, as far as my experience goes, the candid way in which you discuss the subject is unique. The whole will be very useful to me whenever I undertake my volume, though parts take the wind very completely out of my sails; it will be all nuts to me . . . for I have for some time determined to give the arguments on *both* sides (as far as I could), instead of arguing on the mutability side alone.

In my own Cirripedial work (by the way, thank you for the dose of soft solder; it does one—or at least me—a great deal of good)—in my own work I have not felt conscious that disbelieving in the mere *permanence* of species has made much difference one way or the other; in some few cases (if publishing avowedly on doctrine of non-permanence), I should *not* have affixed names, and in some few cases should have affixed names to remarkable varieties. Certainly I have felt it humiliating, discussing and doubting, and examining over and over again, when in my own mind the only doubt has been whether the form varied *to-day or yesterday* (not to put too fine a point on it, as Snagsby* would say). After describing a set of forms as distinct species, tearing up my MS., and making them one species, tearing that up and making them separate, and then making them one again (which has happened to me), I have gnashed my teeth, cursed species, and asked what sin I had committed to be

---

* In 'Bleak House.'

so punished. But I must confess that perhaps nearly the same thing would have happened to me on any scheme of work.

I am heartily glad to hear your Journal * is so much advanced; how magnificently it seems to be illustrated! An "*Oriental Naturalist,*" with lots of imagination and not too much regard to facts, is just the man to discuss species! I think your title of 'A Journal of a Naturalist in the East' very good; but whether "in the Himalaya" would not be better, I have doubted, for the East sounds rather vague. . . .

C. Darwin to J. D. Hooker.

[1853.]

MY DEAR HOOKER,—I have no remarks at all worth sending you, nor, indeed, was it likely that I should, considering how perfect and elaborated an essay it is.† As far as my judgment goes, it is the most important discussion on the points in question ever published. I can say no more. I agree with almost everything you say; but I require much time to digest an essay of such quality. It almost made me gloomy, partly from feeling I could not answer some points which theoretically I should have liked to have been different, and partly from seeing *so far better done* than I *could* have done, discussions on some points which I had intended to have taken up. . . .

I much enjoyed the slaps you have given to the provincial species-mongers. I wish I could have been of the slightest use: I have been deeply interested by the whole essay, and congratulate you on having produced a memoir which I believe will be memorable. I was deep in it when your most considerate note arrived, begging me not to hurry. I thank Mrs. Hooker and yourself most sincerely for your wish to see me. I will not let another summer pass without seeing you at Kew, for indeed I should enjoy it much. . . .

---

* Sir J. D. Hooker's 'Himalayan Journal.'
† 'New Zealand Flora,' 1853.

You do me really more honour than I have any claim to, putting me in after Lyell on ups and downs. In a year or two's 'time, when I shall be at my species book (if I do not break down), I shall gnash my teeth and abuse you for having put so many hostile facts so confoundedly well.

Ever yours affectionately,

C. DARWIN.

C. Darwin to J. D. Hooker.

Down, March 26th [1854].

MY DEAR HOOKER,—I had hoped that you would have had a little breathing-time after your Journal, but this seems to be very far from the case; and I am the more obliged (and somewhat contrite) for the long letter received this morning, *most* juicy with news and *most* interesting to me in many ways. I am very glad indeed to hear of the reforms, &c., in the Royal Society. With respect to the Club,* I am deeply interested; only two or three days ago, I was regretting to my wife, how I was letting drop and being dropped by nearly all my acquaintances, and that I would endeavour to go oftener to London; I was not then thinking of the Club, which, as far as any one thing goes, would answer my exact object in keeping up old and making some new acquaintances.

---

* The Philosophical Club, to which my father was elected (as Professor Bonney is good enough to inform me) on April 24, 1854. He resigned his membership in 1864. The Club was founded in 1847. The number of members being limited to 47, it was proposed to christen it "the Club of 47," but the name was never adopted. The nature of the Club may be gathered from its first rule : " The purpose of the Club is to promote as much as possible the scientific objects of the Royal Society ; to facilitate intercourse between those Fellows who are actively engaged in cultivating the various branches of Natural Science, and who have contributed to its progress ; to increase the attendance at the evening meetings, and to encourage the contribution and discussion of papers." The Club met for dinner (at first) at 6, and the chair was to be quitted at 8.15, it being expected that members would go to the Royal Society. Of late years the dinner has been at 6.30, the Society meeting in the afternoon.

I will therefore come up to London for every (with rare exceptions) Club-day, and then my head, I think, will allow me on an average to go to every other meeting. But it is grievous how often any change knocks me up. I will further pledge myself, as I told Lyell, to resign after a year, if I did not attend pretty often, so that I should *at worst* encumber the Club temporarily. If you can get me elected, I certainly shall be very much pleased. Very many thanks for answers about Glaciers. I am very glad to hear of the second Edit.* so very soon; but am not surprised, for I have heard of several, in our small circle, reading it with very much pleasure. I shall be curious to hear what Humboldt will say: it will, I should think, delight him, and meet with more praise from him than any other book of Travels, for I cannot remember one, which has so many subjects in common with him. What a wonderful old fellow he is. . . . . By the way, I hope, when you go to Hitcham, towards the end of May, you will be forced to have some rest. I am grieved to hear that all the bad symptoms have not left Henslow; it is so strange and new to feel any uneasiness about his health. I am particularly obliged to you for sending me Asa Gray's letter ; how very pleasantly he writes. To see his and your caution on the species-question ought to overwhelm me in confusion and shame; it does make me feel deuced uncomfortable. . . . It is delightful to hear all that he says on Agassiz : how very singular it is that so *eminently* clever a man, with such *immense* knowledge on many branches of Natural History, should write as he does. Lyell told me that he was so delighted with one of his (Agassiz) lectures on progressive development, &c., &c., that he went to him afterwards and told him, "that it was so delightful, that he could not help all the time wishing it was true." I seldom see a Zoological paper from North America, without observing the impress of Agassiz's doctrines—another proof, by the way, of how great a man he is. I was pleased and surprised to see A. Gray's remarks on

---

* Of the Himalayan Journal.

crossing, obliterating varieties, on which, as you know, I have been collecting facts for these dozen years. How awfully flat I shall feel, if when I get my notes together on species, &c., &c., the whole thing explodes like an empty puff-ball. Do not work yourself to death.   Ever yours most truly,

C. DARWIN.

C. Darwin to J. D. Hooker.

Down, Nov. 5th [1854].

MY DEAR HOOKER,—I was delighted to get your note yesterday. I congratulate you very heartily,* and whether you care much or little, I rejoice to see the highest scientific judgment-court in Great Britain recognise your claims. I do hope Mrs. Hooker is pleased, and E. desires me particularly to send her cordial congratulations. . . . I pity you from the very bottom of my heart about your after-dinner speech, which I fear I shall not hear. Without you have a very much greater soul than I have (and I believe that you have), you will find the medal a pleasant little stimulus, when work goes badly, and one ruminates that all is vanity, it is pleasant to have some tangible proof, that others have thought something of one's labours.

Good-bye my dear Hooker, I can assure [you] that we both most truly enjoyed your and Mrs. Hooker's visit here. Farewell.   My dear Hooker, your sincere friend,

C. DARWIN.

C. Darwin to J. D. Hooker.

March 7 [1855].

. . . I have just finished working well at Wollaston's† 'Insecta Maderensia': it is an *admirable* work. There is a very curious point in the astounding proportion of Coleoptera

---

* On the award to him of the Royal Society's Medal.

† Thomas Vernon Wollaston died (in his fifty-seventh year, as I believe) on Jan. 4, 1878. His health forcing him in early manhood to winter in

that are apterous; and I think I have guessed the reason, viz., that powers of flight would be injurious to insects inhabiting a confined locality, and expose them to be blown to the sea: to test this, I find that the insects inhabiting the Dezerte Grande, a quite small islet, would be still more exposed to this danger, and here the proportion of apterous insects is even considerably greater than on Madeira Proper. Wollaston speaks of Madeira and the other Archipelagoes as being " sure and certain witnesses of Forbes' old continent," and of course the Entomological world implicitly follows this view. But to my eyes it would be difficult to imagine facts more opposed to such a view. It is really disgusting and humiliating to see directly opposite conclusions drawn from the same facts.

I have had some correspondence with Wollaston on this and other subjects, and I find that he coolly assumes, (1) that formerly insects possessed greater migratory powers than now, (2) that the old land was *specially* rich in centres of creation, (3) that the uniting land was destroyed before the special creations had time to diffuse, and (4) that the land was broken down before certain families and genera had time to reach from Europe or Africa the points of land in question. Are not these a jolly lot of assumptions? and yet I shall see for the next dozen or score of years Wollaston quoted as proving the former existence of poor Forbes' Atlantis.

---

the south, he devoted himself to a study of the Coleoptera of Madeira, the Cape de Verdes, and St. Helena, whence he deduced evidence in support of the belief in the submerged continent of 'Atlantis.' In an obituary notice by Mr. Rye (' Nature,' 1878) he is described as working persistently "upon a broad conception of the science to which he was devoted," while being at the same time " accurate, elaborate, and precise *ad punctum*, and naturally of a minutely critical habit." His first scientific paper was written when he was an undergraduate at Jesus College, Cambridge. While at the University, he was an Associate and afterwards a Member of the Ray Club: this is a small society which still meets once a week, and where the undergraduate members, or Associates, receive much kindly encouragement from their elders.

I hope I have not wearied you, but I thought you would like to hear about this book, which strikes me as *excellent* in its facts, and the author a most nice and modest man.

Most truly yours,
C. DARWIN.

C. Darwin to W. D. Fox.

Down, March 19th [1855].

MY DEAR FOX,—How long it is since we have had any communication, and I really want to hear how the world goes with you ; but my immediate object is to ask you to observe a point for me, and as I know now you are a very busy man with too much to do, I shall have a good chance of your doing what I want, as it would be hopeless to ask a quite idle man. As you have a Noah's Ark, I do not doubt that you have pigeons. (How I wish by any chance they were fantails !) Now what I want to know is, at what age nestling pigeons have their tail feathers sufficiently developed to be counted. I do not think I ever saw a young pigeon. I am hard at work at my notes collecting and comparing them, in order in some two or three years to write a book with all the facts and arguments, which I can collect, *for and versus* the immutability of species. I want to get the young of our domestic breeds, to see how young, and to what degree the differences appear. I must either breed myself (which is no amusement but a horrid bore to me) the pigeons or buy their young ; and before I go to a seller, whom I have heard of from Yarrell, I am really anxious to know something about their development, not to expose my excessive ignorance, and therefore be excessively liable to be cheated and gulled. With respect to the *one* point of the tail feathers, it is of course in relation to the wonderful development of tail feathers in the adult fantail. If you had any breed of poultry pure, I would beg a chicken with exact age stated, about a week or fortnight old ! to be sent in a box by post, if you could have the heart to kill one ; and secondly, would let me pay postage. . . Indeed, I should be very glad to have a nestling common pigeon sent, for I mean to make skeletons, and have already just begun comparing wild and tame ducks. And I think the results rather curious,* for on weighing the several bones very carefully, when perfectly cleaned the proportional weights of the two have greatly varied, the foot of the tame having largely increased. How I wish I could get a little wild duck of a week old, but that I know is almost impossible.

With respect to ourselves, I have not much to say; we have now a terribly noisy house with the whooping cough, but otherwise are all well. Far the greatest fact about myself is that I have at last quite done with the everlasting barnacles. At the end of the year we had two of our little boys very ill with fever and bronchitis, and all sorts of ailments. Partly for amusement, and partly for change of air, we went to London and took a house for a month, but it turned out a great failure, for that dreadful frost just set in when we went, and all our children got unwell, and E. and I had coughs and colds and rheumatism nearly all the time. We had put down first on our list of things to do, to go and see Mrs. Fox, but literally after waiting some time to see whether the weather would not improve, we had not a day when we both could go out.

I do hope before very long you will be able to manage to pay us a visit. Time is slipping away, and we are getting oldish. Do tell us about yourself and all your large family.

I know you will help me *if you can* with information about the young pigeons; and anyhow do write before very long.

My dear Fox, your sincere old friend,

C. DARWIN.

---

* "I have just been testing practically what disuse does in reducing parts; I have made skeleton of wild and tame duck (oh, the smell of well-boiled, high duck! !) and I find the tame-duck wing ought, according to scale of wild prototype, to have its two wings 360 grains in weight, but it has it only 317."—A letter to Sir J. Hooker, 1855.

P.S.—Amongst all sorts of odds and ends, with which I am amusing myself, I am comparing the seeds of the variations of plants. I had formerly some wild cabbage seeds, which I gave to some one, was it to you? It is a *thousand* to one it was thrown away, if not I should be very glad of a pinch of it.

[The following extract from a letter to Mr. Fox (March 27th, 1855) refers to the same subject as the last letter, and gives some account of the "species work:" "The way I shall kill young things will be to put them under a tumbler glass with a teaspoon of ether or chloroform, the glass being pressed down on some yielding surface, and leave them for an hour or two, young have such power of revivication. (I have thus killed moths and butterflies.) The best way would be to send them as you procure them, in pasteboard chip-box by post, on which you could write and just tie up with string; and you will *really* make me happier by allowing me to keep an account of postage, &c. Upon my word I can hardly believe that *any one* could be so good-natured as to take such trouble and do such a very disagreeable thing as kill babies; and I am very sure I do not know one soul who, except yourself, would do so. I am going to ask one thing more; should old hens of any above poultry (not duck) die or become so old as to be *useless*, I wish you would send her to me per rail, addressed to "C. Darwin, care of Mr. Acton, Post-office, Bromley, Kent." Will you keep this address? as shortest way for parcels. But I do not care so much for this, as I could buy the old birds dead at Baily to make skeletons. I should have written at once even if I had not heard from you, to beg you not to take trouble about pigeons, for Yarrell has persuaded me to attempt it, and I am now fitting up a place, and have written to Baily about prices, &c., &c. *Sometime* (when you are better) I should like very much to hear a little about your "Little Call Duck"; why so called? And where you got it? and what it is like? . . . I was so ignorant I did not even know there were three varieties of Dorking fowl: how do they differ? . . .

I forget whether I ever told you what the object of my present work is,—it is to view all facts that I can master (eheu, eheu, how ignorant I find I am) in Natural History (as on geographical distribution, palæontology, classification, hybridism, domestic animals and plants, &c., &c., &c.) to see how far they favour or are opposed to the notion that wild species are mutable or immutable : I mean with my utmost power to give all arguments and facts on both sides. I have a *number* of people helping me in every way, and giving me most valuable assistance ; but I often doubt whether the subject will not quite overpower me.

So much for the quasi-business part of my letter. I am very very sorry to hear so indifferent account of your health : with your large family your life is very precious, and I am sure with all your activity and goodness it ought to be a happy one, or as happy as can reasonably be expected with all the cares of futurity on one.

One cannot expect the present to be like the old Crux-major days at the foot of those noble willow stumps, the memory of which I revere. I now find my little entomology which I wholly owe to you, comes in very useful. I am very glad to hear that you have given yourself a rest from Sunday duties. How much illness you have had in your life ! Farewell my dear Fox. I assure you I thank you heartily for your proffered assistance."]

C. Darwin to W. D. Fox.

Down, May 7th [1855].

MY DEAR FOX,—My correspondence has cost you a deal of trouble, though this note will not. I found yours on my return home on Saturday after a week's work in London. Whilst there I saw Yarrell, who told me he had carefully examined all points in the Call Duck, and did not feel any doubt about it being specifically identical, and that it had crossed freely with common varieties in St. James's Park. I should therefore be very glad for a seven-days' duckling and

27

for one of the old birds, should one ever die a natural death.
Yarrell told me that Sabine had collected forty varieties of
the common duck ! . . . Well, to return to business ; nobody,
I am sure, could fix better for me than you the characteristic
age of little chickens ; with respect to skeletons, I have feared
it would be impossible to make them, but I suppose I shall
be able to measure limbs, &c., by feeling the joints. What
you say about old cocks just confirms what I thought, and I
will make my skeletons of old cocks. Should an old wild
turkey ever die, please remember me; I do not care for a
baby turkey, nor for a mastiff. Very many thanks for your
offer. I have puppies of bull-dogs and greyhound in salt,
and I have had cart-horse and race-horse young colts carefully measured. Whether I shall do any good I doubt. I
am getting out of my depth. Most truly yours,

C. DARWIN.

[An extract from a letter to Mr. Fox may find a place here,
though of a later date, viz. July, 1855 :

"Many thanks for the seven days' old white Dorking, and
for the other promised ones. I am getting quite a 'chamber
of horrors,' I appreciate your kindness even more than before; for I have done the black deed and murdered an angelic
little fantail and pouter at ten days old. I tried chloroform
and ether for the first, and though evidently a perfectly easy
death, it was prolonged ; and for the second I tried putting
lumps of cyanide of potassium in a very large damp bottle,
half an hour before putting in the pigeon, and the prussic
acid gas thus generated was very quickly fatal."

A letter to Mr. Fox (May 23rd, 1855) gives the first mention of my father's laborious piece of work on the breeding
of pigeons :

"I write now to say that I have been looking at some of
our mongrel chickens, and I should say *one week old* would

do very well. The chief points which I am, and have been
for years, very curious about, is to ascertain whether the
young of our domestic breeds differ as much from each other
as do their parents, and I have no faith in anything short of
actual measurement and the Rule of Three.   I hope and believe I am not giving so much trouble without a motive of
sufficient worth.   I have got my fantails and pouters (choice
birds, I hope, as I paid 20*s.* for each pair from Baily) in a
grand cage and pigeon-house, and they are a decided amusement to me, and delight to H."

In the course of my father's pigeon-fancying enterprise he
necessarily became acquainted with breeders, and was fond
of relating his experiences as a member of the Columbarian
and Philoperistera Clubs, where he met the purest enthusiasts
of the "fancy," and learnt much of the mysteries of their art.
In writing to Mr. Huxley some years afterwards, he quotes
from a book on 'Pigeons' by Mr. J. Eaton, in illustration of
the "extreme attention and close observation" necessary to
be a good fancier.

"In his [Mr. Eaton's] treatise, devoted to the Almond
Tumbler *alone*, which is a sub-variety of the short-faced variety, which is a variety of the Tumbler, as that is of the Rock-
pigeon, Mr. Eaton says : 'There are some of the young fan-
ciers who are over-covetous, who go for all the five properties
at once [*i. e.*, the five characteristic points which are mainly
attended to,—C. D.], they have their reward by getting nothing.'   In short, it is almost beyond the human intellect to
attend to *all* the excellencies of the Almond Tumbler !

"To be a good breeder, and to succeed in improving any
breed, beyond everything enthusiasm is required.   Mr. Eaton
has gained lots of prizes, listen to him.

"'If it was possible for noblemen and gentlemen to know
the amazing amount of solace and pleasure derived from the
Almond Tumbler, when they begin to understand their (*i. e.*,
the tumbler's) properties, I should think that scarce any
nobleman or gentleman would be without their aviaries of
Almond Tumblers.'"

My father was fond of quoting this passage, and always with a tone of fellow-feeling for the author, though, no doubt, he had forgotten his own wonderings as a child that "every gentleman did not become an ornithologist."—('Autobiography,' p. 32.)

To Mr. W. B. Tegetmeier, the well-known writer on poultry, &c., he was indebted for constant advice and co-operation. Their correspondence began in 1855, and lasted to 1881, when my father wrote : "I can assure you that I often look back with pleasure to the old days when I attended to pigeons, fowls, &c., and when you gave me such valuable assistance. I not rarely regret that I have had so little strength that I have not been able to keep up old acquaintances and friendships." My fathers's letters to Mr. Tegetmeier consist almost entirely of series of questions relating to the different breeds of fowls, pigeons, &c., and are not, therefore, interesting. In reading through the pile of letters, one is much struck by the diligence of the writer's search for facts, and it is made clear that Mr. Tegetmeier's knowledge and judgment were completely trusted and highly valued by him. Numerous phrases, such as "your note is a mine of wealth to me," occur, expressing his sense of the value of Mr. Tegetmeier's help, as well as words expressing his warm appreciation of Mr. Tegetmeier's unstinting zeal and kindness, or his "pure and disinterested love of science." On the subject of hive-bees and their combs, Mr. Tegetmeier's help was also valued by my father, who wrote, "your paper on 'Bees-cells,' read before the British Association, was highly useful and suggestive to me."

To work out the problems on the Geographical Distributions of animals and plants on evolutionary principles, he had to study the means by which seeds, eggs, &c., can be transported across wide spaces of ocean. It was this need which gave an interest to the class of experiment to which the following letters allude.]

C. Darwin to W. D. Fox.

Down, May 17th [1855].

My DEAR Fox,—You will hate the very sight of my hand-writing; but after this time I promise I will ask for nothing more, at least for a long time. As you live on sandy soil, have you lizards at all common? If you have, should you think it too ridiculous to offer a reward for me for lizard's eggs to the boys in your school; a shilling for every half-dozen, or more if rare, till you got two or three dozen and send them to me? If snake's eggs were brought in mistake it would be very well, for I want such also; and we have neither lizards nor snakes about here. My object is to see whether such eggs will float on sea water, and whether they will keep alive thus floating for a month or two in my cellar. I am trying experiments on transportation of all organic beings that I can; and lizards are found on every island, and therefore I am very anxious to see whether their eggs stand sea water. Of course this note need not be answered, with-out, by a strange and favourable chance, you can some day answer it with the eggs. Your most troublesome friend,

C. DARWIN.

C. Darwin to J. D. Hooker.

April 13th [1855].

. . . I have had one experiment some little time in pro-gress, which will, I think, be interesting, namely, seeds in salt water immersed in water of $32°-33°$, which I have and shall long have, as I filled a great tank with snow. When I wrote last I was going to triumph over you, for my experiment had in a slight degree succeeded; but this, with infinite baseness, I did not tell, in hopes that you would say that you would eat all the plants which I could raise after immersion. It is very aggravating that I cannot in the least remember what you did formerly say that made me think you scoffed at the experiments vastly; for you now seem to view the experi-

ment like a good Christian.   I have in small bottles out of
doors, exposed to variation of temperature, cress, radish,
cabbages, lettuces, carrots, and celery, and onion seed—four
great families.   These, after immersion for exactly one week,
have all germinated, which I did not in the least expect (and
thought how you would sneer at me) ; for the water of nearly
all, and of the cress especially, smelt very badly, and the
cress seed emitted a wonderful quantity of mucus (the 'Vestiges' would have expected them to turn into tadpoles), so
as to adhere in a mass ; but these seeds germinated and
grew splendidly.   The germination of all (especially cress
and lettuces) has been accelerated, except the cabbages,
which have come up very irregularly, and a good many, I
think, dead.   One would have thought, from their native
habitat, that the cabbage would have stood well.   The Umbelliferæ and onions seem to stand the salt well.   I wash the
seed before planting them.   I have written to the *Gardeners'*
Chronicle,* though I doubt whether it was worth while.   If
my success seems to make it worth while, I will send a seed
list, to get you to mark some different classes of seeds.   To-
day I replant the same seeds as above after fourteen days'
immersion.   As many sea-currents go a mile an hour, even
in a week they might be transported 168 miles ; the Gulf
Stream is said to go fifty and sixty miles a day.   So much
and too much on this head ; but my geese are always
swans. . . .

C. Darwin to J. D. Hooker.

[April 14th, 1855.]

. . . You are a good man to confess that you expected the
cress would be killed in a week, for this gives me a nice little

---

* A few words asking for information.   The results were published in
the 'Gardeners' Chronicle,' May 26, Nov. 24, 1855.   In the same year (p.
789) he sent a P.S. to his former paper, correcting a misprint and adding a few words on the seeds of the Leguminosæ.   A fuller paper on the
germination of seeds after treatment in salt water, appeared in the 'Lin-
næan Soc. Journal,' 1857, p. 130.

triumph. The children at first were tremendously eager, and asked me often, "whether I should beat Dr. Hooker!" The cress and lettuce have just vegetated well after twenty-one days' immersion. But I will write no more, which is a great virtue in me; for it is to me a very great pleasure telling you everything I do.

. . . If you knew some of the experiments (if they may be so-called) which I am trying, you would have a good right to sneer, for they are so *absurd* even in *my* opinion that I dare not tell you.

Have not some men a nice notion of experimentising? I have had a letter telling me that seeds *must* have *great* power of resisting salt water, for otherwise how could they get to islands? This is the true way to solve a problem!

C. Darwin to J. D. Hooker.

Down [1855].

MY DEAR HOOKER,—You have been a very good man to exhale some of your satisfaction in writing two notes to me; you could not have taken a better line in my opinion; but as for showing your satisfaction in confounding my experiments, I assure you I am quite enough confounded—those horrid seeds, which, as you truly observe, if they sink they won't float.

I have written to Scoresby and have had a rather dry answer, but very much to the purpose, and giving me no hopes of any law unknown to me which might arrest their everlasting descent into the deepest depths of the ocean. By the way it was very odd, but I talked to Col. Sabine for half an hour on the subject, and could not make him see with respect to transportal the difficulty of the sinking question! The bore is, if the confounded seeds will sink, I have been taking all this trouble in salting the ungrateful rascals for nothing.

Everything has been going wrong with me lately; the fish at the Zoolog. Soc. ate up lots of soaked seeds, and in imagination they had in my mind been swallowed, fish and all, by a heron, had been carried a hundred miles, been voided on the banks of some other lake and germinated splendidly, when lo and behold, the fish ejected vehemently, and with disgust equal to my own, *all* the seeds from their mouths.*

But I am not going to give up the floating yet : in first place I must try fresh seeds, though of course it seems far more probable that they will sink ; and secondly, as a last resource, I must believe in the pod or even whole plant or branch being washed into the sea ; with floods and slips and earthquakes ; this must continually be happening, and if kept wet, I fancy the pods, &c. &c., would not open and shed their seeds. Do try your Mimosa seed at Kew.

I had intended to have asked you whether the *Mimosa scandens* and *Guilandina bonduc* grows at Kew, to try fresh seeds R. Brown tells me he believes four W. Indian seeds have been washed on shores of Europe. I was assured at Keeling Island that seeds were not rarely washed on shore : so float they must and shall ! What a long yarn I have been spinning.

If you have several of the Loffoden seeds, do soak some in tepid water, and get planted with the utmost care : this is an experiment after my own heart, with chances 1000 to 1 against its success.

---

* In describing these troubles to Mr. Fox, my father wrote :—" All nature is perverse and will not do as I wish it ; and just at present I wish I had my old barnacles to work at, and nothing new." The experiment ultimately succeeded, and he wrote to Sir J. Hooker :—"I find fish will greedily eat seeds of aquatic grasses, and that millet-seed put into fish and given to a stork, and then voided, will germinate. So this is the nursery rhyme of 'this is the stick that beats the pig,' &c., &c."

C. Darwin to J. D. Hooker.

Down, May 11th [1855].

MY DEAR HOOKER,—I have just received your note. I am most sincerely and heartily glad at the news * it contains, and so is my wife. Though the income is but a poor one, yet the certainty, I hope, is satisfactory to yourself and Mrs. Hooker. As it must lead in future years to the Directorship, I do hope you look at it, as a piece of good fortune. For my own taste I cannot fancy a pleasanter position, than the Head of such a noble and splendid place ; far better, I should think, than a Professorship in a great town. The more I think of it, the gladder I am. But I will say no more ; except that I hope Mrs. Hooker is pretty well pleased. . . .

As the *Gardeners' Chronicle* put in my question, and took notice of it, I think I am bound to send, which I had thought of doing next week, my first report to Lindley to give him the option of inserting it ; but I think it likely that he may not think it fit for a Gardening periodical. When my experiments are ended (should the results appear worthy) and should the 'Linnean Journal' not object to the previous publication of imperfect and provisional reports, I should be *delighted* to insert the final report there ; for it has cost me so much trouble, that I should think that probably the result was worthy of more permanent record than a newspaper; but I think I am bound to send it first to Lindley.

I begin to think the floating question more serious than the germinating one ; and am making all the enquiries which I can on the subject, and hope to get some little light on it. . . .

I hope you managed a good meeting at the Club. The Treasurership must be a plague to you, and I hope you will not be Treasurer for long: I know I would much sooner give up the Club than be its Treasurer.

Farewell, Mr. Assistant Director and dear friend,

C. DARWIN.

---

* The appointment of Sir J. D. Hooker as Assistant Director of the Royal Gardens at Kew.

C. Darwin to J. D. Hooker.

June 5th, 1855.

. . . . Miss Thorley* and I are doing *a little Botanical work!* for our amusement, and it does amuse me very much, viz., making a collection of all the plants, which grow in a field, which has been allowed to run waste for fifteen years, but which before was cultivated from time immemorial ; and we are also collecting all the plants in an adjoining and *similar* but cultivated field; just for the fun of seeing what plants have survived or died out.   Hereafter we shall want a bit of help in naming puzzlers.   How dreadfully difficult it is to name plants.

What a *remarkably* nice and kind letter Dr. A. Gray has sent me in answer to my troublesome queries; I retained your copy of his 'Manual' till I heard from him, and when I have answered his letter, I will return it to you.

I thank you much for Hedysarum: I do hope it is not very precious, for as I told you it is for probably a *most* foolish purpose.   I read somewhere that no plant closes its leaves so promptly in darkness, and I want to cover it up daily for half an hour, and see if I can teach it to close by itself, or more easily than at first in darkness. . . . . I cannot make out why you would prefer a continental transmission, as I think you do, to carriage by sea.   I should have thought you would have been pleased at as many means of transmission as possible.   For my own pet theoretic notions, it is quite indifferent whether they are transmitted by sea or land, as long as some tolerably probable way is shown.   But it shocks my philosophy to create land, without some other and independent evidence.   Whenever we meet, by a very few words I should, I think, more clearly understand your views. . . .

I have just made out my first grass, hurrah ! hurrah !   I must confess that fortune favours the bold, for, as good luck

---

* A lady who was for many years a governess in the family.

would have it, it was the easy *Anthoxanthum odoratum :* nevertheless it is a great discovery; I never expected to make out a grass in all my life, so hurrah! It has done my stomach surprising good. . . .

C. Darwin to J. D. Hooker.

Down, [June?] 15th, [1855].

MY DEAR HOOKER,—I just write one line to say that the Hedysarum is come *quite safely*, and thank you for it.

You cannot imagine what amusement you have given me by naming those three grasses: I have just got paper to dry and collect all grasses. If ever you catch quite a beginner, and want to give him a taste of Botany, tell him to make a perfect list of some little field or wood. Both Miss Thorley and I agree that it gives a really uncommon interest to the work, having a nice little definite world to work on, instead of the awful abyss and immensity of all British Plants.

Adios. I was really consummately impudent to express my opinion "on the retrograde step," * and I deserved a good snub, and upon reflection I am very glad you did not answer me in *Gardeners' Chronicle.*

I have been *very much* interested with the Florula.†

[Writing on June 5th to Sir J. D. Hooker, my father mentions a letter from Dr. Asa Gray. The letter referred to was an answer to the following :]

---

* " To imagine such enormous geological changes within the period of the existence of now living beings, on no other ground but to account for their distribution, seems to me, in our present state of ignorance on the means of transportal, an almost retrograde step in science."—Extract from the paper on 'Salt Water and Seeds' in *Gardeners' Chronicle*, May 26, 1855.

† Godron's 'Florula Juvenalis,' which gives an interesting account of plants introduced in imported wool.

*C. Darwin to Asa Gray.**

Down, April 25th [1855.]

MY DEAR SIR,—I hope that you will remember that I had the pleasure of being introduced to you at Kew. I want to beg a great favour of you, for which I well know I can offer no apology. But the favour will not, I think, cause you much trouble, and will greatly oblige me. As I am no botanist, it will seem so absurd to you my asking botanical questions; that I may premise that I have for several years been collecting facts on " variation," and when I find that any general remark seems to hold good amongst animals, I try to test it in Plants. [Here follows a request for information on American Alpine plants, and a suggestion as to publishing on the subject.] I can assure you that I perceive how presumptuous it is in me, not a botanist, to make even the most trifling suggestion to such a botanist as yourself; but from what I saw and have heard of you from our dear and kind friend Hooker, I hope and think that you will forgive me, and believe me, with much respect,

Dear sir, yours very faithfully,

CHARLES DARWIN.

C. Darwin to Asa Gray.

Down, June 8th [1855].

MY DEAR SIR,—I thank you cordially for your remarkably kind letter of the 22d ult., and for the extremely pleasant and obliging manner in which you have taken my rather troublesome questions. I can hardly tell you how much your list of Alpine plants has interested me, and I can now

---

* The well-known American Botanist. My father's friendship with Dr. Gray began with the correspondence of which the present is the first letter. An extract from a letter to Sir J. Hooker, 1857, shows that my father's strong personal regard for Dr. Gray had an early origin: " I have been glad to see A. Gray's letters ; there is always something in them that shows that he is a very lovable man."

in some degree picture to myself the plants of your Alpine summits. The new edit. of your Manual is *capital* news for me. I know from your preface how pressed you are for room, but it would take no space to append (Eu) in brackets to any European plant, and, as far as I am concerned, this would answer every purpose.* From my own experience, whilst making out English plants in our manuals, it has often struck me how much interest it would give if some notion of their range had been given; and so, I cannot doubt, your American inquirers and beginners would much like to know which of their plants were indigenous and which European. Would it not be well in the Alpine plants to append the very same addition which you have now sent me in MS.? though here, owing to your kindness, I do not speak selfishly, but merely *pro bono Americano publico.* I presume it would be too troublesome to give in your manual the habitats of those plants found west of the Rocky Mountains, and likewise those found in Eastern Asia, taking the Yeneseï (?),—which, if I remember right, according to Gmelin, is the main partition line of Siberia. Perhaps Siberia more concerns the northern Flora of North America. The ranges of the plants to the east and west, viz., whether most found are in Greenland and Western Europe, or in E. Asia, appears to me a very interesting point as tending to show whether the migration has been eastward or westward. Pray believe me that I am most entirely conscious that the *only use* of these remarks is to show a botanist what points a non-botanist is curious to learn; for I think every one who studies profoundly a subject often becomes unaware [on] what points the ignorant require information. I am so very glad that you think of drawing up some notice on your geographical distribution, for the area of the Manual strikes me as in some points better adapted for comparison with Europe than that of the whole of North America. You ask me to state definitely some of the points on which I much wish for information; but I really hardly

---

* This suggestion Dr. Gray adopted in subsequent editions.

can, for they are so vague ; and I rather wish to see what results will come out from comparisons, than have as yet defined objects. I presume that, like other botanists, you would give, for your area, the proportion (leaving out introduced plants) to the whole of the great leading families : this is one point I had intended (and, indeed, have done roughly) to tabulate from your book, but of course I could have done it only *very imperfectly*. I should also, of course, have ascertained the proportion, to the whole Flora, of the European plants (leaving out introduced) *and of the separate great families*, in order to speculate on means of transportal. By the way, I ventured to send a few days ago a copy of the *Gardeners' Chronicle* with a short report by me of some trifling experiments which I have been trying on the power of seeds to withstand sea water. I do not know whether it has struck you, but it has me, that it would be advisable for botanists to give in *whole numbers*, as well as in the lowest fraction, the proportional numbers of the families, thus I make out from your Manual that of the *indigenous* plants the proportion of the Umbelliferæ are $\frac{88}{1763} = \frac{1}{20}$; for, without one knows the *whole* numbers, one cannot judge how really close the numbers of the plants of the same family are in two distant countries ; but very likely you may think this superfluous. Mentioning these proportional numbers, I may give you an instance of the sort of points, and how vague and futile they often are, which I *attempt* to work out . . .; reflecting on R. Brown's and Hooker's remark, that near identity of proportional numbers of the great families in two countries, shows probably that they were once continuously united, I thought I would calculate the proportions of, for instance, the *introduced* Compositæ in Great Britain to all the introduced plants, and the result was, $\frac{10}{92} = \frac{1}{9.2}$. In our *aboriginal* or indigenous flora the proportion is $\frac{1}{10}$; and in many other cases I found an equally striking correspondence   I then took your Manual, and worked out the same question ; here I find in the Compositæ an almost equally striking correspondence, viz. $\frac{24}{205} = \frac{1}{8}$ in the introduced plants, and $\frac{223}{1798} = \frac{1}{8}$ in the indigenous; but when I came to the other families I found the proportion entirely different, showing that the co-incidences in the British Flora were probably accidental !

You will, I presume, give the proportion of the species to the genera, *i. e.*, show on an average how many species each genus contains; though I have done this for myself.

If it would not be too troublesome, do you not think it would be very interesting, and give a very good idea of your Flora, to divide the species into three groups, viz., (*a*) species common to the old world, stating numbers common to Europe and Asia; (*b*) indigenous species, but belonging to genera found in the old world; and (*c*) species belonging to genera confined to America or the New World. To make (according to my ideas) perfection perfect, one ought to be told whether there are other cases, like Erica, of genera common in Europe or in Old World not found in your area. But honestly I feel that it is quite ridiculous my writing to you at such length on the subject; but, as you have asked me, I do it gratefully, and write to you as I should to Hooker, who often laughs at me unmercifully, and I am sure you have better reason to do so.

There is one point on which I am *most* anxious for infor-mation, and I mention it with the greatest hesitation, and only in the *full belief* that you will believe me that I have not the folly and presumption to hope for a second that you will give it, without you can with very little trouble. The point can at present interest no one but myself, which makes the case wholly different from geographical distribution. The only way in which, I think, you possibly could do it with little trouble would be to bear in mind, whilst correcting your proof-sheets of the Manual, my question and put a cross or mark to the species, and whenever sending a parcel to Hooker to let me have such old sheets. But this would give you the trouble of remembering my question, and I can hardly hope or expect that you will do it. But I will just mention what I want; it is to have marked the " close species " in a Flora, so as to compare in *different* Floras whether the same genera have "close species," and for other purposes too vague to enumerate.   I have attempted, by Hooker's help, to ascertain in a similar way whether the different species of the same genera in distant quarters of the globe are variable or present varieties.   The definition I should give of a "*close species*" was one that *you* thought specifically distinct, but which you could conceive some other *good* botanist might think only a race or variety; or, again, a species that you had trouble, though having opportunities of knowing it well, in discriminating from some other species.   Supposing that you were inclined to be so very kind as to do this, and could (which I do not expect) spare the time, as I have said, a mere cross to each such species in any useless proof-sheets would give me the information desired, which, I may add, I know must be vague.

How can I apologise enough for all my presumption and the extreme length of this letter?   The great good nature of your letter to me has been partly the cause, so that, as is too often the case in this world, you are punished for your good deeds.   With hearty thanks, believe me,

Yours very truly and gratefully,

CH. DARWIN.

C. Darwin to J. D. Hooker.

Down, 18th [July, 1855].

. . . I think I am getting a *mild* case about Charlock seed; * but just as about salting, ill luck to it, I cannot remember how many years you would allow that Charlock

---

* In the *Gardeners' Chronicle*, 1855, p. 758, appeared a notice (half a column in length) by my father on the "Vitality of Seeds"   The facts related refer to the "Sand-walk"; the wood was planted in 1846 on a piece of pasture land laid down as grass in 1840.   In 1855, on the soil being dug in several places, Charlock (*Brassica sinapistrum*) sprang up freely.   The subject continued to interest him, and I find a note dated July 2nd, 1874, in which my father recorded that forty-six plants of Charlock sprang up in that year over a space (14 × 7 feet) which had been dug to a considerable depth.

seed might live in the ground. Next time you write, show
a bold face, and say in how many years, you think, Charlock
seed would probably all be dead. A man told me the other
day of, as I thought, a splendid instance,—and *splendid* it
was, for according to his evidence the seed came up alive out
of the *lower part* of the *London Clay ! ! !* I disgusted him by
telling him that Palms ought to have come up.

You ask how far I go in attributing organisms to a common descent; I answer I know not; the way in which I intend treating the subject, is to show (*as far as I can*) the facts
and arguments for and against the common descent of the
species of the same genus ; and then show how far the same
arguments tell for or against forms, more and more widely
different : and when we come to forms of different orders
and classes, there remain only some such arguments as those
which can perhaps be deduced from similar rudimentary
structures, and very soon not an argument is left.

[The following extract from a letter to Mr. Fox [Oct.
1855,* gives a brief mention of the last meeting of the British
Association which he attended :] " I really have no news :
the only thing we have done for a long time, was to go to
Glasgow ; but the fatigue was to me more than it was worth,
and E. caught a bad cold. On our return we stayed a single
day at Shrewsbury, and enjoyed seeing the old place. I saw
a little of Sir Philip † (whom I liked much), and he asked me
"why on earth I instigated you to rob his poultry-yard?"
The meeting was a good one, and the Duke of Argyll spoke
excellently."]

---

* In this year he published (' Phil. Mag.' x.) a paper ' On the power of
icebergs to make rectilinear uniformly-directed grooves across a subma ·
rine undulatory surface.' "

† Sir P. Egerton was a neighbour of Mr. Fox.

CHAPTER XII.

THE UNFINISHED BOOK.

May 1856 to June 1858.

[IN the Autobiographical chapter (page 69,) my father wrote:—"Early in 1856 Lyell advised me to write out my views pretty fully, and I began at once to do so on a scale three or four times as extensive as that which was afterwards followed in my 'Origin of Species;' yet it was only an abstract of the materials which I had collected." The letters in the present chapter are chiefly concerned with the preparation of this unfinished book.

The work was begun on May 14th, and steadily continued up to June 1858, when it was interrupted by the arrival of Mr. Wallace's MS. During the two years which we are now considering he wrote ten chapters (that is about one-half) of the projected book. He remained for the most part at home, but paid several visits to Dr. Lane's Water-Cure Establishment at Moor Park, during one of which he made a pilgrimage to the shrine of Gilbert White at Selborne.]

LETTERS.

C. Darwin to C. Lyell.

May 3 [1856].

. . . With respect to your suggestion of a sketch of my views, I hardly know what to think, but will reflect on it, but it goes against my prejudices. To give a fair sketch would be absolutely impossible, for every proposition requires such an array of facts. If I were to do anything, it could only refer to the main agency of change—selection—and perhaps point out a very few of the leading features, which countenance such a view, and some few of the main difficulties. . But I do not know what to think; I rather hate the idea of writing for priority, yet I certainly should be vexed if any one were to publish my doctrines before me. Anyhow, I thank you heartily for your sympathy. I shall be in London next week, and I will call on you on Thursday morning for one hour precisely, so as not to lose much of your time and my own; but will you let me this time come as early as 9 o'clock, for I have much which I must do in the morning in my strongest time? Farewell, my dear old patron.

Yours,
C. DARWIN.

By the way, *three* plants have come up out of the earth, perfectly enclosed in the roots of the trees. And twenty-nine plants in the table-spoonful of mud, out of the little pond ; Hooker was surprised at this, and struck with it, when I showed him how much mud I had scraped off one duck's feet.

If I did publish a short sketch, where on earth should I publish it?

If I do *not* hear, I shall understand that I may come from 9 to 10 on Thursday.

C. Darwin to J. D. Hooker.

May 9th, [1856].

. . . I very much want advice and *truthful* consolation if you can give it. I had a good talk with Lyell about my species work, and he urges me strongly to publish something. I am fixed against any periodical or Journal, as I positively will *not* expose myself to an Editor or a Council, allowing a publication for which they might be abused. If I publish anything it must be a *very thin* and little volume, giving a sketch of my views and difficulties ; but it is really dreadfully unphilosophical to give a *resumé*, without exact references, of an unpublished work.   But Lyell seemed to think I might do this, at the suggestion of friends, and on the ground, which I might state, that I had been at work for eighteen * years, and yet could not publish for several years, and especially as I could point out difficulties which seemed to me to require especial investigation.   Now what think you?   I should be really grateful for advice.   I thought of giving up a couple of months and writing such a sketch, and trying to keep my judgment open whether or no to publish it when completed. It will be simply impossible for me to give exact references; anything important I should state on the authority of the author generally; and instead of giving all the facts on which I ground my opinion, I could give by memory only one or two.   In the Preface I would state that the work could not be considered strictly scientific, but a mere sketch or outline of a future work in which full references, &c., should be given.   Eheu, eheu, I believe I should sneer at any one else doing this, and my only comfort is, that I *truly* never dreamed of it, till Lyell suggested it, and seems deliberately to think it advisable.

I am in a peck of troubles and do pray forgive me for troubling you.

Yours affectionately,
C. DARWIN.

C. Darwin to J. D. Hooker.

May 11th [1856].

. . . Now for a *more important!* subject, viz., my own self : I am extremely glad you think well of a separate " Preliminary Essay " (*i. e.*, if anything whatever is published; for Lyell seemed rather to doubt on this head) †; but I cannot

---

* The interval of eighteen years, from 1837 when he began to collect facts, would bring the date of this letter to 1855, not 1856, nevertheless the latter seems the more probable date.

† The meaning of the sentence in parentheses is obscure.

bear the idea of *begging* some Editor and Council to publish, and then perhaps to have to *apologise* humbly for having led them into a scrape.   In this one respect I am in the state which, according to a very wise saying of my father's, is the only fit state for asking advice, viz., with my mind firmly made up, and then, as my father used to say, *good* advice was very comfortable, and it was easy to reject *bad* advice.   But Heaven knows I am not in this state with respect to publishing at all any preliminary essay.   It yet strikes me as quite unphilosophical to publish results without the full details which have led to such results.

It is a melancholy, and I hope not quite true view of yours that facts will prove anything, and are therefore superfluous! But I have rather exaggerated, I see, your doctrine.   I do not fear being tied down to error, *i. e.*, I feel pretty sure I should give up anything false published in the preliminary essay, in my larger work ; but I may thus, it is very true, do mischief by spreading error, which as I have often heard you say is much easier spread than corrected.   I confess I lean more and more to at least making the attempt and drawing up a sketch and trying to keep my judgment, whether to publish, open.   But I always return to my fixed idea that it is dreadfully unphilosophical to publish without full details. I certainly think my future work in full would profit by hearing what my friends or critics (if reviewed) thought of the outline.

To any one but you I should apologise for such long discussion on so personal an affair ; but I believe, and indeed you have proved it by the trouble you have taken, that this would be superfluous.

Yours truly obliged,
CH. DARWIN.

P. S.   What you say (for I have just re-read your letter) that the Essay might supersede and take away all novelty and value from any future larger Book, is very true; and that would grieve me beyond everything.   On the other hand (again from Lyell's urgent advice), I published a preliminary sketch of the Coral Theory, and this did neither good nor harm. I begin *most heartily* to wish that Lyell had never put this idea of an Essay into my head.

From a letter to Sir C. Lyell [July, 1856].

" I am delighted that I may say (with absolute truth) that my essay is published at your suggestion, but I hope it will not need so much apology as I at first thought ; for I have resolved to make it nearly as complete as my present materials allow. I cannot put in all which you suggest, for it would appear too conceited."

From a letter to W. D. Fox.

Down, June 14th [1856].

". . . What you say about my Essay, I dare say is very true ; and it gave me another fit of the wibber-gibbers : I hope that I shall succeed in making it modest. One great motive is to get information on the many points on which I want it. But I tremble about it, which I should not do, if I allowed some three or four more years to elapse before pub-lishing anything. . . ."

[The following extracts from letters to Mr. Fox are worth giving, as showing how great was the accumulation of mate-rial which now had to be dealt with.

June 14th [1856].

" Very many thanks for the capital information on cats ; I see I had blundered greatly, but I know I had somewhere your orignal notes ; but my notes are so numerous during nineteen years' collection, that it would take me at least a year to go over and classify them."

Nov. 1856. " Sometimes I fear I shall break down, for my subject gets bigger and bigger with each month's work."]

C. Darwin to C. Lyell.

Down, 16th [June, 1856].

MY DEAR LYELL,—I am going to do the most impudent thing in the world. But my blood gets hot with passion and turns cold alternately at the geological strides, which many of your disciples are taking.

Here, poor Forbes made a continent to [*i. e.*, extending to] North America and another (or the same) to the Gulf weed; Hooker makes one from New Zealand to South America and round the World to Kerguelen Land. Here is Wollaston speaking of Madeira and P. Santo "as the sure and certain witnesses of a former continent." Here is Woodward writes to me, if you grant a continent over 200 or 300 miles of ocean depths (as if that was nothing), why not extend a continent to every island in the Pacific and Atlantic Oceans? And all this within the existence of recent species! If you do not stop this, if there be a lower region for the punishment of geologists, I believe, my great master, you will go there. Why, your disciples in a slow and creeping manner beat all the old Catastrophists who ever lived. You will live to be the great chief of the Catastrophists.

There, I have done myself a great deal of good, and have exploded my passion.

So my master, forgive me, and believe me, ever yours,

C. DARWIN.

P. S. Don't answer this, I did it to ease myself.

C. Darwin to J. D. Hooker.

Down [June] 17th, 1856.

. . . I have been very deeply interested by Wollaston's book,[*] though I differ *greatly* from many of his doctrines. Did you ever read anything so rich, considering how very far he goes, as his denunciations against those who go further:

---

[*] 'The Variation of Species,' 1856.

"most mischievous," "absurd," "unsound." Theology is at the bottom of some of this. I told him he was like Calvin burning a heretic. It is a very valuable and clever book in my opinion. He has evidently read very little out of his own line I urged him to read the New Zealand essay. His Geology also is rather *eocene*, as I told him. In fact I wrote most frankly ; I fear too frankly ; he says he is sure that ultra-honesty is my characteristic : I do not know whether he meant it as a sneer ; I hope not. Talking of eocene geology, I got so wrath about the Atlantic continent, more especially from a note from Woodward (who has published a capital book on shells), who does not seem to doubt that every island in the Pacific and Atlantic are the remains of continents, submerged within period of existing species, that I fairly exploded, and wrote to Lyell to protest, and summed up all the continents created of late years by Forbes (the head sinner !) *yourself*, Wollaston, and Woodward, and a pretty nice little extension of land they make altogether ! I am fairly rabid on the question and therefore, if not wrong already, am pretty sure to become so . . .

I have enjoyed your note much.   Adios,

C. DARWIN.

P. S. [June] 18th. Lyell has written me a *capital* letter on your side, which ought to upset me entirely, but I cannot say it does quite.

Though I must try and cease being rabid and try to feel humble, and allow you all to make continents, as easily as a cook does pancakes.

C. Darwin to C. Lyell.

Down, June 25th [1856].

MY DEAR LYELL,—I will have the following tremendous letter copied to make the reading easier, and as I want to keep a copy.

As you say you would like to hear my reasons for being

most unwilling to believe in the continental extensions of late authors, I gladly write them, as, without I am convinced of my error, I shall have to give them condensed in my essay, when I discuss single and multiple creation; I shall therefore be particularly glad to have your general opinion on them. I may *quite likely* have persuaded myself in my wrath that there is more in them than there is. If there was much more reason to admit a continental extension in any one or two instances (as in Madeira) than in other cases, I should feel no difficulty whatever. But if on account of European plants, and littoral sea shells, it is thought necessary to join Madeira to the mainland, Hooker is quite right to join New Holland to New Zealand, and Auckland Island (and Raoul Island to N. E.), and these to S. America and the Falklands, and these to Tristan d'Acunha, and these to Kerguelen Land; thus making, either strictly at the same time, or at different periods, but all within the life of recent beings, an almost circumpolar belt of land. So again Galapagos and Juan Fernandez must be joined to America; and if we trust to littoral sea shells, the Galapagos must have been joined to the Pacific Islands (2400 miles distant) as well as to America, and as Woodward seems to think all the islands in the Pacific into a magnificent continent; also the islands in the Southern Indian Ocean into another continent, with Madagascar and Africa, and perhaps India. In the North Atlantic, Europe will stretch half-way across the ocean to the Azores, and further north right across. In short, we must suppose probably, half the present ocean was land within the period of living organisms. The Globe within this period must have had a quite different aspect. Now the only way to test this, that I can see, is to consider whether the continents have undergone within this same period such wonderful permutations. In all North and South and Central America, we have both recent and miocene (or eocene) shells, quite distinct on the opposite sides, and hence I cannot doubt that *fundamentally* America has held its place since at least, the miocene period. In Africa almost all the living shells are distinct on the opposite sides of the inter-tropical regions, short as the distance is compared to the range of marine mollusca, in un-interrupted seas ; hence I infer that Africa has existed since our present species were created.   Even the isthmus of Suez and the Aralo-Caspian basin have had a great antiquity.   So I imagine, from the tertiary deposits, has India.   In Austra-lia the great fauna of extinct marsupials shows that before the present mammals appeared, Australia was a separate con-tinent.   I do not for one second doubt that very large por-tions of all these continents have undergone *great* changes of level within this period, but yet I conclude that fundament-ally they stood as barriers in the sea, where they now stand ; and therefore I should require the weightiest evidence to make me believe in such immense changes within the period of living organisms in our oceans, where, moreover, from the great depths, the changes must have been vaster in a vertical sense.

Secondly.   Submerge our present continents, leaving a few mountain peaks as islands, and what will the character of the islands be,—Consider that the Pyrenees, Sierra Nevada, Apen-nines, Alps, Carpathians, are non-volcanic, Etna and Caucasus, volcanic.   In Asia, Altai and Himalaya, I believe non-vol-canic.   In North Africa the non-volcanic, as I imagine, Alps of Abyssinia and of the Atlas.   In South Africa, the Snow Mountains,   In Australia, the non-volcanic Alps.   In North America, the White Mountains, Alleghanies and Rocky Mountains—some of the latter alone, I believe, volcanic.   In South America to the east, the non-volcanic [Silla?] of Ca-racas, and Itacolumi of Brazil, further south the Sierra Ven-tanas, and in the Cordilleras, many volcanic but not all.   Now compare these peaks with the oceanic islands ; as far as known all are volcanic, except St. Paul's (a strange bedevilled rock), and the Seychelles, if this latter can be called oceanic, in the line of Madagascar ; the Falklands, only 500 miles off, are only a shallow bank ; New Caledonia, hardly oceanic, is another exception.   This argument has to me great weight. Compare on a Geographical map, islands which, we have *several* reasons to suppose, were connected with mainland, as Sardinia, and how different it appears. Believing, as I am inclined, that continents as continents, and oceans as oceans, are of immense antiquity—I should say that if any of the existing oceanic islands have any relation of any kind to continents, they are forming continents ; and that by the time they could form a continent, the volcanoes would be denuded to their cores, leaving peaks of syenite, diorite, or porphyry. But have we nowhere any last wreck of a continent, in the midst of the ocean ? St. Paul's Rock, and such old battered volcanic islands, as St. Helena, may be ; but I think we can see some reason why we should have less evidence of sinking than of rising continents (if my view in my Coral volume has any truth in it, viz. : that volcanic outbursts accompany rising areas), for during subsidence there will be no compensating agent at work, in rising areas there will be the *additional* element of outpoured volcanic matter.

Thirdly. Considering the depth of the ocean, I was, before I got your letter, inclined vehemently to dispute the vast amount of subsidence, but I must strike my colours. With respect to coral reefs, I carefully guarded against its being supposed that a continent was indicated by the groups of atolls. It is difficult to guess, as it seems to me, the amount of subsidence indicated by coral reefs ; but in such large areas as the Lowe Archipelago, the Marshall Archipelago, and Laccadive group, it would, judging, from the heights of existing oceanic archipelagoes, be odd, if some peaks of from 8000 to 10,000 feet had not been buried. Even after your letter a suspicion crossed me whether it would be fair to argue from subsidences in the middle of the greatest oceans to continents ; but refreshing my memory by talking with Ramsay in regard to the probable thickness in one vertical line of the Silurian and carboniferous formation, it seems there must have been *at least* 10,000 feet of subsidence during these formations in Europe and North America, and therefore during the continuance of nearly the same set of organic beings. But even 12,000 feet would not be enough for the

Azores, or for Hooker's continent; I believe Hooker does not infer a continuous continent, but approximate groups of islands, with, if we may judge from existing continents, not *profoundly* deep sea between them; but the argument from the volcanic nature of nearly every existing oceanic island tell against such supposed groups of islands,—for I presume he does not suppose a mere chain of volcanic islands belting the southern hemisphere.

Fourthly. The supposed continental extensions do not seem to me, perfectly to account for all the phenomena of distribution on islands; as the absence of mammals and Batrachians; the absence of certain great groups of insects on Madeira, and of Acaciæ and Banksias, &c., in New Zealand; the paucity of plants in some cases, &c. Not that those who believe in various accidental means of dispersal, can explain most of these cases; but they may at least say that these facts seem hardly compatible with former continuous land.

Finally. For these several reasons, and especially considering it certain (in which you will agree) that we are extremely ignorant of means of dispersal, I cannot avoid thinking that Forbes' 'Atlantis,' was an ill-service to science, as checking a close study of means of dissemination. I shall be really grateful to hear, as briefly as you like, whether these arguments have any weight with you, putting yourself in the position of an honest judge. I told Hooker that I was going to write to you on this subject; and I should like him to read this; but whether he or you will think it worth time and postage remains to be proved.

Yours most truly,
CHARLES DARWIN.

[On July 8th he wrote to Sir Charles Lyell.

"I am sorry you cannot give any verdict on Continental extensions; and I infer that you think my argument of not much weight against such extensions. I know I wish I could believe so."]

C. Darwin to Asa Gray.

Down, July 20th [1856].

. . . It is not a little egotistical, but I should like to tell you (and I do not *think* I have) how I view my work. Nineteen years (!) ago it occurred to me that whilst otherwise employed on Nat. Hist., I might perhaps do good if I noted any sort of facts bearing on the question of the origin of species, and this I have since been doing. Either species have been independently created, or they have descended from other species, like varieties from one species. I think it can be shown to be probable that man gets his most distinct varieties by preserving such as arise best worth keeping and destroying the others, but I should fill a quire if I were to go on. To be brief, I *assume* that species arise like our domestic varieties with *much* extinction; and then test this hypothesis by comparison with as many general and pretty well-established propositions as I can find made out,—in geographical distribution, geological history, affinities, &c., &c. And it seems to me that, *supposing* that such hypothesis were to explain such general propositions, we ought, in accordance with the common way of following all sciences, to admit it till some better hypothesis be found out. For to my mind to say that species were created so and so is no scientific explanation, only a reverent way of saying it is so and so. But it is nonsensical trying to show how I try to proceed in the compass of a note. But as an honest man, I must tell you that I have come to the heterodox conclusion that there are no such things as independently created species—that species are only strongly defined varieties. I know that this will make you despise me. I do not much underrate the many *huge* difficulties on this view, but yet it seems to me to explain too much, otherwise inexplicable, to be false. Just to allude to one point in your last note, viz., about species of the same genus *generally* having a common or continuous area; if they are actual lineal descendants of one species, this of course would be the case; and the sadly too many exceptions (for me) have to be explained by climatal and geological changes. *A fortiori* on this view (but on exactly same grounds), all the individuals of the same species should have a continous distribution. On this latter branch of the subject I have put a chapter together, and Hooker kindly read it over. I thought the exceptions and difficulties were so great that on the whole the balance weighed against my notions, but I was much pleased to find that it seemed to have considerable weight with Hooker, who said he had never been so much staggered about the permanence of species.

I must say one word more in justification (for I feel sure that your tendency will be to despise me and my crotchets), that all my notions about *how* species change are derived from long continued study of the works of (and converse with) agriculturists and horticulturists; and I believe I see my way pretty clearly on the means used by nature to change her species and *adapt* them to the wondrous and exquis-itely beautiful contingencies to which every living being is exposed. . . .

C. Darwin to J. D. Hooker.

Down, July 30th, 1856.

MY DEAR HOOKER,—Your letter is of *much* value to me. I was not able to get a definite answer from Lyell,* as you will see in the enclosed letters, though I inferred that he thought nothing of my arguments. Had it not been for this correspondence, I should have written sadly too strongly. You may rely on it I shall put my doubts moderately. There never was such a predicament as mine : here you continental extensionists would remove enormous difficulties opposed to me, and yet I cannot honestly admit the doctrine, and must therefore say so. I cannot get over the fact that not a frag-ment of secondary or palæozoic rock has been found on any island above 500 or 600 miles from a mainland. You rather misunderstand me when you think I doubt the *possibility* of

---

* On the continental extensions of Forbes and others.

subsidence of 20,000 or 30,000 feet ; it is only probability, considering such evidence as we have independently of distribution.   I have not yet worked out in full detail the distribution of mammalia, both *identical* and allied, with respect to the *one element of depth of the sea ;* but as far as I have gone, the results are to me surprisingly accordant with my very most troublesome belief in not such great geographical changes as you believe ; and in mammalia we certainly know more of *means* of distribution than in any other class.   Nothing is so vexatious to me, as so constantly finding myself drawing different conclusions from better judges than myself, from the same facts.

I fancy I have lately removed many (not geographical) great difficulties opposed to my notions, but God knows it may be all hallucination.

Please return Lyell's letters.

What a capital letter of Lyell's that to you is, and what a wonderful man he is.   I differ from him greatly in thinking that those who believe that species are *not* fixed will multiply specific names : I know in my own case my most frequent source of doubt was whether others would not think this or that was a God-created Barnacle, and surely deserved a name. Otherwise I should only have thought whether the amount of difference and permanence was sufficient to justify a name : I am, also, surprised at his thinking it immaterial whether species are absolute or not : whenever it is proved that all species are produced by generation, by laws of change, what good evidence we shall have of the gaps in formations.   And what a science Natural History will be, when we are in our graves, when all the laws of change are thought one of the most important parts of Natural History.

I cannot conceive why Lyell thinks such notions as mine or of 'Vestiges,' will invalidate specific centres.   But I must not run on and take up your time.   My MS. will not, I fear, be copied before you go abroad.   With hearty thanks.

Ever yours,

C. DARWIN.

P. S.—After giving much condensed, my argument versus continental extensions, I shall append some such sentence, as that two better judges than myself have considered these arguments, and attach no weight to them.

C. Darwin to J. D. Hooker.

Down, August 5th [1856].

. . . I quite agree about Lyell's letters to me, which, though to me interesting, have afforded me no new light. Your letters, under the *geological* point of view, have been more valuable to me. You cannot imagine how earnestly I wish I could swallow continental extension, but I cannot; the more I think (and I cannot get the subject out of my head), the more difficult I find it. If there were only some half-dozen cases, I should not feel the least difficulty; but the generality of the facts of all islands (except one or two) having a considerable part of their productions in common with one or more mainlands utterly staggers me. What a wonderful case of the Epacridæ! It is most vexatious, also humiliating, to me that I cannot follow and subscribe to the way in which you strikingly put your view of the case. I look at your facts (about Eucalyptus, &c.) as *damning* against continental extension, and if you like also damning against migration, or at least of *enormous* difficulty. I see the ground of our difference (in a letter I must put myself on an equality in arguing) lies, in my opinion, that scarcely anything is known of means of distribution. I quite agree with A. De Candolle's (and I dare say your) opinion that it is poor work putting together the merely *posssible* means of distribution; but I see no other way in which the subject can be attacked, for I think that A. De Candolle's argument, that no plants have been introduced into England except by man's agency, [is] of no weight. I cannot but think that the theory of continental extension does do some little harm as stopping investigation of the means of dispersal, which, whether *negative* or positive, seems to me of value; when negatived, then every

one who believes in single centres will have to admit continental extensions.

. . . I see from your remarks that you do not understand
my notions (whether or no worth anything) about modification; I attribute very little to the direct action of climate,
&c. I suppose, in regard to specific centres, we are at cross
purposes; I should call the kitchen garden in which the red
cabbage was produced, or the farm in which Bakewell made
the Shorthorn cattle, the specific centre of these *species!* And
surely this is centralisation enough!

I thank you most sincerely for all your assistance; and
whether or no my book may be wretched, you have done
your best to make it less wretched. Sometimes I am in very
good spirits and sometimes very low about it. My own mind
is decided on the question of the origin of species; but, good
heavens, how little that is worth! . . .

[With regard to "specific centres," a passage from a letter
dated July 25, 1856, by Sir Charles Lyell to Sir J. D. Hooker
('Life,' ii. p. 216) is of interest :

"I fear much that if Darwin argues that species are phantoms, he will also have to admit that single centres of dispersion are phantoms also, and that would deprive me of much
of the value which I ascribe to the present provinces of animals and plants, as illustrating modern and tertiary changes
in physical geography."

He seems to have recognised, however, that the phantom
doctrine would soon have to be faced, for he wrote in the
same letter: "Whether Darwin persuades you and me to
renounce our faith in species (when geological epochs are
considered) or not, I foresee that many will go over to the
indefinite modifiability doctrine."

In the autumn my father was still working at geographical
distribution, and again sought the aid of Sir J. D. Hooker.

A Letter to Sir J. D. Hooker [Sept., 1856].

"In the course of some weeks, you unfortunate wretch,
you will have my MS. on one point of Geographical Distribu-

tion.   I will, however, never ask such a favour again ; but in regard to this one piece of MS., it is of infinite importance to me for you to see it; for never in my life have I felt such difficulty what to do, and I heartily wish I could slur the whole subject over."

In a letter to Sir J. D. Hooker (June, 1856), the following characteristic passage occurs, suggested, no doubt, by the kind of work which his chapter on Geographical Distribution entailed :

"There is wonderful ill logic in his [E. Forbes'] famous and admirable memoir on distribution, as it appears to me, now that I have got it up so as to give the heads in a page. Depend on it, my saying is a true one, viz., that a compiler is a *great* man, and an original man a commonplace man. Any fool can generalise and speculate ; but, oh, my heavens ! to get up *at second hand* a New Zealand Flora, that is work."]

C. Darwin to W. D. Fox.

Oct. 3 [1856].

. . . I remember you protested against Lyell's advice of writing a *sketch* of my species doctrines.   Well, when I began I found it such unsatisfactory work that I have desisted, and am now drawing up my work as perfect as my materials of nineteen years' collecting suffice, but do not intend to stop to perfect any line of investigation beyond current work. Thus far and no farther I shall follow Lyell's urgent advice. Your remarks weighed with me considerably.   I find to my sorrow it will run to quite a big book.   I have found my careful work at pigeons really invaluable, as enlightening me on many points on variation under domestication.   The copious old literature, by which I can trace the gradual changes in the breeds of pigeons has been extraordinarily useful to me. I have just had pigeons and fowls *alive* from the Gambia ! Rabbits and ducks I am attending to pretty carefully, but less so than pigeons.   I find most remarkable differences in the skeletons of rabbits.   Have you ever kept any odd breeds of rabbits, and can you give me any details? One other question: You used to keep hawks; do you at all know, after eating a bird, how soon after they throw up the pellet?

No subject gives me so much trouble and doubt and difficulty as the means of dispersal of the same species of terrestrial productions on the oceanic islands. Land mollusca drive me mad, and I cannot anyhow get their eggs to experimentise their power of floating and resistance to the injurious action of salt water. I will not apologise for writing so much about my own doings, as I believe you will like to hear. Do sometime, I beg you, let me hear how you get on in health ; and *if so inclined* let me have some words on call-ducks.

> My dear Fox, yours affectionately,
>
> CH. DARWIN.

[With regard to his book he wrote (Nov. 10th) to Sir Charles Lyell :

"I am working very steadily at my big book ; I have found it quite impossible to publish any preliminary essay or sketch ; but am doing my work as completely as my present materials allow without waiting to perfect them. And this much acceleration I owe to you."]

C. Darwin to J. D. Hooker.

Down, Sunday [Oct. 1856.]

MY DEAR HOOKER,—The seeds are come all safe, many thanks for them. I was very sorry to run away so soon and miss any part of my *most* pleasant evening ; and I ran away like a Goth and Vandal without wishing Mrs. Hooker goodbye ; but I was only just in time, as I got on the platform the train had arrived.

I was particularly glad of our discussion after dinner ; fighting a battle with you always clears my mind wonderfully. I groan to hear that A. Gray agrees with you about the condition of Botanical Geography. All I know is that if you had

had to search for light in Zoological Geography you would by contrast, respect your own subject a vast deal more than you now do. The hawks have behaved like gentlemen, and have cast up pellets with lots of seeds in them; and I have just had a parcel of partridge's feet well caked with mud!!!* Adios.

Your insane and perverse friend,

C. DARWIN.

C. Darwin to J. D. Hooker.

Down, Nov. 4th [1856].

MY DEAR HOOKER,—I thank you more *cordially* than you will think probable, for your note. Your verdict† has been a great relief. On my honour I had no idea whether or not you would say it was (and I knew you would say it very kindly) so bad, that you would have begged me to have burnt the whole. To my own mind my MS. relieved me of some few difficulties, and the difficulties seemed to me pretty fairly stated, but I had become so bewildered with conflicting facts, evidence, reasoning and opinions, that I felt to myself that I had lost all judgment. Your general verdict is *incomparably* more favourable than I had anticipated. . . .

C. Darwin to J. D. Hooker.

Down, Nov. 23rd [1856].

MY DEAR HOOKER,—I fear I shall weary you with letters, but do not answer this, for in truth and without flattery, I so value your letters, that after a heavy batch, as of late, I feel that I have been extravagant and have drawn too much money, and shall therefore have to stint myself on another occasion.

When I sent my MS. I felt strongly that some preliminary

---

* The mud in such cases often contains seeds, so that plants are thus transported.

† On the MS. relating to geographical distribution.

questions on the causes of variation ought to have been sent you. Whether I am right or wrong in these points is quite a separate question, but the conclusion which I have come to, quite independently of geographical distribution, is that external conditions (to which naturalists so often appeal) do by themselves *very little*. How much they do is the point of all others on which I feel myself very weak. I judge from the facts of variation under domestication, and I may yet get more light. But at present, after drawing up a rough copy on this subject, my conclusion is that external conditions do *extremely* little, except in causing mere variability. This mere variability (causing the child *not* closely to resemble its parent) I look at as *very* different from the formation of a marked variety or new species. (No doubt the variability is governed by laws, some of which I am endeavouring very obscurely to trace.) The formation of a strong variety or species I look at as almost wholly due to the selection of what may be incorrectly called *chance* variations or variability. This power of selection stands in the most direct relation to time, and in the state of nature can be only excessively slow. Again, the slight differences selected, by which a race or species is at last formed, stands, as I think can be shown (even with plants, and obviously with animals), in a far more important relation to its associates than to external conditions. Therefore, according to my principles, whether right or wrong, I cannot agree with your proposition that time, and altered conditions, and altered associates, are "convertible terms.' I look at the first and the last as *far* more important : time being important only so far as giving scope to selection. God knows whether you will perceive at what I am driving. I shall have to discuss and think more about your difficulty of the temperate and sub-arctic forms in the S. hemisphere than I have yet done. But I am inclined to think that I am right (if my general principles are right), that there would be little tendency to the formation of a new species, during the period of migration, whether shorter or longer, though considerable variability may have supervened. . . .

C. Darwin to J. D. Hooker.

Dec. 24th [1856].

. . . How I do wish I lived near you to discuss matters with. I have just been comparing definitions of species, and stating briefly how systematic naturalists work out their subjects. Aquilegia in the Flora Indica was a capital example for me. It is really laughable to see what different ideas are prominent in various naturalists' minds, when they speak of " species ; " in some, resemblance is everything and descent of little weight—in some, resemblance seems to go for nothing, and Creation the reigning idea—in some, descent is the key,—in some, sterility an unfailing test, with others it is not worth a farthing. It all comes, I believe. from trying to define the undefinable. I suppose you have lost the odd black seed from the birds' dung, which germinated,—anyhow, it is not worth taking trouble over. I have now got about a dozen seeds out of small birds' dung. Adios,

My dear Hooker, ever yours,

C. DARWIN.

C. Darwin to Asa Gray.

Down, Jan. 1st [1857?].

MY DEAR DR GRAY,—I have received the second part of your paper,* and though I have nothing particular to say, I must send you my thanks and hearty admiration. The whole paper strikes me as quite exhausting the subject, and I quite fancy and flatter myself I now appreciate the character of your Flora. What a difference in regard to Europe your remark in relation to the genera makes ! I have been eminently glad to see your conclusion in regard to the species of large genera widely ranging; it is in strict conformity with the results I have worked out in several ways. It is of great importance to my notions. By the way you have paid me a *great*

---

* Statistics of the Flora of the Northern U. States.' *Silliman's Journal,* 1857

compliment : * to be *simply* mentioned even in such a paper I consider a very great honour. One of your conclusions makes me groan, viz., that the line of connection of the strictly alpine plants is through Greenland. I should *extremely* like to see your reasons published in detail, for it " riles " me (this is a proper expression, is it not ?) dreadfully. Lyell told me, that Agassiz having a theory about when Saurians were first created, on hearing some careful observations opposed to this, said he did not believe it, " for Nature never lied." I am just in this predicament, and repeat to you that, " Nature never lies," ergo, theorisers are always right. . . .

Overworked as you are, I dare say you will say that I am an odious plague ; but here is another suggestion ! I was led by one of my wild speculations to conclude (though it has nothing to do with geographical distribution, yet it has with your statistics) that trees would have a strong tendency to have flowers with diœcious, monœcious or polygamous structure. Seeing that this seemed so in Persoon, I took one little British Flora, and discriminating trees from bushes according to Loudon, I have found that the result was in species, genera and families, as I anticipated. So I sent my notions to Hooker to ask him to tabulate the New Zealand Flora for this end, and he thought my result sufficiently curious, to do so ; and the accordance with Britain is very striking, and the more so, as he made three classes of trees, bushes, and herbaceous plants. (He says further he shall work the Tasmanian Flora on the same principle.) The bushes hold an intermediate position between the other two classes. It seems to me a curious relation in itself, and is very much so, if my theory and explanation are correct.†

With hearty thanks, your most troublesome friend,

C. DARWIN.

---

* " From some investigations of his own, this sagacious naturalist inclines to think that [the species of] large genera range over a larger area than the species of small genera do."—Asa Gray, *loc. cit.*

† See ' Origin,' Ed. i., p. 100.

C. Darwin to J. D. Hooker.

Down, April 12th [1857].

MY DEAR HOOKER,—Your letter has pleased me much, for I never can get it out of my head, that I take unfair advantage of your kindness, as I receive all and give nothing. What a splendid discussion you could write on the whole subject of variation! The cases discussed in your last note are valuable to me (though odious and damnable), as showing how profoundly ignorant we are on the causes of variation. I shall just allude to these cases, as a sort of sub-division of polymorphism a little more definite, I fancy, than the variation of, for instance, the Rubi, and equally or more perplexing.

I have just been putting my notes together on variations *apparently* due to the immediate and direct action of external causes; and I have been struck with one result. The most firm sticklers for independent creation admit, that the fur of the *same* species is thinner towards the south of the range of the same species than to the north—that the *same* shells are brighter-coloured to the south than north; that the same [shell] is paler-coloured in deep water—that insects are smaller and darker on mountains—more livid and testaceous near sea —that plants are smaller and more hairy and with brighter flowers on mountains: now in all such, and other cases, distinct species in the two zones follow the same rule, which seems to me to be most simply explained by species, being only strongly marked varieties, and therefore following the same laws as recognised and admitted varieties. I mention all this on account of the variation of plants in ascending mountains ; I have quoted the foregoing remark only generally with no examples, for I add, there is so much doubt and dispute what to call varieties ; but yet I have stumbled on so many casual remarks on *varieties* of plants on mountains being so characterised, that I presume there is some truth in it. What think you ? Do you believe there is *any* tendency in *varieties*, as *generally* so called, of plants to become more hairy and with proportionally larger and brighter-coloured flowers in ascending a mountain?

I have been interested in my "weed garden," of 3 × 2 feet square: I mark each seedling as it appears, and I am astonished at the number that come up, and still more at the number killed by slugs, &c. Already 59 have been so killed; I expected a good many, but I had fancied that this was a less potent check than it seems to be, and I attributed almost exclusively to mere choking, the destruction of the seedlings. Grass-seedlings seem to suffer much less than exogens. . . .

C. Darwin to J. D. Hooker.

Moor Park, Farnham [April (?) 1857].

MY DEAR HOOKER,—Your letter has been forwarded to me here, where I am undergoing hydropathy for a fortnight, having been here a week, and having already received an amount of good which is quite incredible to myself and quite unaccountable. I can walk and eat like a hearty Christian, and even my nights are good. I cannot in the least understand how hydropathy can act as it certainly does on me It dulls one's brain splendidly; I have not thought about a single species of any kind since leaving home. Your note has taken me aback; I thought the hairiness, &c., of Alpine *species* was generally admitted; I am sure I have seen it alluded to a score of times. Falconer was haranguing on it the other day to me Meyen or Gay, or some such fellow (whom you would despise), I remember, makes some remark on Chilian Cordillera plants. Wimmer has written a little book on the same lines, and on *varieties* being so characterised in the Alps. But after writing to you, I confess I was staggered by finding one man (Moquin-Tandon, I think) saying that Alpine flowers are strongly inclined to be white, and Linnæus saying that cold makes plants *apetalous*, even the same species! Are Arctic plants often apetalous? My general belief from my compiling work is quite to agree with what you say about the little direct influence of climate; and I have just alluded to the hairiness of Alpine plants as an *exception*. The odoriferousness would be a good case for me if I knew of *varieties* being more odoriferous in dry habitats.

I fear that I have looked at the hairiness of Alpine plants as so generally acknowledged that I have not marked passages, so as at all to see what kind of evidence authors advance. I must c.nfess, the other day, when I asked Falconer, whether he knew of *individual* plants losing or acquiring hairiness when transported, he did not. But now *this second*, my memory flashes on me, and I am certain I have somewhere got marked a case of hairy plants from the Pyrenees losing hairs when cultivated at Montpellier. Shall you think me very impudent if I tell you that I have sometimes thought that (quite independently of the present case), you are a little too hard on bad observers; that a remark made by a bad observer *cannot* be right; an observer who deserves to be damned you would utterly damn. I feel entire deference to any remark you make out of your own head; but when in opposition to some poor devil, I somehow involuntarily feel not quite so much, but yet much deference for your opinion. I do not know in the least whether there is any truth in this my criticism against you, but I have often thought I would tell you it.

I am really very much obliged for your letter, for, though I intended to put only one sentence and that vaguely, I should probably have put that much too strongly.

Ever, my dear Hooker, yours most truly,

C. DARWIN.

P. S. This note, as you see, has not anything requiring an answer.

The distribution of fresh-water molluscs has been a horrid incubus to me, but I think I know my way now; when first hatched they are very active, and I have had thirty or forty crawl on a dead duck's foot; and they cannot be jerked off, and will live fifteen and even twenty-four hours out of water.

[The following letter refers to the expedition of the Austrian frigate *Novara;* Lyell had asked my father for suggestions.]

C. Darwin to C. Lyell.

Down, Feb. 11th [1857].

My dear Lyell,—I was glad to see in the newspapers about the Austrian Expedition. I have nothing to add geologically to my notes in the Manual.* I do not know whether the Expedition is tied down to call at only fixed spots. But if there be any choice or power in the scientific men to influence the places—this would be most desirable. It is my most deliberate conviction that nothing would aid more, Natural History, than careful collecting and investigating *all the productions* of the most isolated islands, especially of the southern hemisphere. Except Tristan d'Acunha and Kerguelen Land, they are very imperfectly known; and even at Kerguelen Land, how much there is to make out about the lignite beds, and whether there are signs of old Glacial action. Every sea shell and insect and plant is of value from such spots. Some one in the Expedition especially ought to have Hooker's New Zealand Essay. What grand work to explore Rodriguez, with its fossil birds, and little known productions of every kind. Again the Seychelles, which, with the Cocos so near, must be a remnant of some older land. The outer island of Juan Fernandez is little known. The investigation of these little spots by a band of naturalists would be grand; St. Paul's and Amsterdam would be glorious, botanically, and geologically. Can you not recommend them to get my 'Journal' and 'Volcanic Islands' on account of the Galapagos. If they come from the north it will be a shame and a sin if they do not call at Cocos Islet, one of the Galapagos. I always regretted that I was not able to examine the great

---

* The article "Geology" in the Admiralty Manual of Scientific Enquiry.

craters on Albemarle Island, one of the Galapagos. In New Zealand urge on them to look out for erratic boulders and marks of old glaciers.

Urge the use of the dredge in the Tropics; how little or nothing we know of the limit of life downward in the hot seas?

My present work leads me to perceive how much the domestic animals have been neglected in out of the way countries.

The Revillagigedo Island off Mexico, I believe, has never been trodden by foot of naturalist.

If the expedition sticks to such places as Rio, Cape of Good Hope, Ceylon and Australia, &c., it will not do much.

Ever yours most truly,

C. DARWIN.

[The following passage occurs in a letter to Mr. Fox, February 22, 1857, and has reference to the book on Evolution on which he was still at work. The remainder of the letter is made up in details of no interest :

" I am got most deeply interested in my subject; though I wish I could set less value on the bauble fame, either present or posthumous, than I do, but not I think, to any extreme degree : yet; if I know myself, I would work just as hard, though with less gusto, if I knew that my book would be pub-lished for ever anonymously."]

C. Darwin to A. R. Wallace.

Moor Park, May 1st, 1857.

MY DEAR SIR,—I am much obliged for your letter of October 10th, from Celebes, received a few days ago; in a laborious undertaking, sympathy is a valuable and real en-couragement. By your letter and even still more by your

paper* in the Annals, a year or more ago, I can plainly see
that we have thought much alike and to a certain extent have
come to similar conclusions.   In regard to the Paper in the
Annals, I agree to the truth of almost every word of your
paper; and I dare say that you will agree with me that it is
very rare to find oneself agreeing pretty closely with any
theoretical paper; for it is lamentable how each man draws
his own different conclusions from the very same facts.   This
summer will make the 20th year (!) since I opened my first
note-book, on the question how and in what way do species
and varieties differ from each other.   I am now preparing my
work for publication, but I find the subject so very large, that
though I have written many chapters, I do not suppose I shall
go to press for two years.   I have never heard how long you
intend staying in the Malay Archipelago; I wish I might
profit by the publication of your Travels there before my
work appears, for no doubt you will reap a large harvest of
facts.   I have acted already in accordance with your advice
of keeping domestic varieties, and those appearing in a state
of nature, distinct; but I have sometimes doubted of the
wisdom of this, and therefore I am glad to be backed by your
opinion.   I must confess, however, I rather doubt the truth
of the now very prevalent doctrine of all our domestic animals
having descended from several wild stocks; though I do not
doubt that it is so in some cases.   I think there is rather
better evidence on the sterility of hybrid animals than you
seem to admit : and in regard to plants the collection of
carefully recorded facts by Kölreuter and Gaertner (and
Herbert,] is *enormous*.   I most entirely agree with you on the
little effects of " climatal conditions," which one sees referred
to *ad nauseam* in all books : I suppose some very little effect
must be attributed to such influences, but I fully believe that
they are very slight.   It is really *impossible* to explain my
views (in the compass of a letter), on the causes and means

* 'On the law that has regulated the introduction of new species.'—
Ann. Nat. Hist., 1855.

of variation in a state of nature ; but I have slowly adopted a
distinct and tangible idea,—whether true or false others must
judge ; for the firmest conviction of the truth of a doctrine by
its author, seems, alas, not to be the slightest guarantee of
truth ! . . .

C. Darwin to J. D. Hooker.

Moor Park, Saturday [May 2nd, 1857].

MY DEAR HOOKER,—You have shaved the hair off the
Alpine plants pretty effectually. The case of the Anthyllis
will make a " tie " with the believed case of Pyrenees plants
becoming glabrous at low levels. If I *do* find that I have
marked such facts, I will lay the evidence before you. I
wonder how the belief could have originated ! Was it through
final causes to keep the plants warm ? Falconer in talk
coupled the two facts of woolly Alpine plants and mammals.
How candidly and meekly you took my Jeremiad on your
severity to second-class men. After I had sent it off, an ugly
little voice asked me, once or twice, how much of my noble
defence of the poor in spirit and in fact, was owing to your
having not seldom smashed favourite notions of my own. I
silenced the ugly little voice with contempt, but it would
whisper again and again. I sometimes despise myself as a
poor compiler as heartily as you could do, though I do *not*
despise my whole work, as I think there is enough known to
lay a foundation for the discussion on the origin of species.
I have been led to despise and laugh at myself as a compiler,
for having put down that " Alpine plants have large flowers,"
and now perhaps I may write over these very words, " Alpine
plants have small or apetalous flowers ! " . . .

C. Darwin to J. D. Hooker.

Down, [May] 16th [1857].

MY DEAR HOOKER,—You said—I hope honestly—that
you did not dislike my asking questions on general points,
you of course answering or not as time or inclination might

serve. I find in the animal kingdom that the proposition that any part or organ developed normally (*i. e.*, not a monstrosity) in a species in any *high* or *unusual* degree, compared with the same part or organ in allied species, tends to be *highly variable.* I cannot doubt this from my mass of collected facts. To give an instance, the Cross-bill is very abnormal in the structure of its bill compared with other allied Fringillidæ, and the beak is *eminently variable.* The Himantopus, remarkable from the wonderful length of its legs, is *very* variable in the length of its legs. I could give *many* most striking and curious illustrations in all classes; so many that I think it cannot be chance. But I have *none* in the vegetable kingdom, owing, as I believe, to my ignorance. If Nepenthes consisted of *one* or two species in a group with a pitcher developed, then I should have expected it to have been very variable ; but I do not consider Nepenthes a case in point, for when a whole genus or group has an organ, however anomalous, I do not expect it to be variable,—it is only when one or few species differ greatly in some one part or organ from the forms *closely allied* to it in all other respects, that I believe such part or organ to be highly variable. Will you turn this in your mind ? it is an important apparent *law* (!) for me.

Ever yours,
C. DARWIN.

P. S.—I do not know how far you will care to hear, but I find Moquin-Tandon treats in his ' Tératologie ' on villosity of plants, and seems to attribute more to dryness than altitude ; but seems to think that it must be admitted that mountain plants are villose, and that this villosity is only in part explained by De Candolle's remark that the dwarfed condition of mountain plants would condense the hairs, and so give them the *appearance* of being more hairy. He quotes Senebier, ' Physiologie Végétale,' as authority—I suppose the first authority, for mountain plants being hairy.

If I could show positively that the endemic species were

more hairy in dry districts, then the case of the varieties becoming more hairy in dry ground would be a fact for me.

C. Darwin to J. D. Hooker.

Down, June 3rd [1857].

MY DEAR HOOKER,—I am going to enjoy myself by having a prose on my own subjects to you, and this is a greater enjoyment to me than you will readily understand, as I for months together do not open my mouth on Natural History. Your letter is of great value to me, and staggers me in regard to my proposition. I dare say the absence of botanical facts may in part be accounted for by the difficulty of measuring slight variations. Indeed, after writing, this occurred to me; for I have *Crucianella stylosa* coming into flower, and the pistil ought to be very variable in length, and thinking of this I at once felt how could one judge whether it was variable in any high degree. How different, for instance, from the beak of a bird! But I am not satisfied with this explanation, and am staggered. Yet I think there is something in the law; I have had so many instances, as the following: I wrote to Wollaston to ask him to run through the Madeira Beetles and tell me whether any one presented anything very anomalous in relation to its allies. He gave me a unique case of an enormous head in a female, and then I found in his book, already stated, that the size of the head was *astonishingly* variable. Part of the difference with plants may be accounted for by many of my cases being secondary male or *female* characters, but then I have striking cases with hermaphrodite Cirripedes. The cases seem to me far too numerous for accidental coincidences, of great variability and abnormal development. I presume that you will not object to my putting a note saying that you had reflected over the case, and though one or two cases seemed to support, quite as many or more seemed wholly contradictory. This want of evidence

is the more surprising to me, as generally I find any proposition more easily tested by observations in botanical works,
which I have picked up, than in zoological works. I never
dreamed that you had kept the subject at all before your
mind. Altogether the case is one more of my *many* horrid
puzzles. My observations, though on so infinitely a small
scale, on the struggle for existence, begin to make me see a
little clearer how the fight goes on. Out of sixteen kinds of
seed sown on my meadow, fifteen have germinated, but now
they are perishing at such a rate that I doubt whether more
than one will flower. Here we have choking which has taken
place likewise on a great scale, with plants not seedlings, in
a bit of my lawn allowed to grow up. On the other hand, in
a bit of ground, 2 by 3 feet, I have daily marked each seedling weed as it has appeared during March, April and May,
and 357 have come up, and of these 277 have *already* been
killed, chiefly by slugs. By the way, at Moor Park, I saw
rather a pretty case of the effects of animals on vegetation :
there are enormous commons with clumps of old Scotch firs
on the hills, and about eight or ten years ago some of these
commons were enclosed, and all round the clumps nice young
trees are springing up by the million, looking exactly as if
planted, so many are of the same age. In other parts of the
common, not yet enclosed, I looked for miles and not *one*
young tree could be seen. I then went near (within quarter
of a mile of the clumps) and looked closely in the heather,
and there I found tens of thousands of young Scotch firs
(thirty in one square yard) with their tops nibbled off by the
few cattle which occasionally roam over these wretched heaths.
One little tree, three inches high, by the rings appeared to be
twenty-six years old, with a short stem about as thick as a
stick of sealing-wax. What a wondrous problem it is, what
a play of forces, determining the kind and proportion of each
plant in a square yard of turf ! It is to my mind truly wonderful. And yet we are pleased to wonder when some animal
or plant becomes extinct.

     I am so sorry that you will not be at the Club. I see Mrs.

Hooker is going to Yarmouth ; I trust that the health of your children is not the motive.   Good-bye.

My dear Hooker, ever yours,

C. DARWIN.

P. S.—I believe you are afraid to send me a ripe Edwardsia pod, for fear I should float it from New Zealand to Chile ! ! !

C. Darwin to J. D. Hooker.

Down, June 5 [1857].

MY DEAR HOOKER,—I honour your conscientious care about the medals.*   Thank God! I am only an amateur (but a much interested one) on the subject.

It is an old notion of mine that more good is done by giving medals to younger men in the early part of their career, than as a mere reward to men whose scientific career is nearly finished.   Whether medals ever do any good is a question which does not concern us, as there the medals are. I am almost inclined to think that I would rather lower the standard, and give medals to young workers than to old ones with no *especial* claims.   With regard to especial claims, I think it just deserving your attention, that if general claims are once admitted, it opens the door to great laxity in giving them.   Think of the case of a very rich man, who aided *solely* with his money, but to a grand extent—or such an inconceivable prodigy as a minister of the Crown who really cared for science.   Would you give such men medals?   Perhaps medals could not be better applied than *exclusively* to such men.   I confess at present I incline to stick to especial claims which can be put down on paper. . . .

I am much confounded by your showing that there are not obvious instances of my (or rather Waterhouse's) law of abnormal developments being highly variable.   I have been thinking more of your remark about the difficulty of judging

---

* The Royal Society's medals.

or comparing variability in plants from the great general variability of parts. I should look at the law as more completely smashed if you would turn in your mind for a little while for cases of great variability of an organ, and tell me whether it is moderately easy to pick out such cases; *for if they can be picked out*, and, notwithstanding, do not coincide with great or abnormal development, it would be a complete smasher. It is only beginning in your mind at the variability end of the question instead of at the abnormality end. *Perhaps* cases in which a part is highly variable in all the species of a group should be excluded, as possibly being something distinct, and connected with the perplexing subject of polymorphism. Will you perfect your assistance by further considering, for a little, the subject this way?

I have been so much interested this morning in comparing all my notes on the variation of the several species of the genus Equus and the results of their crossing. Taking most strictly analogous facts amongst the blessed pigeons for my guide, I believe I can plainly see the colouring and marks of the grandfather of the Ass, Horse, Quagga, Hemionus and Zebra, some millions of generations ago! Should not I [have] sneer[ed] at any one who made such a remark to me a few years ago; but my evidence seems to me so good that I shall publish my vision at the end of my little discussion on this genus.

I have of late inundated you with my notions, you best of friends and philosophers.

Adios,
C. DARWIN.

C. Darwin to J. D. Hooker.

Moor Park, Farnham, June 25th [1857].

MY DEAR HOOKER,—This requires no answer, but I will ask you whenever we meet. Look at enclosed seedling gorses, especially one with the top knocked off. The leaves succeeding the cotyledons being almost clover-like in shape, seems to me feebly analogous to embryonic resemblances in young animals, as, for instance, the young lion being striped. I shall ask you whether this is so.*. . .

Dr. Lane † and wife, and mother-in-law, Lady Drysdale, are some of the nicest people I have ever met.

I return home on the 30th.   Good-bye, my dear Hooker.

Ever yours,

C. DARWIN.

[Here follows a group of letters, of various dates, bearing on the question of large genera varying.]

C. Darwin to J. D. Hooker.

March 11th [1858].

I was led to all this work by a remark of Fries, that the species in large genera were more closely related to each other than in small genera; and if this were so, seeing that varieties and species are so hardly distinguishable, I concluded that I should find more varieties in the large genera than in the small. . . . Some day I hope you will read my short discussion on the whole subject.   You have done me infinite service, whatever opinion I come to, in drawing my attention to at least the possibility or the probability of botanists recording more varieties in the large than in the small genera.   It will be hard work for me to be candid in coming to my conclusion.

Ever yours, most truly,

C. DARWIN.

P. S.—I shall be several weeks at my present job.   The work has been turning out badly for me this morning, and I am sick at heart ; and, oh ! how I do hate species and varieties.

---

* See 'Power of Movement in Plants,' p. 414.
† The physician at Moor Park.

C. Darwin to J. D. Hooker.

July 14th [1857?].

. . . I write now to supplicate most earnestly a favour, viz., the loan of *Boreau, Flore du centre de la France, either 1st or 2nd edition,* last best ; also " Flora Ratisbonensis," by Dr. Fürnrohr, in ' Naturhist. Topographie von Regensburg, 1839.' If you can *possibly* spare them, will you send them at once to the enclosed address. If you have not them, will you send one line by return of post: as I must try whether Kippist * can anyhow find them, which I fear will be nearly impossible in the Linnean Library, in which I know they are.

I have been making some calculations about varieties, &c., and talking yesterday with Lubbock, he has pointed out to me the grossest blunder which I have made in principle, and which entails two or three weeks' lost work ; and I am at a dead-lock till I have these books to go over again, and see what the result of calculation on the right principle is. I am the most miserable, bemuddled, stupid dog' in all England, and am ready to cry with vexation at my blindness and presumption.

Ever yours, most miserably,

C. DARWIN.

C. Darwin to John Lubbock.

Down, [July] 14th [1857].

MY DEAR LUBBOCK,— You have done me the greatest possible service in helping me to clarify my brains. If I am as muzzy on all subjects as I am on proportion and chance, —what a book I shall produce !

I have divided the New Zealand Flora as you suggested. There are 329 species in genera of 4 and upwards, and 323 in genera of 3 and less.

---

* The late Mr. Kippist was at this time in charge of the Linnean Society's Library.

The 339 species have 51 species presenting one or more varieties. The 323 species have only 37. Proportionately (339 : 323 :: 51 : 48·5) they ought to have had 48½ species presenting vars. So that the case goes as I want it, but not strong enough, without it be general, for me to have much confidence in. I am quite convinced yours is the right way ; I had thought of it, but should never have done it had it not been for my most fortunate conversation with you.

I am quite shocked to find how easily I am muddled, for I had before thought over the subject much, and concluded my way was fair. It is dreadfully erroneous.

What a disgraceful blunder you have saved me from. I heartily thank you.

Ever yours,
C. DARWIN.

P. S.—It is enough to make me tear up all my MS. and give up in despair.

It will take me several weeks to go over all my materials. But oh, if you knew how thankful I am to you !

C. Darwin to J. D. Hooker.

Down, Aug. [1857].

MY DEAR HOOKER,—It is a horrid bore you cannot come soon, and I reproach myself that I did not write sooner. How busy you must be! with such a heap of botanists at Kew. Only think, I have just had a letter from Henslow, saying he will come here between 11th and 15th! Is not that grand ? Many thanks about Fürnrohr. I must humbly supplicate Kippist to search for it : he most kindly got Boreau for me.

I am got extremely interested in tabulating, according to mere size of genera, the species having any varieties marked by Greek letters or otherwise : the result (as far as I have yet gone) seems to me one of the most important arguments I have yet met with, that varieties are only small species—or species only strongly marked varieties. The subject is in many ways so very important for me ; I wish much you would think of any well-worked Floras with from 1000–2000 species, with the varieties marked. It is good to have hair-splitters and lumpers.* I have done, or am doing :—

Babington . . . . . ⎫	
Henslow . . . . . ⎬	British Flora.
London Catalogue. H. C. Watson ⎭	
Boreau	France.
Miquel	Holland.
Asa Gray . . .	N. U. States.
Hooker	⎰ N. Zealand.
	⎱ Fragment of Indian Flora.
Wollaston . . .	Madeira insects.

Has not Koch published a good German Flora? Does he mark varieties? Could you send it me? Is there not some grand Russian Flora, which perhaps has varieties marked? The Floras ought to be well known.

I am in no hurry for a few weeks. Will you turn this in your head when, if ever, you have leisure? The subject is very important for my work, though I clearly see *many* causes of error. . . .

C. Darwin to Asa Gray.

Down, Feb. 21st [1859].

MY DEAR GRAY,—My last letter begged no favour, this one does : but it will really cost you very little trouble to answer to me, and it will be of very *great* service to me, owing to a remark made to me by Hooker, which I cannot credit, and which was suggested to him by one of my letters. He suggested my asking you, and I told him I would not give the least hint what he thought. I generally believe Hooker

---

* Those who make many species are the "splitters," and those who make few are the "lumpers."

implicitly, but he is sometimes, I think, and he confesses it, rather over critical, and his ingenuity in discovering flaws seems to me admirable. Here is my question:—"Do you think that good botanists in drawing up a local Flora, whether small or large, or in making a Prodromus like De Candolle's, would almost universally, but unintentionally and unconsciously, tend to record (*i. e.*, marking with Greek letters and giving short characters) varieties in the large or in the small genera? Or would the tendency be to record the varieties about equally in genera of all sizes? Are you yourself conscious on reflection that you have attended to, and recorded more carefully the varieties in large or small, or very small genera?"

I know what fleeting and trifling things varieties very often are; but my query applies to such as have been thought worth marking and recording. If you could screw time to send me ever so brief an answer to this, pretty soon, it would be a great service to me.

Yours most truly obliged,

CH. DARWIN.

P. S.—Do you know whether any one has ever published any remarks on the geographical range of varieties of plants in comparison with the species to which they are supposed to belong? I have in vain tried to get some vague idea, and with the exception of a little information on this head given me by Mr. Watson in a paper on Land Shells in U. States, I have quite failed; but perhaps it would be difficult for you to give me even a brief answer on this head, and if so I am not so unreasonable, *I assure you*, as to expect it.

If you are writing to England soon, you could enclose other letters [for] me to forward.

Please observe the question is not whether there are more or fewer varieties in larger or smaller genera, but whether there is a stronger or weaker tendency in the minds of botanists to *record* such in large or small genera.

C. Darwin to J. D. Hooker.

Down, May 6th [1858].

. . . I send by this post my MS. on the "commonness," "range," and "variation" of species in large and small genera. You have undertaken a horrid job in so very kindly offering to read it, and I thank you warmly. I have just corrected the copy, and am disappointed in finding how tough and obscure it is; but I cannot make it clearer, and at present I loathe the very sight of it. The style of course requires further correction, and if published I must try, but as yet see not how, to make it clearer.

If you have much to say and can have patience to consider the whole subject, I would meet you in London on the Phil. Club day, so as to save you the trouble of writing. For Heaven's sake, you stern and awful judge and sceptic, remember that my conclusions may be true, notwithstanding that Botanists may have recorded more varieties in large than in small genera. It seems to me a mere balancing of probabilities. Again I thank you most sincerely, but I fear you will find it a horrid job.

Ever yours,

C. DARWIN.

P. S.—As usual, Hydropathy has made a man of me for a short time: I hope the sea will do Mrs. Hooker much good.

C. Darwin to A. R. Wallace.

Down, Dec. 22nd, 1857.

MY DEAR SIR,—I thank you for your letter of Sept. 27th. I am extremely glad to hear that you are attending to distribution in accordance with theoretical ideas. I am a firm believer that without speculation there is no good and original observation. Few travellers have attended to such points as you are now at work on; and, indeed, the whole subject of distribution of animals is dreadfully behind that of plants.

You say that you have been somewhat surprised at no notice having been taken of your paper in the Annals.* I cannot say that I am, for so very few naturalists care for anything beyond the mere description of species. But you must not suppose that your paper has not been attended to : two very good men, Sir C. Lyell, and Mr. E. Blyth at Calcutta, specially called my attention to it. Though agreeing with you on your conclusions in that paper, I believe I go much further than you ; but it is too long a subject to enter on my speculative notions. I have not yet seen your paper on the distribution of animals in the Aru Islands. I shall read it with the utmost interest ; for I think that the most interesting quarter of the whole globe in respect to distribution, and I have long been very imperfectly trying to collect data for the Malay Archipelago. I shall be quite prepared to subscribe to your doctrine of subsidence ; indeed, from the quite independent evidence of the Coral Reefs I coloured my original map (in my Coral volume) of the Aru Islands as one of subsidence, but got frightened and left it uncoloured. But I can see that you are inclined to go much further than I am in regard to the former connection of oceanic islands with continents. Ever since poor E. Forbes propounded this doctrine it has been eagerly followed ; and Hooker elaborately discusses the former connection of all the Antarctic Islands and New Zealand and South America. About a year ago I discussed this subject much with Lyell and Hooker (for I shall have to treat of it), and wrote out my arguments in opposition ; but you will be glad to hear that neither Lyell nor Hooker thought much of my arguments. Nevertheless, for once in my life, I dare withstand the almost preternatural sagacity of Lyell.

You ask about land-shells on islands far distant from continents : Madeira has a few identical with those of Europe, and here the evidence is really good, as some of them are

---

* 'On the law that has regulated the introduction of New Species.. Ann. Nat. Hist., 1855.

sub-fossil. In the Pacific Islands there are cases of identity, which I cannot at present persuade myself to account for by introduction through man's agency; although Dr. Aug. Gould has conclusively shown that many land-shells have thus been distributed over the Pacific by man's agency. These cases of introduction are most plaguing. Have you not found it so in the Malay Archipelago? It has seemed to me in the lists of mammals of Timor and other islands, that *several* in all probability have been naturalised. . . .

You ask whether I shall discuss "man." I think I shall avoid the whole subject, as so surrounded with prejudices ; though I fully admit that it is the highest and most interesting problem for the naturalist. My work, on which I have now been at work more or less for twenty years, will not fix or settle anything; but I hope it will aid by giving a large collection of facts, with one definite end. I get on very slowly, partly from ill-health, partly from being a very slow worker. I have got about half written ; but I do not suppose I shall published under a couple of years. I have now been three whole months on one chapter on Hybridism!

I am astonished to see that you expect to remain out three or four years more. What a wonderful deal you will have seen, and what interesting areas—the grand Malay Archipelago and the richest parts of South America! I infinitely admire and honour your zeal and courage in the good cause of Natural Science ; and you have my very sincere and cordial good wishes for success of all kinds, and may all your theories succeed, except that on Oceanic Islands, on which subject I will do battle to the death.

Pray believe me, my dear sir, yours very sincerely,

C. DARWIN.

C. Darwin to W. D. Fox.

Feb. 8th [1858].

. . . I am working very hard at my book, perhaps too hard. It will be very big, and I am become most deeply interested in the way facts fall into groups. I am like Crœsus overwhelmed with my riches in facts, and I mean to make my book as perfect as ever I can. I shall not go to press at soonest for a couple of years. . . .

C. Darwin to J. D. Hooker.

Feb. 23rd [1858].

. . . I was not much struck with the great Buckle, and I admired the way you stuck up about deduction and induction. I am reading his book,* which, with much sophistry, as it seems to me, is *wonderfully* clever and original, and with astounding knowledge.

I saw that you admired Mrs. Farrer's ' Questa tomba' of Beethoven thoroughly ; there is something grand in her sweet tones.

Farewell. I have partly written this note to drive bee's-cells out of my head ; for I am half-mad on the subject to try to make out some simple steps from which all the wondrous angles may result.†

I was very glad to see Mrs. Hooker on Friday ; how well she appears to be and looks.

Forgive your intolerable but affectionate friend,

C. DARWIN.

C. Darwin to W. D. Fox.

Down, April 16th [1858].

MY DEAR FOX,—I want you to observe one point for me, on which I am extremely much interested, and which will give you no trouble beyond keeping your eyes open, and that is a habit I know full well that you have.

I find horses of various colours often have a spinal band or stripe of different and darker tint than the rest of the body ; rarely transverse bars on the legs, generally on the under-side

---

* ' The History of Civilisation.'

† He had much correspondence on this subject with the late Professor Miller of Cambridge.

of the front legs, still more rarely a very faint transverse shoulder-stripe like an ass.

Is there any breed of Delamere forest ponies? I have found out little about ponies in these respects. Sir P. Egerton has, I believe, some quite thoroughbred chestnut horses; have any of them the spinal stripe? Mouse-coloured ponies, or rather small horses, often have spinal and leg bars. So have dun horses (by dun I mean real colour of cream mixed with brown, bay, or chestnut). So have sometimes chestnuts, but I have not yet got a case of spinal stripe in chestnut, race horse, or in quite heavy cart-horse. Any fact of this nature of such stripes in horses would be *most* useful to me. There is a parallel case in the legs of the donkey, and I have collected some most curious cases of stripes appearing in various crossed equine animals. I have also a large mass of parallel facts in the breeds of pigeons about the wing bars. I *suspect* it will throw light on the colour of the primeval horse. So do help me if occasion turns up. . . . My health has been lately very bad from overwork, and on Tuesday I go for a fortnight's hydropathy. My work is everlasting. Farewell.

My dear Fox, I trust you are well.   Farewell,

C. DARWIN.

C. Darwin to J. D. Hooker.

Moor Park, Farnham [April 26th, 1858].

. . . I have just had the innermost cockles of my heart rejoiced by a letter from Lyell. I said to him (or he to me) that I believed from the character of the flora of the Azores, that icebergs must have been stranded there; and that I expected erratic boulders would be detected embedded between the upheaved lava-beds; and I got Lyell to write to Hartung to ask, and now H. says my question explains what had astounded him, viz., large boulders (and some polished) of mica-schist, quartz, sandstone, &c., some embedded, and some 40 and 50 feet above the level of the sea, so that he had inferred that they had not been brought as ballast. Is this not beautiful?

The water-cure has done me some good, but I [am] nothing to boast of to-day, so good-bye.

My dear friend, yours,

C. D.

C. Darwin to C. Lyell.

Moor Park, Farnham, April 26th [1858].

MY DEAR LYELL,—I have come here for a fortnight's hydropathy, as my stomach had got, from steady work, into a horrid state. I am extremely much obliged to you for sending me Hartung's interesting letter. The erratic boulders are splendid. It is a grand case of floating ice versus glaciers. He ought to have compared the northern and southern shores of the islands. It is eminently interesting to me, for I have written a very long chapter on the subject, collecting briefly all the geological evidence of glacial action in different parts of the world, and then at great length (on the theory of species changing) I have discussed the migration and modification of plants and animals, in sea and land, over a large part of the world. To my mind, it throws a flood of light on the whole subject of distribution, if combined with the modification of species. Indeed, I venture to speak with some little confidence on this, for Hooker, about a year ago, kindly read over my chapter, and though he then demurred gravely to the general conclusion, I was delighted to hear a week or two ago that he was inclined to come round pretty strongly to my views of distribution and change during the glacial period. I had a letter from Thompson, of Calcutta, the other day, which helps me much, as he is making out for me what heat our temperate plants can endure. But it is too long a subject for a note; and I have written thus only because Hartung's note has set the whole subject afloat in my mind again. But I will write no more, for my object here is to think about nothing, bathe much, walk much, eat much, and read much novels. Farewell, with many thanks, and very kind remembrance to Lady Lyell.

Ever yours,
C. DARWIN.

C. Darwin to Mrs. Darwin.

Moor Park, Wednesday, April [1858].

The weather is quite delicious. Yesterday, after writing to you, I strolled a little beyond the glade for an hour and a half, and enjoyed myself—the fresh yet dark-green of the grand Scotch firs, the brown of the catkins of the old birches, with their white stems, and a fringe of distant green from the larches made an excessively pretty view. At last I fell fast asleep on the grass, and awoke with a chorus of birds singing around me, and squirrels running up the trees, and some woodpeckers laughing, and it was as pleasant and rural a scene as ever I saw, and I did not care one penny how any of the beasts or birds had been formed. I sat in the drawing-room till after eight, and then went and read the Chief Justice's summing up, and thought Bernard * guilty, and then read a bit of my novel, which is feminine, virtuous, clerical, philanthropical, and all that sort of thing, but very decidedly flat. I say feminine, for the author is ignorant about money matters, and not much of a lady—for she makes her men say, " My Lady." I like Miss Craik very much, though we have some battles, and differ on every subject. I like also the Hungarian ; a thorough gentleman, formerly attaché at Paris, and then in the Austrian cavalry, and now a pardoned exile, with broken health. He does not seem to like Kossuth, but says, he is certain [he is] a sincere patriot, most clever and eloquent, but weak, with no determination of character. . . .

---

* Simon Bernard was tried in April 1858 as an accessory to Orsini's attempt on the life of the Emperor of the French. The verdict was " not guilty."

CHAPTER XIII.

THE WRITING OF THE 'ORIGIN OF SPECIES.'

June 18, 1858, to November, 1859.

[THE letters given in the present chapter tell their story with sufficient clearness, and need but a few words of explanation. Mr. Wallace's Essay, referred to in the first letter, bore the sub-title, 'On the Tendency of Varieties to depart indefinitely from the Original Type,' and was published in the Linnean Society's Journal (1858, vol. iii. p. 53) as part of the joint paper of "Messrs. C. Darwin and A. Wallace," of which the full title was ' On the Tendency of Species to form Varieties ; and on the Perpetuation of Varieties and Species by Natural Means of Selection.'

My father's contribution to the paper consisted of (1) Extracts from the sketch of 1844 ; (2) part of a letter addressed to Dr. Asa Gray, dated September 5, 1857, and which is given at p. 120. The paper was "communicated" to the Society by Sir Charles Lyell and Sir Joseph Hooker, in whose prefatory letter, a clear account of the circumstances of the case is given.

Referring to Mr. Wallace's Essay, they wrote :

"So highly did Mr. Darwin appreciate the value of the views therein set forth, that he proposed, in a letter to Sir Charles Lyell, to obtain Mr. Wallace's consent to allow the Essay to be published as soon as possible. Of this step we highly approved, provided Mr. Darwin did not withold from the public, as he was strongly inclined to do (in favour of Mr. Wallace), the memoir which he had himself written on the same subject, and which, as before stated, one of us had perused in 1844, and the contents of which we had both of us been privy to for many years. On representing this to Mr. Darwin, he gave us permission to make what use we thought proper of his memoir, &c.; and in adopting our present course, of presenting it to the Linnean Society, we have explained to him that we are not solely considering the relative claims to priority of himself and his friend, but the interests of science generally."]

LETTERS.

C. Darwin to C. Lyell.

Down, 18th [June 1858].

MY DEAR LYELL,—Some year or so ago you recommended me to read a paper by Wallace in the 'Annals,' * which had interested you, and, as I was writing to him, I knew this would please him much, so I told him. He has to-day sent me the enclosed, and asked me to forward it to you. It seems to me well worth reading. Your words have come true with a vengeance—that I should be forestalled. You said this, when I explained to you here very briefly my views of 'Natural Selection' depending on the struggle for existence. I never saw a more striking coincidence; if Wallace had my MS. sketch written out in 1842, he could not have made a better short abstract! Even his terms now stand as heads of my chapters. Please return me the MS., which he does not say he wishes me to publish, but I shall of course, at once write and offer to send to any journal. So all my originality, whatever it may amount to, will be smashed, though my book, if it will ever have any value, will not be deteriorated; as all the labour consists in the application of the theory.

I hope you will approve of Wallace's sketch, that I may tell him what you say.

My dear Lyell, yours most truly,

C. DARWIN.

---

* Annals and Mag. of Nat. Hist., 1855.

C. Darwin to C. Lyell.

Down, Friday [June 25, 1858].

MY DEAR LYELL,—I am very sorry to trouble you, busy as you are, in so merely a personal an affair ; but if you will give me your deliberate opinion, you will do me as great a service as ever man did, for I have entire confidence in your judgment and honour. . . . .

There is nothing in Wallace's sketch which is not written out much fuller in my sketch, copied out in 1844, and read by Hooker some dozen years ago. About a year ago I sent a short sketch, of which I have a copy, of my views (owing to correspondence on several points) to Asa Gray, so that I could most truly say and prove that I take nothing from Wallace. I should be extremely glad now to publish a sketch of my general views in about a dozen pages or so ; but I cannot persuade myself that I can do so honourably. Wallace says nothing about publication, and I enclose his letter. But as I had not intended to publish any sketch, can I do so honourably, because Wallace has sent me an outline of his doctrine? I would far rather burn my whole book, than that he or any other man should think that I had behaved in a paltry spirit. Do you not think his having sent me this sketch ties my hands? . . . If I could honourably publish, I would state that I was induced now to publish a sketch (and I should be very glad to be permitted to say, to follow your advice long ago given) from Wallace having sent me an outline of my general conclusions. We differ only, [in] that I was led to my views from what artificial selection has done for domestic animals. I would send Wallace a copy of my letter to Asa Gray, to show him that I had not stolen his doctrine. But I cannot tell whether to publish now would not be base and paltry. This was my first impression, and I should have certainly acted on it had it not been for your letter.

This is a trumpery affair to trouble you with, but you cannot tell how much obliged I should be for your advice.

By the way, would you object to send this and your answer to Hooker to be forwarded to me, for then I shall have the opinion of my two best and kindest friends. This letter is miserably written, and I write it now, that I may for a time banish the whole subject; and I am worn out with musing . . .

My good dear friend forgive me. This is a trumpery letter, influenced by trumpery feelings.

Yours most truly,

C. DARWIN.

I will never trouble you or Hooker on the subject again.

C. Darwin to C. Lyell.

Down, 26th [June, 1858].

MY DEAR LYELL,—Forgive me for adding a P.S. to make the case as strong as possible against myself.

Wallace might say, "You did not intend publishing an abstract of your views till you received my communication. Is it fair to take advantage of my having freely, though unasked, communicated to you my ideas, and thus prevent me forestalling you?" The advantage which I should take being that I am induced to publish from privately knowing that Wallace is in the field. It seems hard on me that I should be thus compelled to lose my priority of many years' standing, but I cannot feel at all sure that this alters the justice of the case. First impressions are generally right, and I at first thought it would be dishonourable in me now to publish.

Yours most truly,

C. DARWIN.

P. S.—I have always thought you would make a first-rate Lord Chancellor; and I now appeal to you as a Lord Chancellor.

C. Darwin to J. D. Hooker.

Down, Tuesday [June 29, 1858].

. . . . I have received your letters.   I cannot think now*
on the subject, but soon will.   But I can see that you have
acted with more kindness, and so has Lyell, even than I could
have expected from you both, most kind as you are.

I can easily get my letter to Asa Gray copied, but it is too
short.

. . . . God bless you.   You shall hear soon, as soon as I
can think.

Yours affectionately,

C. DARWIN.

C. Darwin to J. D. Hooker.

Tuesday night [June 29, 1858].

MY DEAR HOOKER,—I have just read your letter, and see
you want the papers at once.   I am quite prostrated, and
can do nothing, but I send Wallace, and the abstract † of my
letter to Asa Gray, which gives most imperfectly only the
means of change, and does not touch on reasons for believing
that species do change.   I dare say all is too late.   I hardly
care about it.   But you are too generous to sacrifice so much
time and kindness.   It is most generous, most kind.   I send
my sketch of 1844 solely that you may see by your own
handwriting that you did read it.   I really cannot bear to
look at it.   Do not waste much time.   It is miserable in me
to care at all about priority.

The table of contents will show what it is.

I would make a similar, but shorter and more accurate
sketch for the 'Linnean Journal.'

---

* So soon after the death, from scarlet fever, of his infant child.

† "Abstract" is here used in the sense of "extract;" in this sense also
it occurs in the 'Linnean Journal,' where the sources of my father's paper
are described.

I will do anything. God bless you, my dear kind friend.
I can write no more. I send this by my servant to Kew.

Yours,
C. DARWIN.

[The following letter is that already referred to as forming part of the joint paper published in the Linnean Society's
'Journal,' 1858] :—

C. Darwin to Asa Gray.

Down, Sept.* 5th [1857].

MY DEAR GRAY,—I forget the exact words which I used
in my former letter, but I dare say I said that I thought you
would utterly despise me when I told you what views I had
arrived at, which I did because I thought I was bound as an
honest man to do so. I should have been a strange mortal,
seeing how much I owe to your quite extraordinary kindness,
if in saying this I had meant to attribute the least bad feeling
to you. Permit me to tell you that, before I had ever corresponded with you, Hooker had shown me several of your letters (not of a private nature), and these gave me the warmest
feeling of respect to you ; and I should indeed be ungrateful
if your letters to me, and all I have heard of you, had not
strongly enhanced this feeling. But I did not feel in the least
sure that when you knew whither I was tending, that you
might not think me so wild and foolish in my views (God
knows, arrived at slowly enough, and I hope conscientiously),
that you would think me worth no more notice or assistance.
To give one example : the last time I saw my dear old friend
Falconer, he attacked me most vigorously, but quite kindly,
and told me, "You will do more harm than any ten Naturalists
will do good. I can see that you have already *corrupted* and

---

* The date is given as October in the 'Linnean Journal.' The extracts were printed from a duplicate undated copy in my father's possession, on which he had written, " This was sent to Asa Gray 8 or 9 months
ago, I think October 1857.

half-spoiled Hooker!!" Now when I see such strong feeling in my oldest friends, you need not wonder that I always expect my views to be received with contempt. But enough and too much of this.

I thank you most truly for the kind spirit of your last letter. I agree to every word in it, and think I go as far as almost any one in seeing the grave difficulties against my doctrine. With respect to the extent to which I go, all the arguments in favour of my notions fall *rapidly* away, the greater the scope of forms considered. But in animals, embryology leads me to an enormous and frightful range. The facts which kept me longest scientifically orthodox are those of adaptation—the pollen-masses in asclepias—the mistletoe, with its pollen carried by insects, and seed by birds—the woodpecker, with its feet and tail, beak and tongue, to climb the tree and secure insects. To talk of climate or Lamarckian habit producing such adaptations to other organic beings is futile. This difficulty I believe I have surmounted. As you seem interested in the subject, and as it is an *immense* advantage to me to write to you and to hear, ever so briefly, what you think, I will enclose (copied, so as to save you trouble in reading) the briefest abstract of my notions on the means by which Nature makes her species. Why I think that species have really changed, depends on general facts in the affinities, embryology, rudimentary organs, geological history, and geographical distribution of organic beings. In regard to my Abstract, you must take immensely on trust, each paragraph occupying one or two chapters in my book. You will, perhaps, think it paltry in me, when I ask you not to mention my doctrine; the reason is, if any one, like the author of the 'Vestiges,' were to hear of them, he might easily work them in, and then I should have to quote from a work perhaps despised by naturalists, and this would greatly injure any chance of my views being received by those alone whose opinions I value. [Here follows a discussion on "large genera varying," which has no direct connection with the remainder of the letter.]

I. It is wonderful what the principle of Selection by Man, that is the picking out of individuals with any desired quality, and breeding from them, and again picking out, can do. Even breeders have been astonished at their own results. They can act on differences inappreciable to an uneducated eye. Selection has been *methodically* followed in Europe for only the last half century. But it has occasionally, and even in some degree methodically, been followed in the most ancient times. There must have been also a kind of unconscious selection from t'e most ancient times, namely, in the preservation of the individual animals (without any thought of their offspring) most useful to each race of man in his particular circumstances. The "roguing," as nursery-men call the destroying of varieties, which depart from their type, is a kind of selection. I am convinced that intentional and occasional selection has been the main agent in making our domestic races. But, however this may be, its great power of modification has been indisputedly shown in late times. Selection acts only by the accumulation of very slight or greater varations, caused by external conditions, or by the mere fact that in generation the child is not absolutely similar to its parent. Man, by this power of accumulating variations. adapts living beings to his wants—he *may be said* to make the wool of one sheep good for carpets, and another for cloth, &c.

II. Now, suppose there was a being, who did not judge by mere external appearance, but could study the whole internal organisation—who never was capricious—who should go on selecting for one end during millions of generations, who will say what he might not effect! In nature we have some *slight* variations, occasionally in all parts : and I think it can be shown that a change in the conditions of existence is the main cause of the child not exactly resembling its parents; and in nature, geology shows us what changes have taken place, and are taking place. We have almost unlimited time : no one but a practical geologist can fully appreciate this : think of the Glacial period, during the whole of which the same species of shells at least have existed ; there must have been during this period, millions on millions of generations.

III. I think it can be shown that there is such an unerring power at work, or *Natural Selection* (the title of my book), which selects exclusively for the good of each organic being. The elder De Candolle, W. Herbert, and Lyell, have written strongly on the struggle for life ; but even they have not written strongly enough. Reflect that every being (even the elephant) breeds at such a rate that, in a few years, or at most a few centuries or thousands of years, the surface of the earth would not hold the progeny of any one species. I have found it hard constantly to bear in mind that the increase of every single species is checked during some part of its life, or during some shortly recurrent generation. Only a few of those annually born can live to propagate their kind. What a trifling difference must often determine which shall survive and which perish !

IV. Now take the case of a country undergoing some change ; this will tend to cause some of its inhabitants to vary slightly ; not but what I believe most beings vary at all times enough for selection to act on. Some of its inhabitants will be exterminated, and the remainder will be exposed to the mutual action of a different set of inhabitants, which I believe to be more important to the life of each being than mere climate. Considering the infinitely various ways beings have to obtain food by struggling with other beings, to escape danger at various times of life, to have their eggs or seeds disseminated, &c., &c., I cannot doubt that during millions of generations individuals of a species will be born with some slight variation profitable to some part of its economy ; such will have a better chance of surviving, propagating this variation, which again will be slowly increased by the accumulative action of natural selection ; and the variety thus formed will either coexist with, or more commonly will exterminate its parent form. An organic being like the woodpecker, or the mistletoe, may thus come to be adapted to a score of contingencies; natural selection, accumulating those slight variations in all parts of its structure which are in any way useful to it, during any part of its life.

V. Multiform difficulties will occur to every one on this theory. Most can, I think, be satisfactorily answered.— " Natura non facit saltum " answer some of the most obvious. The slowness of the change, and only a very few undergoing change at any one time answers others. The extreme imperfections of our geological records answers others.

VI. One other principle, which may be called the principle of divergence, plays, I believe, an important part in the origin of species. The same spot will support more life if occupied by very diverse forms : we see this in the many generic forms in a square yard of turf (I have counted twenty species belonging to eighteen genera), or in the plants and insects, on any little uniform islet, belonging to almost as many genera and families as to species. We can understand this with the higher animals, whose habits we best understand. We know that it has been experimentally shown that a plot of land will yield a greater weight, if cropped with several species of grasses, than with two or three species. Now every single organic being, by propagating rapidly, may be said to be striving its utmost to increase in numbers. So it will be with the offspring of any species after it has broken into varieties, or sub-species, or true species. And it follows, I think, from the foregoing facts, that the varying offspring of each species will try (only a few will succeed) to seize on as many and as diverse places in the economy of nature as possible. Each new variety or species when formed will generally take the place of, and so exterminate its less well-fitted parent. This, I believe, to be the origin of the classification or arrangement of all organic beings at all times. These always *seem* to branch and sub-branch like a tree from a common trunk ; the flourishing twigs destroying the less vigorous—the dead and lost branches rudely representing extinct genera and families.

This sketch is *most* imperfect ; but in so short a space I

cannot make it better. Your imagination must fill up many wide blanks. Without some reflection, it will appear all rubbish; perhaps it will appear so after reflection.

C. D.

P. S.—This little abstract touches only the accumulative power of natural selection, which I look at as by far the most important element in the production of new forms. The laws governing the incipient or primordial variation (unimportant except as the groundwork for selection to act on, in which respect it is all important), I shall discuss under several heads, but I can come, as you may well believe, only to very partial and imperfect conclusions.

[The joint paper of Mr. Wallace and my father was read at the Linnean Society on the evening of July 1st. Sir Charles Lyell and Sir J. D. Hooker were present, and both, I believe, made a few remarks, chiefly with a view of impressing on those present the necessity of giving the most careful consideration to what they had heard. There was, however, no semblance of a discussion. Sir Joseph Hooker writes to me: "The interest excited was intense, but the subject was too novel and too ominous for the old school to enter the lists, before armouring. After the meeting it was talked over with bated breath: Lyell's approval, and perhaps in a small way mine, as his lieutenant in the affair, rather overawed the Fellows, who would otherwise have flown out against the doctrine. We had, too, the vantage ground of being familiar with the authors and their theme."]

C. Darwin to J. D. Hooker.

Down, July 5th [1858].

MY DEAR HOOKER,—We are become more happy and less panic-struck, now that we have sent out of the house every child, and shall remove H., as soon as she can move. The first nurse became ill with ulcerated throat and quinsey, and the second is now ill with the scarlet fever, but, thank

God, is recovering. You may imagine how frightened we have been. It has been a most miserable fortnight. Thank you much for your note, telling me that all had gone on prosperously at the Linnean Society. You must let me once again tell you how deeply I feel your generous kindness and Lyell's on this occasion. But in truth it shames me that you should have lost time on a mere point of priority. I shall be curious to see the proofs. I do not in the least understand whether my letter to A. Gray is to be printed ; I suppose not, only your note ; but I am quite indifferent, and place myself absolutely in your and Lyell's hands.

I can easily prepare an abstract of my whole work, but I can hardly see how it can be made scientific for a Journal, without giving facts, which would be impossible. Indeed, a mere abstract cannot be very short. Could you give me any idea how many pages of the Journal could probably be spared me ?

Directly after my return home, I would begin and cut my cloth to my measure. If the Referees were to reject it as not strictly scientific, I could, perhaps, publish it as a pamphlet.

With respect to my big interleaved abstract,* would you send it any time before you leave England, to the enclosed address ? If you do not go till August 7th–10th, I should prefer it left with you. I hope you have jotted criticisms on my MS. on big Genera, &c., sufficient to make you remember your remarks, as I should be infinitely sorry to lose them. And I see no chance of our meeting if you go soon abroad. We thank you heartily for your invitation to join you : I can fancy nothing which I should enjoy more ; but our children are too delicate for us to leave ; I should be mere living lumber.

Lastly, you said you would write to Wallace ; I certainly should much like this, as it would quite exonerate me : if you would send me your note, sealed up, I would forward it with my own, as I know the address, &c.

---

* The Sketch of 1844.

Will you answer me sometime about your notions of the length of my abstract.

If you see Lyell, will you tell him how truly grateful I feel for his kind interest in this affair of mine. You must know that I look at it, as very important, for the reception of the view of species not being immutable, the fact of the greatest Geologist and Botanist in England taking *any sort of interest* in the subject : I am sure it will do much to break down prejudices.

Yours affectionately,

C. DARWIN.

C. Darwin to J. D. Hooker.

Miss Wedgwood's, Hartfield, Tunbridge Wells,
[July 13th, 1858].

MY DEAR HOOKER,—Your letter to Wallace seems to me perfect, quite clear and most courteous. I do not think it could possibly be improved, and I have to day forwarded it with a letter of my own. I always thought it very possible that I might be forestalled, but I fancied that I had a grand enough soul not to care; but I found myself mistaken and punished ; I had, however, quite resigned myself, and had written half a letter to Wallace to give up all priority to him, and should certainly not have changed had it not been for Lyell's and your quite extraordinary kindness. I assure you I feel it, and shall not forget it. I am *more* than satisfied at what took place at the Linnean Society. I had thought that your letter and mine to Asa Gray were to be only an appendix to Wallace's paper.

We go from here in a few days to the sea-side, probably to the Isle of Wight, and on my return (after a battle with pigeon skeletons) I will set to work at the abstract, though how on earth I shall make anything of an abstract in thirty pages of the Journal, I know not, but will try my best. I shall order Bentham; is it not a pity that you should waste time in tabulating varieties? for I can get the Down schoolmaster to do it on my return, and can tell you all the results.

I must try and see you before your journey; but do not think I am fishing to ask you to come to Down, for you will have no time for that.

You cannot imagine how pleased I am that the notion of Natural Selection has acted as a purgative on your bowels of immutability. Whenever naturalists can look at species changing as certain, what a magnificent field will be open,—on all the laws of variation,—on the genealogy of all living beings,—on their lines of migration, &c., &c. Pray thank Mrs. Hooker for her very kind little note, and pray, say how truly obliged I am, and in truth ashamed to think that she should have had the trouble of copying my ugly MS. It was extraordinarily kind in her. Farewell, my dear kind friend.

Yours affectionately,
C. Darwin.

P. S.—I have had some fun here in watching a slave-making ant ; for I could not help rather doubting the wonderful stories, but I have now seen a defeated marauding party, and I have seen a migration from one nest to another of the slave-makers, carrying their slaves (who are *house*, and not field niggers) in their mouths !

I am inclined to think that it is a true generalisation that, when honey is secreted at one point of the circle of the corolla, if the pistil bends, it always bends into the line of the gangway to the honey. The Larkspur is a good instance, in contrast to Columbine,—if you think of it, just attend to this little point.

C. Darwin to C. Lyell.

King's Head Hotel, Sandown, Isle of Wight,
July 18th [1858].

. . . We are established here for ten days, and then go on to Shanklin, which seems more amusing to one, like myself, who cannot walk. We hope much that the sea may do H. and L. good. And if it does, our expedition will answer, but not otherwise.

I have never half thanked you for all the extraordinary trouble and kindness you showed me about Wallace's affair. Hooker told me what was done at the Linnean Society, and I am far more than satisfied, and I do not think that Wallace can think my conduct unfair in allowing you and Hooker to do whatever you thought fair. I certainly was a little annoyed to lose all priority, but had resigned myself to my fate. I am going to prepare a longer abstract; but it is really impossible to do justice to the subject, except by giving the facts on which each conclusion is grounded, and that will, of course, be absolutely impossible. Your name and Hooker's name appearing as in any way the least interested in my work will, I am certain, have the most important bearing in leading people to consider the subject without prejudice. I look at this as so very important, that I am almost glad of Wallace's paper for having led to this.

My dear Lyell, yours most gratefully,

CH. DARWIN.

[The following letter refers to the proof-sheets of the Linnean paper. The 'introduction' means the prefatory letter signed by Sir C. Lyell and Sir J. D. Hooker.]

C. Darwin to J. D. Hooker.

King's Head Hotel, Sandown, Isle of Wight,
July 21st [1858].

MY DEAR HOOKER,—I received only yesterday the proof-sheets, which I now return. I think your introduction cannot be improved.

I am disgusted with my bad writing. I could not improve it, without rewriting all, which would not be fair or worth while, as I have begun on a better abstract for the Linnean Society. My excuse is that it *never* was intended for publication. I have made only a few corrections in the style; but I cannot make it decent, but I hope moderately intelligible. I suppose some one will correct the revise. (Shall I ?)

Could I have a clean proof to send to Wallace?

I have not yet fully considered your remarks on big genera (but your general concurrence is of the *highest possible* interest to me); nor shall I be able till I re-read my MS.; but you may rely on it that you never make a remark to me which is lost from *inattention*. I am particularly glad you do not object to my stating your objections in a modified form, for they always struck me as very important, and as having much inherent value, whether or no they were fatal to my notions. I will consider and reconsider all your remarks. . . .

I have ordered Bentham, for, as ―― says, it will be very curious to see a Flora written by a man who knows nothing of British plants ! !

I am very glad at what you say about my Abstract, but you may rely on it that I will condense to the utmost. I would aid in money if it is too long.* In how many ways you have aided me !

Yours affectionately,
C. DARWIN.

[The 'Abstract' mentioned in the last sentence of the preceding letter was in fact the 'Origin of Species,' on which he now set to work. In his 'Autobiography' (p. 70) he speaks of beginning to write in September, but in his Diary he wrote, "July 20 to Aug. 12, at Sandown, began Abstract of Species book." "Sep. 16, Recommenced Abstract." The book was begun with the idea that it would be published as a paper, or series of papers, by the Linnean Society, and it was only in the late autumn that it became clear that it must take the form of an independent volume.]

---

* That is to say, he would help to pay for the printing, if it should prove too long for the Linnean Society.

C. Darwin to J. D. Hooker.

Norfolk House, Shanklin, Isle of Wight,
Friday [July] 30th [1858].

MY DEAR HOOKER,—Will you give the enclosed scrap to Sir William to thank him for his kindness ; and this gives me an excuse to amuse myself by writing to you a note, which requires no answer.

This is a very charming place, and we have got a very comfortable house. But, alas, I cannot say that the sea has done H. or L. much good. Nor has my stomach recovered from all our troubles. I am very glad we left home, for six children have now died of scarlet fever in Down. We return on the 14th of August.

I have got Bentham,* and am charmed with it, and William (who has just started for a tour abroad) has been making out all sorts of new (to me) plants capitally. The little scraps of information are so capital . . . The English names in the analytical keys drive us mad : give them by all means, but why on earth [not] make them subordinate to the Latin ; it puts me in a passion. W. charged into the Compositæ and Umbelliferæ like a hero, and demolished ever so many in grand style.

I pass my time by doing daily a couple of hours of my Abstract, and I find it amusing and improving work. I am now most heartily obliged to you and Lyell for having set me on this ; for I shall, when it is done, be able to finish my work with greater ease and leisure. I confess I hated the thought of the job ; and now I find it very unsatisfactory in not being able to give my reasons for each conclusion.

I will be longer than I expected ; it will take thirty-five of my MS. folio pages to give an abstract on variation under domestication alone ; but I will try to put in nothing which does not seem to me of some interest, and which was once new to me. It seems a queer plan to give an abstract of an

---

* ' British Flora.'

unpublished work; nevertheless, I repeat, I am extremely glad I have begun in earnest on it.

I hope you and Mrs. Hooker will have a very very pleasant tour. Farewell, my dear Hooker.

Yours affectionately,
C. Darwin.

C. Darwin to J. D. Hooker.

Norfolk House, Shanklin, Isle of Wight,
Thursday [Aug. 5, 1858].

My dear Hooker,—I should think the note apologetical about the style of the abstract was best as a note . . . . But I write now to ask you to send me by return of post the MS. on big genera, that I may make an abstract of a couple of pages in length. I presume that you have quite done with it, otherwise I would not for anything have it back. If you tie it with string, and mark it MS. for printing, it will not cost, I should think, more than 4d. I shall wish much to say that you have read this MS. and concur; but you shall, before I read it to the Society, hear the sentence.

What you tell me after speaking with Busk about the length of the Abstract is an *immense* relief to me; it will make the labour far less, not having to shorten so much every single subject; but I will try not to be too diffusive. I fear it will spoil all interest in my book,* whenever published. The Abstract will do very well to divide into several parts: thus I have just finished "Variation under Domestication," in forty-four MS. pages, and that would do for one evening; but I should be extremely sorry if all could not be published together.

What else you say about my Abstract pleases me highly, but frightens me, for I fear I shall never be able to make it good enough. But how I do run on about my own affairs to you!

---

* The larger book begun in 1856.

32

I was astonished to see Sir W. Hooker's card here two or three days ago : I was unfortunately out walking. Henslow, also, has written to me, proposing to come to Down on the 9th, but alas, I do not return till the 13th, and my wife not till a week later ; so that I am also most sorry to think I shall not see you, for I should not like to leave home so soon. I had thought of going to London and running down for an hour or two to Kew. . . .

C. Darwin to J. D. Hooker.

Norfolk House, Shanklin, Isle of Wight,
[August] [1858].

MY DEAR HOOKER,—I write merely to say that the MS. came safely two or three days ago. I am much obliged for the correction of style : I find it unutterably difficult to write clearly. When we meet I must talk over a few points on the subject.

You speak of going to the sea-side somewhere ; we think this the nicest sea-side place which we have ever seen, and we like Shanklin better than other spots on the south coast of the island, though many are charming and prettier, so that I would suggest your thinking of this place. We are on the actual coast ; but tastes differ so much about places.

If you go to Broadstairs, when there is a strong wind from the coast of France and in fine, dry, warm weather, look out, and you will *probably* (!) see thistle-seeds blown across the Channel. The other day I saw one blown right inland, and then in a few minutes a second one and then a third ; and I said to myself, God bless me, how many thistles there must be in France ; and I wrote a letter in imagination to you. But I then looked at the *low* clouds, and noticed that they were not coming inland, so I feared a screw was loose. I then walked beyond a headland, and found the wind parallel to the coast, and on this very headland a noble bed of thistles, which by every wide eddy were blown far out to

sea, and then came right in at right angles to the shore ! One
day such a number of insects were washed up by the tide,
and I brought to life thirteen species of Coleoptera ; not that
I suppose these came from France. But do you watch for
thistle-seed as you saunter along the coast. . . .

C. Darwin to Asa Gray.

Aug. 11th [1858].

MY DEAR GRAY,—Your note of July 27th has just reached
me in the Isle of Wight. It is a real and great pleasure to
me to write to you about my notions ; and even if it were
not so, I should be a most ungrateful dog, after all the invaluable assistance you have rendered me, if I did not do
anything which you asked.

I have discussed in my long MS. the later changes of
climate and the effect on migration, and I will here give you
an *abstract* of an *abstract* (which latter I am preparing of my
whole work for the Linnean Society). I cannot give you
facts, and I must write dogmatically, though I do not feel so
on any point. I may just mention, in order that you may
believe that I have *some* foundation for my views, that Hooker
has read my MS., and though he at first demurred to my main
point, he has since told me that further reflection and new
facts have made him a convert.

In the older, or perhaps newer, Pliocene age (a little *before* the Glacial epoch) the temperature was higher ; of this
there can be little doubt ; the land, on a *large scale*, held
much its present disposition : the species were mainly, judging from shells, what they are now. At this period when
all animals and plants ranged 10° or 15° nearer the poles, I
believe the northern part of Siberia and of North America,
being almost *continuous*, were peopled (it is quite possible,
considering the shallow water, that Behring Straits were
united, perhaps a little southward) by a nearly uniform
fauna and flora, just as the Arctic regions now are. The
climate then became gradually colder till it became what it

now is ; and then the temperate parts of Europe and America would be separated, as far as migration is concerned, just as they now are. Then came on the Glacial period, driving far south all living things ; middle or even southern Europe being peopled with Arctic productions ; as the warmth returned, the Arctic productions slowly crawled up the mountains as they became denuded of snow ; and we now see on their summits the remnants of a once continuous flora and fauna. This is E. Forbes' theory, which, however, I may add, I had written out four years before he published.

Some facts have made me vaguely *suspect* that between the glacial and the present temperature there was a period of *slightly* greater warmth. According to my modification-doctrines, I look at many of the species of North America which *closely* represent those of Europe, as having become modified since the Pliocene period, when in the northern part of the world there was nearly free communication between the old and new worlds. But now comes a more important consideration ; there is a considerable body of geological evidence that during the Glacial epoch the whole world was colder ; I inferred that, many years ago, from erratic boulder phenomena carefully observed by me on both the east and west coast of South America. Now I am so bold as to believe that at the height of the Glacial epoch, *and when all Tropical productions must have been considerably distressed*, that several temperate forms slowly travelled into the heart of the Tropics, and even reached the southern hemisphere ; and some few southern forms penetrated in a reverse direction northward. (Heights of Borneo with Australian forms, Abyssinia with Cape forms.) Wherever there was nearly continuous *high* land, this migration would have been immensely facilitated ; hence the European character of the plants of Tierra del Fuego and summits of Cordilleras ; hence ditto on Himalaya. As the temperature rose, all the temperate intruders would crawl up the mountains. Hence the European forms on Nilgherries, Ceylon, summit of Java, Organ Mountains of Brazil. But these intruders being surrounded with new forms would be very liable to be improved or modified by natural selection, to adapt them to the new forms with which they had to compete; hence most of the forms on the mountains of the Tropics are not identical, but *representative* forms of North temperate plants.

There are similar classes of facts in marine productions. All this will appear very rash to you, and rash it may be; but I am sure not so rash as it will at first appear to you: Hooker could not stomach it at all at first, but has become largely a convert. From mammalia and shallow sea, I believe Japan to have been joined to main land of China within no remote period; and then the migration north and south before, during, and after the Glacial epoch would act on Japan, as on the corresponding latitude of China and the United States.

I should beyond anything like to know whether you have any Alpine collections from Japan, and what is their character. This letter is miserably expressed, but perhaps it will suffice to show what I believe have been the later main migrations and changes of temperature. . . .

C. Darwin to J. D. Hooker.

[Down] Oct. 6th, 1858.

. . . If you have or can make leisure, I should very much like to hear news of Mrs. Hooker, yourself, and the children. Where did you go, and what did you do and are doing? There is a comprehensive text.

You cannot tell how I enjoyed your little visit here. It did me much good. If Harvey is still with you, pray remember me very kindly to him.

. . . I am working most steadily at my Abstract, but it grows to an inordinate length; yet fully to make my view clear (and never giving briefly more than a fact or two, and slurring over difficulties), I cannot make it shorter. It will yet take me three or four months; so slow do I work, though never idle. You cannot imagine what a service you have done me in making me make this Abstract; for though I thought I had got all clear, it has clarified my brains very much, by making me weigh the relative importance of the several elements.

I have been reading with much interest your (as I believe it to be) capital memoir of R. Brown in the *Gardeners' Chronicle*. . . .

C. Darwin to J. D. Hooker.

Down, Oct. 12th, 1858.

. . . I have sent eight copies* by post to Wallace, and will keep the others for him, for I could not think of any one to send any to.

I pray you not to pronounce too strongly against Natural Selection, till you have read my abstract, for though I dare say you will strike out *many* difficulties, which have never occurred to me; yet you cannot have thought so fully on the subject as I have.

I expect my Abstract will run into a small volume, which will have to be published separately. . . .

What a splendid lot of work you have in hand.

Ever yours,
C. DARWIN.

C. Darwin to J. D. Hooker.

Down, Oct. 13th, 1858.

. . . I have been a little vexed at myself at having asked you not "to pronounce too strongly against Natural Selection." I am sorry to have bothered you, though I have been much interested by your note in answer. I wrote the sentence without reflection. But the truth is, that I have so accustomed myself, partly from being quizzed by my non-naturalist relations, to expect opposition and even contempt, that I forgot for the moment that you are the one living soul

---

* Of the joint paper by C. Darwin and A. R. Wallace.

from whom I have constantly received sympathy. Believe [me] that I never forget for even a minute how much assistance I have received from you. You are quite correct that I never even suspected that my speculations were a "jam-pot" to you; indeed, I thought, until quite lately, that my MS. had produced no effect on you, and this has often staggered me. Nor did I know that you had spoken in general terms about my work to our friends, excepting to dear old Falconer, who some few years ago once told me that I should do more mischief than any ten other naturalists would do good, [and] that I had half spoiled you already! All this is stupid egotistical stuff, and I write it only because you may think me ungrateful for not having valued and understood your sympathy; which God knows is not the case. It is an accursed evil to a man to become so absorbed in any subject as I am in mine.

I was in London yesterday for a few hours with Falconer, and he gave me a magnificent lecture on the age of man. We are not upstarts; we can boast of a pedigree going far back in time coeval with extinct species. He has a grand fact of some large molar tooth in the Trias.

I am quite knocked up, and am going next Monday to revive under Water-cure at Moor Park.

My dear Hooker, yours affectionately,

C. DARWIN.

C. Darwin to J. D. Hooker.

Nov. 1858.

. . . . I had vowed not to mention my everlasting Abstract to you again, for I am sure I have bothered you far more than enough about it; but, as you allude to its previous publication, I may say that I have the chapters on Instinct and Hybridism to abstract, which may take a fortnight each; and my materials for Palæontology, Geographical Distribution, and Affinities, being less worked up, I dare say each of these will take me three weeks, so that I shall not have done

at soonest till April, and then my Abstract will in bulk make
a small volume. I never give more than one or two instances,
and I pass over briefly all difficulties, and yet I cannot make
my Abstract shorter, to be satisfactory, than I am now doing,
and yet it will expand to a small volume. . . . .

[About this time my father revived his old knowledge of
beetles in helping his boys in their collecting. He sent a
short notice to the 'Entomologist's Weekly Intelligencer,'
June 25th, 1859, recording the capture of *Licinus silphoides,
Clytus mysticus, Panagæus 4-pustulatus.* The notice begins
with the words, "We three very young collectors having lately
taken in the parish of Down," &c., and is signed by three of
his boys, but was clearly not written by them. I have a vivid
recollection of the pleasure of turning out my bottle of dead
beetles for my father to name, and the excitement, in which
he fully shared, when any of them proved to be uncommon
ones. The following letters to Mr. Fox (November 13, 1858),
and to Sir John Lubbock, illustrate this point :]

C. Darwin to W. D. Fox.

Down, Nov. 13th [1858].

. . . . W., my son, is now at Christ's College, in the rooms
above yours. My old Gyp, Impey, was astounded to hear
that he was my son, and very simply asked, "Why, has he
been long married?" What pleasant hours those were when
I used to come and drink coffee with you daily! I am reminded of old days by my third boy having just begun
collecting beetles, and he caught the other day *Brachinus
crepitans,* of immortal Whittlesea Mere memory. My blood
boiled with old ardour when he caught a Licinus—a prize
unknown to me. . . .

C. Darwin to John Lubbock.

Thursday [before 1857].

DEAR LUBBOCK,—I do not know whether you care about
beetles, but for the chance I send this in a bottle, which I

never remember having seen ; though it is excessively rash to speak from a twenty-five-year old remembrance. Whenever we meet you can tell me whether you know it. . . .

I feel like an old war-horse at the sound of the trumpet, when I read about the capturing of rare beetles—is not this a magnanimous simile for a decayed entomologist ?—It really almost makes me long to begin collecting again. Adios.

" Floreat Entomologia " !—to which toast at Cambridge I have drunk many a glass of wine. So again, " Floreat Entomologia." N. B. I have *not* now been drinking any glasses full of wine. Yours,

C. D.

C. Darwin to Herbert Spencer.

Down, Nov. 25th [1858].

DEAR SIR,—I beg permission to thank you sincerely for your very kind present of your Essays.* I have already read several of them with much interest. Your remarks on the general argument of the so-called development theory seems to me admirable. I am at present preparing an Abstract of a larger work on the changes of species ; but I treat the subject simply as a naturalist, and not from a general point of view, otherwise, in my opinion, your argument could not have been improved on, and might have been quoted by me with great advantage. Your article on Music has also interested me much, for I had often thought on the subject, and had come to nearly the same conclusion with you, though unable to support the notion in any detail. Furthermore, by a curious coincidence, expression has been for years a persistent subject with me for *loose* speculation, and I must entirely agree with you that all expression has some biological meaning. I hope to profit by your criticism on style, and with very best thanks, I beg leave to remain, dear Sir,

Yours truly obliged,

C. DARWIN.

---

* ' Essays, Scientific, Political, and Speculative,' by Herbert Spencer, 1858–74.

C. Darwin to J. D. Hooker.

Down, Dec. 24th [1858].

MY DEAR HOOKER,—Your news about your unsolicited salary and house is jolly, and creditable to the Government. My room (28 × 19), with divided room above, with *all fixtures* (and painted), not furniture, and plastered outside, cost about £500. I am heartily glad of this news.

Your facts about distribution are, indeed, very striking. I remember well that none of your many wonderful facts in your several works, perplexed me, for years, more than the migration having been mainly from north to south, and not in the reverse direction. I have now at last satisfied *myself* (but that is very different from satisfying others) on this head; but it would take a little volume to fully explain myself. I did not for long see the bearing of a conclusion, at which I had arrived, with respect to this subject. It is, that species inhabiting a very large area, and therefore existing in large numbers, and which have been subjected to the severest competition with many other forms, will have arrived, through natural selection, at a higher stage of perfection than the inhabitants of a small area. Thus I explain the fact of so many anomalies, or what may be called "living fossils," inhabiting now only fresh water, having been beaten out, and exterminated in the sea, by more improved forms; thus all existing Ganoid fishes are fresh water, as [are] Lepidosiren and Ornithorhynchus, &c. The plants of Europe and Asia, as being the largest territory, I look at as the most "improved," and therefore as being able to withstand the less-perfected Australian plants; [whilst] these could not resist the Indian. See how all the productions of New Zealand yield to those of Europe. I dare say you will think all this utter bosh, but I believe it to be solid truth.

You will, I think, admit that Australian plants, flourishing so in India, is no argument that they could hold their own against the ten thousand natural contingencies of other plants, insects, animals, &c., &c. With respect to South West Australia and the Cape, I am shut up, and can only d—n the whole case.

. . . You say you should like to see my MS., but you did read and approve of my long Glacial chapter, and I have not yet written my Abstract on the whole of the Geographical Distribution, nor shall I begin it for two or three weeks. But either Abstract or the old MS. I should be *delighted* to send you, especially the Abstract chapter. . . .

I have now written 330 folio pages of my abstract, and it will require 150–200 [more] ; so that it will make a printed volume of 400 pages, and must be printed separately, which I think will be better in many respects. The subject really seems to me too large for discussion at any Society, and I believe religion would be brought in by men whom I know.

I am thinking of a 12mo volume, like Lyell's fourth or fifth edition of the ' Principles.' . . .

I have written you a scandalously long note. So now good bye, my dear Hooker,

Ever yours,
C. DARWIN.

C. Darwin to J. D. Hooker.

Down, Jan. 20th, 1859.

MY DEAR HOOKER,—I should very much like to borrow Heer at some future time, for I want to read nothing perplexing at present till my Abstract is done. Your last very instructive letter shall make me very cautious on the hyperspeculative points we have been discussing.

When you say you cannot master the train of thoughts, I know well enough that they are too doubtful and obscure to be mastered. I have often experienced what you call the humiliating feeling of getting more and more involved in doubt the more one thinks of the facts and reasoning on doubtful points. But I always comfort myself with thinking of the future, and in the full belief that the problems which we are just entering on, will some day be solved ; and if we just break the ground we shall have done some service, even if we reap no harvest.

I quite agree that we only differ in *degree* about the means of dispersal, and that I think a satisfactory amount of accordance. You put in a very striking manner the mutation of our continents, and I quite agree; I doubt only about our oceans.

I also agree (I am in a very agreeing frame of mind) with your *argumentum ad hominem*, about the highness of the Australian Flora from the number of species and genera; but here comes in a superlative bothering element of doubt, viz., the effect of isolation.

The only point in which I *presumptuously* rather demur is about the status of the naturalised plants in Australia. I think Müller speaks of their having spread largely beyond cultivated ground; and I can hardly believe that our European plants would occupy stations so barren that the native plants could not live there. I should require much evidence to make me believe this. I have written this note merely to thank you, as you will see it requires no answer.

I have heard to my amazement this morning from Phillips that the Geological Council have given me the Wollaston Medal!!!

Ever yours,
C. DARWIN.

C. Darwin to J. D. Hooker.

Down, Jan. 23d, 1859.

. . . I enclose letters to you and me from Wallace. I admire extremely the spirit in which they are written. I never felt very sure what he would say. He must be an amiable man. Please return that to me, and Lyell ought to be told how well satisfied he is. These letters have vividly brought before me how much I owe to your and Lyell's most kind and generous conduct in all this affair.

. . . How glad I shall be when the Abstract is finished, and I can rest! . . .

C. Darwin to A. R. Wallace.

Down, Jan. 25th [1859].

MY DEAR SIR,—I was extremely much pleased at receiving three days ago your letter to me and that to Dr. Hooker. Permit me to say how heartily I admire the spirit in which they are written. Though I had absolutely nothing whatever to do in leading Lyell and Hooker to what they thought a fair course of action, yet I naturally could not but feel anxious to hear what your impression would be. I owe indirectly much to you and them; for I almost think that Lyell would have proved right, and I should never have completed my larger work, for I have found my Abstract hard enough with my poor health, but now, thank God, I am in my last chapter but one. My Abstract will make a small volume of 400 or 500 pages. Whenever published, I will, of course, send you a copy, and then you will see what I mean about the part which I believe selection has played with domestic productions. It is a very different part, as you suppose, from that played by "Natural Selection." I sent off, by the same address as this note, a copy of the 'Journal of the Linnean Society,' and subsequently I have sent some half-dozen copies of the paper. I have many other copies at your disposal. . . .

I am glad to hear that you have been attending to birds' nests. I have done so, though almost exclusively under one point of view, viz., to show that instincts vary, so that selection could work on and improve them. Few other instincts, so to speak, can be preserved in a Museum.

Many thanks for your offer to look after horses' stripes; if there are any donkeys, pray add them. I am delighted to hear that you have collected bees' combs. . . . . This is an especial hobby of mine, and I think I can throw a light on the subject. If you can collect duplicates, at no very great expense, I should be glad of some specimens for myself with some bees of each kind. Young, growing, and irregular combs, and those which have not had pupæ, are most valuable for measurements and examination. Their edges should be well protected against abrasion.

Every one whom I have seen has thought your paper very well written and interesting. It puts my extracts (written in 1839, now just twenty years ago!), which I must say in apology were never for an instant intended for publication, into the shade.

You ask about Lyell's frame of mind. I think he is somewhat staggered, but does not give in, and speaks with horror, often to me, of what a thing it would be, and what a job it would be for the next edition of 'The Principles,' if he were "*per*verted." But he is most candid and honest, and I think will end by being *per*verted. Dr. Hooker has become almost as heterodox as you or I, and I look at Hooker as *by far* the most capable judge in Europe.

Most cordially do I wish you health and entire success in all your pursuits, and, God knows, if admirable zeal and energy deserve success, most amply do you deserve it. I look at my own career as nearly run out. If I can publish my Abstract and perhaps my greater work on the same subject, I shall look at my course as done.

Believe me, my dear sir, yours very sincerely,

C. DARWIN.

C. *Darwin to J. D. Hooker.*

Down, March 2nd [1859].

MY DEAR HOOKER,—Here is an odd, though very little, fact. I think it would be hardly possible to name a bird which apparently could have less to do with distribution than a Petrel. Sir W. Milner, at St. Kilda, cut open some young nestling Petrels, and he found large, curious nuts in their crops; I suspect picked up by parent birds from the Gulf stream. He seems to value these nuts excessively. I have asked him (but I doubt whether he will) to send a nut to Sir William Hooker (I gave this address for grandeur sake) to see if any of you can name it and its native country. Will you *please mention* this to Sir William Hooker, and if the nut does arrive, will you oblige me by returning it to "Sir W. Milner, Bart., Nunappleton, Tadcaster," in a registered letter, and I will repay you postage. Enclose slip of paper with the name and country if you can, and let me hereafter know. Forgive me asking you to take this much trouble; for it is a funny little fact after my own heart.

Now for another subject. I have finished my Abstract of the chapter on Geographical Distribution, as bearing on my subject. I should like you much to read it; but I say this, believing that you will not do so, if, as I believe to be the case, you are extra busy. On my honour, I shall not be mortified, and I earnestly beg you not to do it, if it will bother you. I want it, because I here feel especially unsafe, and errors may have crept in. Also, I should much like to know what parts you will *most vehemently* object to. I know we do, and must, differ widely on several heads. Lastly, I should like particularly to know whether I have taken anything from you, which you would like to retain for first publication; but I think I have chiefly taken from your published works, and, though I have several times, in this chapter and elsewhere, acknowledged your assistance, I am aware that it is not possible for me in the Abstract to do it sufficiently.* But again let me say that you must not offer to read it if very irksome. It is long—about ninety pages, I expect, when fully copied out.

I hope you are all well. Moor Park has done me some good.   Yours affectionately,

                                                  C. Darwin.

P. S.—Heaven forgive me, here is another question : How far am I right in supposing that with plants, the most impor-

---

* "I never did pick any one's pocket, but whilst writing my present chapter I keep on feeling (even when differing most from you) just as if I were stealing from you, so much do I owe to your writings and conversation, so much more than mere acknowledgments show."—Letter to Sir J. D. Hooker, 1859.

tant characters for main divisions are Embryological? The seed itself cannot be considered as such, I suppose, nor the albumens, &c. But I suppose the Cotyledons and their position, and the position of the plumule and the radicle, and the position and form of the whole embryo in the seed are embryological, and how far are these very important? I wish to instance plants as a case of high importance of embryological characters in classification. In the Animal Kingdom there is, of course, no doubt of this.

C. Darwin to J. D. Hooker.

Down, March 5th [1859].

MY DEAR HOOKER,—Many thanks about the seed . . . it is curious. Petrels at St. Kilda apparently being fed by seeds raised in the West Indies. It should be noted whether it is a nut ever imported into England. I am *very* glad you will read my Geographical MS.; it is now copying, and it will (I presume) take ten days or so in being finished; it shall be sent as soon as done. . . .

I shall be very glad to see your embryological ideas on plants; by the sentence which I sent you, you will see that I only want one sentence; if facts are at all, as I suppose, and I shall see this from your note, for sending which very many thanks.

I have been so poorly, the last three days, that I sometimes doubt whether I shall ever get my little volume done, though so nearly completed. . . .

C. Darwin to J. D. Hooker.

Down, March 15th [1859].

MY DEAR HOOKER,—I am *pleased* at what you say of my chapter. You have not attacked it nearly so much as I feared you would. You do not seem to have detected *many* errors. It was nearly all written from memory, and hence I was particularly fearful; it would have been better if the whole had first been carefully written out, and abstracted afterwards. I look at it as morally certain that it must include much error in some of its general views. I will just run over a few points in your note, but do not trouble yourself to reply without you have something important to say. . . .

. . . I should like to know whether the case of Endemic bats in islands struck you; it has me especially; perhaps too strongly.

With hearty thanks, ever yours,

C. DARWIN.

P. S. You cannot tell what a relief it has been to me your looking over this chapter, as I felt very shaky on it.

I shall to-morrow finish my last chapter (except a recapitulation) on Affinities, Homologies, Embryology, &c., and the facts seem to me to come out *very* strong for mutability of species.

I have been much interested in working out the chapter.

I shall now, thank God, begin looking over the old first chapters for press.

But my health is now so very poor, that even this will take me long.

C. Darwin to W. D. Fox.

Down [March] 24th [1859].

MY DEAR FOX,—It was very good of you to write to me in the midst of all your troubles, though you seem to have got over some of them, in the recovery of your wife's and your own health. I had not heard lately of your mother's health, and am sorry to hear so poor an account. But as she does not suffer much, that is the great thing; for mere life I do not think is much valued by the old. What a time you must have had of it, when you had to go backwards and forwards.

We are all pretty well, and our eldest daughter is improving. I can see daylight through my work, and am now finally

33

correcting my chapters for the press ; and I hope in a month or six weeks to have proof-sheets. I am weary of my work. It is a very odd thing that I have no sensation that I over-work my brain ; but facts compel me to conclude that my brain was never formed for much thinking. We are resolved to go for two or three months, when I have finished, to Ilkley, or some such place, to see if I can anyhow give my health a good start, for it certainly has been wretched of late, and has incapacitated me for everything. You do me injustice when you think that I work for fame ; I value it to a certain extent; but, if I know myself, I work from a sort of instinct to try to make out truth. How glad I should be if you could sometime come to Down ; especially when I get a little better, as I still hope to be. We have set up a billiard table, and I find it does me a deal of good, and drives the horrid species out of my head. Farewell, my dear old friend.

Yours affectionately,

C. DARWIN.

C. Darwin to C. Lyell.

Down, March 28th [1859].

MY DEAR LYELL,—If I keep decently well, I hope to be able to go to press with my volume early in May. This being so, I want much to beg a little advice from you. From an expression in Lady Lyell's note, I fancy that you have spoken to Murray. Is it so? And is he willing to publish my Ab-stract? If you will tell me whether anything, and what has passed, I will then write to him. Does he know at all of the subject of the book? Secondly, can you advise me, whether I had better state what terms of publication I should prefer, or first ask him to propose terms? And what do you think would be fair terms for an edition? Share profits, or what?

Lastly, will you be so very kind as to look at the enclosed title and give me your opinion and any criticisms; you must remember that, if I have health and it appears worth doing, I have a much larger and full book on the same subject nearly ready.

My Abstract will be about five hundred pages of the size of your first edition of the ' Elements of Geology.'

Pray forgive me troubling you with the above queries; and you shall have no more trouble on the subject. I hope the world goes well with you, and that you are getting on with your various works.

I am working very hard for me, and long to finish and be free and try to recover some health.

My dear Lyell, ever yours,
C. DARWIN.

Very sincere thanks to you for standing my proxy for the Wollaston Medal.

P. S. Would you advise me to tell Murray that my book is not more *un*-orthodox than the subject makes inevitable. That I do not discuss the origin of man. That I do not bring in any discussion about Genesis, &c., &c., and only give facts, and such conclusions from them as seem to me fair.

Or had I better say *nothing* to Murray, and assume that he cannot object to this much unorthodoxy, which in fact is not more than any Geological Treatise which runs slap counter to Genesis.

Inclosure.

AN ABSTRACT OF AN ESSAY

ON THE

ORIGIN

OF

SPECIES AND VARIETIES

THROUGH NATURAL SELECTION

BY

CHARLES DARWIN, M.A.

FELLOW OF THE ROYAL GEOLOGICAL AND LINNEAN SOCIETIES

———

LONDON :

&c.,   &c.,   &c.,   &c.

1859.

C. Darwin to C. Lyell.

Down, March 30th [1859].

MY DEAR LYELL,—You have been uncommonly kind in all you have done. You not only have saved me much trouble and some anxiety, but have done all incomparably better than I could have done it. I am much pleased at all you say about Murray. I will write either to-day or to-morrow to him, and will send shortly a large bundle of MS., but unfortunately I cannot for a week, as the first three chapters are in the copyists' hands.

I am sorry about Murray objecting to the term Abstract, as I look at it as the only possible apology for *not* giving references and facts in full, but I will defer to him and you. I am also sorry about the term "natural selection." I hope to retain it with explanation somewhat as thus —

"Through natural selection, or the preservation of favoured Races."

Why I like the term is that it is constantly used in all works on breeding, and I am surprised that it is not familiar to Murray; but I have so long studied such works that I have ceased to be a competent judge.

I again most truly and cordially thank you for your really valuable assistance.

Yours most truly,

C. DARWIN.

C. Darwin to J. D. Hooker.

Down, April 2nd [1859].

. . . . I wrote to him [Mr. Murray] and gave him the headings of the chapters, and told him he could not have the MS. for ten days or so ; and this morning I received a letter, offering me handsome terms, and agreeing to publish without seeing the MS. ! So he is eager enough ; I think I should have been cautious, anyhow, but, owing to your letter, I told him most *explicitly* that I accept his offer solely on condition that, after he has seen part or all the MS., he has full power of retracting. You will think me presumptuous, but I think my book will be popular to a certain extent (enough to ensure [against] heavy loss) amongst scientific and semi-scientific men ; why I think so is, because I have found in conversation so great and surprising an interest amongst such men, and some o-scientific [non-scientific] men on this subject, and all my chapters are not *nearly* so dry and dull as that which you have read on geographical distribution. Anyhow, Murray ought to be the best judge, and if he chooses to pub-lish it, I think I may wash my hands of all responsibility. I am sure my friends, *i. e.*, Lyell and you, have been *extraordinarily* kind in troubling yourselves on the matter.

I shall be delighted ·to see you the day before Good Friday ; there would be one advantage for you in any other day—as I believe both my boys come home on that day—and it would be almost impossible that I could send the carriage for you. There will, I believe, be some relations in the house—but I hope you will not care for that, as we shall easily get as much talking as my *imbecile state* allows. I shall deeply enjoy seeing you.

. . . . I am tired, so no more.

My dear Hooker, your affectionate,

C. DARWIN.

P. S.—Please to send, well *tied up* with strong string, my Geographical MS., towards the latter half of next week—*i.e.*, 7th or 8th—that I may send it with more to Murray ; and God help him if he tries to read it.

. . . . I cannot help a little doubting whether Lyell would take much pains to induce Murray to publish my book ; this was not done at my request, and it rather grates against my pride.

I know that Lyell has been *infinitely* kind about my affair, but your dashed [*i. e.*, underlined] "*induce*" gives the idea that Lyell had unfairly urged Murray.

C. Darwin to Asa Gray.

April 4th [1859].

. . . . You ask to see my sheets as printed off ; I assure you that it will be the *highest* satisfaction to me to do so : I look at the request as a high compliment. I shall not, you may depend, forget a request which I look at as a favour. But (and it is a heavy " but " to me) it will be long before I go to press ; I can truly say I am *never* idle ; indeed, I work too hard for my much weakened health ; yet I can do only three hours of work daily, and I cannot at all see when I shall have finished : I have done eleven long chapters, but I have got some other very difficult ones : as palæontology, classifications, and embryology, &c., and I have to correct and add largely to all those done. I find, alas ! each chapter takes me on an average three months, so slow I am. There is no end to the necessary digressions. I have just finished a chapter on Instinct, and here I found grappling with such a subject as bees' cells, and comparing all my notes made during twenty years, took up a despairing length of time.

But I am running on about myself in a most egotistical style. Yet I must just say how useful I have again and again found your letters, which I have lately been looking over and quoting ! but you need not fear that I shall quote anything you would dislike, for I try to be very cautious on this head. I most heartily hope you may succeed in getting your " incubus " of old work off your hands, and be in some degree a free man. . . .

Again let me say that I do indeed feel grateful to you . . .

C. Darwin to J. Murray.

Down, April 5th [1859].

MY DEAR SIR,—I send by this post, the Title (with some remarks on a separate page), and the first three chapters. If you have patience to read all Chapter I., I honestly think you will have a fair notion of the interest of the whole book.

It may be conceit, but I believe the subject will interest the public, and I am sure that the views are original.   If you think otherwise, I must repeat my request that you will freely reject my work ; and though I shall be a little disappointed, I shall be in no way injured.

If you choose to read Chapters II. and III., you will have a dull and rather abstruse chapter, and a plain and interesting one, in my opinion.

As soon as you have done with the MS., please to send it by *careful messenger, and plainly directed*, to Miss G. Tollett, 14, Queen Anne Street, Cavendish Square.

This lady, being an excellent judge of style, is going to look out for errors for me.

You must take your own time, but the sooner you finish, the sooner she will, and the sooner I shall get to press, which I so earnestly wish.

I presume you will wish to see Chapter IV., the key-stone of my arch, and Chapters X. and XI., but please to inform me on this head.

My dear Sir, yours sincerely,
C. DARWIN.

C. Darwin to J. D. Hooker.

Down, April 11th [1859].

. . . I write one line to say that I heard from Murray yesterday, and he says he has read the first three chapters of one MS. (and this includes a very dull one), and he abides by his offer.   Hence he does not want more MS., and you can send my Geographical chapter when it pleases you. . . .

[Part of the MS. seems to have been lost on its way back to my father; he wrote (April 14) to Sir J. D. Hooker :]

" I have the old MS., otherwise, the loss would have killed me !   The worst is now that it will cause delay in getting to press, and *far worst* of all, lose all advantage of your having looked over my chapter, except the third part returned. I am very sorry Mrs. Hooker took the trouble of copying the two pages."

C. Darwin to J. D. Hooker.

[April or May, 1859.]

. . . Please do not say to any one that I thought my book on Species would be fairly popular, and have a fairly remu-nerative sale (which was the height of my ambition), for if it prove a dead failure, it would make me the more ridiculous.

I enclose a criticism, a taste of the future—

Rev. S. Haughton's Address to the Geological Society, Dublin.[*]

" This speculation of Messrs. Darwin and Wallace would not be worthy of notice were it not for the weight of authority of the names (*i. e.* Lyell's and yours), under whose auspices it has been brought forward. If it means what it says, it is a truism ; if it means anything more, it is contrary to fact."

Q. E. D.

C. Darwin to J. D. Hooker.

Down, May 11th [1859].

MY DEAR HOOKER,— Thank you for telling me about obscurity of style. But on my life no nigger with lash over him could have worked harder at clearness than I have done. But the very difficulty to me, of itself leads to the probability that I fail. Yet one lady who has read all my MS. has found only two or three obscure sentences, but Mrs. Hooker having so found it, makes me tremble. I will do my best in proofs. You are a good man to take the trouble to write about it.

With respect to our mutual muddle, † I never for a moment

---

* Feb. 9, 1859.

† " When I go over the chapter I will see what I can do, but I hardly know how I am obscure, and I think we are somehow in a mutual muddle with respect to each other, from starting from some fundamentally differ-ent notions."—Letter of May 6, 1859.

thought we could not make our ideas clear to each other by talk, or if either of us had time to write in extenso.

I imagine from some expressions (but if you ask me what, I could not answer) that you look at variability as some necessary contingency with organisms, and further that there is some necessary tendency in the variability to go on diverging in character or degree. *If you do*, I do not agree. "Reversion" again (a form of inheritance), I look at as in no way directly connected with Variation, though of course inheritance is of fundamental importance to us, for if a variation be not inherited, it is of no significance to us. It was on such points as these *I fancied* that we perhaps started differently.

I fear that my book will not deserve at all the pleasant things you say about it; and Good Lord, how I do long to have done with it!

Since the above was written, I have received and have been *much interested* by A. Gray. I am delighted at his note about my and Wallace's paper. He will go round, for it is futile to give up very many species, and stop at an arbitrary line at others. It is what my grandfather called Unitarianism, "a feather bed to catch a falling Christian." . . .

C. Darwin to J. D. Hooker.

Down, May 18th [1859].

MY DEAR HOOKER,—My health has quite failed. I am off to-morrow for a week of Hydropathy. I am very very sorry to say that I cannot look over any proofs * in the week, as my object is to drive the subject out of my head. I shall return to-morrow week. If it be worth while, which probably it is not, you could keep back any proofs till my return home.

In haste, ever yours,

C. DARWIN.

---

* Of Sir J. Hooker's Introduction to the ' Flora of Australia.'

[Ten days later he wrote to Sir J. D. Hooker :

". . . I write one word to say that I shall return on Saturday, and if you have any proof-sheets to send, I shall be glad to do my best in any criticisms.

I had . . . great prostration of mind and body, but entire rest, and the douche, and 'Adam Bede,' have together done me a world of good."]

C. Darwin to J. Murray.

Down, June 14th [1859].

My dear Sir,—The diagram will do very well, and I will send it shortly to Mr. West to have a few trifling corrections made.

I get on very slowly with proofs. I remember writing to you that I thought there would be not much correction. I honestly wrote what I thought, but was most grievously mistaken. I find the style incredibly bad, and most difficult to make clear and smooth. I am extremely sorry to say, on account of expense, and loss of time for me, that the corrections are very heavy, as heavy as possible. But from casual glances, I still hope that later chapters are not so badly written. How I could have written so badly is quite inconceivable, but I suppose it was owing to my whole attention being fixed on the general line of argument, and not on details. All I can say is, that I am very sorry.

Yours very sincerely,

C. Darwin.

P. S. I have been looking at the corrections, and considering them. It seems to me that I shall put you to a quite unfair expense. If you please I should like to enter into some such arrangement as the following : When work completed, you to allow in the account a fairly moderately heavy charge for corrections, and all excess over that to be deducted from my profits, or paid by me individually.

C. Darwin to C. Lyell.

Down, June 21st [1859].

I am working very hard, but get on slowly, for I find that my corrections are terrifically heavy, and the work most difficult to me. I have corrected 130 pages, and the volume will be about 500. I have tried my best to make it clear and striking, but very much fear that I have failed—so many discussions are and must be very perplexing. I have done my best. If you had all my materials, I am sure you would have made a splendid book. I long to finish, for I am nearly worn out.

My dear Lyell, ever yours most truly,

C. DARWIN.

C. Darwin to J. D. Hooker.

Down, 22nd [June, 1859].

MY DEAR HOOKER,—I did not answer your pleasant note, with a good deal of news to me, of May 30th, as I have been expecting proofs from you. But now, having nothing particular to do, I will fly a note, though I have nothing particular to say or ask. Indeed, how can a man have anything to say, who spends every day in correcting accursed proofs; and such proofs! I have fairly to blacken them, and fasten slips of paper on, so miserable have I found the style. You say that you dreamt that my book was *entertaining ;* that dream is pretty well over with me, and I begin to fear that the public will find it intolerably dry and perplexing. But I will never give up that a better man could have made a splendid book out of the materials. I was glad to hear about Prestwich's paper.* My doubt has been (and I see Wright has inserted the same in the 'Athenæum') whether the pieces of flint are really tools; their numbers make me doubt, and when I formerly looked at Boucher de Perthe's drawings, I

---

* Mr. Prestwich wrote on the occurrence of flint instruments associated with the remains of extinct animals in France.—(Proc. R. Soc., 1859.)

came to the conclusion that they were angular fragments broken by ice action.

Did crossing the Acacia do any good? I am so hard worked, that I can make no experiments. I have got only to 150 pages in first proof.

Adios, my dear Hooker, ever yours,

C. DARWIN.

C. Darwin to J. Murray.

Down, July 25th [1859].

MY DEAR SIR,—I write to say that five sheets are returned to the printers ready to strike off, and two more sheets require only a revise; so that I presume you will soon have to decide what number of copies to print off.

I am quite incapable of forming an opinion. I think I have got the style *fairly* good and clear, with infinite trouble. But whether the book will be successful to a degree to satisfy you, I really cannot conjecture. I heartily hope it may.

My dear Sir, yours very sincerely,

C. DARWIN.

C. Darwin to A. R. Wallace.

Down, Aug. 9th, 1859.

MY DEAR MR. WALLACE,—I received your letter and memoir * on the 7th, and will forward it to-morrow to the Linnean Society. But you will be aware that there is no meeting till the beginning of November. Your paper seems to me *admirable* in matter, style, and reasoning; and I thank you for allowing me to read it. Had I read it some months ago, I should have profited by it for my forthcoming volume. But my two chapters on this subject are in type, and, though not yet corrected, I am so wearied out and weak in health, that I am fully resolved not to add one word, and merely improve the style. So you will see that my views are nearly

---

* This seems to refer to Mr. Wallace's paper, "On the Zoological Geography of the Malay Archipelago," 'Linn. Soc. Journ,' 1860.

the same with yours, and you may rely on it that not one word shall be altered owing to my having read your ideas. Are you aware that Mr. W. Earl* published several years ago the view of distribution of animals in the Malay Archipelago, in relation to the depth of the sea between the islands? I was much struck with this, and have been in the habit of noting all facts in distribution in that archipelago, and elsewhere, in this relation. I have been led to conclude that there has been a good deal of naturalisation in the different Malay islands, and which I have thought, to a certain extent, would account for anomalies. Timor has been my greatest puzzle. What do you say to the peculiar Felis there? I wish that you had visited Timor; it has been asserted that a fossil mastodon's or elephant's tooth (I forget which) has been found there, which would be a grand fact. I was aware that Celebes was very peculiar; but the relation to Africa is quite new to me, and marvellous, and almost passes belief. It is as anomalous as the relation of *plants* in S. W. Australia to the Cape of Good Hope. I differ *wholly* from you on the colonisation of oceanic islands, but you will have *every one* else on your side. I quite agree with respect to all islands not situated far in the ocean. I quite agree on the little occasional intermigration between lands [islands?] when once pretty well stocked with inhabitants, but think this does not apply to rising and ill-stocked islands. Are you aware that *annually* birds are blown to Madeira, the Azores (and to Bermuda from America). I wish I had given a fuller abstract of my reasons for not believing in Forbes' great continental extensions; but it is too late, for I will alter nothing—I am worn out, and must have rest. Owen, I do not doubt, will bitterly oppose us. . . . Hooker is publishing a grand introduction to the Flora of Australia, and goes the whole length. I have seen proofs of about half. With every good wish.

Believe me, yours very sincerely,

C. DARWIN.

---

* Probably Mr. W. Earle's paper, Geographical Soc. Journal, 1845.

C. Darwin to J. D. Hooker.

Down, Sept. 1st [1859].

. . . I am not surprised at your finding your Introduction very difficult. But do not grudge the labour, and do not say you "have burnt your fingers," and are "deep in the mud"; for I feel sure that the result will be well worth the labour. Unless I am a fool, I must be a judge to some extent of the value of such general essays, and I am fully convinced that yours are the most valuable ever published.

I have corrected all but the last two chapters of my book, and hope to have done revises and all in about three weeks, and then I (or we all) shall start for some months' hydropathy; my health has been very bad, and I am becoming as weak as a child, and incapable of doing anything whatever, except my three hours daily work at proof-sheets. God knows whether I shall ever be good at anything again, perhaps a long rest and hydropathy may do something.

I have not had A. Gray's Essay, and should not feel up to criticise it, even if I had the impertinence and courage. You will believe me that I speak strictly the truth when I say that your Australian Essay is *extremely* interesting to me, rather too much so. I enjoy reading it over, and if you think my criticisms are worth anything to you, I beg you to send the sheets (if you can give me time for good days); but unless I can render you any little, however little assistance, I would rather read the essay when published. Pray understand that I should be *truly* vexed not to read them, if you wish it for your own sake.

I had a terribly long fit of sickness yesterday, which makes the world rather extra gloomy to-day, and I have an insanely strong wish to finish my accursed book, such corrections every page has required as I never saw before. It is so weariful, killing the whole afternoon, after 12 o'clock doing nothing whatever. But I will grumble no more. So farewell, we shall meet in the winter I trust.

Farewell, my dear Hooker, your affectionate friend,

C. DARWIN.

C. Darwin to C. Lyell.

Down, Sept. 2nd [1859].

. . . I am very glad you wish to see my clean sheets: I should have offered them, but did not know whether it would bore you; I wrote by this morning's post to Murray to send them. Unfortunately I have not got to the part which will interest you, I think most, and which tells most in favour of the view, viz., Geological Succession, Geographical Distribution, and especially Morphology, Embryology and Rudimentary Organs. I will see that the remaining sheets, when printed off, are sent to you. But would you like for me to send the last and perfect revises of the sheets as I correct them? if so, send me your address in a blank envelope. I hope that you will read all, whether dull (especially latter part of Chapter II.) or not, for I am convinced there is not a sentence which has not a bearing on the whole argument. You will find Chapter IV. perplexing and unintelligible, without the aid of the enclosed queer diagram,* of which I send an old and useless proof. I have, as Murray says, corrected so heavily, as almost to have re-written it; but yet I fear it is poorly written. Parts are intricate; and I do not think that even you could make them quite clear. Do not, I beg, be in a hurry in committing yourself (like so many naturalists) to go a certain length and no further; for I am deeply convinced that it is absolutely necessary to go the whole vast length, or stick to the creation of each separate species; I argue this point briefly in the last chapter. Remember that your verdict will probably have more influence than my book in deciding whether such views as I hold will be admitted or rejected at present; in the future I cannot doubt about their admittance, and our posterity will marvel as much about the current belief as we do about fossil shells having been thought to have been created as we now see them. But forgive me for running on about my hobby-horse. . . .

---

* The diagram illustrates descent with divergence.

C. Darwin to J. D. Hooker.

Down, [Sept.] 11th [1859].

MY DEAR HOOKER,—I corrected the last proof yesterday, and I have now my revises, index, &c., which will take me near to the end of the month. So that the neck of my work, thank God, is broken.

I write now to say that I am uneasy in my conscience about hesitating to look over your proofs, but I was feeling miserably unwell and shattered when I wrote. I do not suppose I could be of hardly any use, but if I could, pray send me any proofs. I should be (and fear I was) the most ungrateful man to hesitate to do anything for you after some fifteen or more years' help from you.

As soon as ever I have fairly finished I shall be off to Ilkley, or some other Hydropathic establishment. But I shall be some time yet, as my proofs have been so utterly obscured with corrections, that I have to correct heavily on revises.

Murray proposes to publish the first week in November. Oh, good heavens, the relief to my head and body to banish the whole subject from my mind!

I hope to God, you do not think me a brute about your proof-sheets.

Farewell, yours affectionately,

C. DARWIN.

C. Darwin to C. Lyell.

Down, Sept. 20th [1859].

MY DEAR LYELL,—You once gave me intense pleasure, or rather delight, by the way you were interested, in a manner I never expected, in my Coral Reef notions, and now you have again given me similar pleasure by the manner you have noticed my species work.* Nothing could be more satisfac-

---

* Sir Charles was President of the Geological section at the meeting of the British Association at Aberdeen in 1859. The following passage

tory to me, and I thank you for myself, and even more for the subject's sake, as I know well that the sentence will make many fairly consider the subject, instead of ridiculing it. Although your previously felt doubts on the immutability of species, may have more influence in converting you (if you be converted) than my book ; yet as I regard your verdict as far more important in my own eyes, and I believe in the eyes of the world than of any other dozen men, I am naturally very anxious about it. Therefore let me beg you to keep your mind open till you receive (in perhaps a fortnight's time) my latter chapters, which are the most important of all on the favourable side. The last chapter, which sums up and balances in a mass all the arguments contra and pro, will, I think, be useful to you. I cannot too strongly express my conviction of the general truth of my doctrines, and God knows I have never shirked a difficulty. I am foolishly anxious for your verdict, not that I shall be disappointed if you are not converted ; for I remember the long years it took me to come round; but I shall be most deeply delighted if you do come round, especially if I have a fair share in the conversion, I shall then feel that my career is run, and care little whether I ever am good for anything again in this life.

Thank you much for allowing me to put in the sentence about your grave doubt.* So much and too much about myself.

---

occurs in the address : "On this difficult and mysterious subject a work will very shortly appear by Mr. Charles Darwin, the result of twenty years of observations and experiments in Zoology, Botany, and Geology, by which he had been led to the conclusion that those powers of nature which give rise to races and permanent varieties in animals and plants, are the same as those which in much longer periods produce species, and in a still longer series of ages give rise to differences of generic rank. He appears to me to have succeeded by his investigations and reasonings in throwing a flood of light on many classes of phenomena connected with the affinities, geographical distribution, and geological succession of organic beings, for which no other hypothesis has been able, or has even attempted to account."

    * As to the immutability of species, ' Origin,' Ed. i., p. 310.

     34

I have read with extreme interest in the Aberdeen paper about the flint tools; you have made the whole case far clearer to me ; I suppose that you did not think the evidence sufficient about the Glacial period.

With cordial thanks for your splendid notice of my book.

Believe me, my dear Lyell, your affectionate disciple,

CHARLES DARWIN.

C. Darwin to W. D. Fox.

Down, Sept. 23rd [1859].

MY DEAR FOX,—I was very glad to get your letter a few days ago. I was wishing to hear about you, but have been in such an absorbed, slavish, overworked state, that I had not heart without compulsion to write to any one or do anything beyond my daily work. Though your account of yourself is better, I cannot think it at all satisfactory, and I wish you would soon go to Malvern again. My father used to believe largely in an old saying that, if a man grew thinner between fifty and sixty years of age, his chance of long life was poor, and that on the contrary it was a very good sign if he grew fatter ; so that your stoutness, I look at as a very good omen. My health has been as bad as it well could be all this summer; and I have kept on my legs, only by going at short intervals to Moor Park ; but I have been better lately, and, thank Heaven, I have at last as good as done my book, having only the index and two or three revises to do. It will be published in the first week in November, and a copy shall be sent you. Remember it is only an Abstract (but has cost me above thirteen months to write ! !), and facts and authorities are far from given in full. I shall be curious to hear what you think of it, but I am not so silly as to expect to convert you. Lyell has read about half of the volume in clean sheets, and gives me very great *kudos.* He is wavering so much about the immutability of species, that I expect he will come round. Hooker has come round, and will publish his belief soon. So much for my abominable volume, which has cost me so much labour that I almost hate it. On October 3rd I start for Ilkley, but shall take three days for the journey! It is so late that we shall not take a house; but I go there alone for three or four weeks, then return home for a week and go to Moor Park for three or four weeks, and then I shall get a moderate spell of hydropathy: and I intend, if I can keep to my resolution, of being idle this winter. But I fear *ennui* will be as bad as a bad stomach. . . .

C. Darwin to C. Lyell.

Down, Sept. 25th [1859].

MY DEAR LYELL,—I send by this post four corrected sheets. I have altered the sentence about the Eocene fauna being beaten by recent, thanks to your remark. But I imagined that it would have been clear that I supposed the climate to be nearly similar; you do not doubt, I imagine, that the climate of the eocene and recent periods in *different* parts of the world could be matched. Not that I think climate nearly so important as most naturalists seem to think. In my opinion no error is more mischievous than this.

I was very glad to find that Hooker, who read over, in MS., my Geographical chapters, quite agreed in the view of the greater importance of organic relations. I should like you to consider p. 77 and reflect on the case of any organism in the midst of its range.

I shall be curious hereafter to hear what you think of distribution during the glacial and preceding warmer periods. I am so glad you do not think the Chapter on the Imperfection of the Geological Record exaggerated; I was more fearful about this chapter than about any part.

Embryology in Chapter VIII. is one of my strongest points I think. But I must not bore you by running on. My mind is so wearisomely full of the subject.

I do thank you for your eulogy at Aberdeen. I have been so wearied and exhausted of late that I have for months doubted whether I have not been throwing away time and labour for nothing. But now I care not what the universal world says; I have always found you right, and certainly on this occasion I am not going to doubt for the first time. Whether you go far, or but a very short way with me and others who believe as I do, I am contented, for my work cannot be in vain. You would laugh if you knew how often I have read your paragraph, and it has acted like a little dram. . . .

Farewell,
C. DARWIN.

C. Darwin to C. Lyell.

Down, Sept. 30th [1859].

MY DEAR LYELL,—I sent off this morning the last sheets, but without index, which is not in type. I look at you as my Lord High Chancellor in Natural Science, and therefore I request you, after you have finished, just to *rerun* over the heads in the Recapitulation-part of last chapter. I shall be deeply anxious to hear what you decide (if you are able to decide) on the balance of the pros and contras given in my volume, and of such other pros and contras as may occur to you. I hope that you will think that I have given the difficulties fairly. I feel an entire conviction that if you are now staggered to any moderate extent, that you will come more and more round, the longer you keep the subject at all before your mind. I remember well how many long years it was before I could look into the faces of some of the difficulties and not feel quite abashed. I fairly struck my colours before the case of neuter insects.

I suppose that I am a very slow thinker, for you would be surprised at the number of years it took me to see clearly what some of the problems were which had to be solved, such as the necessity of the principle of divergence of character, the extinction of intermediate varieties, on a continuous area, with graduated conditions; the double problem of sterile first crosses and sterile hybrids, &c., &c.

Looking back, I think it was more difficult to see what

the problems were than to solve them, so far as I have succeeded in doing, and this seems to me rather curious. Well,
good or bad, my work, thank God, is over; and hard work, I
can assure you, I have-had, and much work which has never
borne fruit. You can see, by the way I am scribbling, that
I have an idle and rainy afternoon. I was not able to start
for Ilkley yesterday as I was too unwell; but I hope to get
there on Tuesday or Wednesday. Do, I beg you, when you
have finished my book and thought a little over it, let me
hear from you. Never mind and pitch into me, if you think
it requisite ; some future day, in London possibly, you may
give me a few criticisms in detail, that is, if you have scribbled any remarks on the margin, for the chance of a second
edition.

Murray has printed 1250 copies, which seems to me rather
too large an edition, but I hope he will not lose.

I make as much fuss about my book as if it were my first.
Forgive me, and believe me, my dear Lyell,

Yours most sincerely,

C. DARWIN.

C. Darwin to J. D. Hooker.

Ilkley, Yorkshire, Oct. 15th [1859].

MY DEAR HOOKER,—Be a good man and screw out time
enough to write me a note and tell me a little about yourself,
your doings, and belongings.

Is your Introduction fairly finished ? I know you will
abuse it, and I know well how much I shall like it. I have
been here nearly a fortnight, and it has done me very much
good, though I sprained my ankle last Sunday, which has
quite stopped walking. All my family come here on Monday
to stop three or four weeks, and then I shall go back to the
great establishment, and stay a fortnight; so that if I can
keep my spirits, I shall stay eight weeks here, and thus give
hydropathy a fair chance. Before starting here I was in an
awful state of stomach, strength, temper, and spirits. My

book has been completely finished some little time; as soon
as copies are ready, of course one will be sent you. I hope
you will mark your copy with scores, so that I may profit by
any criticisms. I should like to hear your general impression.
From Lyell's letters, he thinks favourably of it, but seems
staggered by the lengths to which I go. But if you go any
considerable length in the admission of modification, I can
see no possible means of drawing the line, and saying here
you must stop. Lyell is going to reread my book, and I yet
entertain hopes that he will be converted, or perverted, as he
calls it. Lyell has been *extremely* kind in writing me three
volume-like letters; but he says nothing about dispersal during the glacial period. I should like to know what he thinks
on this head. I have one question to ask : Would it be any
good to send a copy of my book to Decaisne? and do you
know any philosophical botanists on the Continent, who read
English and care for such subjects? if so, give their addresses.
How about Andersson in Sweden? You cannot think how
refreshing it is to idle away the whole day, and hardly ever
think in the least about my confounded book which half-
killed me. I much wish I could hear of your taking a real
rest. I know how very strong you are, mentally, but I never
will believe you can go on working as you have worked of
late with impunity. You will some day stretch the string too
tight. Farewell, my good, and kind, and dear friend,

Yours affectionately,

C. DARWIN.

C. Darwin to T. H. Huxley.

Ilkley, Otley, Yorkshire, Oct. 15th [1859].

MY DEAR HUXLEY,—I am here hydropathising and coming to life again, after having finished my accursed book,
which would have been easy work to any one else, but half-
killed me. I have thought you would give me one bit of
information, and I know not to whom else to apply; viz., the
addresses of Barrande, Von Siebold, Keyserling (I dare say
Sir Roderick would know the latter).

Can you tell me of any good and *speculative* foreigners to whom it would be worth while to send copies of my book, on the 'Origin of Species'? I doubt whether it is worth sending to Siebold. I should like to send a few copies about, but how many I can afford I know not yet till I hear what price Murray affixes.

I need not say that I will send, of course, one to you, in the first week of November. I hope to send copies abroad immediately. I shall be *intensely* curious to hear what effect the book produces on you. I know that there will be much in it which you will object to, and I do not doubt many errors. I am very far from expecting to convert you to many of my heresies ; but if, on the whole, you and two or three others think I am on the right road, I shall not care what the mob of naturalists think. The penultimate chapter,* though I believe it includes the truth, will, I much fear, make you savage. Do not act and say, like Macleay versus Fleming, "I write with aqua fortis to bite into brass."

Ever yours,
C. Darwin.

C. Darwin to C. Lyell.

Ilkley, Yorkshire,
Oct. 20th [1859].

My dear Lyell,—I have been reading over all your letters consecutively, and I do not feel that I have thanked you half enough for the extreme pleasure which they have given me, and for their utility. I see in them evidence of fluctuation in the degree of credence you give to the theory; nor am I at all surprised at this, for many and many fluctuations I have undergone.

There is one point in your letter which I did not notice, about the animals (and many plants) naturalised in Australia, which you think could not endure without man's aid. I cannot see how man does aid the feral cattle. But, letting that

---

* Chapter XIII. is on Classification, Morphology, Embryology, and Rudimentary Organs.

pass, you seem to think, that because they suffer prodigious destruction during droughts, that they would all be destroyed. In the "gran secos" of La Plata, the indigenous animals, such as the American deer, die by thousands, and suffer apparently as much as the cattle. In parts of India, after a drought, it takes ten or more years before the indigenous mammals get up to their full number again. Your argument would, I think, apply to the aborigines as well as to the feral.

An animal or plant which becomes feral in one small territory might be destroyed by climate, but I can hardly believe so, when once feral over several large territories. Again, I feel inclined to swear at climate : do not think me impudent for attacking you about climate. You say you doubt whether man could have existed under the Eocene climate, but man can now withstand the climate of Esquimaux-land and West Equatorial Africa; and surely you do not think the Eocene climate differed from the present throughout all Europe, as much as the Arctic regions differ from Equatorial Africa?

With respect to organisms being created on the American type in America, it might, I think, be said that they were so created to prevent them being too well created, so as to beat the aborigines ; but this seems to me, somehow, a monstrous doctrine.

I have reflected a good deal on what you say on the necessity of continued intervention of creative power. I cannot see this necessity; and its admission, I think, would make the theory of Natural Selection valueless. Grant a simple Archetypal creature, like the Mud-fish or Lepidosiren, with the five senses and some vestige of mind, and I believe natural selection will account for the production of every vertebrate animal.

Farewell ; forgive me for indulging in this prose, and believe me, with cordial thanks,

Your ever attached disciple,

C. DARWIN.

P. S.—When, and if, you reread, I supplicate you to write on the margin the word "expand," when too condensed, or "not clear," or "?." Such marks would cost you little trouble, and I could copy them and reflect on them, and their value would be infinite to me.

My larger book will have to be wholly re-written, and not merely the present volume expanded; so that I want to waste as little time over this volume as possible, if another edition be called for; but I fear the subject will be too perplexing, as I have treated it, for general public.

C. Darwin to J. D. Hooker.

Ilkley, Yorkshire,
Sunday [Oct. 23rd, 1859].

MY DEAR HOOKER,—I congratulate you on your 'Introduction'* being in fact finished. I am sure from what I read of it (and deeply I shall be interested in reading it straight through), that it must have cost you a prodigious amount of labour and thought. I shall like very much to see the sheet, which you wish me to look at. Now I am so completely a gentleman, that I have sometimes a little difficulty to pass the day; but it is astonishing how idle a three weeks I have passed. If it is any comfort to you, pray delude yourself by saying that you intend "sticking to humdrum science." But I believe it just as much as if a plant were to say that, "I have been growing all my life, and, by Jove, I will stop growing." You cannot help yourself; you are not clever enough for that. You could not even remain idle, as I have done, for three weeks! What you say about Lyell pleases me exceedingly; I had not at all inferred from his letters that he had come so much round. I remember thinking, above a year ago, that if ever I lived to see Lyell, yourself, and Huxley come round, partly by my book, and partly by their own reflections, I should feel that the subject is safe, and all the world might rail, but that ultimately the theory of Natural Selection (though, no doubt, imperfect in its present condi-

---

* Australian Flora.

tion, and embracing many errors) would prevail. Nothing will ever convince me that three such men, with so much diversified knowledge, and so well accustomed to search for truth, could err greatly. I have spoken of you here as a convert made by me; but I know well how much larger the share has been of your own self-thought. I am intensely curious to hear Huxley's opinion of my book. I fear my long discussion on Classification will disgust him; for it is much opposed to what he once said to me.

But, how I am running on. You see how idle I am ; but I have so enjoyed your letter that you must forgive me. With respect to migration during the glacial period: I think Lyell quite comprehends, for he has given me a supporting fact. But, perhaps, he unconsciously hates (do not say so to him) the view as slightly staggering him on his favourite theory of all changes of climate being due to changes in the relative position of land and water.

I will send copies of my book to all the men specified by you; . . . would you be so kind as to add title, as Doctor, or Professor, or Monsieur, or Von, and initials (when wanted), and addresses to the names on the enclosed list, and let me have it pretty *soon*, as towards the close of this week Murray says the copies to go abroad will be ready. I am anxious to get my view generally known, and not, I hope and think, for mere personal conceit. . . . .

C. Darwin to C. Lyell.

Ilkley, Yorkshire, Oct. 25th [1859].

. . . . . Our difference on "principle of improvement" and "power of adaptation" is too profound for discussion by letter. If I am wrong, I am quite blind to my error. If I am right, our difference will be got over only by your re-reading carefully and reflecting on my first four chapters. I supplicate you to read these again carefully. The so-called improvement of our Shorthorn cattle, pigeons, &c., does not presuppose or require any aboriginal "power of adaptation," or "principle of improvement;" it requires only diversified variability, and man to select or take advantage of those modifications which are useful to him; so under nature any slight modification which *chances* to arise, and is useful to any creature, is selected or preserved in the struggle for life ; any modification which is injurious is destroyed or rejected ; any which is neither useful nor injurious will be left a fluctuating element. When you contrast natural selection and "improvement," you seem always to overlook (for I do not see how you can deny) that every step in the natural selection of each species implies improvement in that species in relation to its conditions of life. No modification can be selected without it be an improvement or advantage. Improvement implies, I suppose, each form obtaining many parts or organs, all excellently adapted for their functions. As each species is improved, and as the number of forms will have increased, if we look to the whole course of time, the organic condition of life for other forms will become more complex, and there will be a necessity for other forms to become improved, or they will be exterminated ; and I can see no limit to this process of improvement, without the intervention of any other and direct principle of improvement. All this seems to me quite compatible with certain forms fitted for simple conditions, remaining unaltered, or being degraded.

If I have a second edition, I will reiterate " Natural Selection," and, as a general consequence, " Natural Improvement."

As you go, as far as you do, I begin strongly to think, judging from myself, that you will go much further. How slowly the older geologists admitted your grand views on existing geological causes of change !

If at any time you think I can answer any question, it is a real pleasure to me to write.

Yours affectionately,

C. DARWIN.

C. Darwin to J. Murray.

Ilkley, Yorkshire [1859].

MY DEAR SIR,—I have received your kind note and the copy ; I am infinitely pleased and proud at the appearance of my child.

I quite agree to all you propose about price. But you are really too generous about the, to me, scandalously heavy corrections. Are you not acting unfairly towards yourself ? Would it not be better at least to share the £72 8s. ? I shall be fully satisfied, for I had no business to send, though quite unintentionally and unexpectedly, such badly composed MS. to the printers.

Thank you for your kind offer to distribute the copies to my friends and assistors as soon as possible. Do not trouble yourself much about the foreigners, as Messrs. Williams and Norgate have most kindly offered to do their best, and they are accustomed to send to all parts of the world.

I will pay for my copies whenever you like. I am so glad that you were so good as to undertake the publication of my book.

My dear Sir, yours very sincerely,

CHARLES DARWIN.

P. S.—Please do not forget to let me hear about two days before the copies are distributed.

I do not know when I shall leave this place, certainly not for several weeks. Whenever I am in London I will call on you.

CHAPTER XIV.

BY PROFESSOR HUXLEY.

ON THE RECEPTION OF THE 'ORIGIN OF SPECIES.'

To the present generation, that is to say, the people a few years on the hither and thither side of thirty, the name of Charles Darwin stands alongside of those of Isaac Newton and Michael Faraday ; and, like them, calls up the grand ideal of a searcher after truth and interpreter of Nature. They think of him who bore it as a rare combination of genius, industry, and unswerving veracity, who earned his place among the most famous men of the age by sheer native power, in the teeth of a gale of popular prejudice, and uncheered by a sign of favour or appreciation from the official fountains of honour ; as one who in spite of an acute sensitiveness to praise and blame, and notwithstanding provocations which might have excused any outbreak, kept himself clear of all envy, hatred, and malice, nor dealt otherwise than fairly and justly with the unfairness and injustice which was showered upon him ; while, to the end of his days, he was ready to listen with patience and respect to the most insignificant of reasonable objectors.

And with respect to that theory of the origin of the forms of life peopling our globe, with which Darwin's name is bound up as closely as that of Newton with the theory of gravitation, nothing seems to be further from the mind of the present generation than any attempt to smother it with ridicule or to crush it by vehemence of denunciation. " The struggle for existence," and " Natural selection," have become household words and every-day conceptions. The reality and the

ON THE RECEPTION OF

importance of the natural processes on which Darwin founds
his deductions are no more doubted than those of growth
and multiplication ; and, whether the full potency attributed
to them is admitted or not, no one doubts their vast and far-
reaching significance. Wherever the biological sciences are
studied, the ' Origin of Species ' lights the paths of the in-
vestigator; wherever they are taught it permeates the course
of instruction. Nor has the influence of Darwinian ideas
been less profound, beyond the realms of Biology. The
oldest of all philosophies, that of Evolution, was bound hand
and foot and cast into utter darkness during the millennium
of theological scholasticism. But Darwin poured new life-
blood into the ancient frame ; the bonds burst, and the re-
vivified thought of ancient Greece has proved itself to be a
more adequate expression of the universal order of things
than any of the schemes which have been accepted by the
credulity and welcomed by the superstition of seventy later
generations of men.

To any one who studies the signs of the times, the emer-
gence of the philosophy of Evolution, in the attitude of
claimant to the throne of the world of thought, from the
limbo of hated and, as many hoped, forgotten things, is the
most portentous event of the nineteenth century. But the
most effective weapons of the modern champions of Evolution were fabricated by Darwin; and the ' Origin of Species '
has enlisted a formidable body of combatants, trained in the
severe school of Physical Science, whose ears might have long
remained deaf to the speculations of *à priori* philosophers.

I do not think any candid or instructed person will deny
the truth of that which has just been asserted. He may hate
the very name of Evolution, and may deny its pretensions
as vehemently as a Jacobite denied those of George the
Second. But there it is—not only as solidly seated as the
Hanoverian dynasty, but happily independent of Parlia-
mentary sanction—and the dullest antagonists have come to
see that they have to deal with an adversary whose bones are
to be broken by no amount of bad words.

Even the theologians have almost ceased to pit the plain
meaning of Genesis against the no less plain meaning of
Nature. Their more candid, or more cautious, representatives
have given up dealing with Evolution as if it were a damnable
heresy, and have taken refuge in one of two courses. Either
they deny that Genesis was meant to teach scientific truth,
and thus save the veracity of the record at the expense of its
authority ; or they expend their energies in devising the cruel
ingenuities of the reconciler, and torture texts in the vain
hope of making them confess the creed of Science. But when
the *peine forte et dure* is over, the antique sincerity of the venerable sufferer always reasserts itself. Genesis is honest to
the core, and professes to be no more than it is, a repository
of venerable traditions of unknown origin, claiming no scientific authority and possessing none.

As my pen finishes these passages, I can but be amused
to think what a terrible hubbub would have been made (in
truth was made) about any similar expressions of opinion a
quarter of a century ago. In fact, the contrast between the
present condition of public opinion upon the Darwinian question ; between the estimation in which Darwin's views are
now held in the scientific world ; between the acquiescence,
or at least quiescence, of the theologians of the self-respecting
order at the present day and the outburst of antagonism on
all sides in 1858–9, when the new theory respecting the origin
of species first became known to the older generation to which
I belong, is so startling that, except for documentary evidence,
I should be sometimes inclined to think my memories dreams.
I have a great respect for the younger generation myself
(they can write our lives, and ravel out all our follies, if they
choose to take the trouble, by and by), and I should be glad
to be assured that the feeling is reciprocal; but I am afraid
that the story of our dealings with Darwin may prove a great
hindrance to that veneration for our wisdom which I should
like them to display. We have not even the excuse that,
thirty years ago, Mr. Darwin was an obscure novice, who had
no claims on our attention. On the contrary, his remarkable

zoological and geological investigations had long given him
an assured position among the most eminent and original
investigators of the day; while his charming 'Voyage of a
Naturalist' had justly earned him a wide-spread reputation
among the general public. I doubt if there was any man
then living who had a better right to expect that anything
he might choose to say on such a question as the Origin of
Species would be listened to with profound attention, and
discussed with respect; and there was certainly no man whose
personal character should have afforded a better safeguard
against attacks, instinct with malignity and spiced with shame-
less impertinences.

Yet such was the portion of one of the kindest and truest
men that it was ever my good fortune to know; and years
had to pass away before misrepresentation, ridicule, and denunciation, ceased to be the most notable constituents of the
majority of the multitudinous criticisms of his work which
poured from the press. I am loth to rake any of these ancient scandals from their well-deserved oblivion; but I must
make good a statement which may seem overcharged to the
present generation, and there is no *pièce justificative* more apt
for the purpose, or more worthy of such dishonour, than the
article in the 'Quarterly Review' for July, 1860.* Since
Lord Brougham assailed Dr. Young, the world has seen no
such specimen of the insolence of a shallow pretender to a
Master in Science as this remarkable production, in which
one of the most exact of observers, most cautious of reason-
ers, and most candid of expositors, of this or any other age,
is held up to scorn as a "flighty" person, who endeavours
"to prop up his utterly rotten fabric of guess and speculation,"

---

* I was not aware when I wrote these passages that the authorship of
the article had been publicly acknowledged. Confession unaccompanied
by penitence, however, affords no ground for mitigation of judgment; and
the kindliness with which Mr. Darwin speaks of his assailant, Bishop Wil-
berforce (vol. ii. p. 125), is so striking an exemplification of his singular
gentleness and modesty, that it rather increases one's indignation against
the presumption of his critic.

and whose "mode of dealing with nature" is reprobated as
"utterly dishonourable to Natural Science." And all this
high and mighty talk, which would have been indecent in one
of Mr. Darwin's equals, proceeds from a writer whose want
of intelligence, or of conscience, or of both, is so great, t at,
by way of an objection to Mr. Darwin's views, he can ask,
"Is it credible that all favourable varieties of turnips are
tending to become men;" who is so ignorant of paleontology,
that he can talk of the "flowers and fruits" of the plants of
the carboniferous epoch; of comparative anatomy, that he
can gravely affirm the poison apparatus of the venomous
snakes to be "entirely separate from the ordinary laws of
animal life, and peculiar to themselves;" of the rudiments
of physiology, that he can ask, "what advantage of life could
alter the shape of the corpuscles into which the blood can
be evaporated?" Nor does the reviewer fail to flavour this
outpouring of preposterous incapacity with a little stimu-
lation of the *odium theologicum.* Some inkling of the history of the conflicts between Astronomy, Geology, and
Theology, leads him to keep a retreat open by the proviso
that he cannot "consent to test the truth of Natural Science by the word of Revelation;" but, for all that, he
devotes pages to the exposition of his conviction that Mr.
Darwin's theory "contradicts the revealed relation of the
creation to its Creator," and is "inconsistent with the fulness
of his glory."

If I confine my retrospect of the reception of the 'Origin
of Species' to a twelvemonth, or thereabouts, from the time
of its publication, I do not recollect anything quite so foolish
and unmannerly as the 'Quarterly Review' article, unless,
perhaps, the address of a Reverend Professor to the Dublin
Geological Society might enter into competition with it. But
a large proportion of Mr. Darwin's critics had a lamentable
resemblance to the 'Quarterly' reviewer, in so far as they
lacked either the will, or the wit, to make themselves masters
of his doctrine; hardly any possessed the knowledge required
to follow him through the immense range of biological and
35

geological science which the 'Origin' covered ; while, too commonly, they had prejudiced the case on theological grounds, and, as seems to be inevitable when this happens, eked out lack of reason by superfluity of railing.

But it will be more pleasant and more profitable to consider those criticisms, which were acknowledged by writers of scientific authority, or which bore internal evidence of the greater or less competency and, often, of the good faith, of their authors. Restricting my survey to a twelvemonth, or thereabouts, after the publication of the 'Origin,' I find among such critics Louis Agassiz ; * Murray, an excellent entomologist ; Harvey, a botanist of considerable repute ; and the author of an article in the 'Edinburgh Review,' all strongly adverse to Darwin. Pictet, the distinguished and widely learned paleontogist of Geneva, treats Mr. Darwin with a respect which forms a grateful contrast to the tone of some of the preceding writers, but consents to go with him only a very little way.† On the other hand, Lyell, up to that time a pillar of the anti-transmutationists (who regarded

---

* "The arguments presented by Darwin in favor of a universal derivation from one primary form of all the peculiarities existing now among living beings have not made the slightest impression on my mind."

"Until the facts of Nature are shown to have been mistaken by those who have collected them, and that they have a different meaning from that now generally assigned to them. I shall therefore consider the transmutation theory as a scientific mistake, untrue in its facts, unscientific in its method, and mischievous in its tendency."—Silliman's 'Journal,' July, 1860, pp. 143, 154. Extract from the 3rd vol. of 'Contributions to the Natural History of the United States.'

† "I see no serious objections to the formation of varieties by natural selection in the existing world, and that, so far as earlier epochs are concerned, this law may be assumed to explain the origin of closely allied species, supposing for this purpose a very long period of time."

"With regard to simple varieties and closely allied species, I believe that Mr. Darwin's theory may explain many things, and throw a great light upon numerous questions."—'Sur l'Origine de l'Espèce. Par Charles Darwin.' 'Archives des Sc. de la Bibliothèque Universelle de Genève,' pp. 242, 243, Mars 1860.

him, ever afterwards, as Pallas Athene may have looked at
Dian, after the Endymion affair), declared himself a Darwinian, though not without putting in a serious *caveat*. Nevertheless, he was a tower of strength, and his courageous stand
for truth as against consistency, did him infinite honour, As
evolutionists, *sans phrase*, I do not call to mind among the
biologists more than Asa Gray, who fought the battle splendidly in the United States; Hooker, who was no less vigorous
here; the present Sir John Lubbock and myself. Wallace
was far away in the Malay Archipelago; but, apart from his
direct share in the promulgation of the theory of natural
selection, no enumeration of the influences at work, at the
time I am speaking of, would be complete without the mention of his powerful essay 'On the Law which has regulated
the Introduction of New Species,' which was published in
1855. On reading it afresh, I have been astonished to recollect how small was the impression it made.

In France, the influence of Elie de Beaumont and of
Flourens—the former of whom is said to have " damned himself to everlasting fame " ,by inventing the nickname of "*la
science moussante*" for Evolutionism,*—to say nothing of the
ill-will of other powerful members of the Institut, produced
for a long time the effect of a conspiracy of silence; and
many years passed before the Academy redeemed itself from
the reproach that the name of Darwin was not to be found
on the list of its members. However, an accomplished
writer, out of the range of academical influences, M. Laugel,
gave an excellent and appreciative notice of the ' Origin ' in
the ' Revue des Deux Mondes.' Germany took time to consider ; Bronn produced a slightly Bowdlerized translation of
the ' Origin '; and ' Kladderadatsch ' cut his jokes upon the
ape origin of man; but I do not call to mind that any scien-

---

* One is reminded of the effect of another small academic epigram.
The so-called vertebral theory of the skull is said to have been nipped in
the bud in France by the whisper of an academician to his neighbor, that,
in that case, one's head was a "*vertèbre pensante.*'

tific notability declared himself publicly in 1860.* None of us dreamed that, in the course of a few years, the strength (and perhaps I may add the weakness) of " Darwinismus " would have its most extensive and most brilliant illustrations in the land of learning. If a foreigner may presume to speculate on the cause of this curious interval of silence, I fancy it was that one moiety of the German biologists were orthodox at any price, and the other moiety as distinctly heterodox. The latter were evolutionists, à priori, already, and they must have felt the disgust natural to deductive philosophers at being offered an inductive and experimental foundation for a conviction which they had reached by a shorter cut. It is undoubtedly trying to learn that, though your conclusions may be all right, your reasons for them are all wrong, or, at any rate, insufficient.

On the whole, then, the supporters of Mr. Darwin's views in 1860 were numerically extremely insignificant. There is not the slightest doubt that, if a general council of the Church scientific had been held at that time, we should have been condemned by an overwhelming majority. And there is as little doubt that, if such a council gathered now, the decree would be of an exactly contrary nature. It would indicate a lack of sense, as well as of modesty, to ascribe to the men of that generation less capacity or less honesty than their successors possess. What, then, are the causes which led instructed and fair-judging men of that day to arrive at a judgment so different from that which seems just and fair to those who follow them? That is really one of the most interesting of all questions connected with the history of science, and I shall try to answer it. I am afraid that in order to do so I must run the risk of appearing egotistical. How-

---

* However, the man who stands next to Darwin in his influence on modern biologists, K. E. von Bär, wrote to me, in August 1860, expressing his general assent to evolutionist views. His phrase, " J'ai énoncé les mêmes idées . . . que M. Darwin " (vol. ii. p. 122), is shown by his subsequent writings to mean no more than this.

ever, if I tell my own story it is only because I know it better than that of other people.

I think I must have read the 'Vestiges' before I left England in 1846; but, if I did, the book made very little impression upon me, and I was not brought into serious contact with the 'Species' question until after 1850. At that time, I had long done with the Pentateuchal cosmogony, which had been impressed upon my childish understanding as Divine truth, with all the authority of parents and instructors, and from which it had cost me many a struggle to get free. But my mind was unbiassed in respect of any doctrine which presented itself, if it professed to be based on purely philosophical and scientific reasoning. It seemed to me then (as it does now) that "creation," in the ordinary sense of the word, is perfectly conceivable. I find no difficulty in imagining that, at some former period, this universe was not in existence; and that it made its appearance in six days (or instantaneously, if that is preferred), in consequence of the volition of some pre-existent Being. Then, as now, the so-called *à priori* arguments against Theism; and, given a Deity, against the possibility of creative acts, appeared to me to be devoid of reasonable foundation. I had not then, and I have not now, the smallest *à priori* objection to raise to the account of the creation of animals and plants given in 'Paradise Lost,' in which Milton so vividly embodies the natural sense of Genesis. Far be it from me to say that it is untrue because it is impossible. I confine myself to what must be regarded as a modest and reasonable request for some particle of evidence that the existing species of animals and plants did originate in that way, as a condition of my belief in a statement which appears to me to be highly improbable.

And, by way of being perfectly fair, I had exactly the same answer to give to the evolutionists of 1851–8. Within the ranks of the biologists, at that time, I met with nobody, except Dr. Grant, of University College, who had a word to say for Evolution—and his advocacy was not calculated to advance the cause. Outside these ranks, the only person

known to me whose knowledge and capacity compelled respect, and who was, at the same time, a thorough-going evolutionist, was Mr. Herbert Spencer, whose acquaintance I
made, I think, in 1852, and then entered into the bonds of a
friendship which, I am happy to think, has known no inter-
ruption.   Many and prolonged were the battles we fought on
this topic.   But even my friend's rare dialectic skill and co-
piousness of apt illustration could not drive me from my agnostic position.   I took my stand upon two grounds : firstly,
that up to that time, the evidence in favor of transmutation
was wholly insufficient ; and, secondly, that no suggestion respecting the causes of the transmutation assumed, which had
been made, was in any way adequate to explain the phenomena.   Looking back at the state of knowledge at that time, I
really do not see that any other conclusion was justifiable.

In those days I had never even heard of Treviranus'
'Biologie.'   However, I had studied Lamarck attentively
and I had read the 'Vestiges' with due care ; but neither of
them afforded me any good ground for changing my negative and critical attitude.   As for the 'Vestiges,' I confess
that the book simply irritated me by the prodigious ignorance
and thoroughly unscientific habit of mind manifested by the
writer.   If it had any influence on me at all, it set me against
Evolution ; and the only review I ever have qualms of conscience about, on the ground of needless savagery, is one I
wrote on the 'Vestiges' while under that influence.

With respect to the 'Philosophie Zoologique,' it is no reproach to Lamarck to say that the discussion of the Species
question in that work, whatever might be said for it in 1809,
was miserably below the level of the knowledge of half a
century later.   In that interval of time the elucidation of the
structure of the lower animals and plants had given rise to
wholly new conceptions of their relations ; histology and
embryology, in the modern sense, had been created ; physiology had been reconstituted ; the facts of distribution, geological and geographical, had been prodigiously multiplied
and reduced to order.   To any biologist whose studies had

carried him beyond mere species-mongering in 1850, one-half of Lamarck's arguments were obsolete and the other half erroneous, or defective, in virtue of omitting to deal with the various classes of evidence which had been brought to light since his time. Moreover his one suggestion as to the cause of the gradual modification of species—effort excited by change of conditions—was, on the face of it, inapplicable to the whole vegetable world. I do not think that any impartial judge who reads the 'Philosophie Zoologique' now, and who afterwards takes up Lyell's trenchant and effectual criticism (published as far back as 1830), will be disposed to allot to Lamarck a much higher place in the establishment of biological evolution than that which Bacon assigns to himself in relation to physical science generally,—*buccinator tantum.**

But, by a curious irony of fate, the same influence which led me to put as little faith in modern speculations on this subject, as in the venerable traditions recorded in the first two chapters of Genesis, was perhaps more potent than any other in keeping alive a sort of pious conviction that Evolution, after all, would turn out true. I have recently read afresh the first edition of the 'Principles of Geology'; and when I consider that this remarkable book had been nearly thirty years in everybody's hands, and that it brings home to any reader of ordinary intelligence a great principle and a great fact—the principle, that the past must be explained by the present, unless good cause be shown to the contrary; and the fact, that, so far as our knowledge of the past history of life on our globe goes, no such cause can be shown †—I cannot but believe that Lyell, for others, as for myself, was

---

* Erasmus Darwin first promulgated Lamarck's fundamental conceptions, and, with greater logical consistency, he had applied them to plants. But the advocates of his claims have failed to show that he, in any respect, anticipated the central idea of the 'Origin of Species.'

† The same principle and the same fact guide and result from all sound historical investigation. Grote's 'History of Greece' is a product of the same intellectual movement as Lyell's 'Principles.'

the chief agent for smoothing the road for Darwin. For consistent uniformitarianism postulates evolution as much in the organic as in the inorganic world. The origin of a new species by other than ordinary agencies would be a vastly greater " catastrophe " than any of those which Lyell successfully eliminated from sober geological speculation.

In fact, no one was better aware of this than Lyell himself.* If one reads any of the earlier editions of the ' Principles ' carefully (especially by the light of the interesting series of letters recently published by Sir Charles Lyell's biographer), it is easy to see that, with all his energetic opposition to Lamarck, on the one hand, and to the ideal quasi-progressionism of Agassiz, on the other, Lyell, in his own mind, was strongly disposed to account for the origination of all past and present species of living things by natural·causes. But he would have liked, at the same time, to keep the name of creation for a natural process which he imagined to be incomprehensible. ·

In a letter addressed to Mantell (dated March 2, 1827), Lyell speaks of having just read Lamarck ; he expresses his delight at Lamarck's theories, and his personal freedom from any objection based on theological grounds. And though he is evidently alarmed at the pithecoid origin of man involved in Lamarck's doctrine, he observes :—

---

* Lyell, with perfect right, claims this position for himself. He speaks of having "advocated a law of continuity even in the organic world, so far as possible without adopting Lamarck's theory of transmutation." . . .

"But while· I taught that as often as certain forms of animals and plants disappeared, for reasons quite intelligible to us, others took their place by virtue of a causation which was beyond our comprehension ; it remained for Darwin to accumulate proof that there is no break between the incoming and the outgoing species, that they are the work of evolution, and not of special creation. . . .

"I had certainly prepared the way in this country, in six editions of my work before the ' Vestiges of Creation ' appeared in 1842 [1844], for the reception of Darwin's gradual and insensible evolution of species."— ' Life and Letters,' Letter to Haeckel, vol. ii. p. 436. Nov. 23, 1868.

" But, after all, what changes species may really undergo! How impossible will it be to distinguish and lay down a line, beyond which some of the so-called extinct species have never passed into recent ones."

Again, the following remarkable passage occurs in the postscript of a letter addressed to Sir John Herschel in 1836 :—

" In regard to the origination of new species, I am very glad to find that you think it probable that it may be carried on through the intervention of intermediate causes. I left this rather to be inferred, not thinking it worth while to offend a certain class of persons by embodying in words what would only be a speculation."* He goes on to refer to the criticisms which have been directed against him on the ground that, by leaving species to be originated by miracle, he is inconsistent with his own doctrine of uniformitarianism ; and he leaves it to be understood that he had not replied, on the ground of his general objection to controversy.

Lyell's contemporaries were not without some inkling of his esoteric doctrine. Whewell's ' History of the Inductive Sciences,' whatever its philosophical value, is always worth reading and always interesting, if under no other aspect than that of an evidence of the speculative limits within which a highly-placed divine might, at that time, safely range at will. In the course of his discussion of uniformitarianism, the encyclopædic Master of Trinity observes :—

" Mr. Lyell, indeed, has spoken of an hypothesis that

---

* In the same sense, see the letter to Whewell, March 7, 1837, vol. ii., p. 5 :—

" In regard to this last subject [the changes from one set of animal and vegetable species to another] . . . you remember what Herschel said in his letter to me. If I had stated as plainly as he has done the possibility of the introduction or origination of fresh species being a natural, in contradistinction to a miraculous process, I should have raised a host of prejudices against me, which are unfortunately opposed at every step to any philosopher who attempts to address the public on these mysterious subjects." See also letter to Sedgwick, Jan. 20, 1838, ii. p. 35.

the successive creation of species may constitute a regulai part of the economy of nature,' but he has nowhere, I think, so described this process as to make it appear in what department of science we are to place the hypothesis. Are these new species created by the production, at long intervals, of an offspring different in species from the parents? Or are the species so created produced without parents? Are they gradually evolved from some embryo substance? Or do they suddenly start from the ground, as in the creation of the poet? . . .

"Some selection of one of these forms of the hypothesis, rather than the others, with evidence for the selection, is requisite to entitle us to place it among the known causes of change, which in this chapter we are considering. The bare conviction that a creation of species has taken place, whether once or many times, so long as it is unconnected with our organical sciences, is a tenet of Natural Theology rather than of Physical Philosophy." *

The earlier part of this criticism appears perfectly just and appropriate; but, from the concluding paragraph, Whewell evidently imagines that by "creation" Lyell means a preternatural intervention of the Deity; whereas the letter to Herschel shows that, in his own mind, Lyell meant natural causation; and I see no reason to doubt † that, if Sir Charles

---

* Whewell's ' History,' vol. iii. p. 639–640 (Ed. 2, 1847).

† The following passages in Lyell's letters appear to me decisive on this point :—

To Darwin, Oct. 3, 1859 (ii, 325), on first reading the ' Origin.'

" I have long seen most clearly that if any concession is made, all that you claim in your concluding pages will follow.

" It is this which has made me so long hesitate, always feeling that the case of Man and his Races, and of other animals, and that of plants, is one and the same, and that if a *vera causa* be admitted for one instant, [instead] of a purely unknown and imaginary one, such as the word ' creation,' all the consequences must follow."

To Darwin, March 15, 1863 (vol. ii. p. 365).

" I remember that it was the conclusion he [Lamarck] came to about man that fortified me thirty years ago against the great impression which

could have avoided the inevitable corollary of the pithecoid origin of man—for which, to the end of his life, he entertained a profound antipathy—he would have advocated the efficiency of causes now in operation to bring about the condition of the organic world, as stoutly as he championed that doctrine in reference to inorganic nature.

The fact is, that a discerning eye might have seen that some form or other of the doctrine of transmutation was inevitable, from the time when the truth enunciated by William Smith that successive strata are characterised by different kinds of fossil remains, became a firmly established law of nature. No one has set forth the speculative consequences of this generalisation better than the historian of the 'Inductive Sciences':—

"But the study of geology opens to us the spectacle of many groups of species which have, in the course of the earth's history, succeeded each other at vast intervals of time ; one set of animals and plants disappearing, as it would seem, from the face of our planet, and others, which did not before

---

his arguments at first made on my mind, all the greater because Constant Prévost, a pupil of Cuvier's forty years ago, told me his conviction ' that Cuvier thought species not real, but that science could not advance without assuming that they were so.' "

To Hooker, March 9, 1863 (vol. ii. p. 361,), in reference to Darwin's feeling about the ' Antiquity of Man.'

" He [Darwin] seems much disappointed that I do not go farther with him, or do not speak out more. I can only say that I have spoken out to the full extent of my present convictions, and even beyond my state of *feeling* as to man's unbroken descent from the brutes, and I find I am half converting not a few who were in arms against Darwin, and are even now against Huxley." He speaks of having had to abandon " old and long cherished ideas, which constituted the charm to me of the theoretical part of the science in my earlier day, when I believed with Pascal in the theory, as Hallam terms it, of ' the arch-angel ruined.' "

See the same sentiment in the letter to Darwin, March 11, 1863, p. 363 :—

" I think the old ' creation ' is almost as much required as ever, but of course it takes a new form if Lamarck's views improved by yours are adopted."

exist, becoming the only occupants of the globe. And the dilemma then presents itself to us anew :— either we must accept the doctrine of the transmutation of species, and must suppose that the organized species of one geological epoch were transmuted into those of another by some long-continued agency of natural causes; or else, we must believe in many successive acts of creation and extinction of species, out of the common course of nature ; acts which, therefore, we may properly call miraculous." *

Dr. Whewell decides in favour of the latter conclusion. And if any one had plied him with the four questions which he puts to Lyell in the passage already cited, all that can be said now is that he would certainly have rejected the first. But would he really have had the courage to say that a *Rhinoceros tichorhinus*, for instance, " was produced without parents ; " or was " evolved from some embryo substance ; " or that it suddenly started from the ground like Milton's lion "pawing to get free his hinder parts." I permit myself to doubt whether even the Master of Trinity's well-tried courage —physical, intellectual, and moral—would have been equal to this feat. No doubt the sudden concurrence of half-a-ton of inorganic molecules into a live rhinoceros is conceivable, and therefore may be possible. But does such an event lie sufficiently within the bounds of probability to justify the belief in its occurrence on the strength of any attainable, or, indeed, imaginable, evidence ?

In view of the assertion (often repeated in the early days of the opposition to Darwin) that he had added nothing to Lamarck, it is very interesting to observe that the possibility of a fifth alternative, in addition to the four he has stated, has not dawned upon Dr. Whewell's mind. The suggestion that new species may result from the selective action of external conditions upon the variations from their specific type which individuals present—and which we call "spontaneous," be-

---

* Whewell's ' History of the Inductive Sciences.' Ed. ii., 1847, vol. iii. pp. 624–625. See for the author's verdict, pp. 638–39.

cause we are ignorant of their causation—is as wholly unknown to the historian of scientific ideas as it was to biological specialists before 1858. But that suggestion is the central
idea of the 'Origin of Species,' and contains the quintessence
of Darwinism.

Thus, looking back into the past, it seems to me that my
own position of critical expectancy was just and reasonable,
and must have been taken up, on the same grounds, by many
other persons. If Agassiz told me that the forms of life
which had successively tenanted the globe were the incarna-
tions of successive thoughts of the Deity; and that he had
wiped out one set of these embodiments by an appalling
geological catastrophe as soon as His ideas took a more
advanced shape, I found myself not only unable to admit the
accuracy of the deductions from the facts of paleontology,
upon which this astounding hypothesis was founded, but I
had to confess my want of any means of testing the correctness of his explanation of them. And besides that, I could
by no means see what the explanation explained. Neither
did it help me to be told by an eminent anatomist that species
had succeeded one another in time, in virtue of "a continuously operative creational law." That seemed to me to be
no more than saying that species had succeeded one another,
in the form of a vote-catching resolution, with "law" to please
the man of science, and "creational" to draw the orthodox.
So I took refuge in that "*thätige Skepsis*" which Goethe has
so well defined; and, reversing the apostolic precept to be
all things to all men, I usually defended the tenability of the
received doctrines, when I had to do with the transmutationists; and stood up for the possibility of transmutation among
the orthodox — thereby, no doubt, increasing an already
current, but quite undeserved, reputation for needless com-
bativeness.

I remember, in the course of my first interview with Mr.
Darwin, expressing my belief in the sharpness of the lines of
demarcation between natural groups and in the absence of
transitional forms, with all the confidence of youth and im-

perfect knowledge. I was not aware, at that time, that he had then been many years brooding over the species-question ; and the humorous smile which accompanied his gentle answer, that such was not altogether his view, long haunted and puzzled me. But it would seem that four or five years' hard work had enabled me to understand what it meant ; for Lyell,[*] writing to Sir Charles Bunbury (under date of April 30, 1856), says :—

"When Huxley, Hooker, and Wollaston were at Darwin's last week they (all four of them) ran a tilt against species— further, I believe, than they are prepared to go."

I recollect nothing of this beyond the fact of meeting Mr. Wollaston ; and except for Sir Charles' distinct assurance as to "all four," I should have thought my *outrecuidance* was probably a counterblast to Wollaston's conservatism. With regard to Hooker, he was already, like Voltaire's Habbakuk, "*capable de tout*" in the way of advocating Evolution.

As I have already said, I imagine that most of those of my contemporaries who thought seriously about the matter, were very much in my own state of mind—inclined to say to both Mosaists and Evolutionists, "a plague on both your houses!" and disposed to turn aside from an interminable and apparently fruitless discussion, to labour in the fertile fields of ascertainable fact. And I may, therefore, further suppose that the publication of the Darwin and Wallace papers in 1858, and still more that of the 'Origin' in 1859, had the effect upon them of the flash of light, which to a man who has lost himself in a dark night, suddenly reveals a road which, whether it takes him straight home or not, certainly goes his way. That which we were looking for, and could not find, was a hypothesis respecting the origin of known organic forms, which assumed the operation of no causes but such as could be proved to be actually at work. We wanted, not to pin our faith to that or any other speculation, but to get hold of clear and definite conceptions which could be

---

* 'Life and Letters,' vol. ii. p. 212.

brought face to face with facts and have their validity tested. The 'Origin' provided us with the working hypothesis we sought. Moreover, it did the immense service of freeing us for ever from the dilemma—refuse to accept the creation hypothesis, and what have you to propose that can be accepted by any cautious reasoner? In 1857, I had no answer ready, and I do not think that any one else had. A year later, we reproached ourselves with dulness for being perplexed by such an inquiry. My reflection, when I first made myself master of the central idea of the 'Origin,' was, "How extremely stupid not to have thought of that!" I suppose that Columbus' companions said much the same when he made the egg stand on end. The facts of variability, of the struggle for existence, of adaptation to conditions, were notorious enough ; but none of us had suspected that the road to the heart of the species problem lay through them, until Darwin and Wallace dispelled the darkness, and the beacon-fire of the 'Origin' guided the benighted.

Whether the particular shape which the doctrine of evolution, as applied to the organic world, took in Darwin's hands, would prove to be final or not, was, to me, a matter of indifference. In my earliest criticisms of the 'Origin' I ventured to point out that its logical foundation was insecure so long as experiments in selective breeding had not produced varieties which were more or less infertile ; and that insecurity remains up to the present time. But, with any and every critical doubt which my sceptical ingenuity could suggest, the Darwinian hypothesis remained incomparably more probable than the creation hypothesis. And if we had none of us been able to discern the paramount significance of some of the most patent and notorious of natural facts, until they were, so to speak, thrust under our noses, what force remained in the dilemma—creation or nothing? It was obvious that, hereafter, the probability would be immensely greater, that the links of natural causation were hidden from our purblind eyes, than that natural causation should be incompetent to produce all the phenomena of nature. The only rational course for those who had no other object than the attainment of truth, was to accept " Darwinism " as a working hypothesis, and see what could be made of it. Either it would prove its capacity to elucidate the facts of organic life, or it would break down under the strain. This was surely the dictate of common sense ; and, for once, common sense carried the day. The result has been that complete *volte-face* of the whole scientific world, which must seem so surprising to the present generation. I do not mean to say that all the leaders of biological science have avowed themselves Darwinians; but I do not think that there is a single zoologist, or botanist, or palæontologist, among the multitude of active workers of this generation, who is other than an evolutionist, profoundly influenced by Darwin's views. Whatever may be the ultimate fate of the particular theory put forth by Darwin, I venture to affirm that, so far as my knowledge goes, all the ingenuity and all the learning of hostile critics have not enabled them to adduce a solitary fact, of which it can be said, this is irreconcilable with the Darwinian theory. In the prodigious variety and complexity of organic nature, there are multitudes of phenomena which are not deducible from any generalisations we have yet reached. But the same may be said of every other class of natural objects. I believe that astronomers cannot yet get the moon's motions into perfect accordance with the theory of gravitation.

It would be inappropriate, even if it were possible, to discuss the difficulties and unresolved problems which have hitherto met the evolutionist, and which will probably continue to puzzle him for generations to come, in the course of this brief history of the reception of Mr. Darwin's great work. But there are two or three objections of a more general character, based, or supposed to be based, upon philosophical and theological foundations, which were loudly expressed in the early days of the Darwinian controversy, and which, though they have been answered over and over again, crop up now and then to the present day.

The most singular of these, perhaps immortal, fallacies, which live on, Tithonus-like, when sense and force have long deserted them, is that which charges Mr. Darwin with having attempted to reinstate the old pagan goddess, Chance. It is said that he supposes variations to come about "by chance," and that the fittest survive the "chances" of the struggle for existence. and thus "chance" is substituted for providential design.

It is not a little wonderful that such an accusation as this should be brought against a writer who has, over and over again, warned his readers that when he uses the word "spontaneous," he merely means that he is ignorant of the cause of that which is so termed ; and whose whole theory crumbles to pieces if the uniformity and regularity of natural causation for illimitable past ages is denied. But probably the best answer to those who talk of Darwinism meaning the reign of "chance," is to ask them what they themselves understand by "chance"? Do they believe that anything in this universe happens without reason or without a cause? Do they really conceive that any event has no cause, and could not have been predicted by any one who had a sufficient insight into the order of Nature? If they do, it is they who are the inheritors of antique superstition and ignorance, and whose minds have never been illumined by a ray of scientific thought. The one act of faith in the convert to science, is the confession of the universality of order and of the absolute validity in all times and under all circumstances, of the law of causation. This confession is an act of faith, because, by the nature of the case, the truth of such propositions is not susceptible of proof. But such faith is not blind, but reasonable ; because it is invariably confirmed by experience, and constitutes the sole trustworthy foundation for all action.

If one of these people, in whom the chance-worship of our remoter ancestors thus strangely survives, should be within reach of the sea when a heavy gale is blowing, let him betake himself to the shore and watch the scene. Let him note the infinite variety of form and size of the tossing waves

36

out at sea ; or of the curves of their foam-crested breakers,
as they dash against the rocks ; let him listen to the roar and
scream of the shingle as it is cast up and torn down the
beach ; or look at the flakes of foam as they drive hither and
thither before the wind ; or note the play of colours, which
answers a gleam of sunshine as it falls upon the myriad bub-
bles.   Surely here, if anywhere, he will say that chance is
supreme, and bend the knee as one who has entered the very
penetralia of his divinity.   But the man of science knows that
here, as everywhere, perfect order is manifested ; that there
is not a curve of the waves, not a note in the howling chorus,
not a rainbow-glint on a bubble, which is other than a necessary consequence of the ascertained laws of nature ; and that
with a sufficient knowledge of the conditions, competent
physico-mathematical skill could account for, and indeed
predict, every one of these "chance" events.

A second very common objection to Mr. Darwin's views
was (and is), that they abolish Teleology, and eviscerate the
argument from design.   It is nearly twenty years since I
ventured to offer some remarks on this subject, and as my
arguments have as yet received no refutation, I hope I may
be excused for reproducing them.   I observed, "that the
doctrine of Evolution is the most formidable opponent of all
the commoner and coarser forms of Teleology.   But perhaps
the most remarkable service to the Philosophy of Biology
rendered by Mr. Darwin is the reconciliation of Teleology
and Morphology, and the explanation of the facts of both,
which his views offer.   The teleology which supposes that
the eye, such as we see it in man, or one of the higher verte-
brata, was made with the precise structure it exhibits, for the
purpose of enabling the animal which possesses it to see, has
undoubtedly received its death-blow.   Nevertheless, it is
necessary to remember that there is a wider teleology which
is not touched by the doctrine of Evolution, but is actually
based upon the fundamental proposition of Evolution.   This
proposition is that the whole world, living and not living, is
the result of the mutual interaction, according to definite

laws, of the forces* possessed by the molecules of which the primitive nebulosity of the universe was composed. If this be true, it is no less certain that the existing world lay potentially in the cosmic vapour, and that a sufficient intelligence could, from a knowledge of the properties of the molecules of that vapour, have predicted, say the state of the fauna of Britain in 1869, with as much certainty as one can say what will happen to the vapour of the breath on a cold winter's day. . . . .

. . . . The teleological and the mechanical views of nature are not, necessarily, mutually exclusive. On the contrary, the more purely a mechanist the speculator is, the more firmly does he assume a primordial molecular arrangement of which all the phenomena of the universe are the consequences, and the more completely is he thereby at the mercy of the teleologist, who can always defy him to disprove that this primordial molecular arrangement was not intended to evolve the phenomena of the universe." †

The acute champion of Teleology, Paley, saw no difficulty in admitting that the " production of things " may be the result of trains of mechanical dispositions fixed beforehand by intelligent appointment and kept in action by a power at the centre, ‡ that is to say, he proleptically accepted the modern doctrine of Evolution ; and his successors might do well to follow their leader, or at any rate to attend to his weighty reasonings, before rushing into an antagonism which has no reasonable foundation.

Having got rid of the belief in chance and the disbelief in design, as in no sense appurtenances of Evolution, the third libel upon that doctrine, that it is anti-theistic, might perhaps be left to shift for itself. But the persistence with which many people refuse to draw the plainest consequences

---

* I should now like to substitute the word powers for " forces."
† The " Genealogy of Animals " (' The Academy,' 1869), reprinted in ' Critiques and Addresses."
‡ ' Natural Theology,' chap. xxiii.

from the propositions they profess to accept, renders it advisable to remark that the doctrine of Evolution is neither Anti-theistic nor Theistic. It simply has no more to do with Theism than the first book of Euclid has. It is quite certain that a normal fresh-laid egg contains neither cock nor hen; and it is also as certain as any proposition in physics or morals, that if such an egg is kept under proper conditions for three weeks, a cock or hen chicken will be found in it. It is also quite certain that if the shell were transparent we should be able to watch the formation of the young fowl, day by day, by a process of evolution, from a microscopic cellular germ to its full size and complication of structure. Therefore Evolution, in the strictest sense, is actually going on in this and analogous millions and millions of instances, wherever living creatures exist. Therefore, to borrow an argument from Butler, as that which now happens must be consistent with the attributes of the Deity, if such a Being exists, Evolution must be consistent with those attributes. And, if so, the evolution of the universe, which is neither more nor less explicable than that of a chicken, must also be consistent with them. The doctrine of Evolution, therefore, does not even come into contact with Theism, considered as a philosophical doctrine. That with which it does collide, and with which it is absolutely inconsistent, is the conception of creation, which theological speculators have based upon the history narrated in the opening of the book of Genesis.

There is a great deal of talk and not a little lamentation about the so-called religious difficulties which physical science has created. In theological science, as a matter of fact, it has created none. Not a solitary problem presents itself to the philosophical Theist, at the present day, which has not existed from the time that philosophers began to think out the logical grounds and the logical consequences of Theism. All the real or imaginary perplexities which flow from the conception of the universe as a determinate mechanism, are equally involved in the assumption of an Eternal, Omnipotent and Omniscient Deity. The theological equivalent of the scientific conception of order is Providence ; and the doctrine of determinism follows as surely from the attributes of foreknowledge assumed by the theologian, as from the universality of natural causation assumed by the man of science. The angels in ' Paradise Lost ' would have found the task of enlightening Adam upon the mysteries of " Fate, Foreknowledge, and Free-will," not a whit more difficult, if their pupil had been educated in a " Real-schule " and trained in every laboratory of a modern university. In respect of the great problems of Philosophy, the post-Darwinian generation is, in one sense, exactly where the præ-Darwinian generations were. They remain insoluble. But the present generation has the advantage of being better provided with the means of freeing itself from the tyranny of certain sham solutions.

The known is finite, the unknown infinite ; intellectually we stand on an islet in the midst of an illimitable ocean of inexplicability. Our business in every generation is to reclaim a little more land, to add something to the extent and the solidity of our possessions. And even a cursory glance at the history of the biological sciences during the last quarter of a century is sufficient to justify the assertion, that the most potent instrument for the extension of the realm of natural knowledge which has come into men's hands, since the publication of Newton's ' Principia,' is Darwin's ' Origin of Species.'

It was badly received by the generation to which it was first addressed, and the outpouring of angry nonsense to which it gave rise is sad to think upon. But the present generation will probably behave just as badly if another Darwin should arise, and inflict upon them that which the generality of mankind most hate—the necessity of revising their convictions. Let them, then, be charitable to us ancients ; and if they behave no better than the men of my day to some new benefactor, let them recollect that, after all, our wrath did not come to much, and vented itself chiefly in the bad language of sanctimonious scolds. Let them as speedily perform a strategic right-about-face, and follow the truth wherever it leads. The opponents of the new truth will discover, as those of Darwin are doing, that, after all, theories do not alter facts, and that the universe remains unaffected even though texts crumble. Or, it may be, that, as history repeats itself, their happy ingenuity will also discover that the new wine is exactly of the same vintage as the old, and that (rightly viewed) the old bottles prove to have been expressly made for holding it.

END OF VOLUME ONE.

Printed in the United States
89328LV00003B/253-255/A